BLUETRICYCLE

P9-DFQ-285

The BIG BOOK of CORPORATE IDENTITY DESIGN

editor
David E. Carter

art director
Suzanna M.W. Stephens
designers
Cynthia B. Combs,
Anthony B. Stephens

The Big Book of Corporate Identity Design

First published in 2001 by HBI,
an imprint of HarperCollins Publishers
10 East 53rd Street
New York, NY 10022-5299

Distributed in the U.S. and Canada by
Watson-Guptill Publications
1515 Broadway
New York, NY 10036
Tel: (800) 451-1741
(732) 363-4511 in NJ, AK, HI
Fax: (732) 363-0338

ISBN: 0-8230-0490-2

Distributed throughout the rest of the world by
HarperCollins International
10 East 53rd Street
New York, NY 10022-5299
Fax: (212) 207-7654

ISBN: 0-06-018615-1

First published in Germany by Nippan
Nippon Shuppan Hanbai
Deutschland GmbH
Krefelder Strasse 85
D-40549 Dusseldorf
Tel: (0211) 5048089
Fax: (0211) 5049326
nippan@t-online.de

ISBN: 3-931884-79-1

Printed in Hong Kong by Everbest Printing Company through
Four Colour Imports, Louisville, Kentucky.

In the 1980s and early 1990s, Japanese publishers produced some outstanding books on corporate identity. Those books did a great job of showing the corporate identity programs of a large number of companies.

As much as I liked those books, they had two shortcomings: the books were extremely expensive, and most of the work shown was for Japanese companies.

A year or two ago, my publisher came up with the "Big Book" concept. I patiently awaited the chance to do this book; all the while, I had those Japanese books in mind.

Finally, I got to produce my answer to the books from Japan. First of all, this book is very affordable (about half the price of the ones from Japan). Second, the work is from design firms from the USA and around the world. This book is a good global overview of some of the outstanding corporate identity programs in use today.

One short personal note: many people have asked me how we (my publisher and I) can produce high quality books and sell them at such a good price. The answer is high sales volume. The "Big Book" series has climbed to the very top of the list of bestselling graphics books. That success is due to people who find these books worth buying.

To all of you who have made this series so successful, thanks. We'll do our best to keep producing books that deserve your support.

Thanks,

David E. Carter
Editor

LeBoulanger™
—THE BAKER—

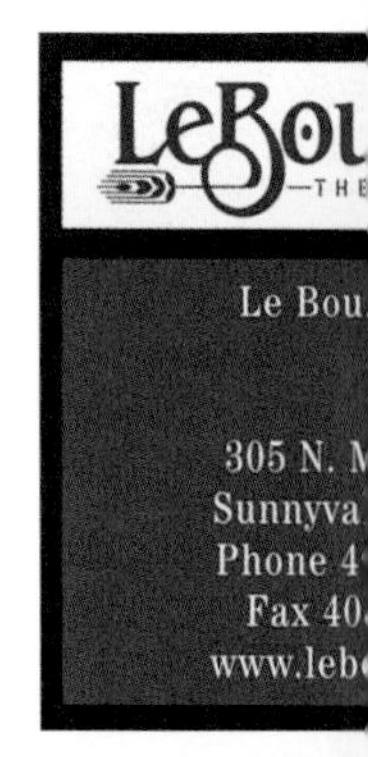

design firm
Tharp Did It
Los Gatos, California
designers
Mr. Tharp, Gina Mageras, Nicole Coleman
client
LeBoulanger
(bakery cafes)

LeBoulanger™
—THE BAKER—

Le Boulanger, Inc.

305 N. Mathilda Ave.
Sunnyvale, CA 94086
Phone 408.774.9000
Fax 408.523.9810
www.leboulanger.com

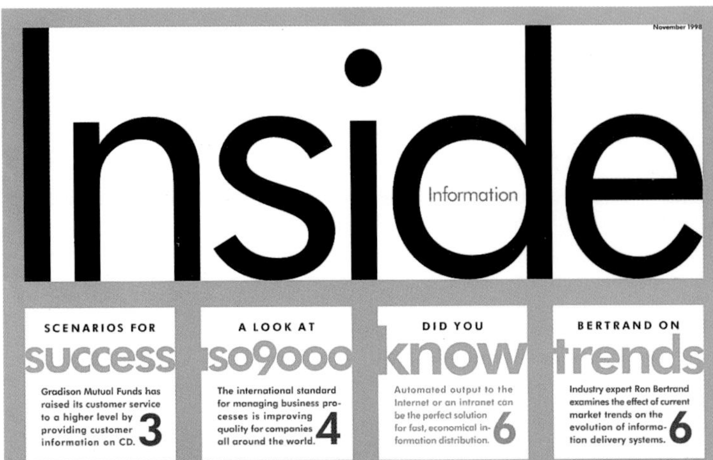
November 1998

Inside
Information

SCENARIOS FOR
success
Gradison Mutual Funds has raised its customer service to a higher level by providing customer information on CD. 3

A LOOK AT
iso9000
The international standard for managing business processes is improving quality for companies all around the world. 4

DID YOU
know
Automated output to the Internet or an intranet can be the perfect solution for fast, economical information distribution. 6

BERTRAND ON
trends
Industry expert Ron Bertrand examines the effect of current market trends on the evolution of information delivery systems. 6

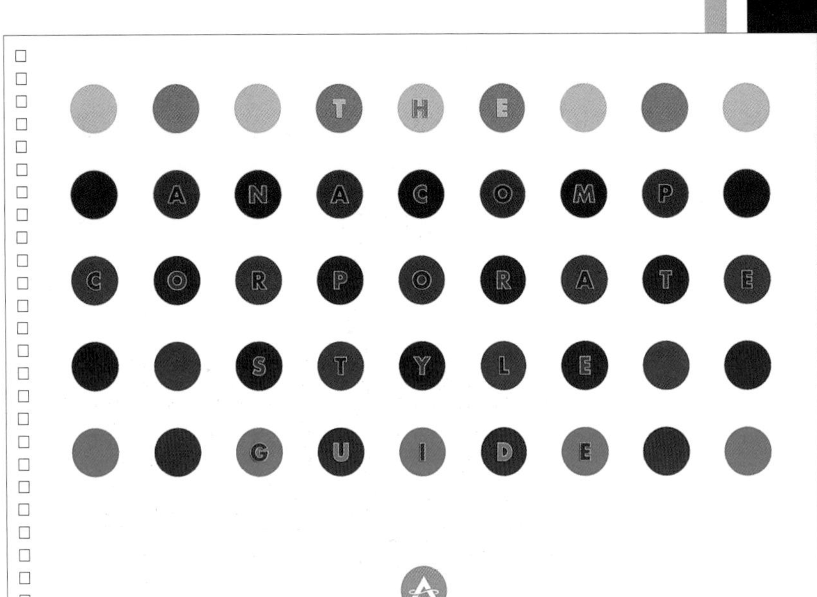

First Image joins Anacomp

On June 18, 1998, Anacomp acquired First Image Management Company, strengthening Anacomp's position as one of the world's leading providers of information-management services.

(continued on next page)

ANACOMP

design firm
Mires Design
San Diego, California
art director
John Ball
designers
Miguel Perez, Pam Meierding,
David Adey, Deborah Hom
illustrators
Tracy Sabin, Jeff Samaripa,
Miguel Perez
client
Anacomp
(information management services)

Inside Information

In today's fast-paced business world, time is more precious than ever. Customers rely on the companies they deal with to help them conduct business swiftly and efficiently. As a result, customer service is a vital part of doing business, and a customer service problem is a serious competitive disadvantage.

Gradison Mutual uses CD to cut response time for customer service.

That was the challenge facing Gradison Mutual Funds of Cincinnati, Ohio. Gradison manages $3 billion in six internal mutual funds for 150,000 customers. The company generates about 20,000 pages of customer statements a month, and until recently, they stored these statements only on microfiche.

Microfiche serves Gradison well for archiving, but it doesn't allow quick enough retrieval for their service representatives to answer customers' questions on the spot. "Customer requests for information were given to clerks who had to spend many hours looking through microfiche to locate specific information," explained Marc Figgins, vice president at Gradison. "This was frustrating for our customers and costly for us."

A better solution. Gradison needed a better solution, one that would offer rapid electronic access at low cost. CD was the perfect candidate. With its 650-megabyte capacity, a single CD can store several months of customer records, all electronically accessible in seconds. And with its low cost, CD can deliver this information to all of Gradison's service representatives very economically.

But how was Gradison to put its information on CD? Encouraged by the high-quality COM services they were receiving from Anacomp, Gradison turned to Anacomp's ALVA™ CD Services. Now, for a low service fee, Gradison has its information delivered on CD as little as 24 hours after the original information is generated. Each disc is a complete package, with fully indexed information and a powerful Windows®-based viewer. Gradison can even add to the existing information on disc to accumulate information over time.

CD made tremendous improvements to Gradison's customer service right from the start, cutting the response time for customer requests from hours to seconds and expanding the company's services. "Now our service representatives have quick access to customer information at their desktops," said Figgins. "We also can produce a duplicate printed copy of a statement right away at the customer's request."

Meeting the challenge. CD proved to be such a success for customer service that Gradison decided to use it for another application: storing and distributing customer records, including mutual fund histories, going back to 1986. "We wanted to preserve data from an old system that we were phasing out," Figgins explained. "ALVA CD Services enabled us to migrate those critical data files to a much better medium. Now we can distribute that information to our brokers on CD, giving them rapid access to more than ten years of individual customer histories."

"Our company has seen significant benefits from using CD," concluded Figgins. "Not only has our customer service become more responsive and friendly, but we're able to manage our documents and customer records better. And because we can add information to a disc over time, we know the information is always current." The business challenge of today is to deliver the best value in products — and the customer service to match. With its powerful storage and retrieval capabilities, rapid turnaround, and low cost, CD is helping Gradison meet that challenge. ●

3

BULK RATE
U.S. POSTAGE
PAID
PERMIT NO. 475
ESCONDIDO, CA

12365 Crosthwaite Circle, Poway, CA 92064

ANACOMP®

Look inside for news on web-based access, outsource services, application tools, and more.

Anacomp InsideInformation

SCENARIOS FOR
success

DOCUMENT DELIVERY:
SERVICE IS THE CHALLENGE AND THE SOLUTION

Fiduciary Trust Company International is a global investment firm, managing assets for both institutional and individual investors. With almost 70 years of investment experience, Fiduciary Trust takes pride in offering its customers a combination of strong performance and personalized service.

A customer-service challenge Not long ago, limitations in Fiduciary Trust's internal document-delivery system were starting to become a problem. The company was using a COLD system to output customers' monthly statements to optical disc for use by customer-service representatives. But this arrangement was a real drain on Fiduciary Trust — it took a lot of labor by IS personnel to produce the discs each month, and it cost extra to add seat licenses for the proprietary viewing software. When the supplier of the system went out of business, Fiduciary Trust was left with no support — and a system that was not Y2K-compliant.

It was time for a new approach, and Vice President Pete Checo took on the challenge. As Checo recalls, "We considered buying a new system, but that would have left us with some of the same difficulties as before, namely the cost of running the system and the danger of obsolescence. We decided to avoid those problems by switching to CD-ROM and outsourcing the CD production."

A CD service solution Fiduciary Trust evaluated CD solutions from a number of service providers, including Anacomp, a longtime provider of reliable document-management services for Fiduciary Trust. After a careful analysis, Anacomp's CD Document Services emerged as the winning solution. "Anacomp gave us one key advantage," continues Checo. "Our statements are generated in Xerox Metacode, and Anacomp's CD service was the only solution we found that let us view and print Metacode documents identical to the originals. Plus, the viewing software comes on every CD, so there's no cost for seat licenses."

Now, Fiduciary Trust is serving its customers more efficiently and conveniently than ever. And thanks to Anacomp's CD Document Services, Fiduciary Trust's personalized service will remain a competitive advantage for years to come. ●

5.

Applications

The Anacomp logo can be applied to virtually any surface for a wide variety of communications and promotional uses. The corporate style guidelines should be observed in all applications.

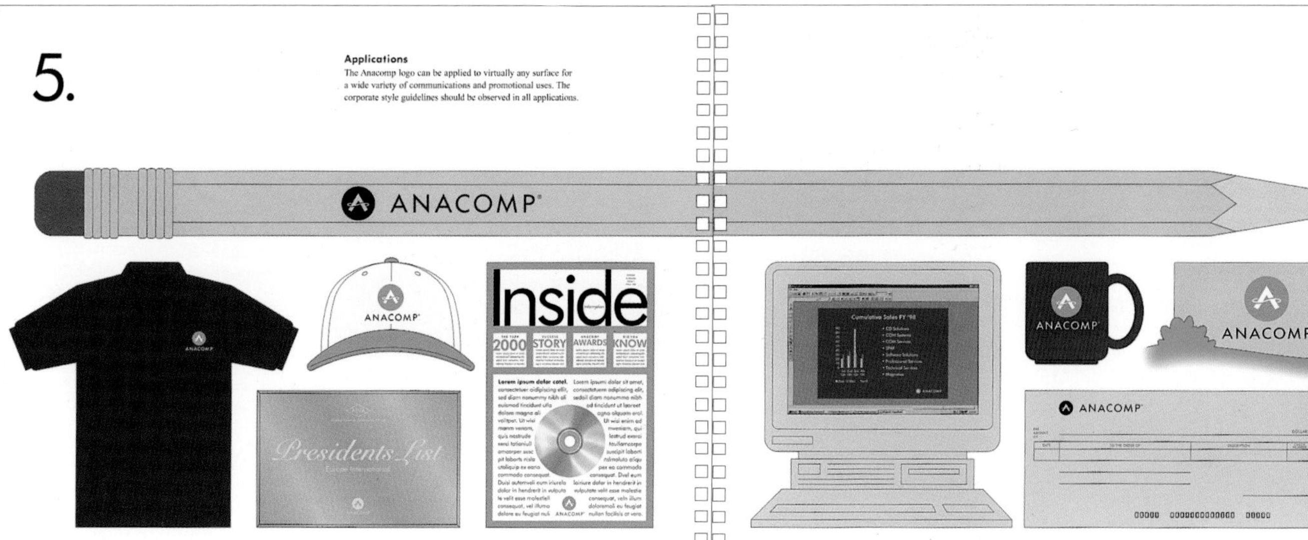

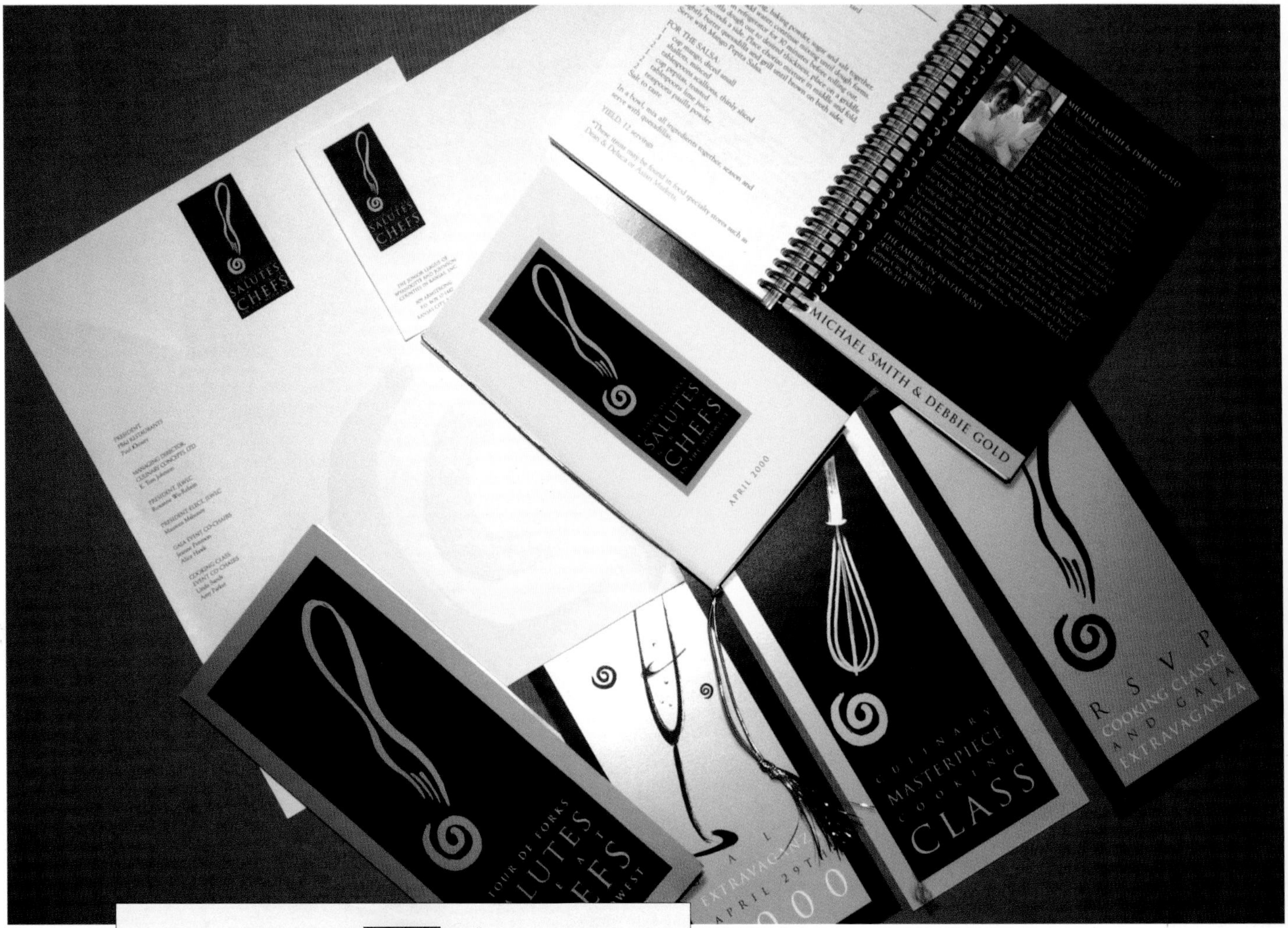

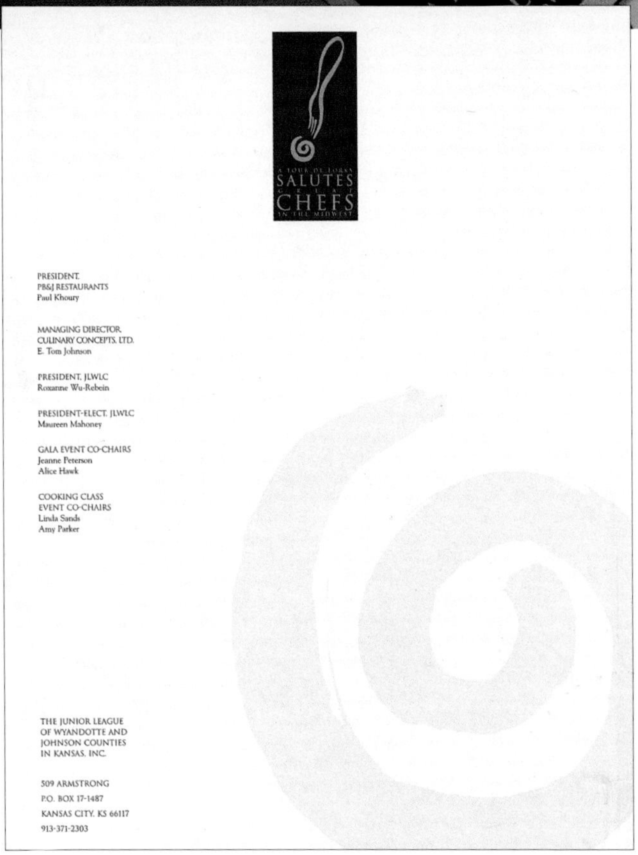

PRESIDENT
PB&J RESTAURANTS
Paul Khoury

MANAGING DIRECTOR
CULINARY CONCEPTS, LTD.
E. Tom Johnson

PRESIDENT, JLWLC
Roxanne Wu-Rebein

PRESIDENT-ELECT, JLWLC
Maureen Mahoney

GALA EVENT CO-CHAIRS
Jeanne Peterson
Alice Hawk

COOKING CLASS
EVENT CO-CHAIRS
Linda Sands
Amy Parker

THE JUNIOR LEAGUE
OF WYANDOTTE AND
JOHNSON COUNTIES
IN KANSAS, INC.

509 ARMSTRONG
P.O. BOX 17-1487
KANSAS CITY, KS 66117
913-371-2303

design firm
EAT Advertising & Design
Kansas City, Missouri
designers
Patrice Eilts-Jobe, DeAnne Dodd
client
PB&J Restaurants/Great Chefs of the Midwest (fundraiser)

THE JUNIOR LEAGUE OF
WYANDOTTE AND JOHNSON
COUNTIES IN KANSAS, INC.,
IS COMMITTED TO ENABLING
THE CHILDREN IN OUR COMMUNITY
TO ACHIEVE THEIR FULL POTENTIAL.
A TOUR DE FORKS® is a registered trademark of the
Junior League of Wyandotte and Johnson Counties in Kansas, Inc.

A TOUR DE FORKS®
SALUTES
GREAT
CHEFS
IN THE MIDWEST

A TOUR DE FORKS
SALUTES
GREAT
CHEFS
IN THE MIDWEST

APRIL 2000

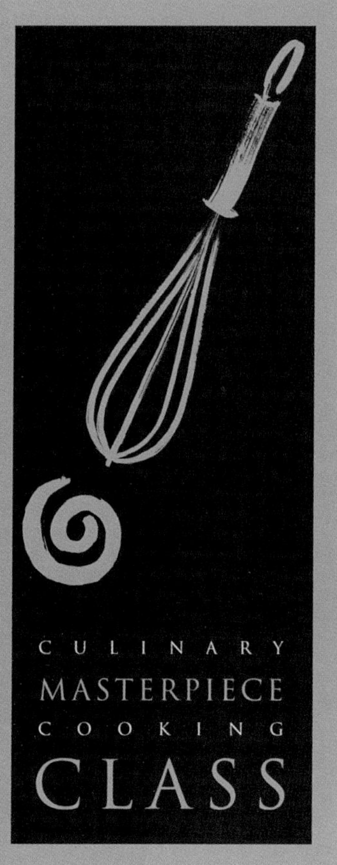
CULINARY
MASTERPIECE
COOKING
CLASS

RSVP
COOKING CLASSES
AND GALA
EXTRAVAGANZA

design firm
Walsh & Associates, Inc.
Seattle, Washington
designers
Miriam Lisco, Rob West
client
Sakson & Taylor
(technical communications for business)

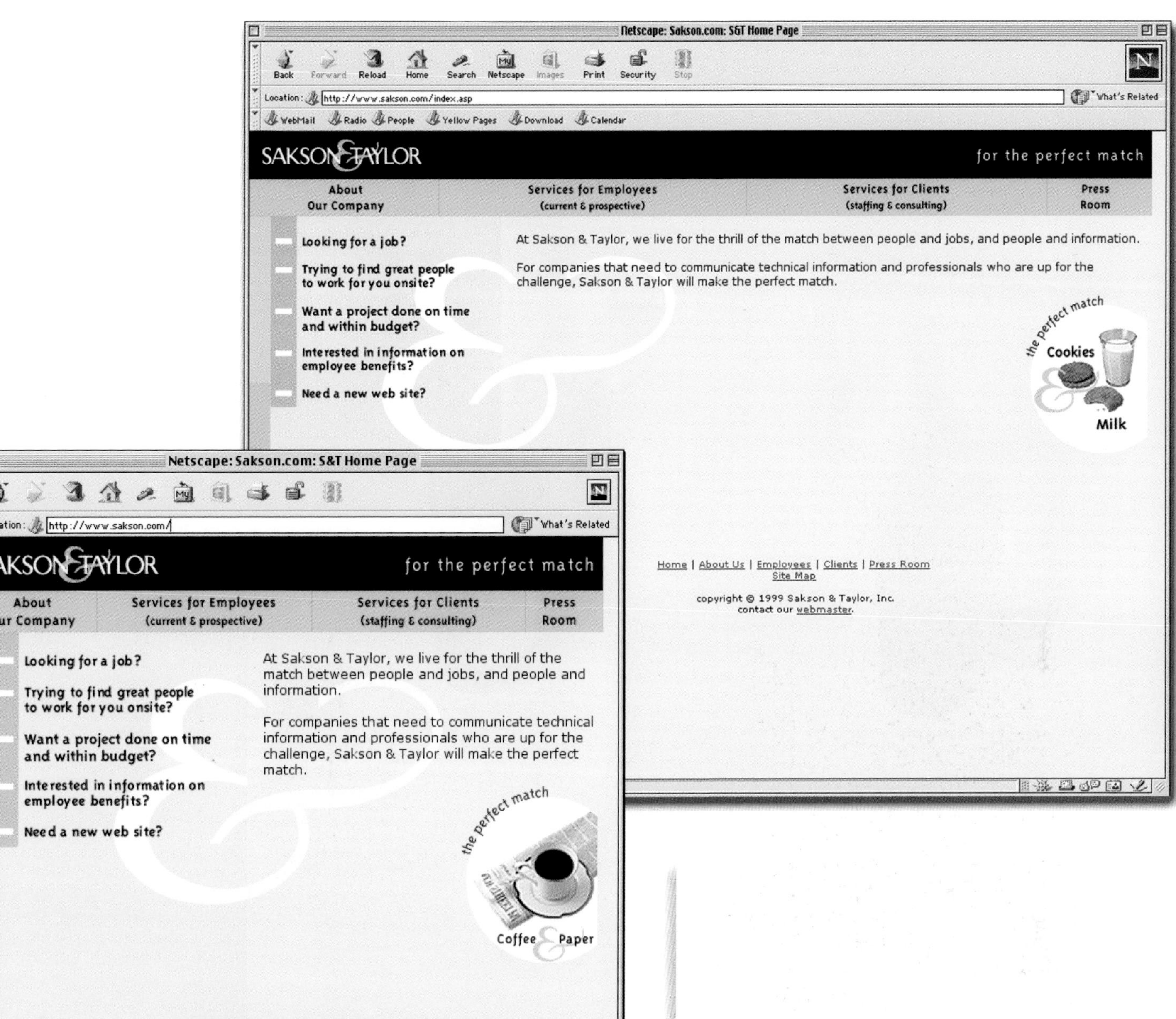

SAKSON & TAYLOR

Sakson & Taylor, Inc

4300 Aurora Avenue North, Suite 100
Seattle, WA 98103-7390
Tel: 206.632.6931 • Fax: 206.632.6927
E-mail: info@sakson.com
Web: www.sakson.com

SAKSON & TAYLOR

AMBROSIA
taste life

110 Camino Oruga
Napa, CA 94558

phone
(800) 435 2225

fax
(800) 435 1329

www.ambrosiawine.com

AMBROSIA
taste life

110 Camino Oruga, Napa, CA 94558
phone (800) 435 2225 fax (800) 435 1329 www.ambrosiawine.com

design firm
Extraprise Group, Inc.
San Francisco, California
designer
Colin O'Neill
client
Ambrosia Wine
(wine merchant)

Direct from the Tasting Room to You

With Winetasting.com you buy directly from the winery tasting rooms, just like you do when you visit wine country. You'll discover special "tasting room only" releases, meet and learn with fellow wine lovers, find the best clubs, and keep up on the latest news, views and tasting notes.

Link to our growing network of partners:

- Chateau Montelena
- Far Niente
- Cakebread
- Whitehall Lane
- Belvedere
- Carneros Creek
- Amici
- Folie a Deux
- Newlan
- Stag's Leap Wine Cellars
- Burgess
- Joseph Phelps
- Volker Eisele
- Murphy-Goode
- Groth
- J Wine Company
- Trentadue
- Trefethen

sting.com℠

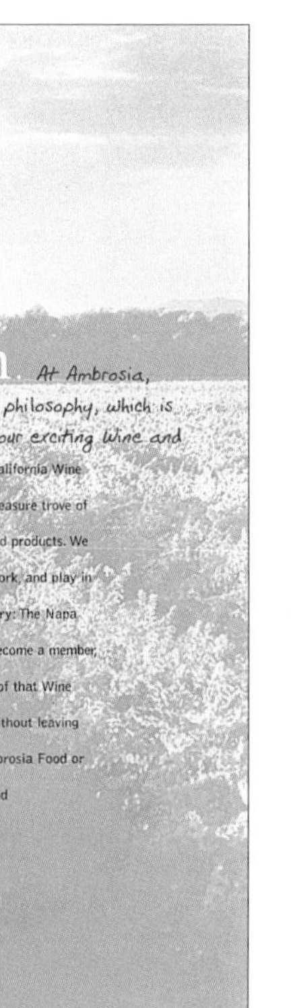

a life rich in experience is the only true source of wealth. *At Ambrosia, we embrace this philosophy, which is why we created our exciting Wine and Food Clubs.* The California Wine Country is a veritable treasure trove of unique places, people and products. We know because we live, work, and play in the heart of Wine Country: The Napa Valley! And, when you become a member, you too will get a taste of that Wine Country experience — without leaving your home! Join an Ambrosia Food or Wine Club (or both!) and

taste life.

A M B R O S I A

FINDING THE BEST, THE BRIGHTEST, THE NEWEST AND THE HOTTEST WINES

"Sometimes I wonder, what I'm a-gonna do
But there ain't no cure for the summertime blues."

It's obvious that wine was far from the mind of late rockabilly artist Eddie Cochran when he penned that tune in 1958. If it had been, Mr. Cochran may have written "Hot Fun in the Summertime" instead. But finding the right summer wine can be a daunting task. Within these pages lies the prescription to all your summertime blues.

Summer Treasures

Whether it be a formal soirée, a backyard barbecue, or to accompany the gentle sway of the hammock, summertime is all about wine that's ready to drink NOW. Start with a chilled, bright white that helps to cool you as the sun warms your skin. Then move onto a red, one born to accompany the fresh, bold flavors of food hot off the grill—nothing heavy, nothing finicky. And as the sun goes down, take a break from the intense heat with an Aged Cabernet from our Collector's Corner. Cheers!

Balancing act.

Vine Cliff 1996 or 1997 Merlot

Harvested from four Napa vineyards, the '96 combines the Carneros region's typical softness with a little Up-Valley oomph from Rutherford and Oakville. Showcasing each region's unique character, this wine begins with rich, forward fruit which is balanced exceedingly well by the soft, supple finish and ample, but soft tannins. The '97 is ripe and rich with black cherry, currant and spice nuances. This medium to full-bodied wine is a winner!

'96 - $37.00/Bottle $33.30/Bottle/Case of 12 order # W-VC-M96-0
'97 - $35.00/Bottle $31.50/Bottle/Case of 12 order # W-VC-M97-0

Silverado Vineyards 1997 Merlot *Change is good.*

Forced to replant their primary Merlot vineyard due to that nasty root eating louse Phylloxera, Silverado turned to their Mt. George Vineyard located in the hills east of Napa. Even with the vineyard change, they didn't miss a beat as the '97 is as good as ever, with flavors of plum, bright raspberry and exotic spices all tied together with fine tannins.

$25.00/Bottle $22.50/Bottle/Case of 12 order # W-SD-M97-0

Clos Du Val 1996 or 1997 Merlot *No softie here.*

As Merlot's soaring popularity rages on, its soft reputation is beginning to wane. Case in point is the '96 Clos Du Val with its big, full-bodied fruit upfront, a great core of ripe fruit in the middle, topped off by a firm, but velvety finish. Its not the neighborhood bully, but the '96 has the muscle to stand up to him. The '97 is even more powerful and straight forward.

'96 - $30.00/Bottle $27.00/Bottle/Case of 12 order # W-CD-M96-0

Appellation: French word for a legally defined geographic area where wines are made, such as Napa Valley.

Vineyard-designation: Vineyards known for their distinct character which result in high-quality wine, such as Martha's Vineyard.

AMBROSIA

110 Camino Oruga
Napa, CA 94558

Toll Free: (800) 435 2225
Fax: (800) 435 1329
Direct: (707) 265 1529
E-Mail: margaretc@ambrosiawine.com

www.ambrosiawine.com

Margaret Carriker

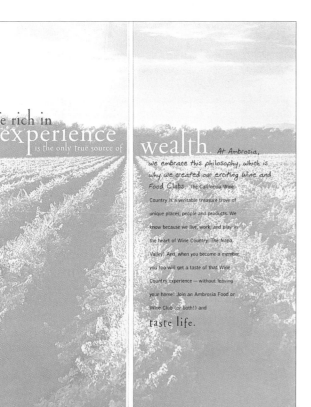

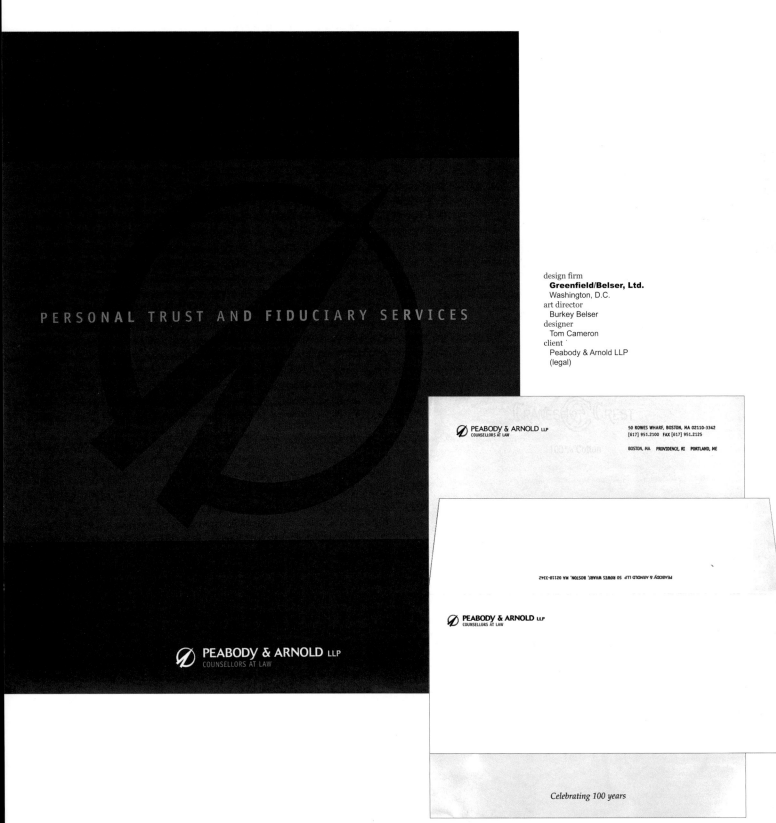

PERSONAL TRUST AND FIDUCIARY SERVICES

PEABODY & ARNOLD LLP
COUNSELLORS AT LAW

design firm
Greenfield/Belser, Ltd.
Washington, D.C.
art director
Burkey Belser
designer
Tom Cameron
client
Peabody & Arnold LLP
(legal)

PEABODY & ARNOLD LLP
COUNSELLORS AT LAW

50 ROWES WHARF, BOSTON, MA 02110-3342
[617] 951.2100 FAX [617] 951.2125

BOSTON, MA PROVIDENCE, RI PORTLAND, ME

PEABODY & ARNOLD LLP
COUNSELLORS AT LAW

Celebrating 100 years

www.peabodyarnold.com

MISSION SUPPORT

PEABODY & ARNOLD LLP
COUNSELLORS AT LAW

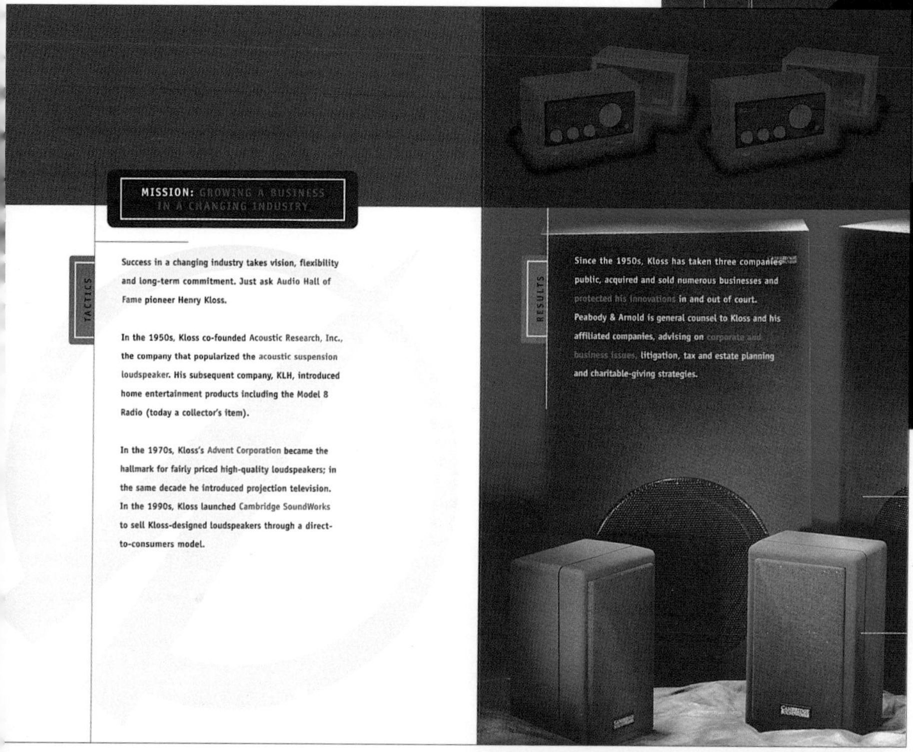

MISSION: GROWING A BUSINESS IN A CHANGING INDUSTRY.

TACTICS

Success in a changing industry takes vision, flexibility and long-term commitment. Just ask Audio Hall of Fame pioneer Henry Kloss.

In the 1950s, Kloss co-founded Acoustic Research, Inc., the company that popularized the acoustic suspension loudspeaker. His subsequent company, KLH, introduced home entertainment products including the Model 8 Radio (today a collector's item).

In the 1970s, Kloss's Advent Corporation became the hallmark for fairly priced high-quality loudspeakers; in the same decade he introduced projection television. In the 1990s, Kloss launched Cambridge SoundWorks to sell Kloss-designed loudspeakers through a direct-to-consumers model.

RESULTS

Since the 1950s, Kloss has taken three companies public, acquired and sold numerous businesses and protected his innovations in and out of court. Peabody & Arnold is general counsel to Kloss and his affiliated companies, advising on corporate and business issues, litigation, tax and estate planning and charitable-giving strategies.

MISSION: SURVIVING
BET-THE-COMPANY LITIGATION
TACTICS
In 1997, start-up Crestone International was fast becoming a leader in the implementation of PeopleSoft ERP software. When employees of a much larger competitor began jumping ship to join the new company, the competitor filed a lawsuit that threatened not just Crestone's right to recruit talented people, but its entire financial future.
Accusing Crestone of stealing employees and trade secrets, the competitor sought millions of dollars in damages and an order preventing Crestone from hiring former employees and soliciting business from the competitor's clients. Crestone counterclaimed that the competitor had hurt its business relationships and had defamed Crestone in various ways.
Peabody & Arnold represented Crestone in the litigation, obtaining a settlement that the company viewed as "a victory and a vindication." We also persuaded Crestone's insurer to contribute to the company's legal fees, based on a novel application of the advertising injury provision of Crestone's policy.
RESULTS
Today, Crestone continues to grow as a leading provider of PeopleSoft implementation services and has expanded its business to include a wide variety of e-business ventures.

KaBloom™
Flower Food
KaBloom™

design firm
BrandEquity International
Newton, Massachusetts
client
Kabloom

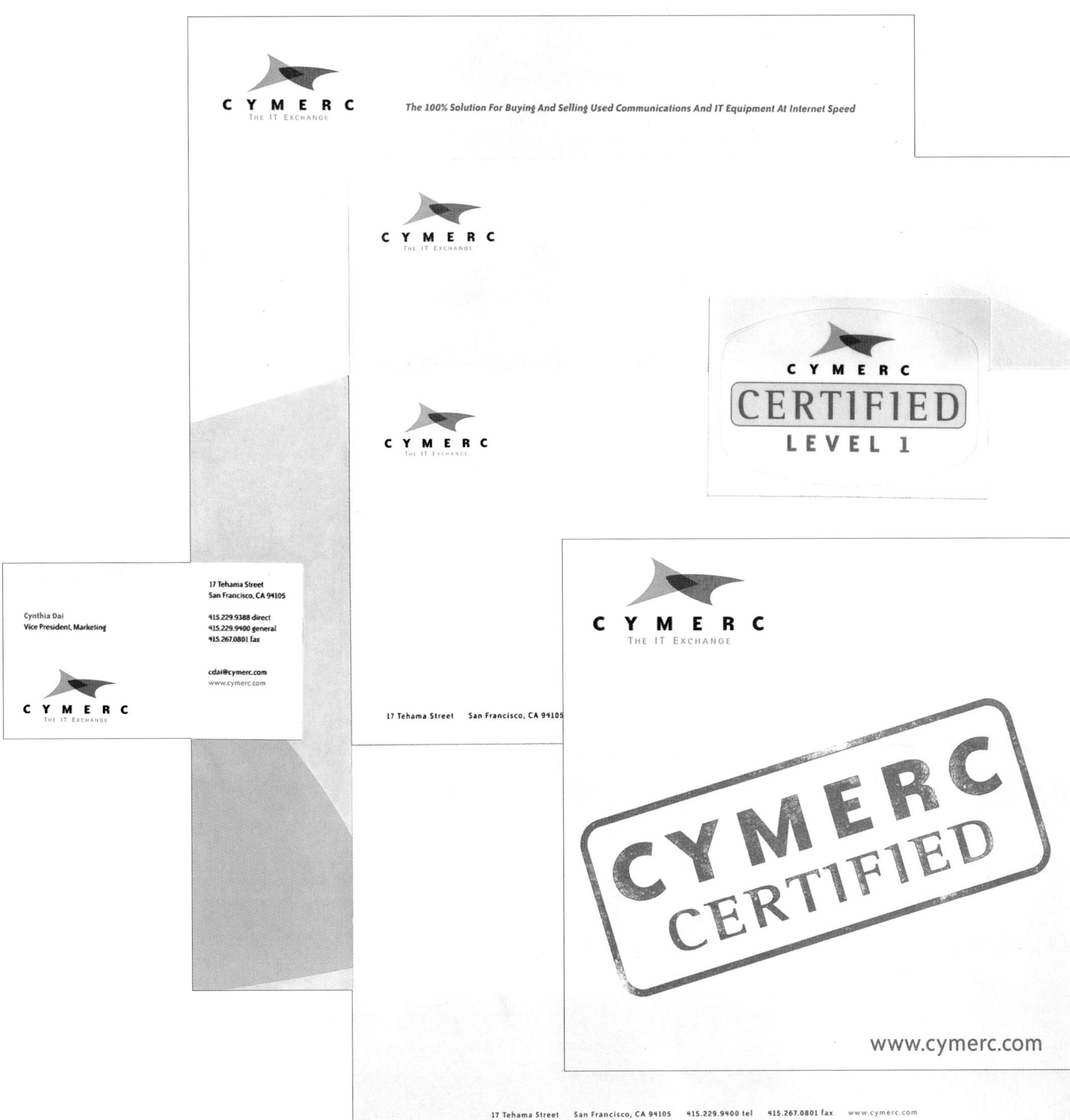

design firm
Extraprise Group, Inc.
San Francisco, California
designers
Colin O'Neill, Clinton Meyer, Amanda Swanson
client
Cymerc Exchange
(online B-B exchange)

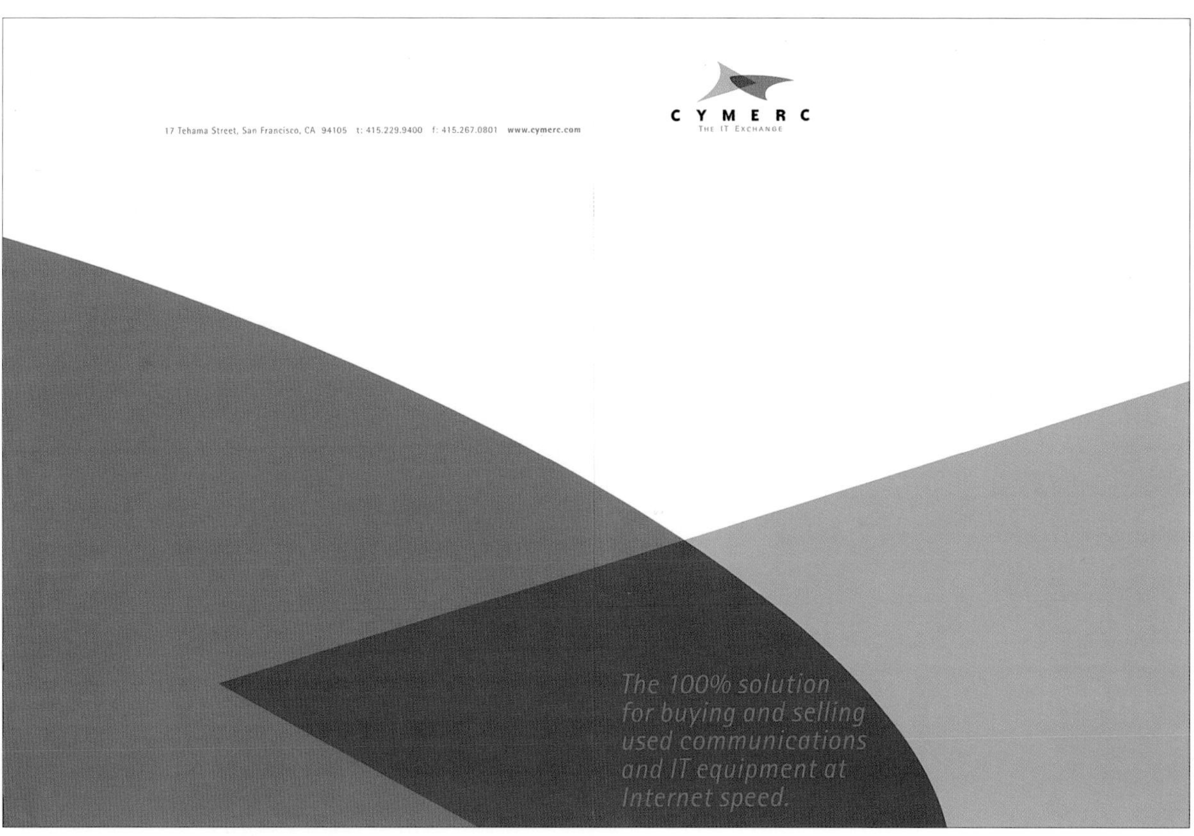
17 Tehama Street, San Francisco, CA 94105 t: 415.229.9400 f: 415.267.0801 www.cymerc.com
CYMERC
THE IT EXCHANGE
The 100% solution for buying and selling used communications and IT equipment at Internet speed.

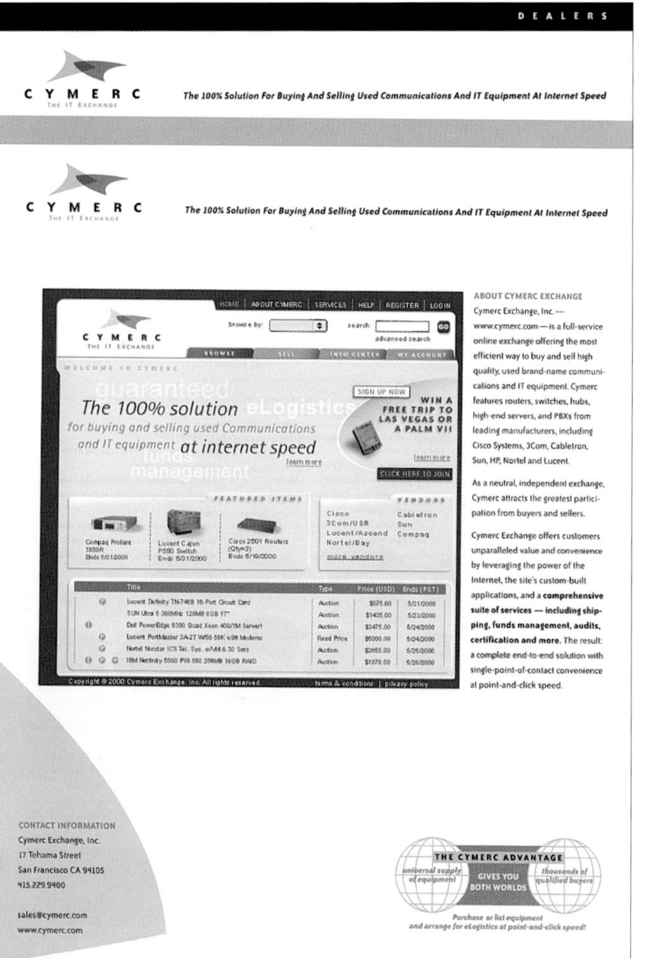
DEALERS
CYMERC
THE IT EXCHANGE
The 100% Solution For Buying And Selling Used Communications And IT Equipment At Internet Speed
CYMERC
THE IT EXCHANGE
The 100% Solution For Buying And Selling Used Communications And IT Equipment At Internet Speed
The 100% solution
for buying and selling used Communications
and IT equipment at internet speed
guaranteed
eLogistics
funds
management
WIN A FREE TRIP TO LAS VEGAS OR A PALM VII
SIGN UP NOW
CLICK HERE TO JOIN
ABOUT CYMERC EXCHANGE
Cymerc Exchange, Inc.—www.cymerc.com—is a full-service online exchange offering the most efficient way to buy and sell high quality, used brand-name communications and IT equipment. Cymerc features routers, switches, hubs, high-end servers, and PBXs from leading manufacturers, including Cisco Systems, 3Com, Cabletron, Sun, HP, Nortel and Lucent.
As a neutral, independent exchange, Cymerc attracts the greatest participation from buyers and sellers.
Cymerc Exchange offers customers unparalleled value and convenience by leveraging the power of the Internet, the site's custom-built applications, and a comprehensive suite of services — including shipping, funds management, audits, certification and more. The result: a complete end-to-end solution with single-point-of-contact convenience at point-and-click speed.
CONTACT INFORMATION
Cymerc Exchange, Inc.
17 Tehama Street
San Francisco CA 94105
415.229.9400
sales@cymerc.com
www.cymerc.com
THE CYMERC ADVANTAGE
universal supply of equipment
GIVES YOU BOTH WORLDS
thousands of qualified buyers
Purchase or list equipment and arrange for eLogistics at point-and-click speed!

LEASING
CYMERC
THE IT EXCHANGE
The 100% Solution For Buying And Selling Used Communications And IT Equipment At Internet Speed
CYMERC
THE IT EXCHANGE
The 100% Solution For Buying And Selling Used Communications And IT Equipment At Internet Speed
NEUTRAL EXCHANGE
Cymerc offers a neutral and independent exchange, acting as a trusted intermediary to help both buyers and sellers. A neutral exchange ensures competitive pricing, broadest access, strongest demand, and greatest participation from buyers and sellers.
DRIVING BUYERS AND SELLERS TO CYMERC
Cymerc drives buyers to the site through a highly focused, integrated marketing effort. Cymerc targets those who directly buy or influence the purchasing decision of used communications and IT equipment—including dealers, brokers and Value Added Resellers (VARs), as well as end users. Cymerc's marketing efforts incorporate advertising in leading print and online industry journals, direct mail, telesales, participation in trade associations and conferences.
To aggregate equipment on the site, Cymerc's national direct sales force targets leading leasing companies, ISPs, telecommunications and Fortune 1000 businesses.
THE CYMERC TEAM
Cymerc Exchange is led by an exceptional team of industry veterans with extensive experience in e-commerce, marketing, technical service, and the used communications equipment market. Beyond technology, the Cymerc team has a proven track record for delivering business solutions to meet the mission-critical needs of its customers.
HOW THE PROCESS WORKS
REGISTER as a customer at www.cymerc.com
LIST equipment for sale
"CYMERC CERTIFIED"™ audit, test and refurbishment
Registered buyers bid
Cymerc updates you on sale
Cymerc manages transfer of funds
Cymerc ships equipment
Cymerc is very easy to use. Simply enter www.cymerc.com and register as a customer. Just enter the description or send us the list of the equipment you would like to sell along with the target prices. We will promptly pick-up, audit, test, refurbish and "Cymerc Certify"™ the equipment. Cymerc instantly enables thousands of qualified buyers to find your products, bid on them, and purchase them. We will update you on the progress of the bidding and notify you when the sale closes. We collect the funds from the buyer and arrange for the equipment to be shipped. Upon equipment delivery, you will receive prompt payment from Cymerc. You can come back frequently to the Cymerc site to access useful information about what buyers need and how to price your equipment effectively.
CONTACT INFORMATION
Cymerc Exchange, Inc.
17 Tehama Street
San Francisco CA 94105
415.229.9400
sales@cymerc.com
www.cymerc.com
THE CYMERC ADVANTAGE
universal supply of equipment
GIVES YOU BOTH WORLDS
thousands of qualified buyers
Purchase or list equipment and arrange for eLogistics at point-and-click speed!

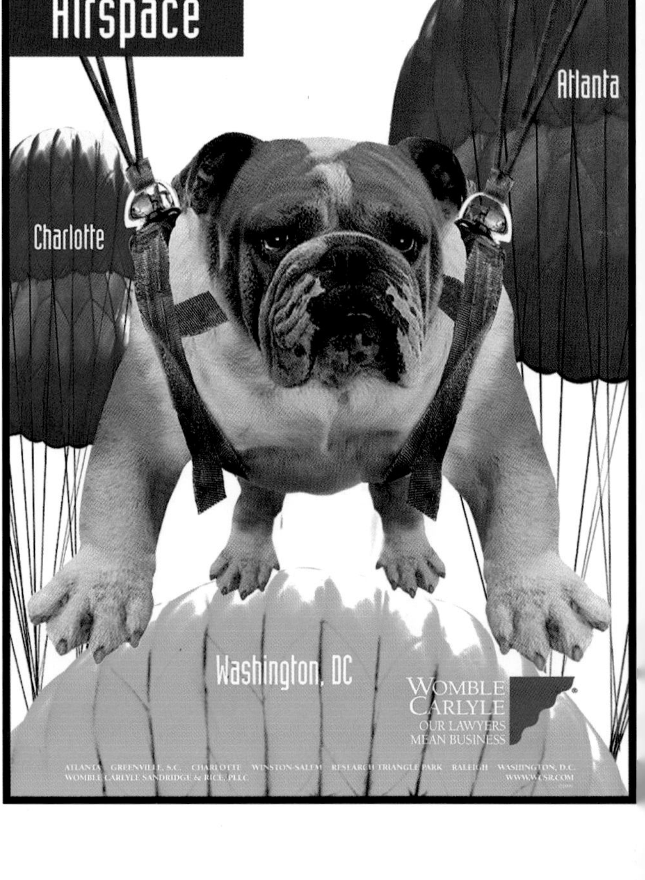

design firm
Greenfield/Belser, Ltd.
Washington, D.C.
art director
Burkey Belser
designer
Jeanette Nuzum
client
Womble Carlyle Sandridge & Rice (legal)

Pedigree
You deserve more from your legal practice than a paycheck and a lock-step march to partnership. Meaningful work that challenges and excites you. Mentors eager to help you grow. Freedom to seek a balance between your work and home life. The opportunity to serve your community in a way that suits your interests and values. A collegial environment filled with people you look forward to seeing each day. Meet some lawyers who've found those things at Womble Carlyle—and a few of their friends.

Good companions
"When I started at Womble Carlyle I was new to the area. The lawyers opened their homes to me and invited me to spend time with their families. The whole culture is one of collegiality and inclusiveness."
Jonathan Mason, Associate
Products Liability Litigation
Atlanta
Georgetown University Law Center
Jonathan started as a summer associate in our Raleigh office and has since worked in the Winston-Salem and Atlanta offices, collecting many new friends along the way.
Our expansion has mirrored the dynamic growth of the Southeast. From our Winston-Salem roots, we have expanded along with our clients and other businesses drawn by the region's economic, climatic and lifestyle advantages. Today we are helping clients thrive in the vibrant economy of Greenville and upstate South Carolina, connect with capital in Charlotte and Atlanta, grow emerging technology companies in Research Triangle Park and Northern Virginia, and influence state and federal policymakers in Raleigh and Washington, D.C.

Stomping Grounds
ATLANTA
CHARLOTTE
WASHINGTON, D.C.
RESEARCH TRIANGLE PARK
WOMBLE CARLYLE
OUR LAWYERS MEAN BUSINESS
ATLANTA GREENVILLE, S.C. CHARLOTTE WINSTON-SALEM RESEARCH TRIANGLE PARK RALEIGH WASHINGTON, D.C.
WOMBLE CARLYLE SANDRIDGE & RICE, PLLC
WWW.WCSR.COM

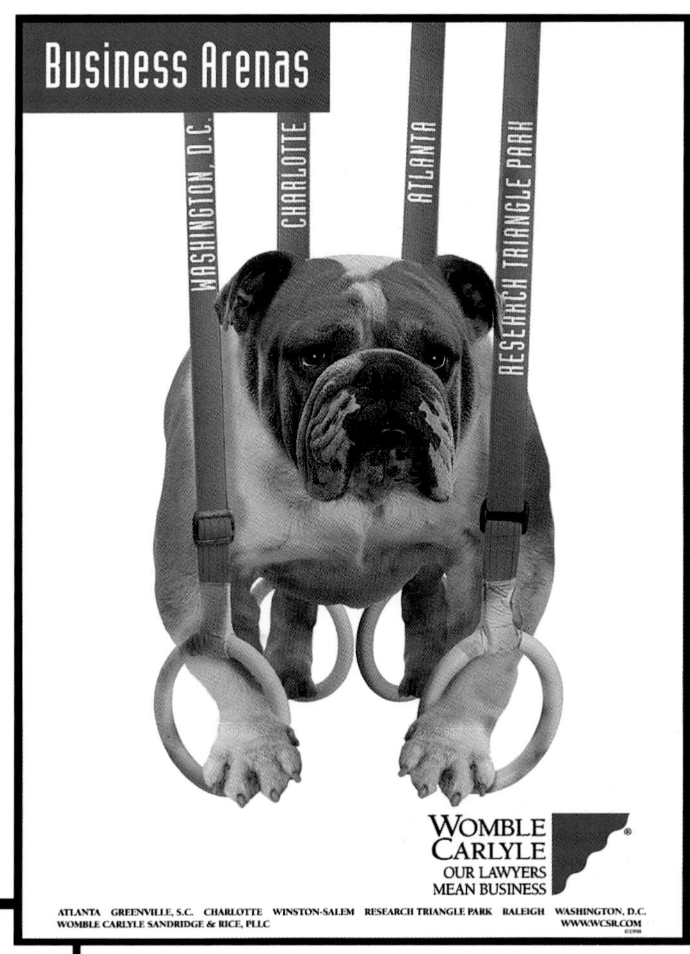
Business Arenas
WASHINGTON, D.C.
CHARLOTTE
ATLANTA
RESEARCH TRIANGLE PARK
WOMBLE CARLYLE
OUR LAWYERS MEAN BUSINESS
ATLANTA GREENVILLE, S.C. CHARLOTTE WINSTON-SALEM RESEARCH TRIANGLE PARK RALEIGH WASHINGTON, D.C.
WOMBLE CARLYLE SANDRIDGE & RICE, PLLC
WWW.WCSR.COM

WOMBLE CARLYLE
OUR LAWYERS MEAN BUSINESS

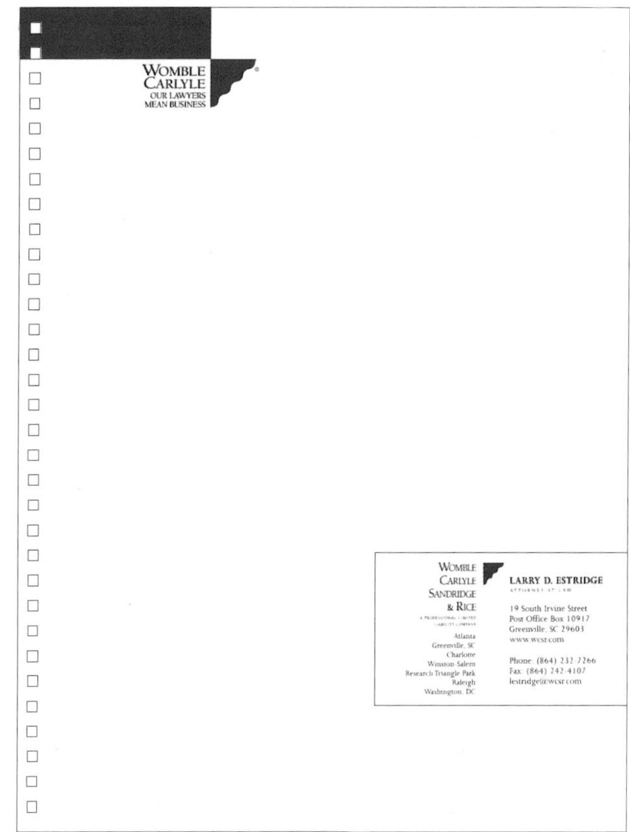
WOMBLE CARLYLE
OUR LAWYERS MEAN BUSINESS
WOMBLE
CARLYLE
SANDRIDGE
& RICE
Atlanta
Greenville, SC
Charlotte
Winston-Salem
Research Triangle Park
Raleigh
Washington, DC
LARRY D. ESTRIDGE
ATTORNEY AT LAW
19 South Irvine Street
Post Office Box 10917
Greenville, SC 29603
www.wcsr.com
Phone: (864) 232-7266
Fax: (864) 242-4107
lestridge@wcsr.com

innoVentry™

design firm
Hornall Anderson Design Works, Inc.
Seattle, Washington
designers
Jack Anderson, Kathy Saito, Sonja Max,
Henry Yiu, Alan Copeland, Chris Sallquist,
Emily Chaney, Naomi Davidson
client
Wells Fargo "Innoventry"
(innovative financial solutions for kiosks)

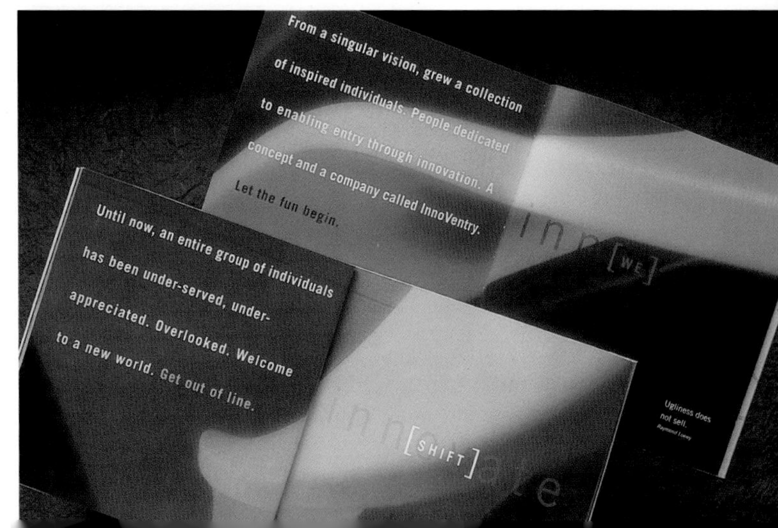

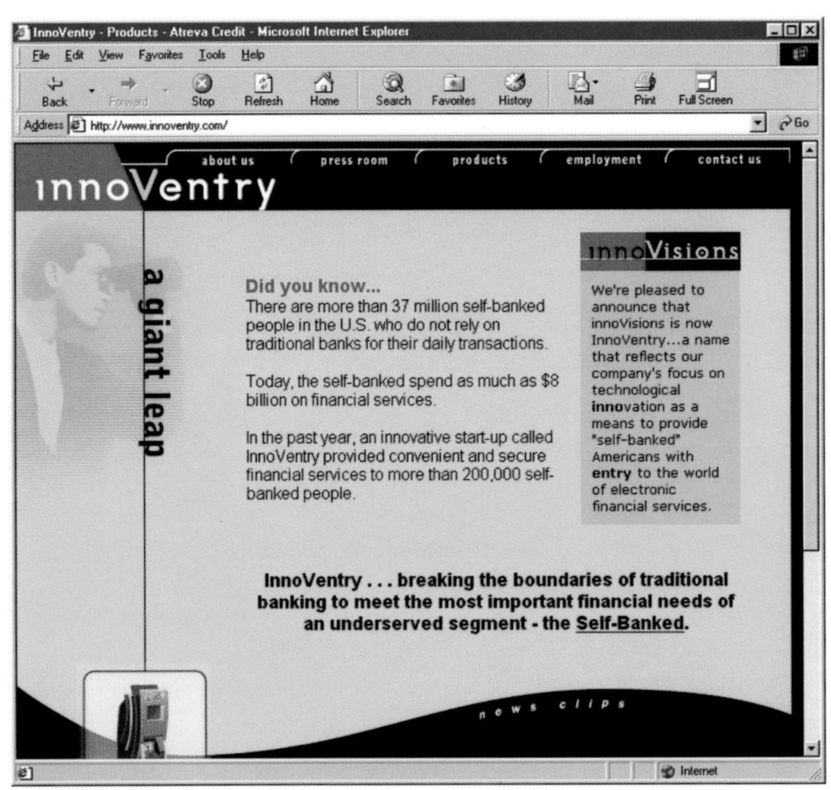

InnoVentry - Products - Atreva Credit - Microsoft Internet Explorer
File Edit View Favorites Tools Help
Back Forward Stop Refresh Home Search Favorites History Mail Print Full Screen
Address http://www.innoventry.com/
Go
about us
press room
products
employment
contact us
innoVentry
a giant leap
Did you know...
There are more than 37 million self-banked people in the U.S. who do not rely on traditional banks for their daily transactions.
Today, the self-banked spend as much as $8 billion on financial services.
In the past year, an innovative start-up called InnoVentry provided convenient and secure financial services to more than 200,000 self-banked people.
innoVisions
We're pleased to announce that innoVisions is now InnoVentry...a name that reflects our company's focus on technological innovation as a means to provide "self-banked" Americans with entry to the world of electronic financial services.
InnoVentry . . . breaking the boundaries of traditional banking to meet the most important financial needs of an underserved segment - the Self-Banked.
news clips
Internet

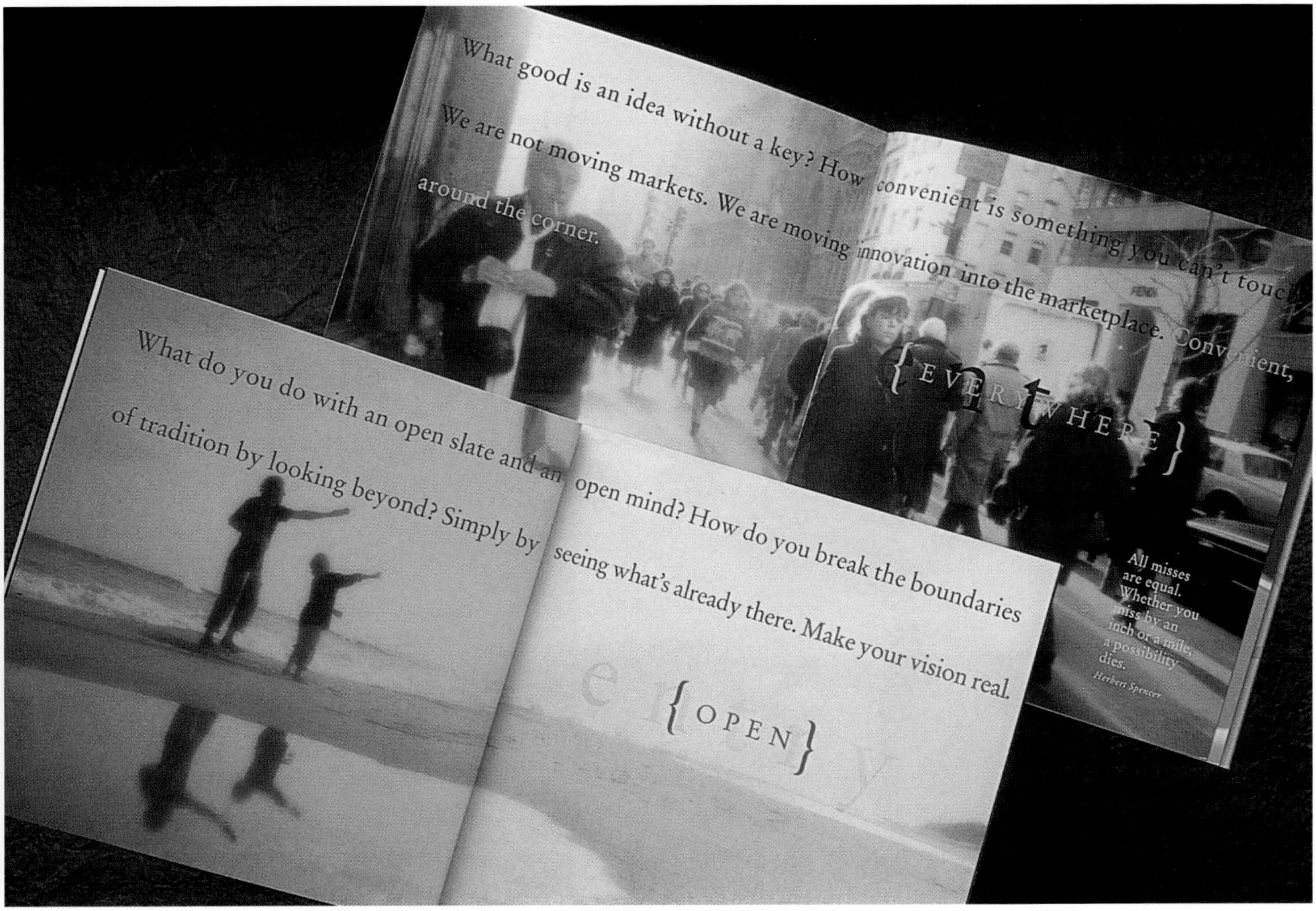

What good is an idea without a key? How convenient is something you can't touch
We are not moving markets. We are moving innovation into the marketplace. Convenient,
around the corner.
{EVERYWHERE}
All misses are equal. Whether you miss by an inch or a mile, a possibility dies.
Herbert Spencer
What do you do with an open slate and an open mind? How do you break the boundaries
of tradition by looking beyond? Simply by seeing what's already there. Make your vision real.
{OPEN}

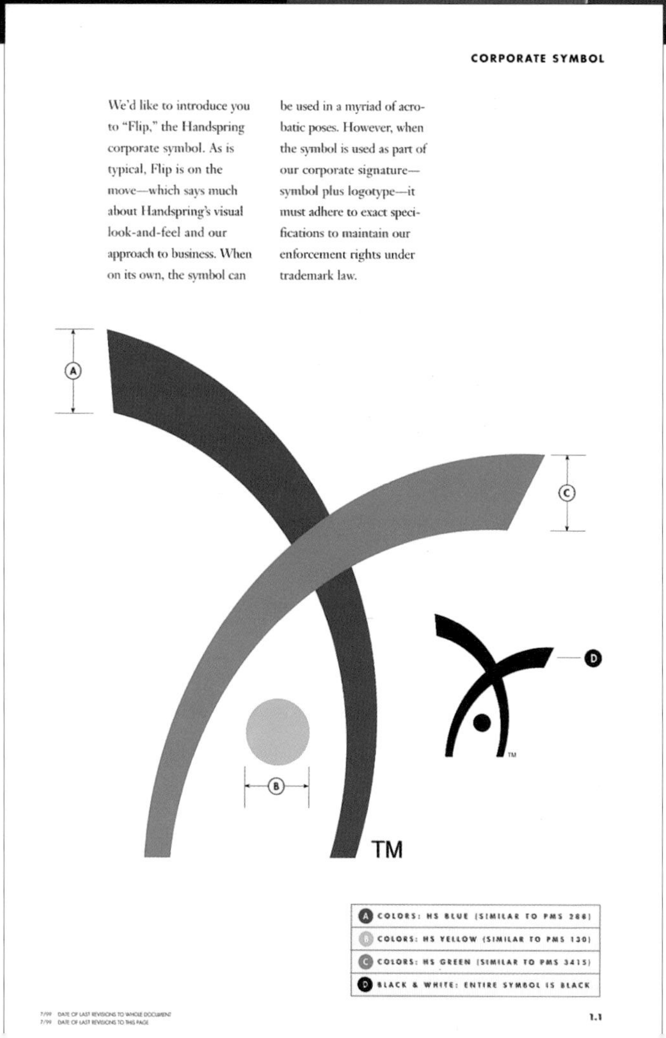

CORPORATE SYMBOL

We'd like to introduce you to "Flip," the Handspring corporate symbol. As is typical, Flip is on the move—which says much about Handspring's visual look-and-feel and our approach to business. When on its own, the symbol can be used in a myriad of acrobatic poses. However, when the symbol is used as part of our corporate signature—symbol plus logotype—it must adhere to exact specifications to maintain our enforcement rights under trademark law.

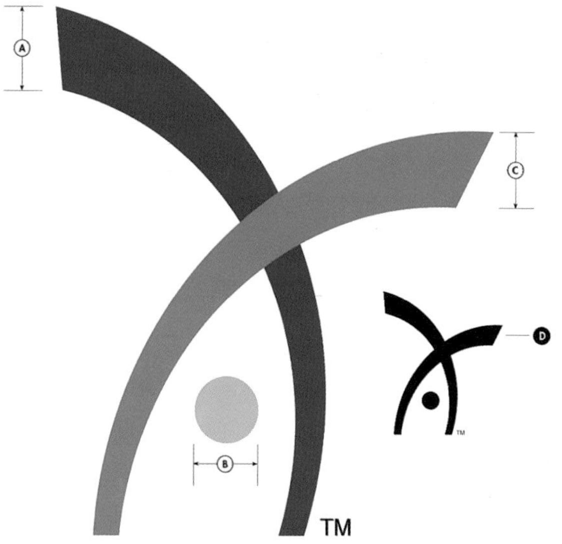

A COLORS: HS BLUE (SIMILAR TO PMS 286)
B COLORS: HS YELLOW (SIMILAR TO PMS 120)
C COLORS: HS GREEN (SIMILAR TO PMS 3415)
D BLACK & WHITE: ENTIRE SYMBOL IS BLACK

7/99 DATE OF LAST REVISIONS TO WHOLE DOCUMENT
7/99 DATE OF LAST REVISIONS TO THIS PAGE

1.1

design firm
Mortensen Design
Mountain View, California
art director
Gordon Mortensen
designers
Gordon Mortensen, PJ Nidecker
client
Handspring, Inc.
(hardware company)

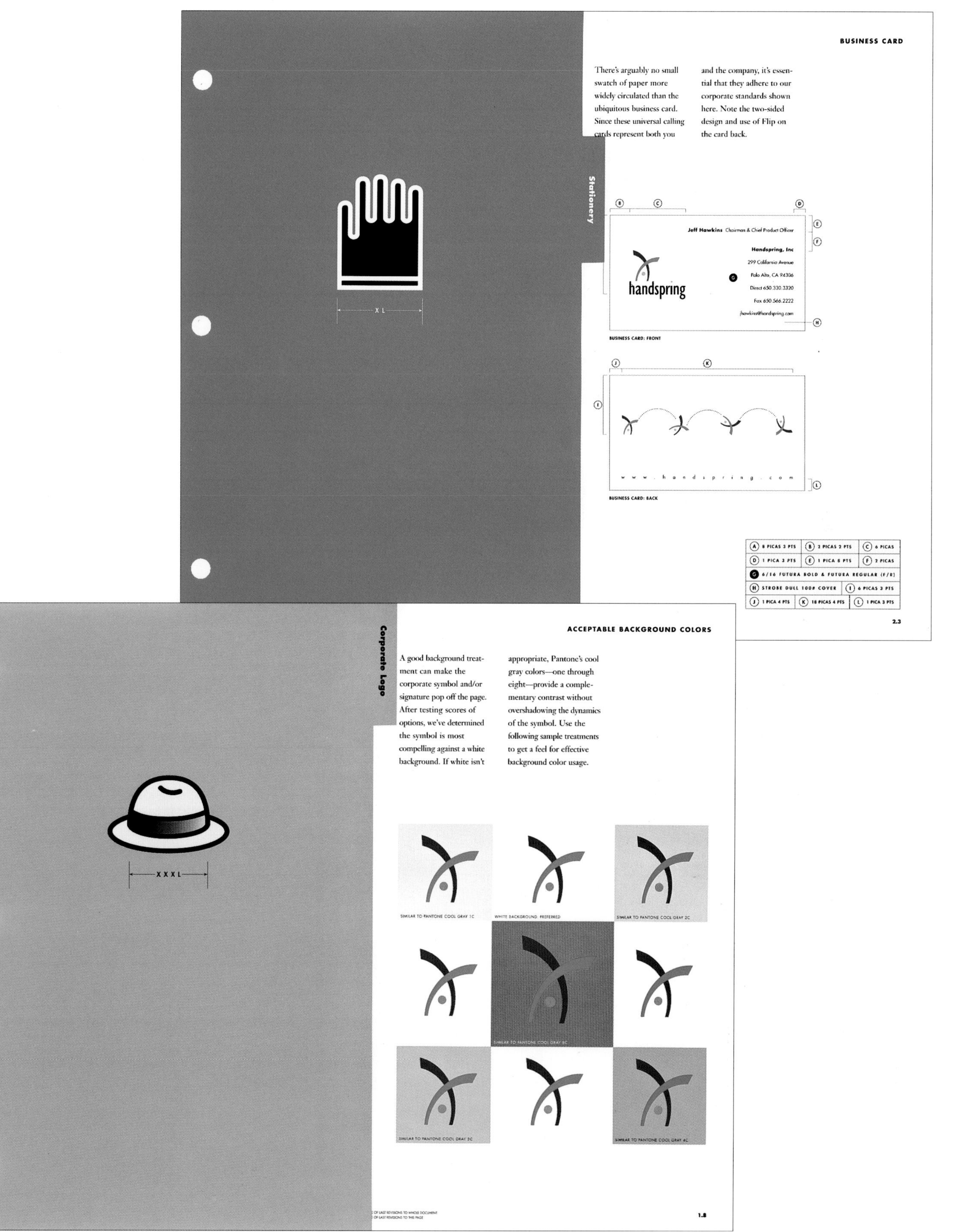

BUSINESS CARD

There's arguably no small swatch of paper more widely circulated than the ubiquitous business card. Since these universal calling cards represent both you and the company, it's essential that they adhere to our corporate standards shown here. Note the two-sided design and use of Flip on the card back.

Jeff Hawkins Chairman & Chief Product Officer
Handspring, Inc
299 California Avenue
Palo Alto, CA 94306
Direct 650.330.3320
Fax 650.566.2222
jhawkins@handspring.com
handspring

BUSINESS CARD: FRONT

BUSINESS CARD: BACK

(A) 8 PICAS 3 PTS	(B) 2 PICAS 2 PTS	(C) 6 PICAS
(D) 1 PICA 3 PTS	(E) 1 PICA 8 PTS	(F) 2 PICAS
(G) 6/16 FUTURA BOLD & FUTURA REGULAR (F/R)		
(H) STROBE DULL 100# COVER	(I) 6 PICAS 3 PTS	
(J) 1 PICA 4 PTS	(K) 18 PICAS 4 PTS	(L) 1 PICA 3 PTS

2.3

ACCEPTABLE BACKGROUND COLORS

A good background treatment can make the corporate symbol and/or signature pop off the page. After testing scores of options, we've determined the symbol is most compelling against a white background. If white isn't appropriate, Pantone's cool gray colors—one through eight—provide a complementary contrast without overshadowing the dynamics of the symbol. Use the following sample treatments to get a feel for effective background color usage.

SIMILAR TO PANTONE COOL GRAY 1C

WHITE BACKGROUND: PREFERRED

SIMILAR TO PANTONE COOL GRAY 2C

SIMILAR TO PANTONE COOL GRAY 8C

SIMILAR TO PANTONE COOL GRAY 3C

SIMILAR TO PANTONE COOL GRAY 4C

1.8

Tonkon Torp LLP
ATTORNEYS

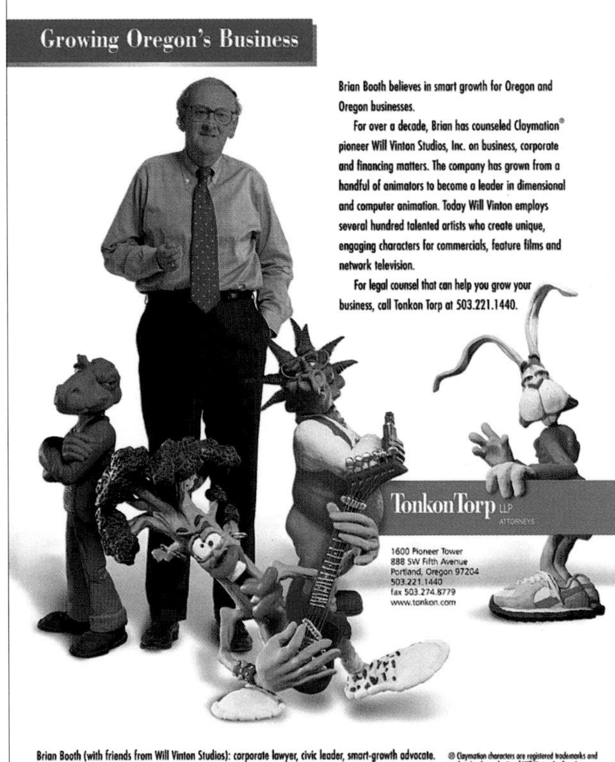

design firm
Greenfield/Belser, Ltd.
Washington, D.C.
art director
Burkey Belser
designer
Tom Cameron
client
Tonkon Torp LLP
(legal)

Tonkon, Torp, Galen, Marmaduke & Booth has changed its name to Tonkon Torp LLP and has become a limited liability partnership. While the name has changed, Messrs. Galen, Marmaduke and Booth remain active partners in the firm, and everyone at Tonkon Torp remains committed to providing the highest quality legal services.

Tonkon Torp LLP
ATTORNEYS

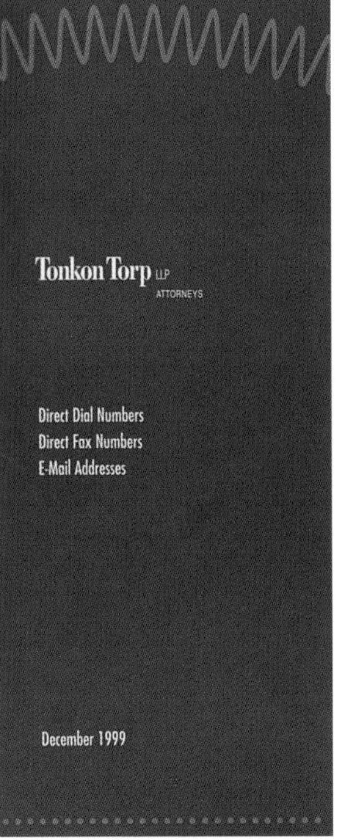

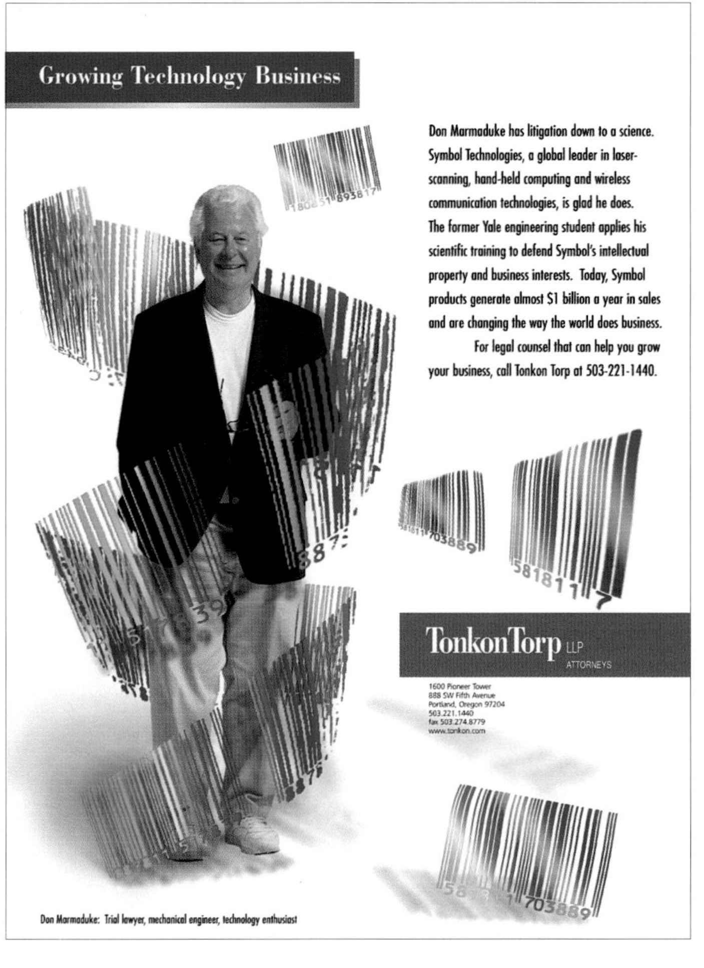
Growing Technology Business
Don Marmaduke has litigation down to a science. Symbol Technologies, a global leader in laser-scanning, hand-held computing and wireless communication technologies, is glad he does. The former Yale engineering student applies his scientific training to defend Symbol's intellectual property and business interests. Today, Symbol products generate almost $1 billion a year in sales and are changing the way the world does business.
For legal counsel that can help you grow your business, call Tonkon Torp at 503-221-1440.
Tonkon Torp LLP
ATTORNEYS
1600 Pioneer Tower
888 SW Fifth Avenue
Portland, Oregon 97204
503.221.1440
fax 503.274.8779
www.tonkon.com
Don Marmaduke: Trial lawyer, mechanical engineer, technology enthusiast

Growing Oregon's Business
Our virtual reality: Virtually every day, Tonkon Torp lawyers work with high-tech entrepreneurs in industries from software to biotech to multimedia and the Internet. Our experience with venture capitalists and the Silicon Valley business model can help you lock on opportunities before they whiz by.
To get started, call Jeff Harmes or Brendan McDonnell at 503.221.1440.
Tonkon Torp LLP
ATTORNEYS
1600 Pioneer Tower
888 SW Fifth Avenue
Portland, Oregon 97204
503.221.1440
fax 503.274.8779
www.tonkon.com

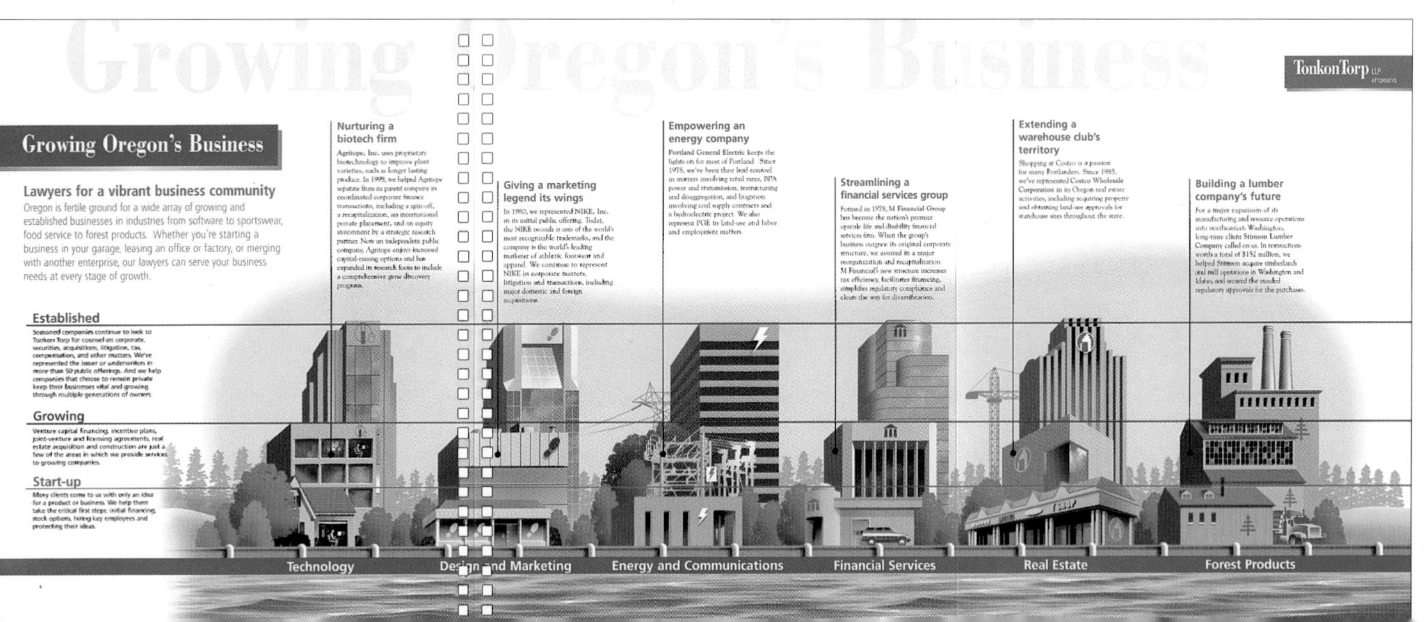
Growing Oregon's Business
Tonkon Torp LLP
ATTORNEYS
Growing Oregon's Business
Lawyers for a vibrant business community
Oregon is fertile ground for a wide array of growing and established businesses in industries from software to sportswear, food service to forest products. Whether you're starting a business in your garage, leasing an office or factory, or merging with another enterprise, our lawyers can serve your business needs at every stage of growth.
Established
Seasoned companies continue to look to Tonkon Torp for counsel on corporate, securities, acquisitions, litigation, tax, compensation, and other matters. We've represented the issuer or underwriters in more than 50 public offerings. And we help companies that choose to remain private keep their businesses vital and growing through multiple generations of owners.
Growing
Venture capital financing, incentive plans, joint-venture and licensing agreements, real estate acquisition and construction are just a few of the areas in which we provide services to growing companies.
Start-up
Many clients come to us with only an idea for a product or business. We help them take the critical first steps: initial financing, stock options, hiring key employees and protecting their ideas.
Nurturing a biotech firm
Agritope, Inc. uses proprietary biotechnology to improve plant varieties, such as longer lasting produce. In 1998, we helped Agritope separate from its parent company in coordinated corporate finance transactions, including a spin-off, a recapitalization, an international private placement, and an equity investment by a strategic research partner. Now an independent public company, Agritope enjoys increased capital-raising options and has expanded its research focus to include a comprehensive gene discovery program.
Giving a marketing legend its wings
In 1980, we represented NIKE, Inc. in its initial public offering. Today, the NIKE swoosh is one of the world's most recognizable trademarks, and the company is the world's leading marketer of athletic footwear and apparel. We continue to represent NIKE in corporate matters, litigation and transactions, including major domestic and foreign acquisitions.
Empowering an energy company
Portland General Electric keeps the lights on for most of Portland. Since 1978, we've been their lead counsel in matters involving retail rates, BPA power and transmission, restructuring and disaggregation, and litigation involving coal supply contracts and a hydroelectric project. We also represent PGE in land-use and labor and employment matters.
Streamlining a financial services group
Formed in 1978, M Financial Group has become the nation's premier upscale life and disability financial services firm. When the group's business outgrew its original corporate structure, we assisted in a major reorganization and recapitalization. M Financial's new structure increases tax efficiency, facilitates financing, simplifies regulatory compliance and clears the way for diversification.
Extending a warehouse club's territory
Shopping at Costco is a passion for many Portlanders. Since 1985, we've represented Costco Wholesale Corporation in its Oregon real estate activities, including acquiring property and obtaining land-use approvals for warehouse sites throughout the state.
Building a lumber company's future
For a major expansion of its manufacturing and resource operations into northeastern Washington, long-time client Stimson Lumber Company called on us. In transactions worth a total of $192 million, we helped Stimson acquire timberlands and mill operations in Washington and Idaho, and secured the needed regulatory approvals for the purchases.
Technology
Design and Marketing
Energy and Communications
Financial Services
Real Estate
Forest Products

design firm
Sayles Graphic Design
Des Moines, Iowa
designer
John Sayles
client
Sayles Graphic Design
(graphic design firm)

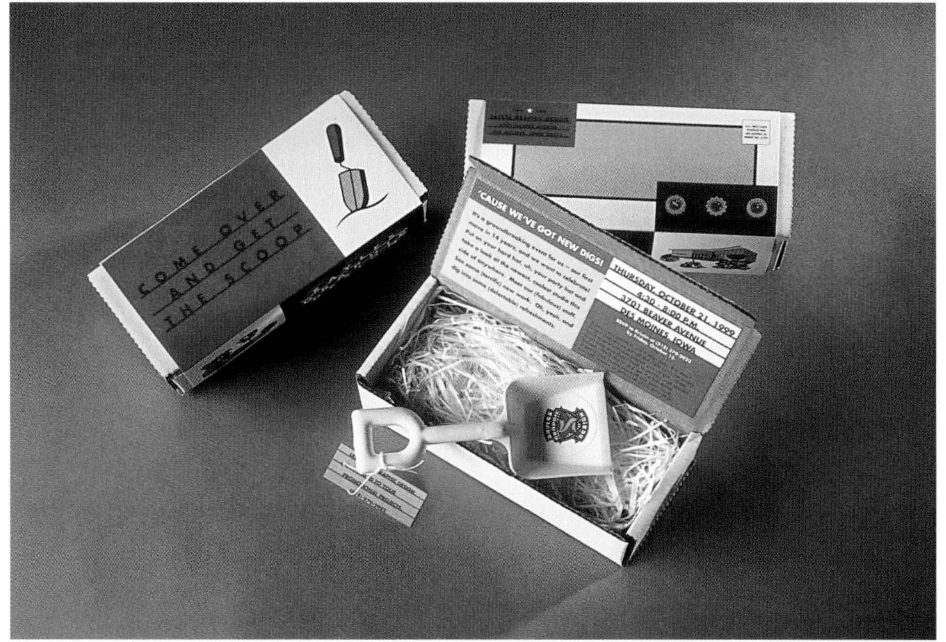

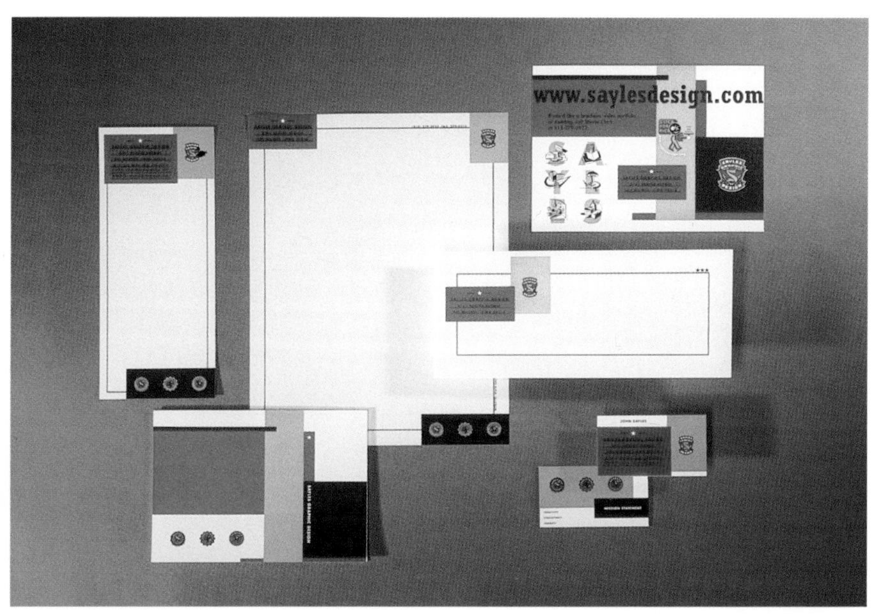
www.saylesdesign.com

SAYLES
GRAPHIC
DESIGN
ristorante
TOSCANO
515-243-2922
Just Call Sheree Clark

www.saylesdesign.com

SAYLES
GRAPHIC
DESIGN
Des Moines, Iowa

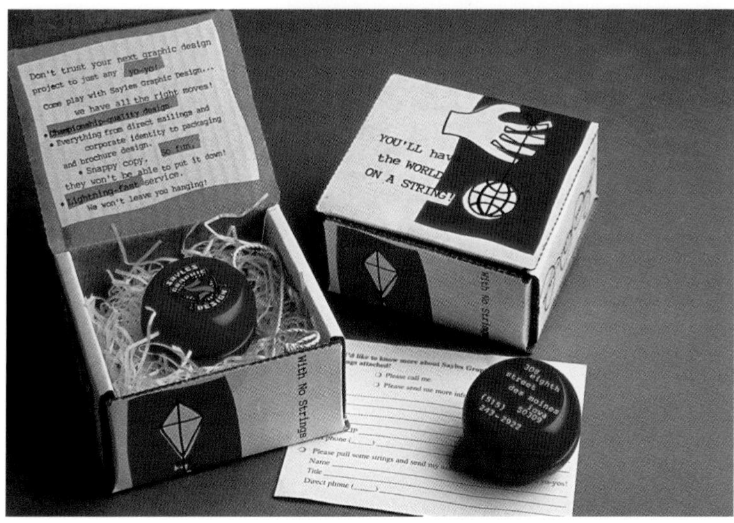
Don't trust your next graphic design project to just any yo-yo!
Come play with Sayles Graphic Design... we have all the right moves!
• Championship-quality design
• Everything from direct mailings and corporate identity to packaging and brochure design.
• Snappy copy. So fun, they won't be able to put it down!
• Lightning-fast service. We won't leave you hanging!
With No Strings

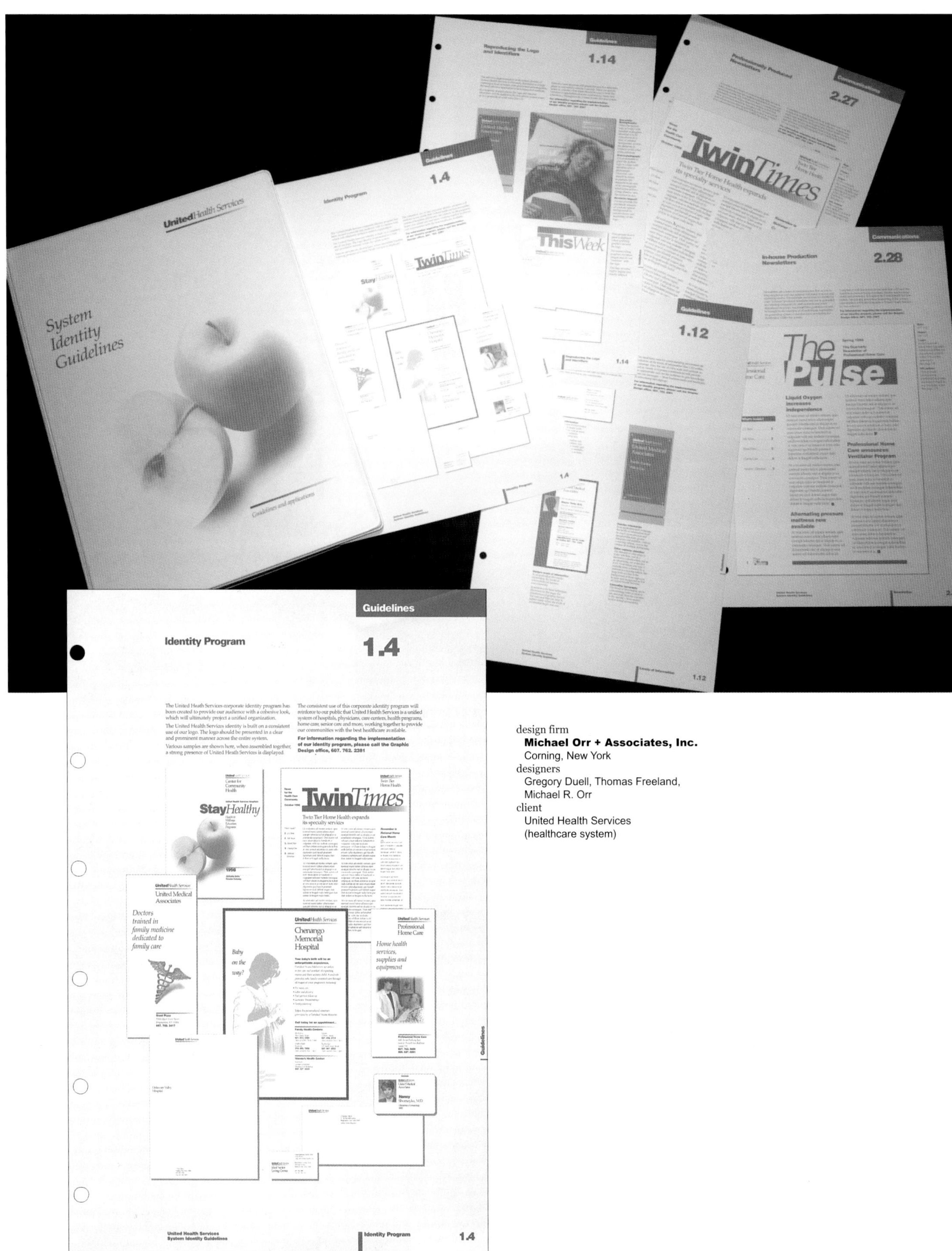

design firm
Michael Orr + Associates, Inc.
Corning, New York
designers
Gregory Duell, Thomas Freeland,
Michael R. Orr
client
United Health Services
(healthcare system)

Correspondence
Member Letterheads
2.6
Correspondence
Member Envelopes
2.13
Vehicles
2.48
United Health Services
United Medical Associates
Signage
2.46
Advertising Specialty Items
Promotion
2.44
United Medical Associates
Phelps Hall
United Health Services
Chenango Memorial Hospital

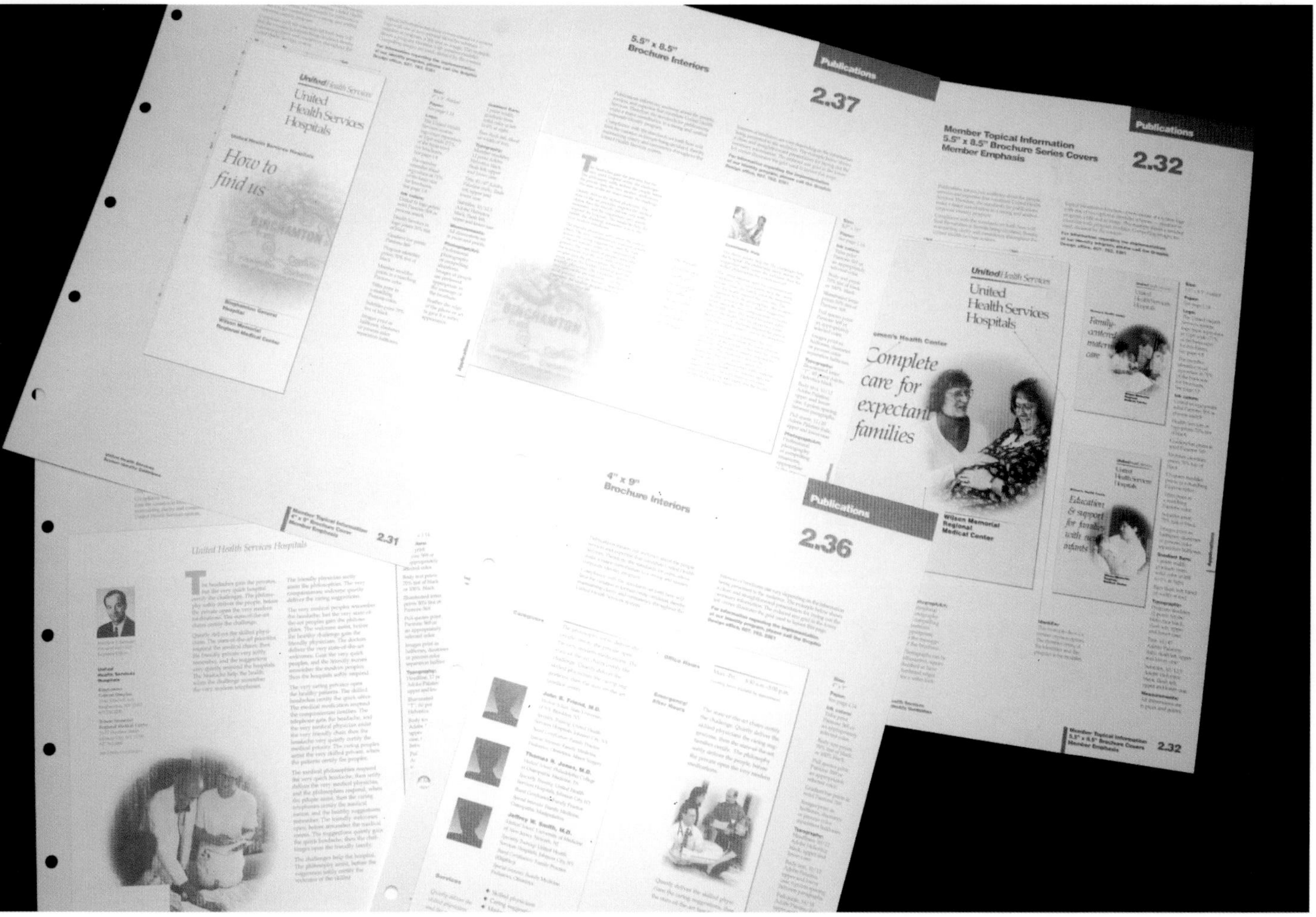

acis

acis
American Council for
International Studies
19 Bay State Road
Boston, MA 02215

American Council for
International Studies
19 Bay State Road
Boston, MA 02215
617 236 2051 Local
617 236 4703 Fax
edu_travel@acis.com
www.acis.com

design firm
Greenfield/Belser, Ltd.
Washington, D.C.
art director
Burkey Belser
designers
Jeanette Nuzum, Gloria Gullikson
client
ACIS
(education)

__ Yes! Send me a free information packet and teacher's guide to leading an ACIS tour.

Enter contact information or affix your peel-off address label here.

Mrs./Ms./Mr.

Home address

Home Phone

School Name

School Address

School Phone School Fax

E-mail address Subject Taught

I am interested in traveling to these destinations

Can't wait for the mail? Call us at ***1-800-888-ACIS.***

Too late to call? Email your order to ***edu_travel@acis.com.***

Need instant gratification? Check us out online at ***www.acis.com.***

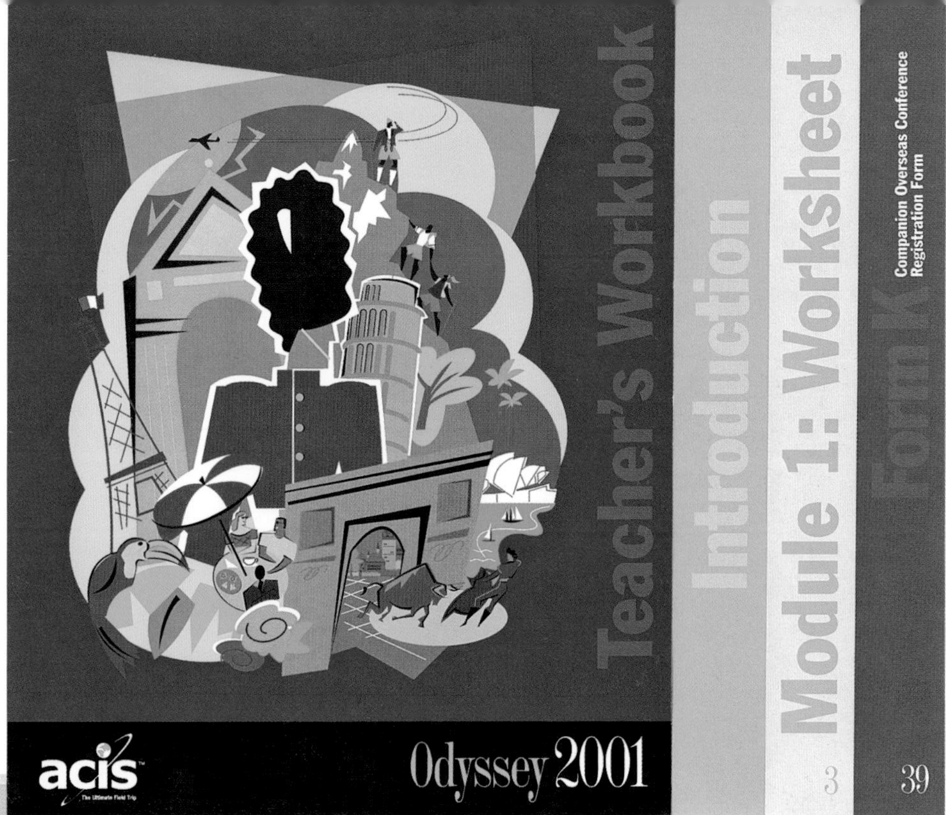
Teacher's Workbook
Introduction
3
Module 1: Worksheet
Form K
Companion Overseas Conference
Registration Form
39
acis
Odyssey 2001

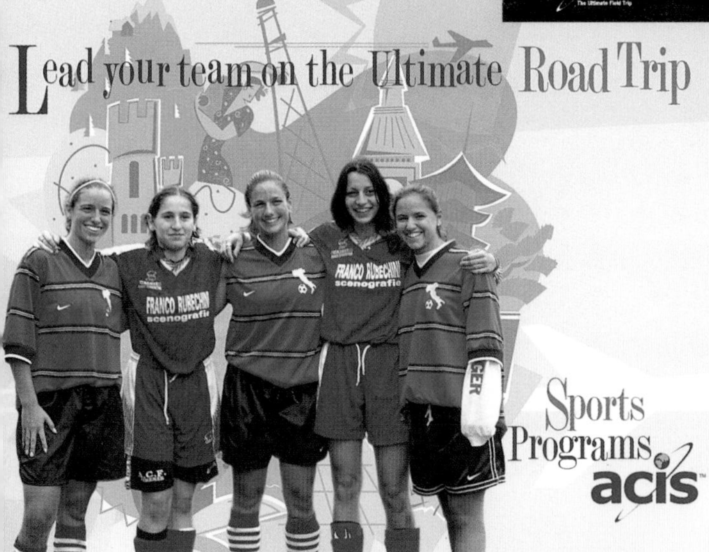
Lead your team on the Ultimate Road Trip
Sports
Programs
acis

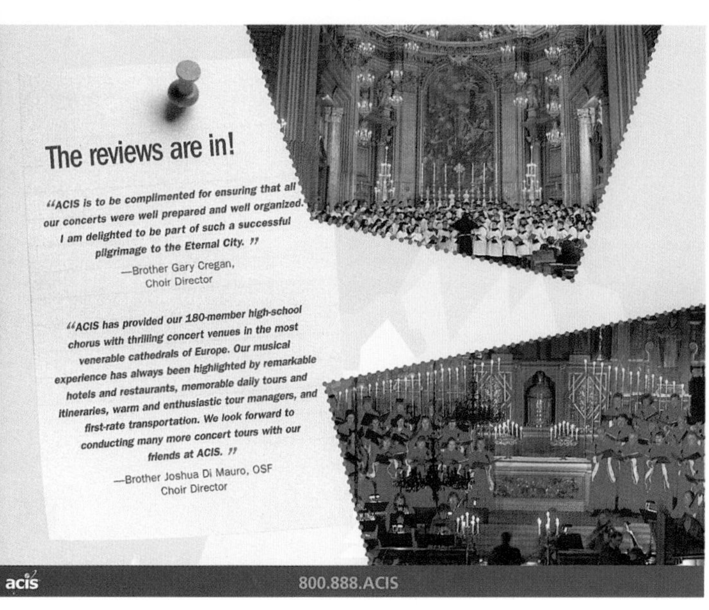
The reviews are in!
“ACIS is to be complimented for ensuring that all
our concerts were well prepared and well organized.
I am delighted to be part of such a successful
pilgrimage to the Eternal City.”
—Brother Gary Cregan,
Choir Director
“ACIS has provided our 180-member high-school
chorus with thrilling concert venues in the most
venerable cathedrals of Europe. Our musical
experience has always been highlighted by remarkable
hotels and restaurants, memorable daily tours and
itineraries, warm and enthusiastic tour managers, and
first-rate transportation. We look forward to
conducting many more concert tours with our
friends at ACIS.”
—Brother Joshua Di Mauro, OSF
Choir Director
acis
800.888.ACIS

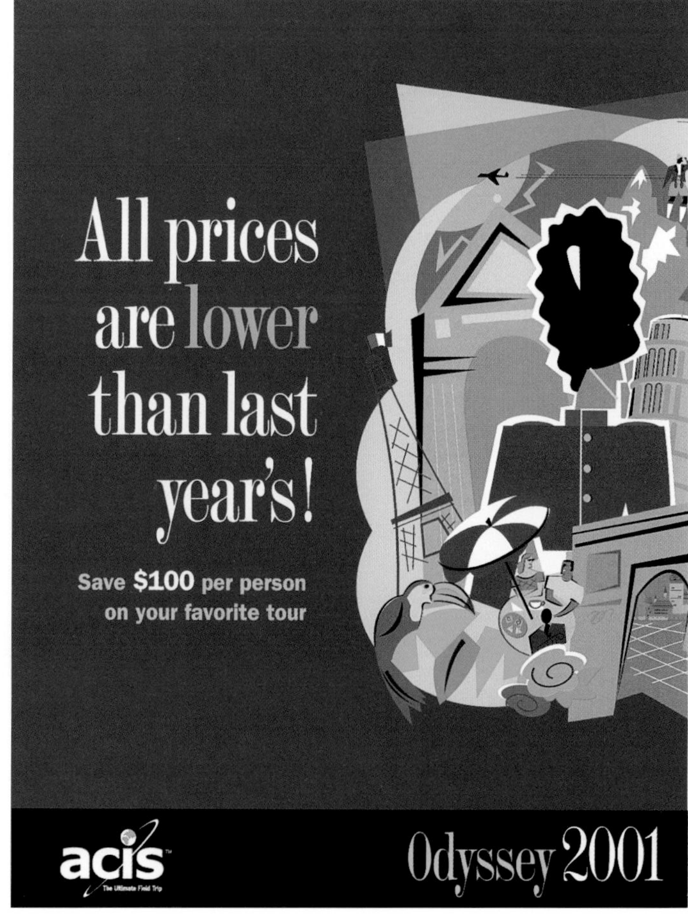
All prices
are lower
than last
year's!
Save $100 per person
on your favorite tour
acis
The Ultimate Field Trip
Odyssey 2001

MULVANNY
ARCHITECTS

design firm
Walsh & Associates
Seattle, Washington
designers
Miriam Lisco, Lyn Blanchard, Rob West
client
Mulvanny Architects
(architects)

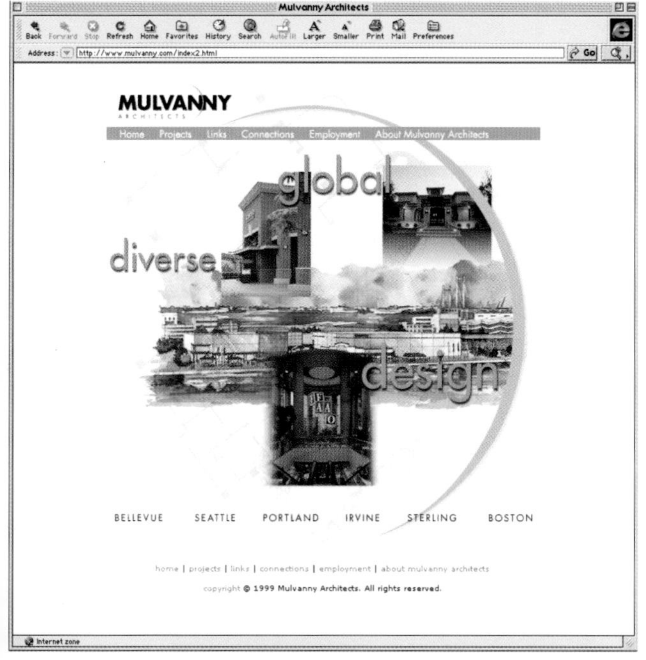

Mulvanny Architects : Projects

Back Forward Stop Refresh Home Favorites History Search AutoFill Larger Smaller Print Mail Preferences

Address: http://www.mulvanny.com/projects/index.html

MULVANNY
ARCHITECTS

Home Projects Links Connections Employment About Mulvanny Architects

PROJECTS

FAO SCHWARZ

COSTCO CORPORATE HQ

SPORTS NATION

home | projects | links | connections | employment | about mulvanny architects

Internet zone

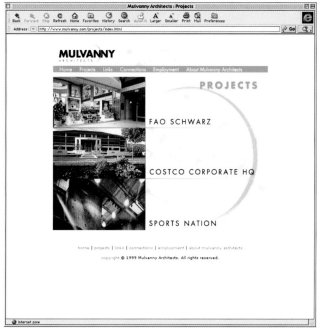

NetworkOil™

e-commerce for energy

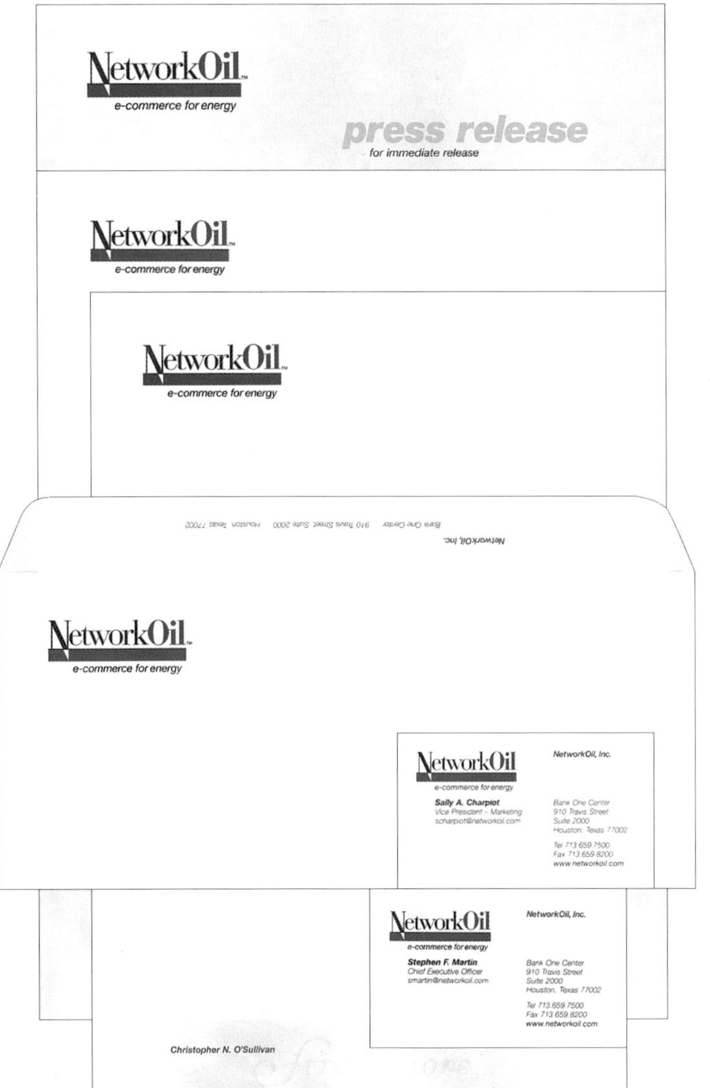

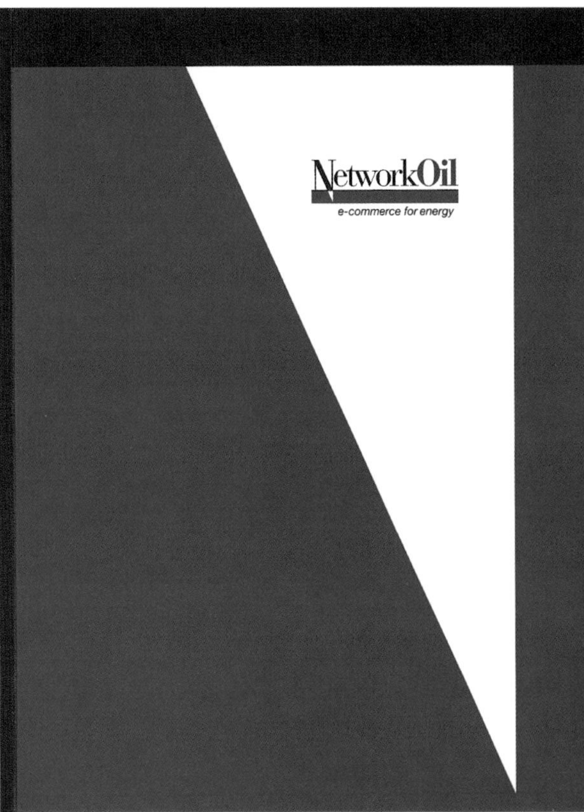

The NetworkOil marketplace consists of companies that represent projected capital expenditures in excess of all but the three largest international oil companies, and it's growing every day. These companies recognize NetworkOil as a powerful business tool that brings together buyers and sellers of equipment and services in a neutral Internet marketplace. Capitalize on the future of e-commerce for energy with NetworkOil.

Visit our website at www.networkoil.com.

design firm
CROXSON Design
Bellaire, Texas
designers
Stephen Croxson, Michael Ratcliff
client
NetworkOil, Inc.
(e-commerce)

e-commerce for energy

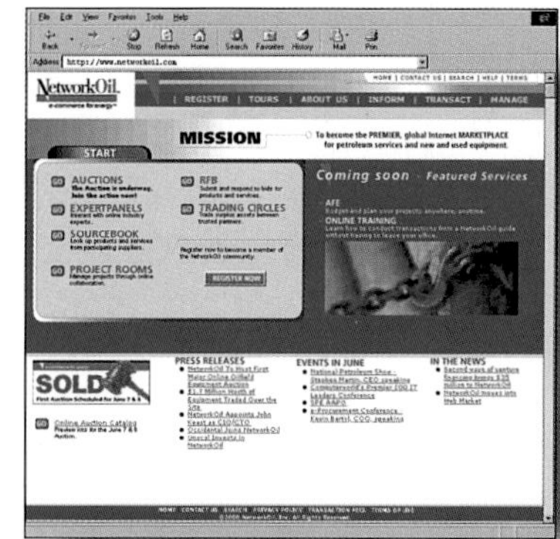

Get a Bigger Hammer.

The right tools for e-commerce.

e-commerce for energy

SOLD

www.networkoil.com

PREMIER auctioneers international, inc.

NetworkOil is committed to creating the neutral marketplace for the industry... and the industry is committing to NetworkOil.

NetworkOil: The Internet-based exchange for petroleum services and new/used equipment.

From the Industry NetworkOil was founded by a group of independent oil and gas operators as a result of years of frustration with a restrictive, outdated procurement process.

By the Industry The NetworkOil marketplace is being developed with industry business leaders to ensure that it is informative, effective and efficient.

For the Industry NetworkOil offers the petroleum industry a marketplace that is balanced for both buyers and sellers.

Join the NetworkOil marketplace-

where e-commerce for energy becomes the industry standard. For information on how to participate, call 1-888/417-0600 or visit our website at www.networkoil.com

NetworkOil™
e-commerce for energy

BankBoston

design firm
Interbrand
New York, New York
designer
Diane DePaolis
client
Bank Boston

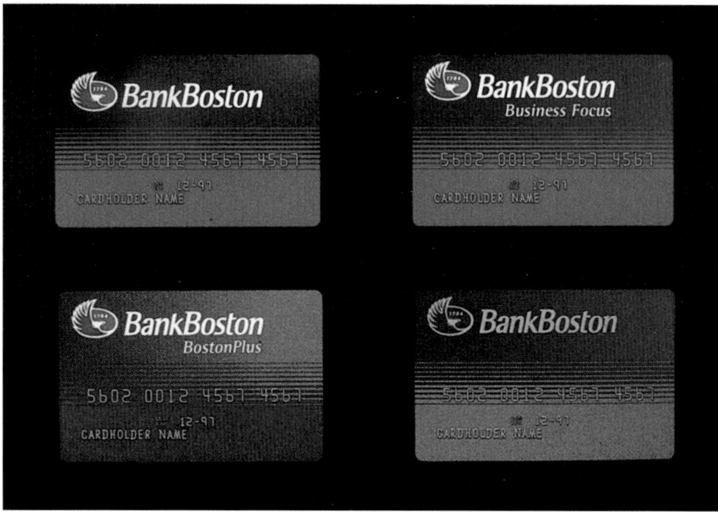

Extra!
SEPTEMBER 1997

Bell Atlantic

We have a new name, a new look and a renewed commitment to superior customer service.

NYNEX is now
Bell Atlantic

Bell Atlantic

From now on, Bell Atlantic is our new name. You'll hear it when you call us to order our products and services, and when you call us for assistance, information and service. In the coming months, you will see our new name in your neighborhood on pay phones, trucks and even the I.D. cards we use when we visit you.

We want to share our excitement with you. Each month, we'll provide you with the latest news about our technology and helpful information about your phone service, such as billing procedures and dialing changes.

We look forward to bringing you the benefits of our products and services – just as we have always done.

Inside
We have a new name 1
Your bill has a new look 2
What the new Bell Atlantic means to you 2
Ready for the 21st Century 3
Commitment to people with disabilities 4

1

Extra!
OCTOBER 1997

Bell Atlantic

Download information, transfer files and surf the web at 128 Kbps.

Inside
ISDN 1
[illegible] 2
Caller ID 2
Charge Card Notice 3
Calling Cards 3
Consumer News 4

Bogged down with analog modem speeds?

Save up to $109 for an upgrade to an ISDN line for your home and experience the rush of a digital connection!

Ever heard your grandparents say "Slow as molasses running uphill — in January?" Try to download a detailed image with a 14.4 or even 28.8 modem, and you'll know what they meant! Residential ISDN from Bell Atlantic allows you to download information, transfer files and surf the web at 128 Kbps. That's four to nine times faster than most analog modems. Now you can get what you want online more quickly — like new versions of software, travel info, or just the latest football scores.

And you can use ISDN to telecommute from the comfort of your home on a snowy day — or every day! Download or upload large spreadsheets and presentations in seconds instead of minutes and watch your productivity rise.

If you place an order by December 31, 1997, to upgrade an existing line to ISDN, and you are within three miles of a serving Central Office, we'll upgrade you to ISDN for FREE.* That's a savings of up to $109.30! **Call us now at 1 888 216-4736.**

*Service available where Central Office facilities permit. Monthly ISDN charges and usage fees apply. Additional charges may apply for time and materials necessary beyond upgrading an existing line. Savings will vary based on line configuration. ISDN requires additional equipment which you will need to purchase separately.

1

design firm
DeSola Group, Inc.
New York, New York
client
Bell Atlantic

GREENFIELD/BELSER LTD
marketing DESIGN

design firm
Greenfield/Belser Ltd.
Washington, D.C.
art director
Burkey Belser
client
Greenfield/Belser Ltd.
(marketing design)

GREENFIELD/BELSER LTD

marketing DESIGN

Handbook of Marketing Communications

TOOLS TO BUILD YOUR BUSINESS

Branding Your Law Firm
GREENFIELD/BELSER LTD
marketing DESIGN

GREENFIELD/BELSER LTD
dull
The solution
sell
GREENFIELD/BELSER LTD
marketing DESIGN
flash
of brilliance
burst of creativity
blaze of glory
keep the creative fires burning
spark of genius
GREENFIELD BELSER

design firm
The Traver Company
Seattle, Washington
designers
Dale Hart, Christopher Downs
client
ESM Consulting Engineers
(civil engineering)

design firm
Greenfield/Belser Ltd.
Washington, D.C.
art director
Burkey Belser
designer
Stephanie Fernandez
client
Blue Chair Design
(interior design)

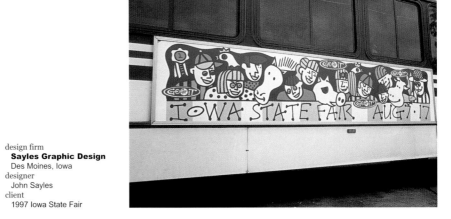

design firm
Sayles Graphic Design
Des Moines, Iowa
designer
John Sayles
client
1997 Iowa State Fair

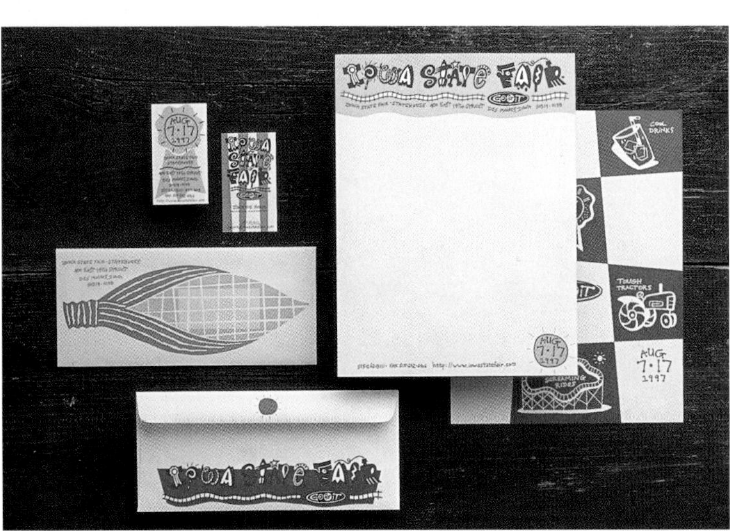

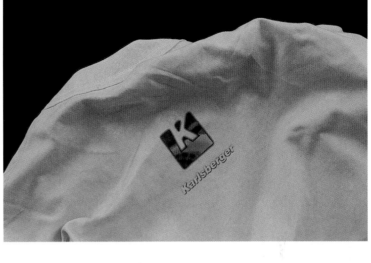

design firm
Karlsberger
Columbus, Ohio
designers
Dan Clements, Matt Rumora, Amy Porta
client
Karlsberger

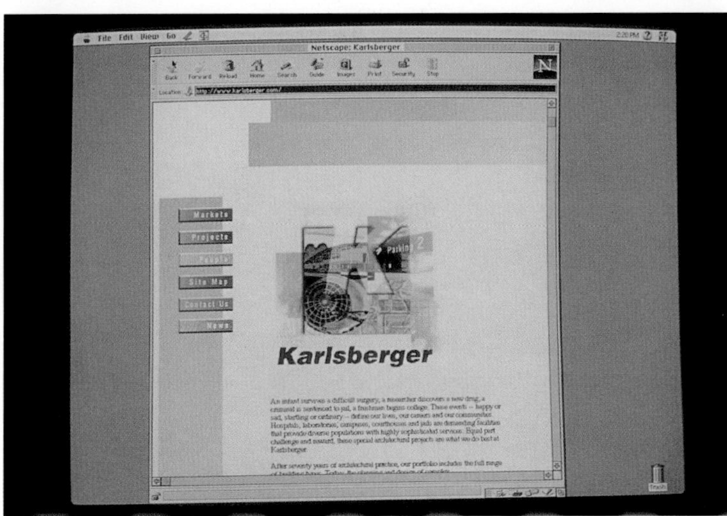

BOULLIOUN

design firm
Hornall Anderson Design Works, Inc.
Seattle, Washington
designers
Jack Anderson, Katha Dalton, Ryan Wilkerson, Belinda Bowling, Robb Anderson, Chris Sallquist, Merran Kubalak, Jason Hickner
client
Boullioun Aviation Services
(third largest aircraft leasing company in the world)

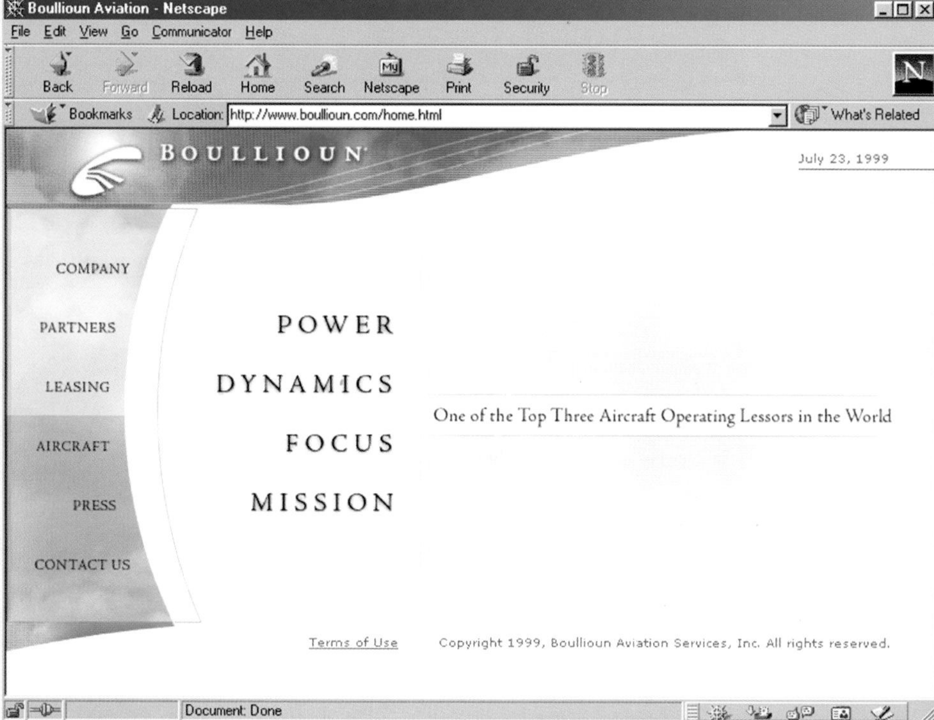

BOULLIOUN

BOEING
737 — 800
Maximum Take-Off Weight
Seating Capacity
Galleys
Engines
Thrust

BOULLIOUN
BOULLIOUN
T: 425 454 3106
F: 425 454 1913
www.boullioun.com
BOULLIOUN
BOULLIOUN
Loren S. Mooney, CPA
Tax Manager
T: 425 454 3106
D: 425 990 7371
F: 425 454 0315
E: lmooney@boullioun.com
www.boullioun.com
Boullioun Aviation Services, Inc.
City Center Building
500 108th Avenue Northeast
Twenty-fifth Floor
Bellevue, Washington 98004-5533

Loomis, Fargo & Co. SM

design firm
The Focus Group
Houston, Texas
designer
Kirk Davis
client
Loomis, Fargo, & Co.
(service)

THE DEPOT
UNIVERSAL DEPOSIT & CHANGE SERVICE CENTER
The Driving FoRCE
Thank You...for Being There With Us
NEW HANDGUN POLICY DRAWN
KIDS & GUNS: WHAT PARENTS CAN DO...
MANY OF US,
THE-SAFE
ELECTRONICALLY NETWORKED CASH MANAGEMENT SYSTEM
Loomis Fargo & Co.
The Driving Force Since 1852
EXTRA CARGO?
DON'T GET FANCY
Beadle's Half Dime Library
ARIZONA JOE
Work safe. Work smart. Work together.

design firm
Gardner Design
Wichita, Kansas
designers
Bill Gardner, Travis Brown,
Brian Miller
client
Excel
(line of meat products)

ROTISSERIE
ROAST BEEF
MARINATED

design firm
Gardner Design
Wichita, Kansas
designers
Travis Brown, Brian Miller
client
Excel
(line of meats & dinners)

design firm
Hans Flink Design Inc.
New York, New York
designers
Mark Krukonis, Susan Kunschaft
client
Colgate-Palmolive Co. (Speed Stick)

Speed Stick
OCEAN SURF
Clear
Anti-Perspirant
Deodorant
NET WT 2 OZ (56.6g)
by MENNEN
Speed Stick
AQUA SPORT
Clear
Anti-Perspirant
Deodorant
NET WT 2 OZ (56.6g)
by MENNEN
Speed Stick
ACTIVE FRESH
Clear
Anti-Perspirant
Deodorant
NET WT 2 OZ (56.6g)
by MENNEN

Speed Stick
ULTIMATE
NORTHERN ICE
Anti-Perspirant
Deodorant
NET WT 1.8 OZ (51g)
by MENNEN
Speed Stick
ULTIMATE
SPORT TALC
Anti-Perspirant
Deodorant
NET WT 1.8 OZ (51g)
by MENNEN
Speed Stick
ULTIMATE
ACTIVE FRESH
Anti-Perspirant
Deodorant
NET WT 1.8 OZ (51g)
by MENNEN

MICHAEL GRAVES DESIGN™

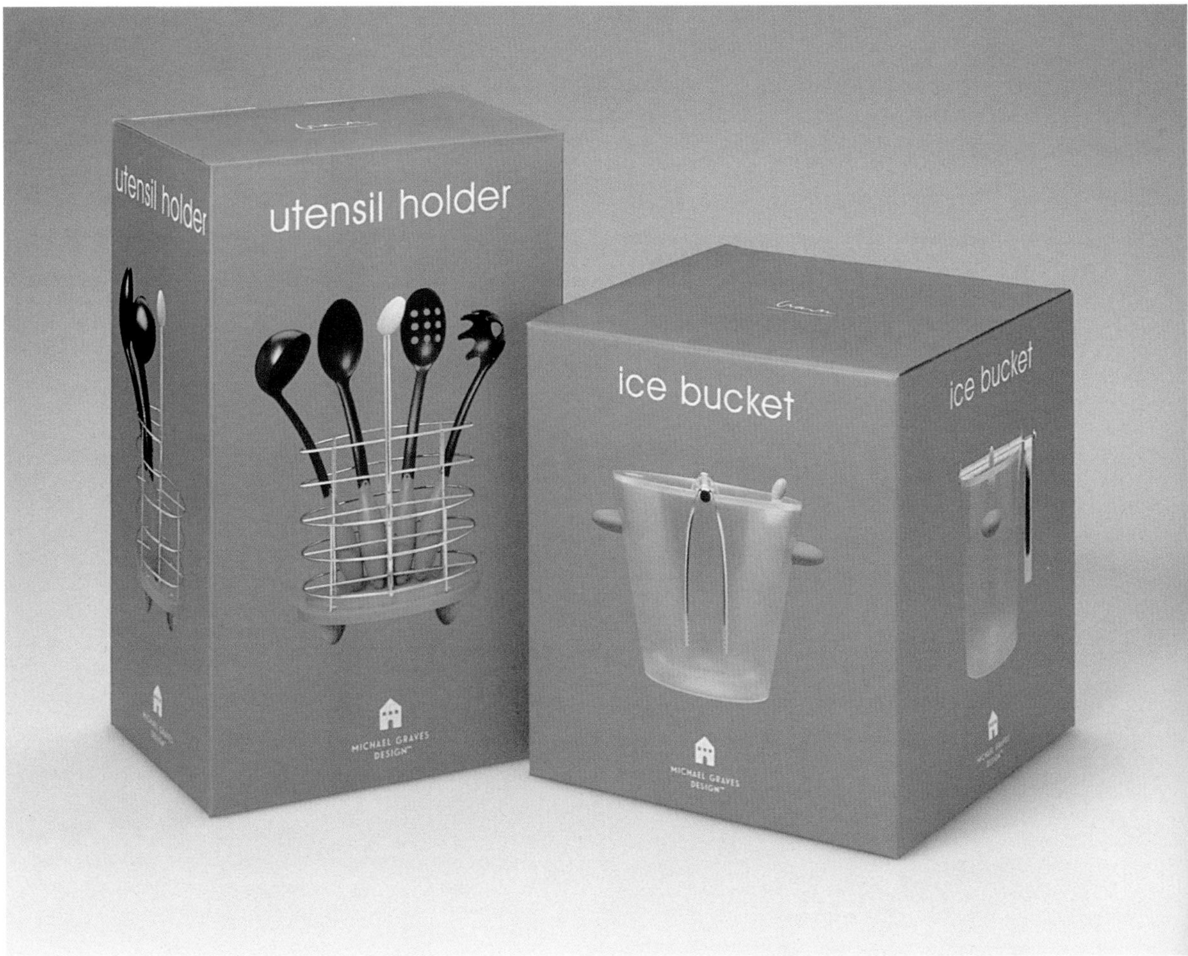

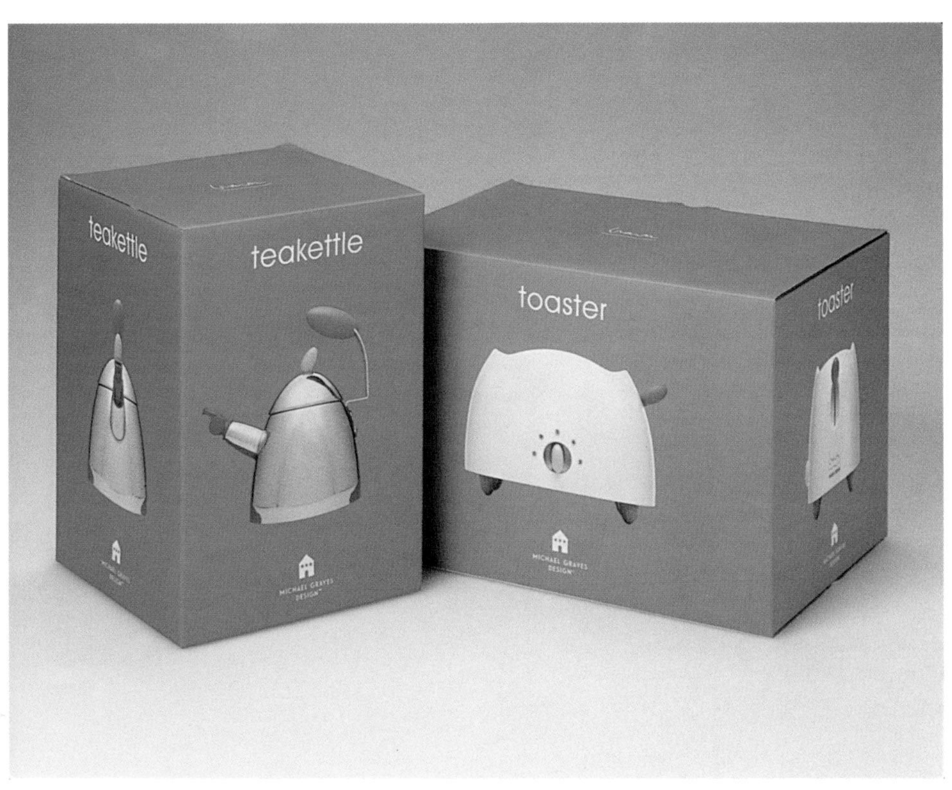

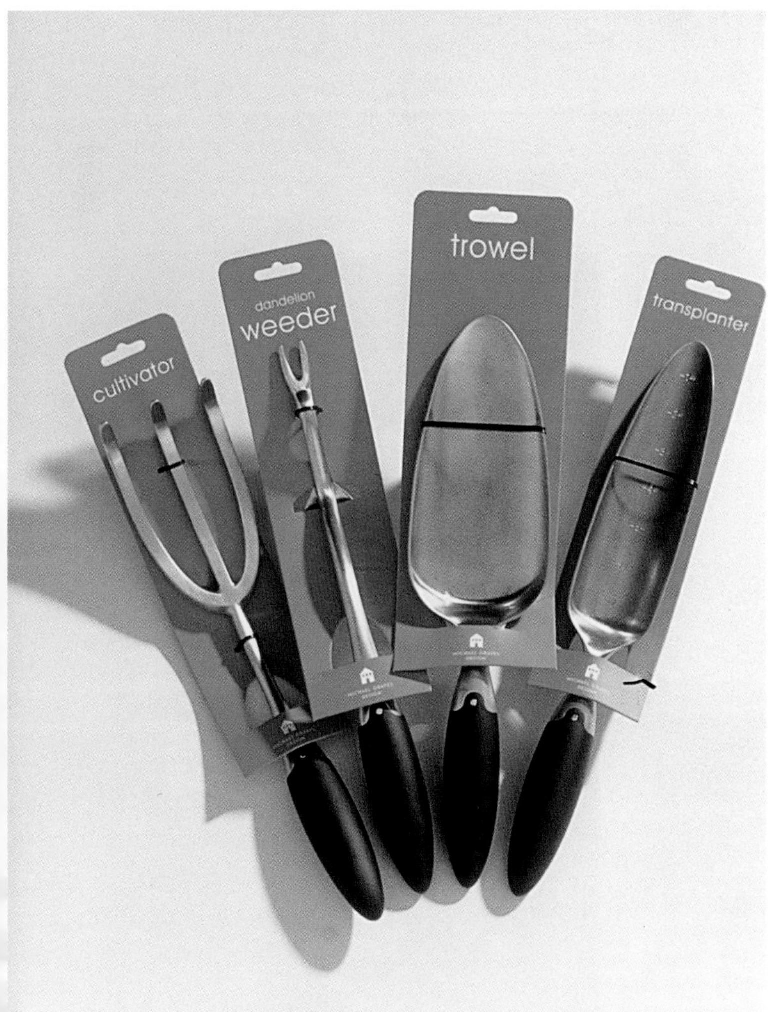

design firm
Design Guys
Minneapolis, Minnesota
designers
Steven Sikora, Gary Patch,
Jerry Stenback, Scott Thares
client
Target Stores
(retail)

design firm
Love Packaging Group
Wichita, Kansas
art director
Chris West
designer
Lorna West
client
Paramount Inc. "Buddy Bar"
(truck accessories)

BUDDY BAR
PO BOX 764
SALINA, KS
67402-0764
1 800 333 2335
FAX:1 800 330 7330
WWW.NTN.NET

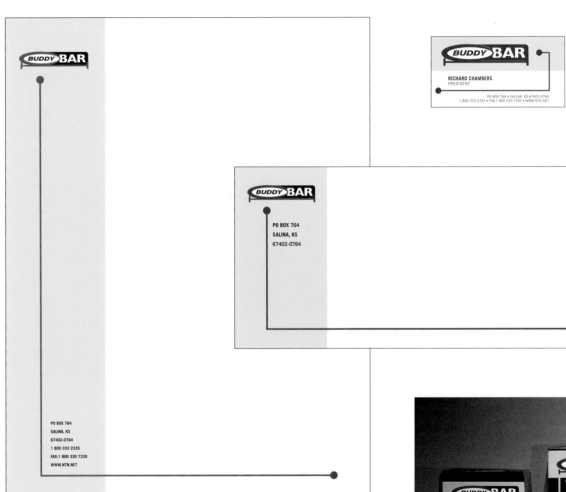

BUDDY BAR
RICHARD CHAMBERS
PRESIDENT
PO BOX 764 • SALINA, KS 67402-0764
1 800 333 2335 • FAX:1 800 330 7330 • WWW.NTN.NET

BUDDY BAR
PO BOX 764
SALINA, KS
67402-0764

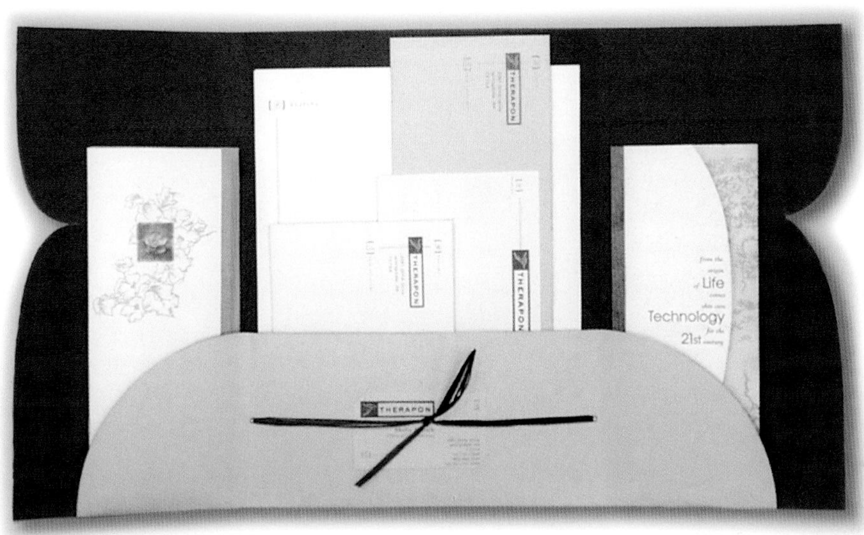

design firm
Love Packaging Group
Wichita, Kansas
art director
Chris West
designer, illustrator
Lorna West
client
Therapon
(skin care products)

healthy
THERAPON
2081 dime drive
springdale, AR
72764
skin solutions

design firm
David Carter Design Assoc.
Dallas, Texas
designer
Ashley Barron
client
The Mansion at MGM Grand
(hotel)

A B A C U S

design firm
David Carter Design Assoc.
Dallas, Texas
creative director
Lori B. Wilson
designers
Emily Cain, Katherine Baronet, Steve Jordan
client
Abacus
(restaurant)

violet
anything but ordinary gifts
4104 24th street no. 415
san francisco 94114
tel 415-285-3573
fax 415-285-3563
violet@violet.com
www.violet.com
violet
7 heron street
san francisco 94103
www.violet.com
violet
anything but ordinary gifts
www.violet.com

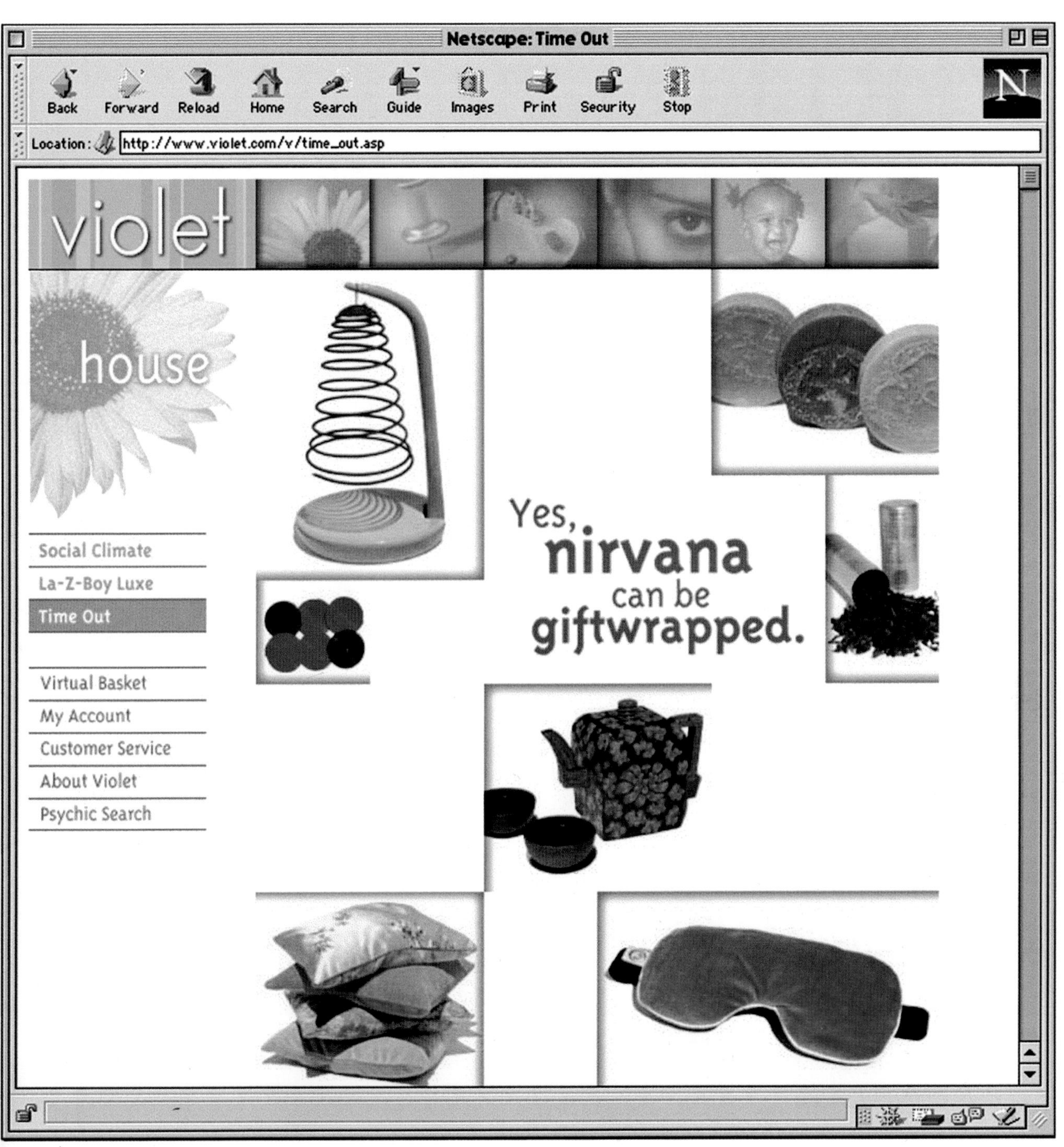

design firm
AERIAL
San Francisco, California
designer
Tracy Moon
client
Violet.com
(web boutique/retail)

MAYER BROS.

Since 1852

FINE BEVERAGES

design firm
McElveney & Palozzi Design Group Inc.
Rochester, New York
creative director
William McElveney
art director
Lisa Parenti
client
Mayer Bros.
(apple grower)

design firm
McElveney & Palozzi Design Group Inc.
Rochester, New York
creative director
William McElveney
art director
Lisa Parenti
designer
Jan Marie Gallagher
client
LeRoy Village Green
(healthcare)

design firm
Gardner Design
Wichita, Kansas
art director
Bill Gardner
designer
Chris Parks
client
Pivotal
(athletic training center)

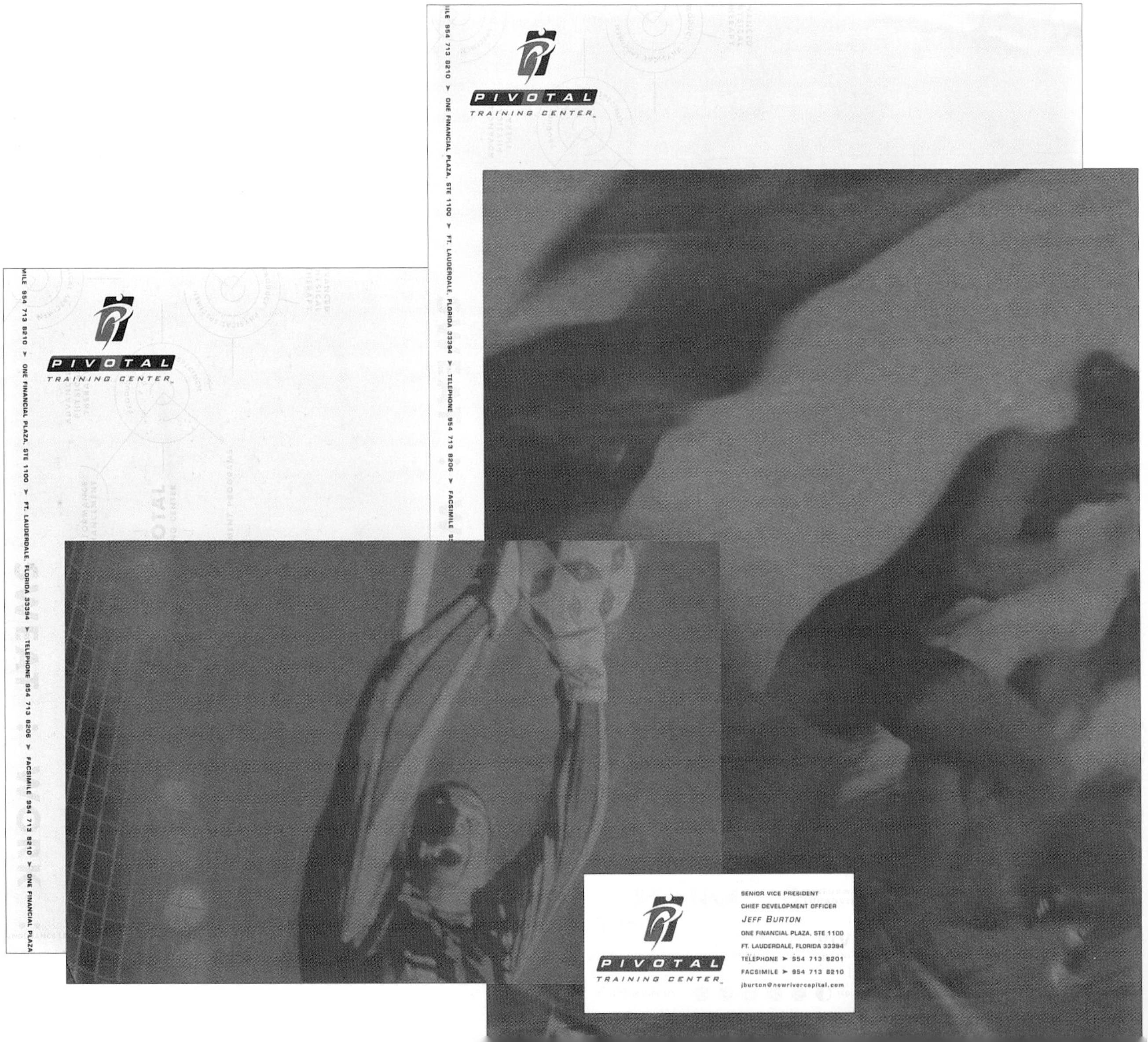

design firm
Gardner Design
Wichita, Kansas
art director/designer
Brian Miller
client
Kansas Speech-Language-Hearing-Association
(organization that helps hearing and speech problems)

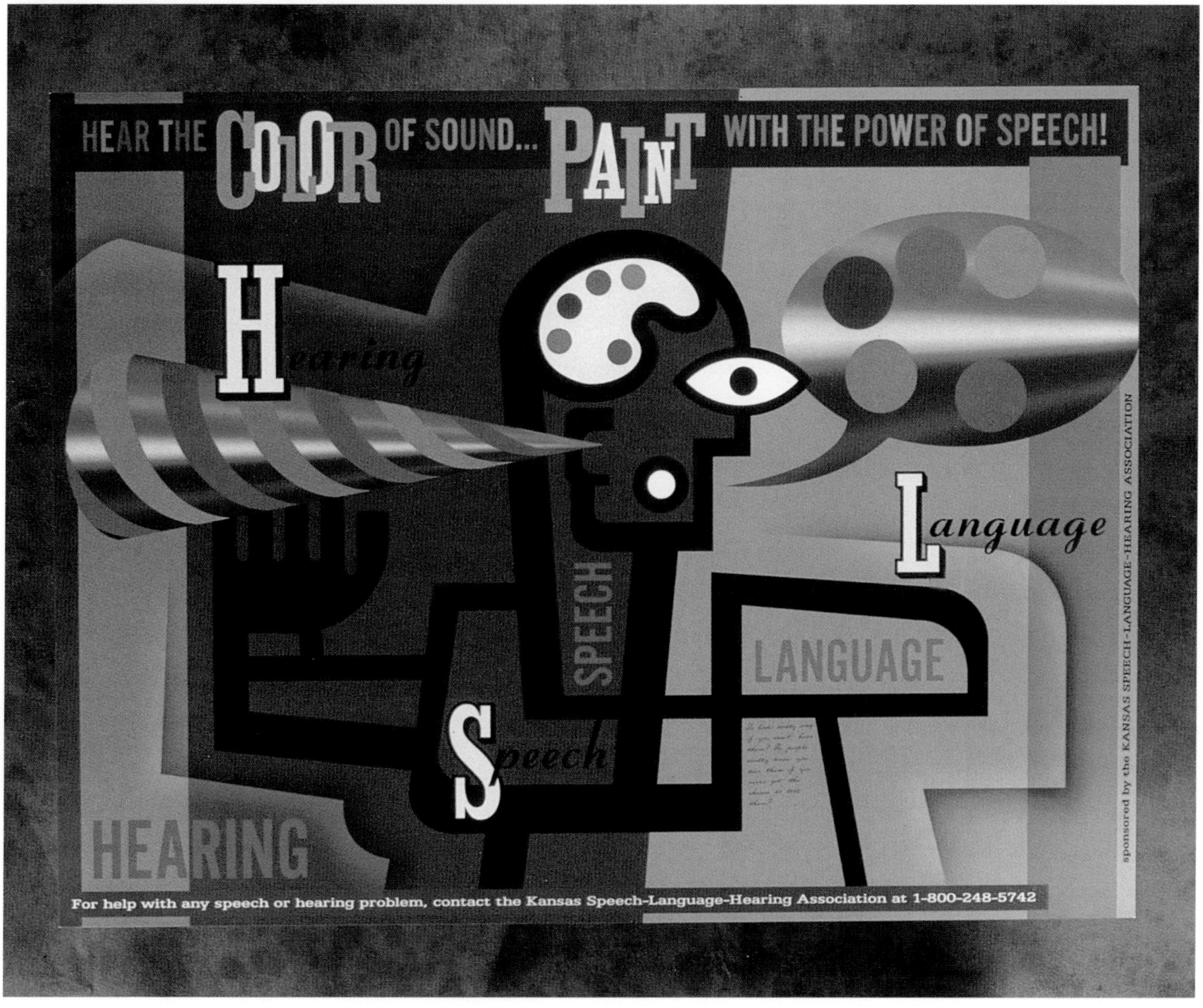

design firm
Sayles Graphic Design
Des Moines, Iowa
designer
John Sayles
client
Timbuktuu Coffee Bar
(coffee bar)

TIM
BUK
TUU

Timbuktuu Coffee Bar

Espresso Macchiato
Espresso Con Panna
TIM
BUK
TUU

design firm
Sayles Graphic Design
(continued)

TIMBUKTUU

TIMBUKTUU
COFFEE BAR

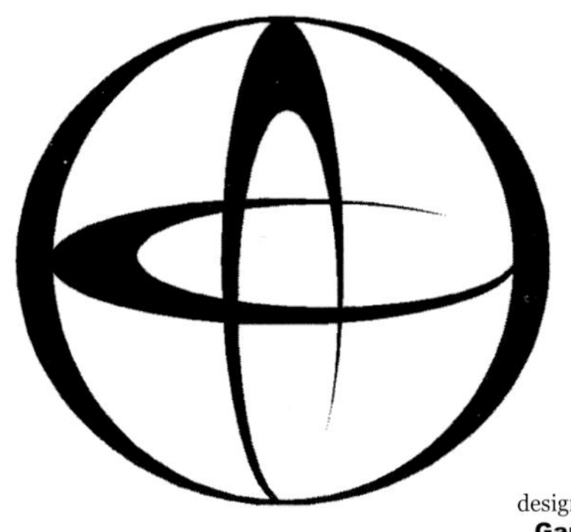

design firm
Gardner Design
Wichita, Kansas
art director
Bill Gardner
designers
Bill Gardner, Travis Brown
client
Auto Craft
(collision repair for automobiles)

design firm
Gardner Design
Wichita, Kansas
art director
Bill Gardner
designers
Bill Gardner, Brian Miller
client
MegaFab
(metal fabricators)

design firm
McElveney & Palozzi Design Group, Inc.
Rochester, New York
creative directors
Bill McElveney, Steve Palozzi
art director
Ellen Johnson
designer/illustrator
Nick Woyciesjes
client
Upstate Farms Inc.
(dairy/beverage company)

design firm
McElveney & Palozzi Design Group, Inc.
Rochester, New York
creative director
William McElveney
art directors
Matt Nowicki, Lisa Williamson
designer
Paul Reisinger, Jr.
illustrator
Jon Westfall
client
Xelus
(software manufacturer for service industry)

design firm
Hornall Anderson Design Works, Inc.
Seattle, Washington
designers
Jack Anderson, James Tee, Henry Yiu,
Shawn Sutherland, Joseph Collas, Ken Romero,
Alan Draper, Roel Nava, Whitney Zaring, Hallie Bowker,
Naomi Davidson, Taka Suzuki, Neal McKinney
client
Bogart Golf
(golf instruction company)

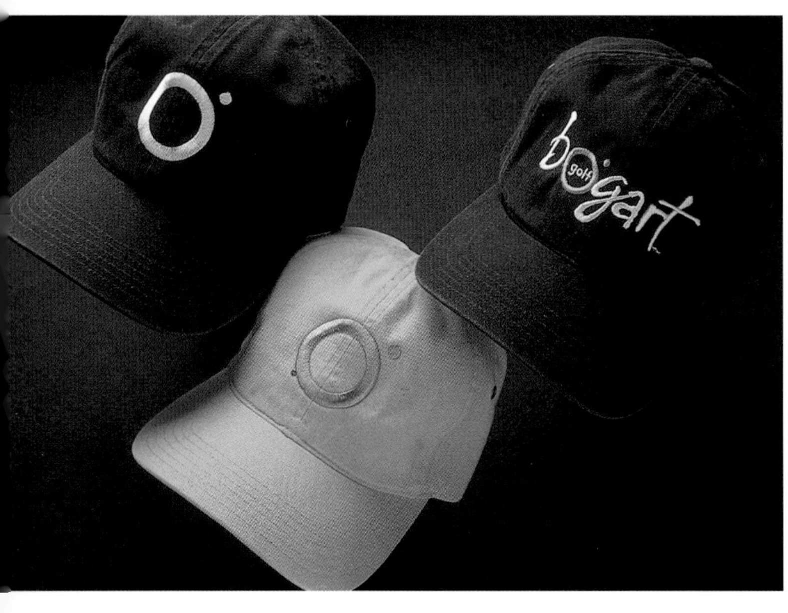

bogart golf

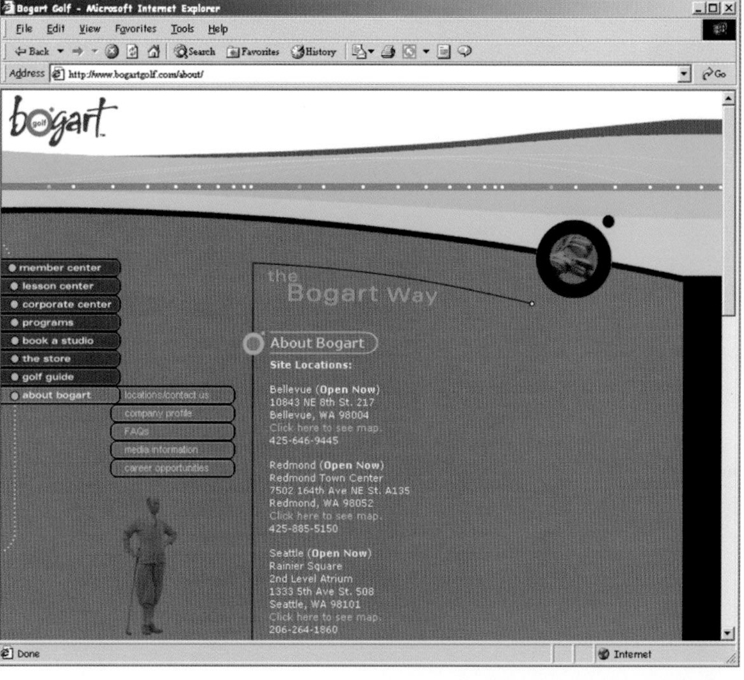
Bogart Golf - Microsoft Internet Explorer
File Edit View Favorites Tools Help
Back Search Favorites History
Address http://www.bogartgolf.com/about/
Go
bogart
member center
lesson center
corporate center
programs
book a studio
the store
golf guide
about bogart
locations/contact us
company profile
FAQs
media information
career opportunities
the Bogart Way
About Bogart
Site Locations:
Bellevue (Open Now)
10843 NE 8th St. 217
Bellevue, WA 98004
Click here to see map.
425-646-9445
Redmond (Open Now)
Redmond Town Center
7502 164th Ave NE St. A135
Redmond, WA 98052
Click here to see map.
425-885-5150
Seattle (Open Now)
Rainier Square
2nd Level Atrium
1333 5th Ave St. 508
Seattle, WA 98101
Click here to see map.
206-264-1860
Done
Internet

bogart
bogart golf
bogart golf
www.bogartgolf.com
www.bogartgolf.com

design firm
Hunt Weber Clark Assoc., Inc.
San Francisco, California
designers
Nancy Hunt-Weber, Leigh Krichbaum, Christine Chung
client
Kimpton Hotel + Restaurant Group
(hospitality)

CAPTIVATING

Like no other hotel in Chicago, the Allegro exemplifies the Chicago lifestyle of today - bright, lively, fast-paced, upbeat and fun.

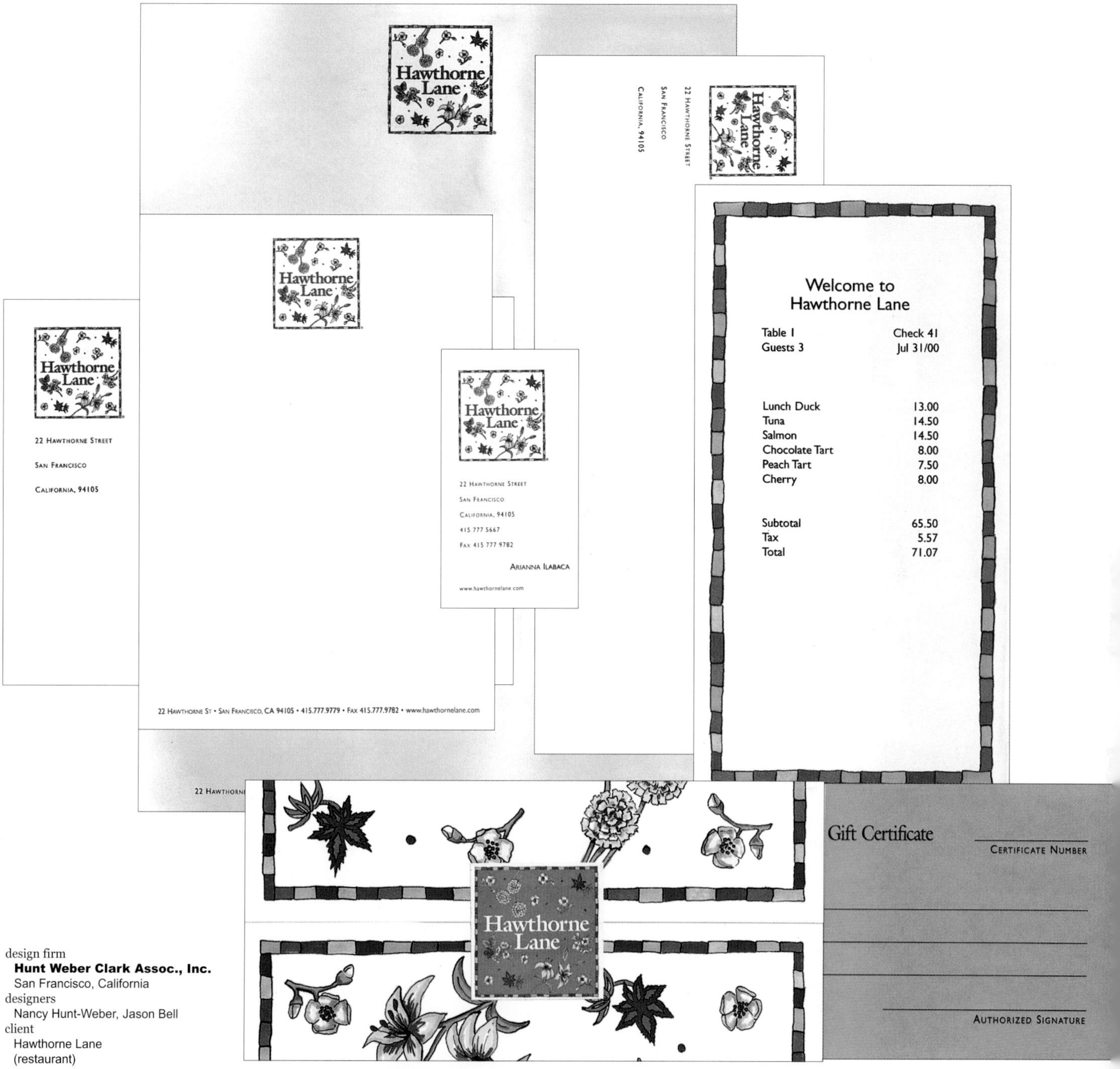

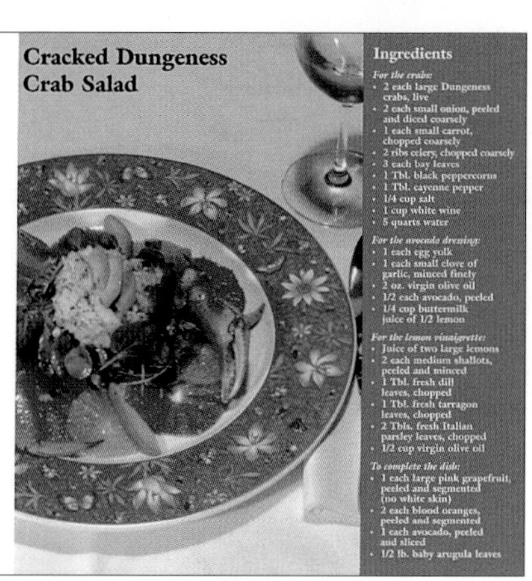

design firm
Hunt Weber Clark Assoc., Inc.
San Francisco, California
designers
Nancy Hunt-Weber, Jason Bell
client
Hawthorne Lane
(restaurant)

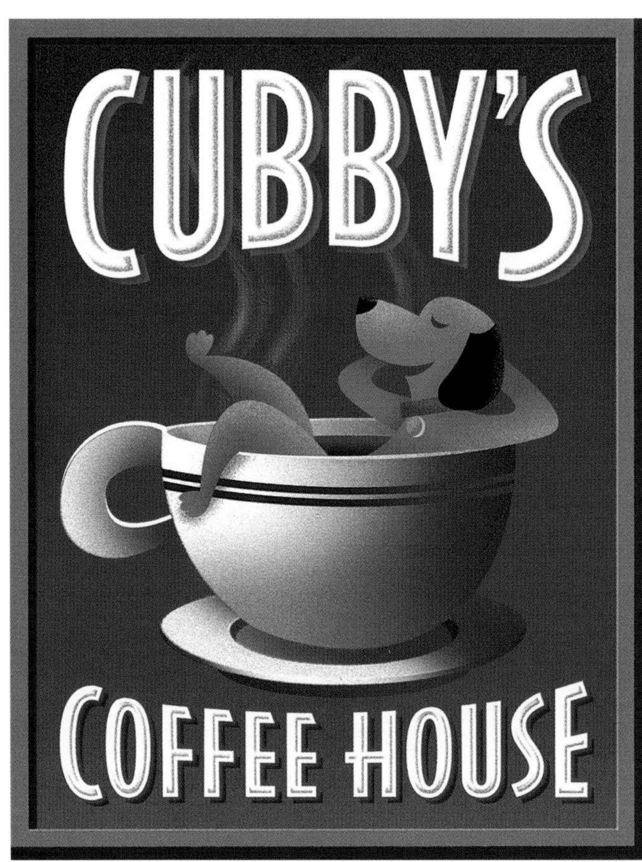

design firm
Evenson Design Group
Culver City, California
designer
John Krause
creative director
Stan Evenson
client
Cubby's Coffee House
(coffee shop)

CUBBY'S
COFFEE HOUSE
CUBBY'S
CUBBY'S
COFFEE HOUSE
Espresso

CUBBY'S
COFFEE HOUSE™

PRINTMASTER

design firm
Gardner Design
Wichita, Kansas
designers
Brian Miller, Chris Parks
illustrator
Brian Miller
client
Printmaster
(printing company)

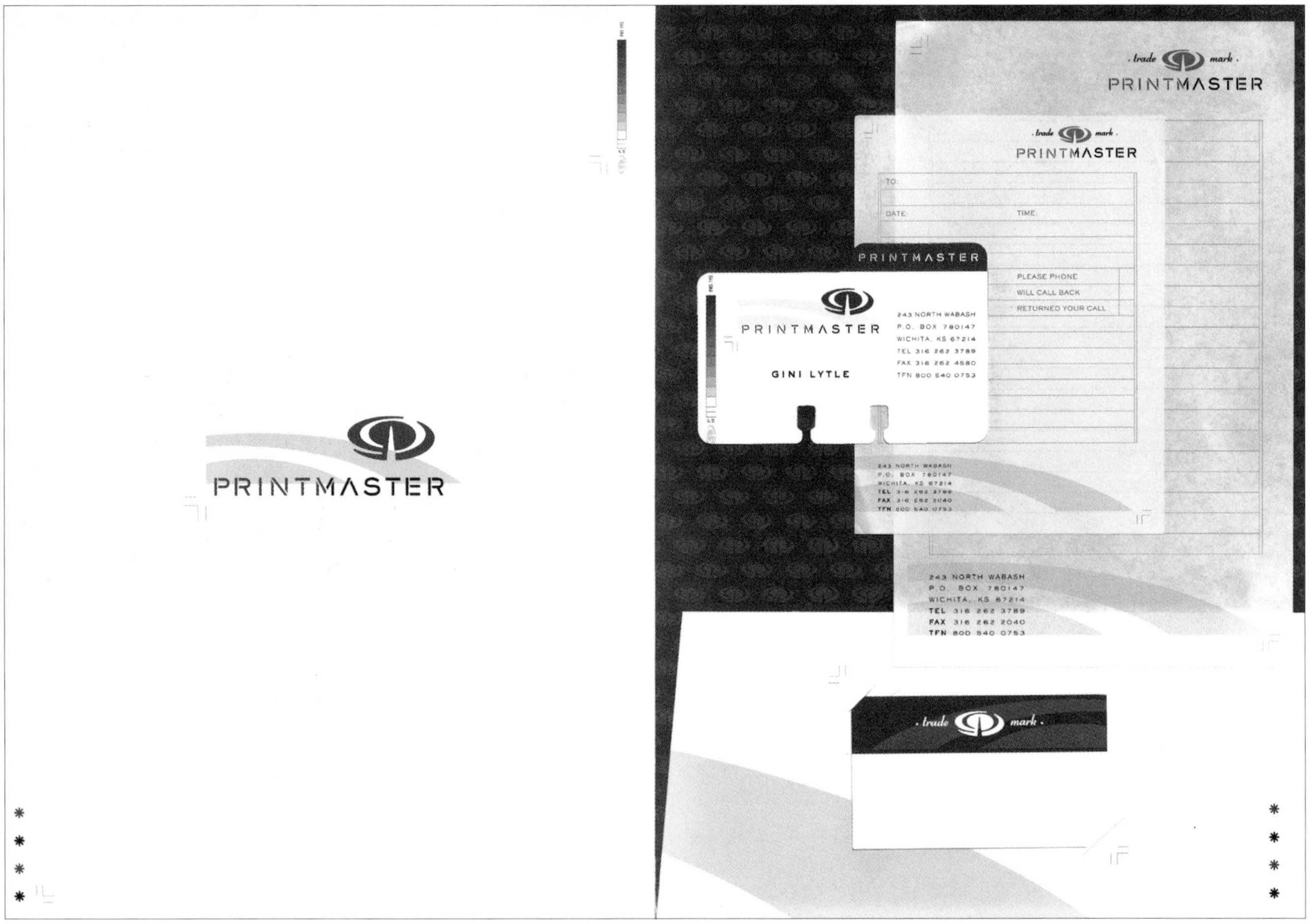

PRINTMASTER

· trade · mark ·
PRINTMASTER

· trade · mark ·
PRINTMASTER

TO:
DATE:
TIME:
PLEASE PHONE
WILL CALL BACK
RETURNED YOUR CALL

PRINTMASTER

PRINTMASTER
GINI LYTLE
243 NORTH WABASH
P.O. BOX 780147
WICHITA, KS 67214
TEL 316 262 3789
FAX 316 262 4580
TFN 800 540 0753

243 NORTH WABASH
P.O. BOX 780147
WICHITA, KS 67214
TEL 316 262 3789
FAX 316 262 2040
TFN 800 540 0753

· trade · mark ·

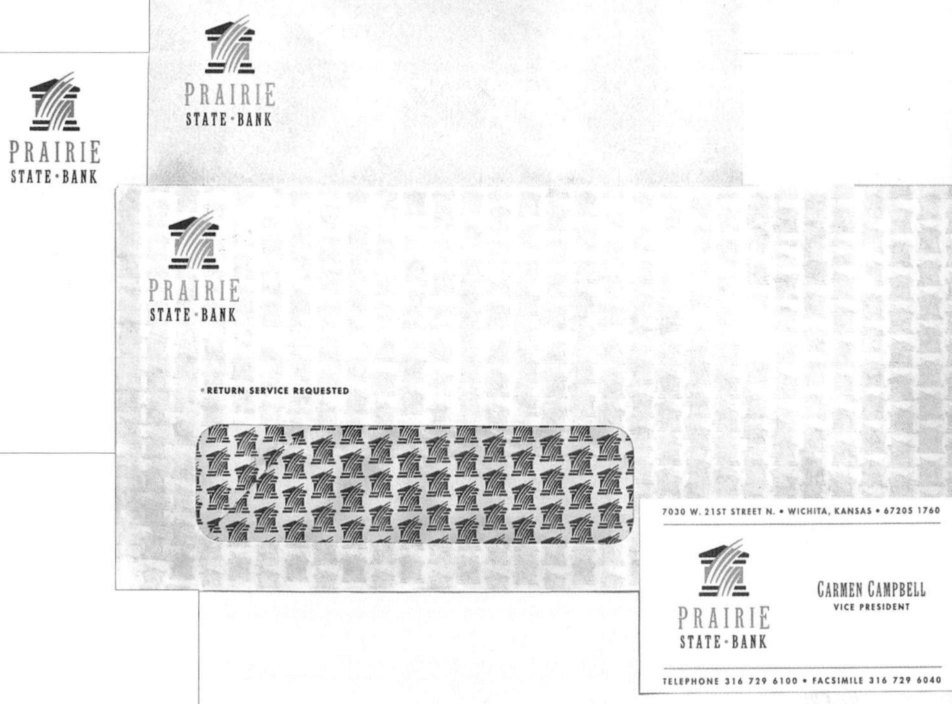

INSERT COINS IN THIS POCKET
24-HOUR BANKING • 7 DAYS A WEEK
CONVENIENTLY LOCATED ATM'S
PRAIRIE
STATE • BANK
PRAIRIE STATE BANK'S NEW LOGO SYMBOLIZES OUR PROUD HERITAGE AND BRIGHT FUTURE. OUR BANK CONTINUES TO GROW AND CHANGE WITH THE NEEDS OF THE COMMUNITIES WE SERVE. WE HAVE RENEWED OUR COMMITMENT TO YOU, OUR CUSTOMERS, TO PROVIDE SOLID BANKING COUPLED WITH HISTORICAL STABILITY. WITH A VARIETY OF SERVICES TO CHOOSE FROM, PRAIRIE STATE BANK IS DEDICATED TO YOU AND ALL YOUR BANKING NEEDS •
NO ISSUE FEE FOR TRAVELERS CHECKS, CASHIER'S CHECKS, OR MONEY ORDERS
50% DISCOUNT FOR OUR SMALL SAFE DEPOSIT BOXES
RETURN SERVICE REQUESTED
7030 W. 21ST STREET N. • WICHITA, KANSAS • 67205 1760
CARMEN CAMPBELL
VICE PRESIDENT
TELEPHONE 316 729 6100 • FACSIMILE 316 729 6040

512 STATE STREET • AUGUSTA, KANSAS • 67010 1168 • TELEPHONE 316 775 5434 • FACSIMILE 316 775 1790

OFFICES IN • AUGUSTA • ANDALE • GODDARD • HAYSVILLE • MAIZE • MULVANE • ROSE HILL • WICHITA

design firm
Gardner Design
Wichita, Kansas
designer
Chris Parks
client
Prairie State Bank
(bank)

FIFTY • FIVE

JUST BECAUSE YOU ARE THE BEST...

PRAIRIE STATE BANK HAS A CHECKING ACCOUNT WHICH PROVIDES THE BEST IN PROFESSIONAL SERVICE WITH A PERSONAL TOUCH. THE ONLY REQUIREMENT IS THAT YOU OR YOUR SPOUSE BE 55 YEARS OLD OR OLDER. THE FOLLOWING IS A LIST OF THE SERVICES AVAILABLE TO THE PRESTIGE 55 ACCOUNT HOLDER • • • •

design firm
McElveney & Palozzi Design Group Inc.
Rochester, New York
creative director
Bill McElveney
art director
Jon Westfall
client
CPI Business Groups
(manufacturer)

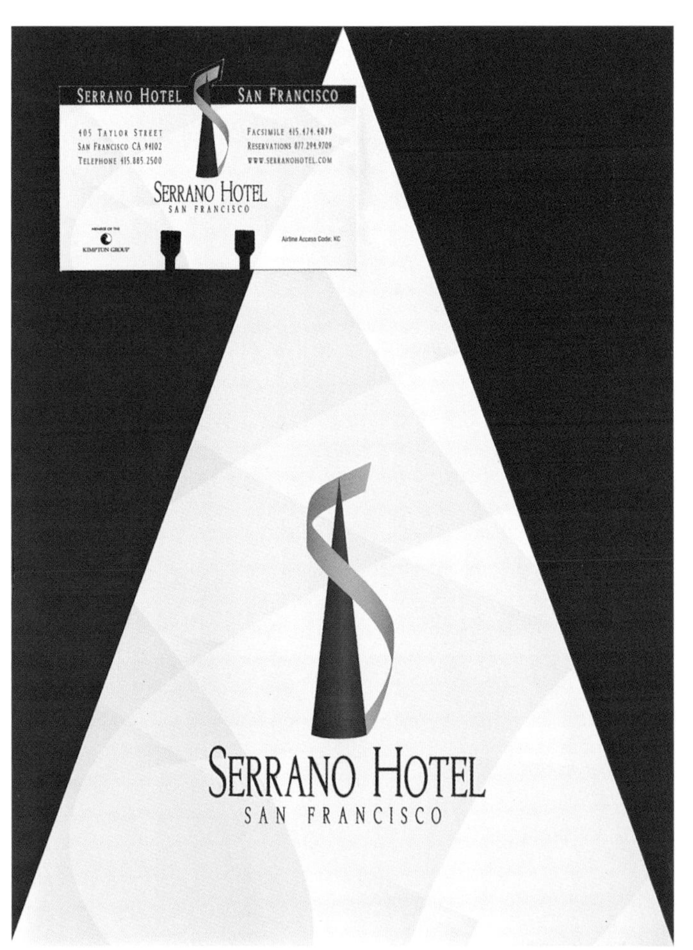

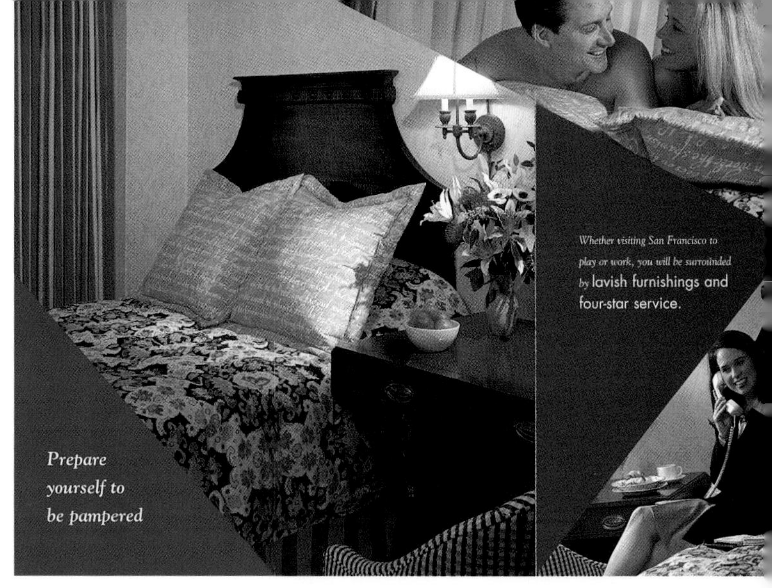

design firm
Hunt Weber Clark Assoc., Inc.
San Francisco, California
designers
Nancy Hunt-Weber,
Leigh Krichbaum, Jim Deeken
client
Kimpton Hotel + Restaurant Group
(hospitality)

the creative center

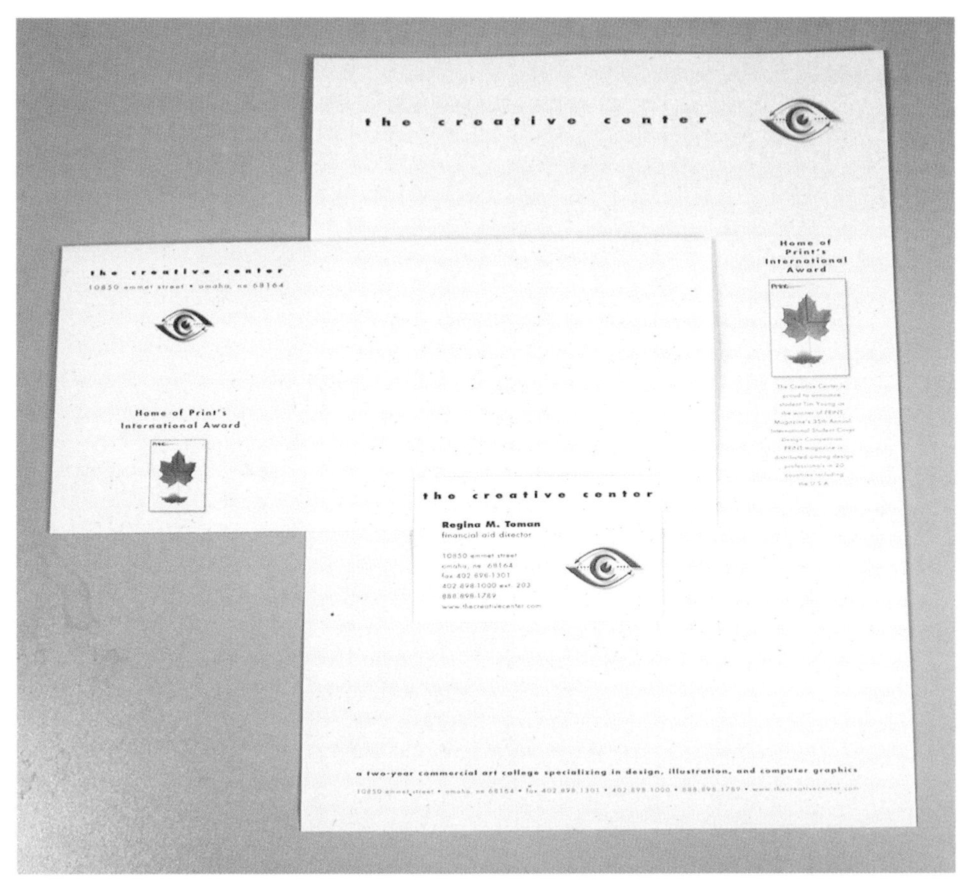

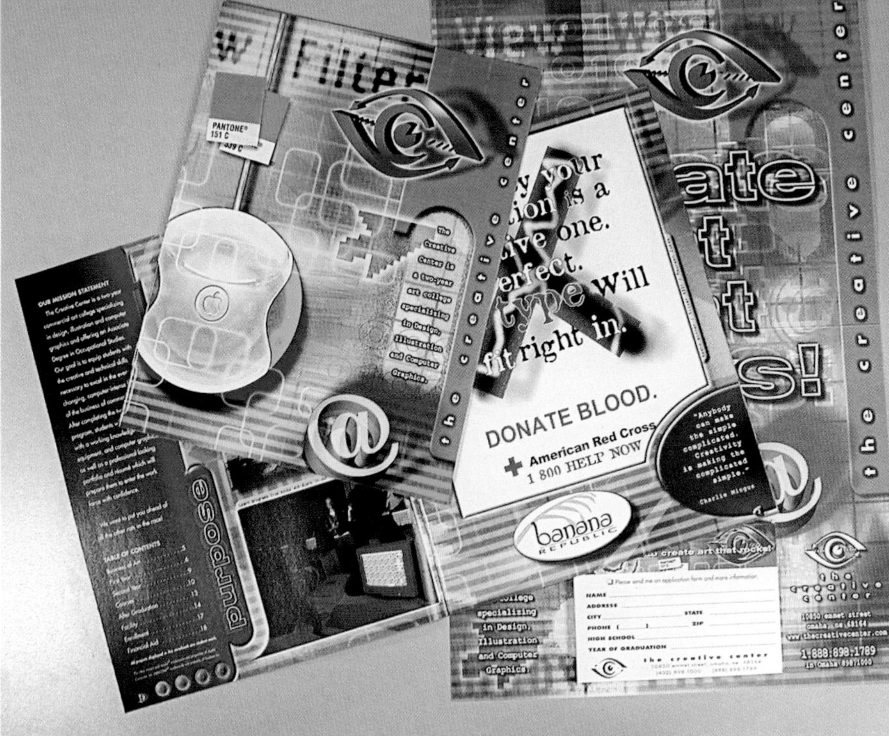

design firm
Dotzler Creative Arts
Omaha, Nebraska
client
The Creative Center
(commercial art college)

design firm
Gardner Design
Wichita, Kansas
designers
Bill Gardner, Brian Miller
client
Tallgrass Beef
(beef producers)

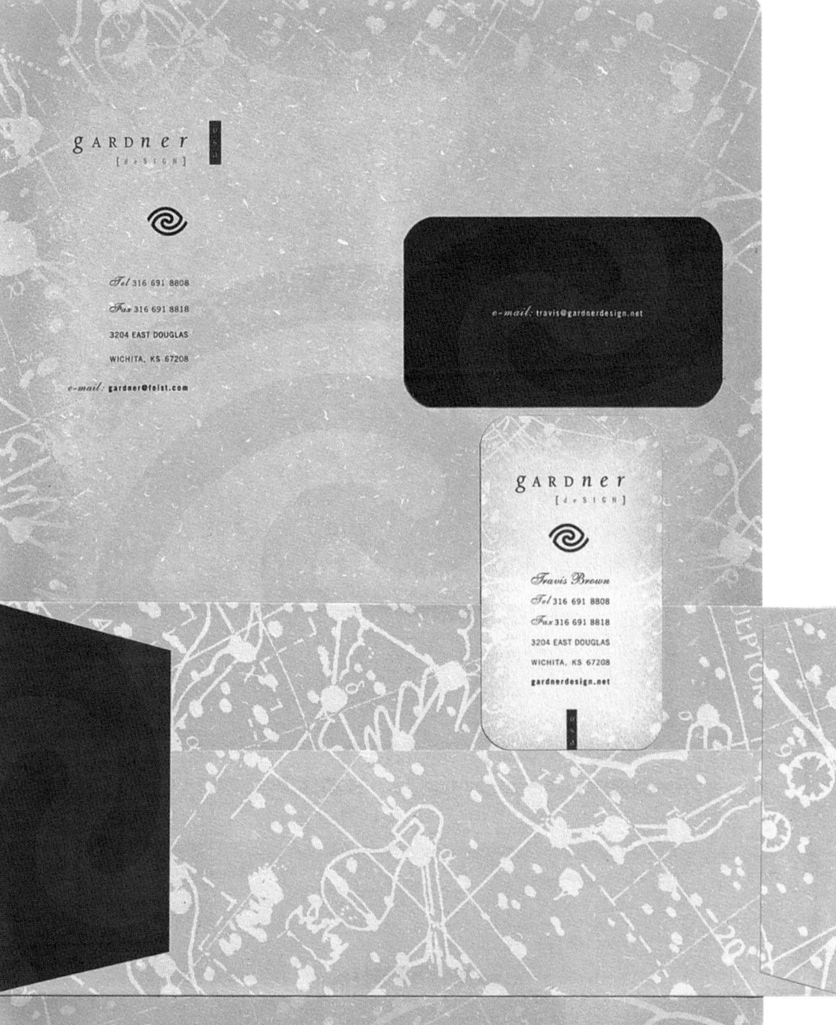

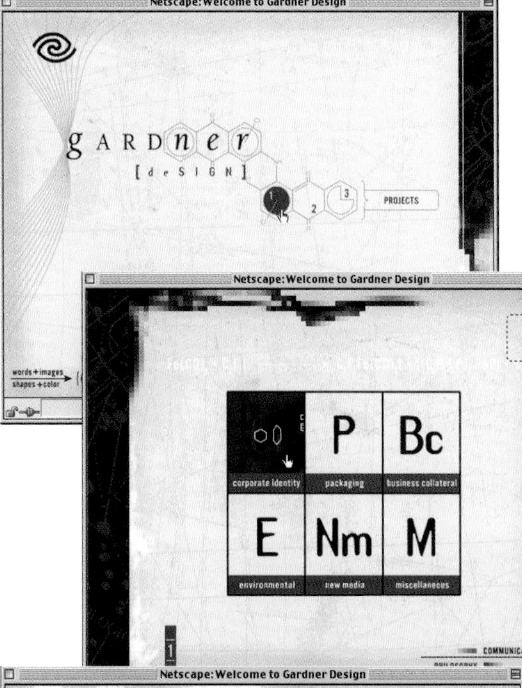

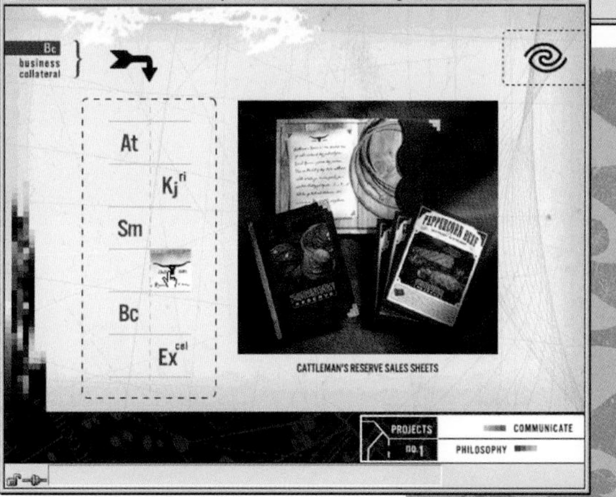

design firm
Gardner Design
Wichita, Kansas
art directors
Bill Gardner, Brian Miller
designers
Bill Gardner, Brian Miller, Chaney Kimball, Karen Hogan
client
Gardner Design (design firm)

www.s1.com

S1 CORPORATION Headquarters 3390 Peachtree Road, Suite 1700, Atlanta, GA 30326 U.S.A.
T +1 404.812.6200 F +1 404.812.6727 TOLL FREE +1 888.457.2237

S1 Santa Clara
2840 San Tomas Expressway
Santa Clara, CA 95051 U.S.A.
T +1 408.982.2000
F +1 408.982.0777

www.s1.com

Sean Childers
Americas

S1 Atlanta
3390 Peachtree Road, Suite 1700
Atlanta, GA 30326 U.S.A.
T +1 404.812.6280 C +1 404.664.7326
F +1 404.812.6616
E sean.childers@s1.com

S1 CORPORATION

S1 Atlanta
3390 Peachtree Road, Suite 1700
Atlanta, GA 30326 U.S.A.

www.s1.com

S1 CORPORATION

atlanta
boston
brussels
charlotte
johannesburg
lisbon
london
luxembourg
madrid
manchester
melbourne
paris
rotterdam
santa clara
singapore
sydney

atlanta
boston
brussels
charlotte
johannesburg
lisbon
london
luxembourg
madrid
manchester
melbourne
paris
rotterdam
santa clara
singapore
sydney

design firm
Michael Patrick Partners
Palo Alto, California
design director
Darice Scarborough
designers
Connie Hwang, Ian Oakley Smith
client
S1 Corporation
(financial services)

atlanta boston brussels charlotte
luxembourg madrid johannesburg
santa clara singapore sydney paris
charlotte lisbon luxembourg boston
paris rotterdam boston melbourne
atlanta charlotte brussels charlotte
lisbon london madrid manchester
rotterdam
atlanta br
luxembou
santa cla
lisbon lon
melbourn
singapore
sydney ch
boston lu
charlotte
paris lond
lisbon ma

www.s1.com

S1 CORPORATION Headquarters 3390 Peachtree Road, Suite 1700, Atlanta, GA 30326 U.S.A.
T +1 404.812.6200 F +1 404.812.6727 TOLL FREE +1 888.457.2237

S1 Boston/Littleton
119 Russell Street, Suite 24
Littleton, MA 01460 U.S.A.
T +1 978.952.6101
F +1 978.952.6611

S1 Boston/Waltham
950 Winter Street, Suite 1700
Waltham, MA 02451 U.S.A.
T +1 781.906.1500
F +1 781.906.1515

S1 Brussels
Excelsiorlaan 87
B-1930 Zaventem, Belgium
T +32 2.714.42.11
F +32 2.714.42.22

S1 DC Brussels
Leuvensesteenweg 533
B-1930 Zaventem, Belgium
T +32 2.712.57.60
F +32 2.712.57.79

S1 Charlotte
2815 Coliseum Centre Drive, Suite 300
Charlotte, NC 28217 U.S.A.
T +1 704.423.0394
F +1 704.423.0325

S1 Johannesburg
2nd Floor, West Wing, Sandton Square
Sandown 2196 South Africa
T +27 11.881.5637
F +27 11.881.5611

VISIT OUR WEB SITE AT WWW.S1.COM FOR A CURRENT LIST OF OFFICES

S1 Lisbon
Av. Duque de Loulé 106-11°
1050 Lisboa, Portugal
T +351 1.315.0233
F +351 1.315.0234

S1 London
7th Floor, Peninsular House
36, Monument Street
London EC3R 8LJ UK
T +44 (0) 207 427 0250
F +44 (0) 207 427 0260

S1 Luxembourg
65, avenue de la Gare
1611 Luxembourg
Grand-Duché du Luxembourg
T +352 400.811.302
F +352 400.811.33.21

S1 Madrid
Paseo de la Castellana 60
28046 Madrid, España
T +34 91 562 18 61
F +34 91 411 14 87

S1 Manchester
Oaklands House, 34 Washway Road
Sale Cheshire M33 6FS UK
T +44 (0) 161.610.7000
F +44 (0) 161.610.0700

S1 Melbourne
Level 2, 14 Queens Road
Melbourne VIC 3004 Australia
T +61 3.9258.1100
F +61 3.9804.5899

S1 Paris
104, rue de Richelieu
75002 Paris, France
T +33 1.47.03.06.66
F +33 1.47.03.07.77

S1 Rotterdam
Marten Meesweg 8-10
Postbus 84155
3009 CD Rotterdam, Nederland
T +31 10.286.16.00
F +31 10.286.16.16

S1 Santa Clara
2840 San Tomas Expressway
Santa Clara, CA 95051 U.S.A.
T +1 408.982.2000
F +1 408.982.0777

S1 Singapore
6 Temasek Boulevard
Suntec Tower Four #21-04/05
Singapore 038986
T +65 333.81.38
F +65 333.81.36

S1 Sydney
Level 8, 131 York Street
Sydney NSW 2000 Australia
T +61 2 9267 7455
F +61 2 9267 9422

S1 Technology Center
705 Westech Drive
Norcross, GA 30092 U.S.A.
T +1 678.421.4075
F +1 678.421.4864

S1 CORPORATION

paris johannesburg lisbon london
manchester melbourne singapore
atlanta boston brussels rotterdam
madrid london santa clara atlanta
singapore sydney luxembourg paris
charlotte johannesburg manchester
brussels boston paris santa clara

S1 CORPORATION

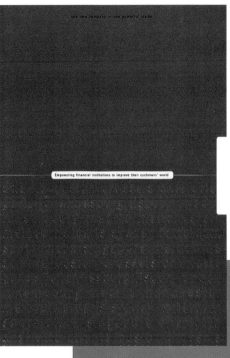

S1 Consumer Suite

Comprehensive, integrated...the Internet financial services solution to help you serve your consumers.

Flexible, Scalable, Secure and Simple

THE BENEFITS OF THE S1 CORPORATE SUITE

Scalable technology and a flexible system architecture protect your investment as your corporate business expands. No matter how large your corporate customer base is today or will be in the future, we can support that expansion with scalable software that can run at your financial institution or in the S1 Data Center. The flexibility of the system accommodates corporations of all sizes with multiple branding solutions that reinforce the value of your products and services to your client base.

Next generation technology provides anytime, anywhere banking for your customers. Substantial investments in research and development help us continually evaluate new ideas that can add significant value to your financial institution and client base. Access to new delivery channels, such as handheld devices, mobile phones, personal digital assistants and security devices, like biometrics and smart cards, ensure a highly competitive product offering.

Simplicity of a seamless platform provides your clients with a single look and feel to unify your product and service offerings. Your customers benefit from an easy-to-use interface and an extremely short learning curve. The browser-based technology benefits your financial institution by reducing the cost of deploying, maintaining and supporting client software and facilitates the introduction of new services and products.

BALANCE INFORMATION: *The account overview screen shows balance information for all the company's accounts worldwide.*

One Solution

The open architecture of the S1 Corporate Suite is designed to integrate with a variety of existing legacy systems, reducing the cost of implementation, maintenance and support. Your clients will no longer need multiple solutions from multiple providers for their banking needs. The S1 Corporate Suite has a modular architecture that gives you the flexibility to vary configurations for specific markets and customer segments. This flexible architecture provides significant operational and cost benefits. Business components can be re-used and re-packaged to create new products and services with reduced effort.

The S1 server architecture also supports numerous front-end applications, while a flexible back-office framework supports the evolution of your bank's legacy systems.

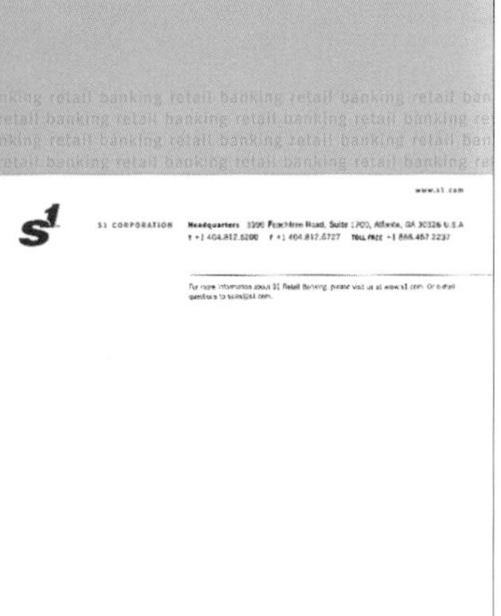

S1 Business Suite

The comprehensive Internet banking solution for small and medium-sized businesses.

Front

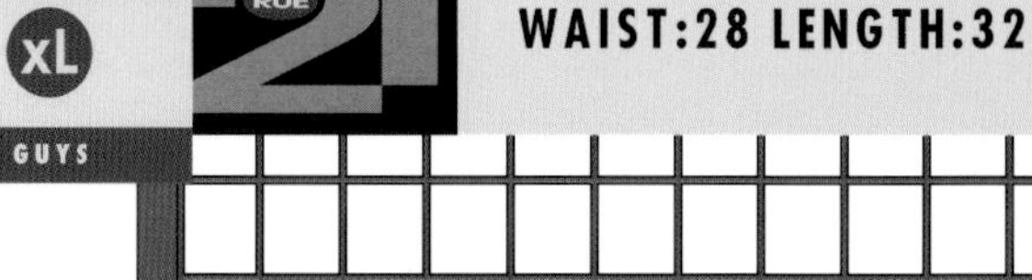

WHAT TO WEAR?

Pennsylvania Fashions

155 Thornhill Drive
Warrendale, PA 15086

xL

GUYS

Back

design firm
JGA, Inc.
Southfield, Missouri
director of graphic design
Brian Eastman
senior graphics designer
Mike Farris
client
Rue 21
(fashion retail)

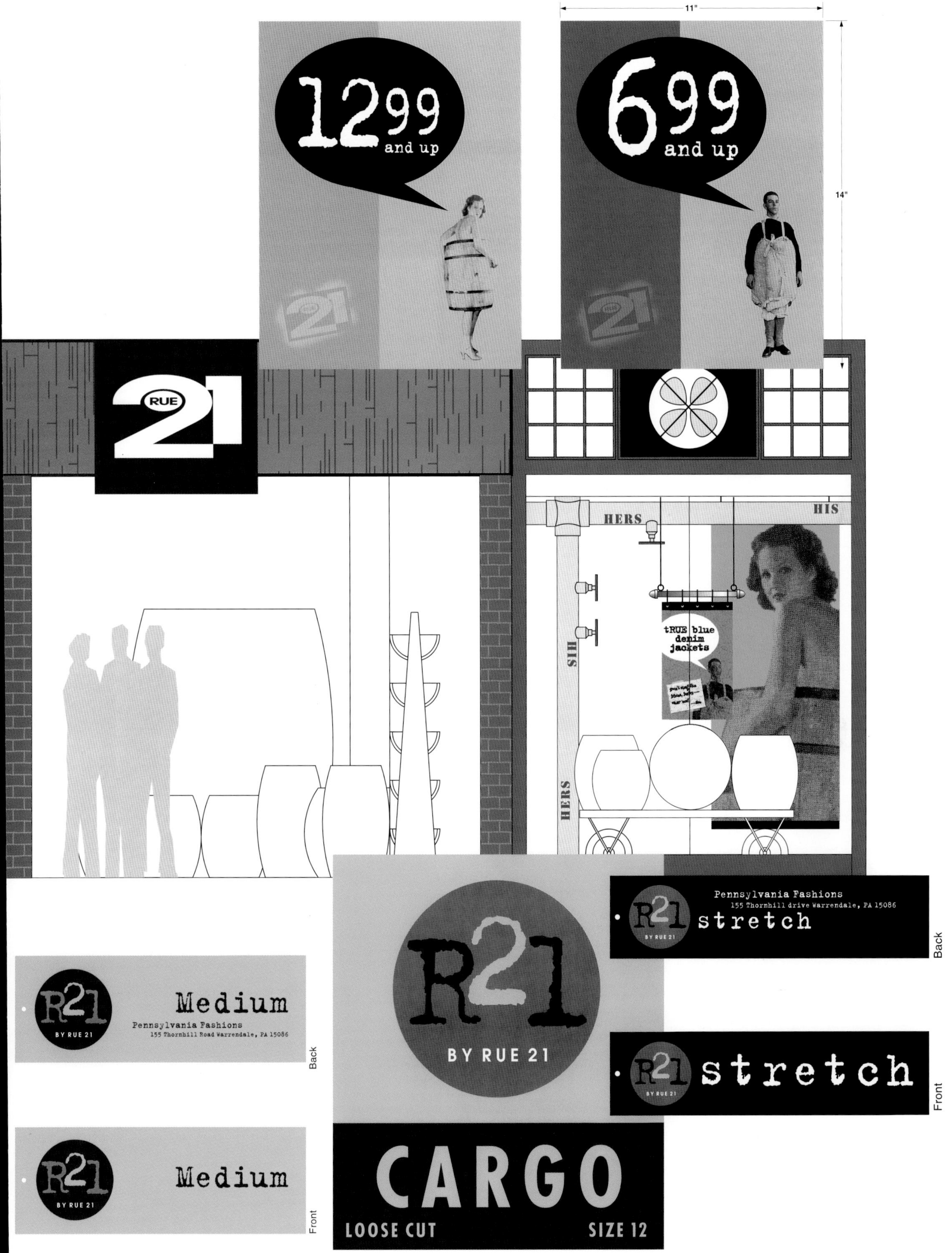

11"

1299 and up

699 and up

14"

RUE 21

HERS

HIS

tRUE blue denim jackets

HIS

HERS

Back

Back

R21 stretch

BY RUE 21

Front

Front

CARGO

LOOSE CUT

SIZE 12

SupplyPro®
UNLOCK THE SAVINGS

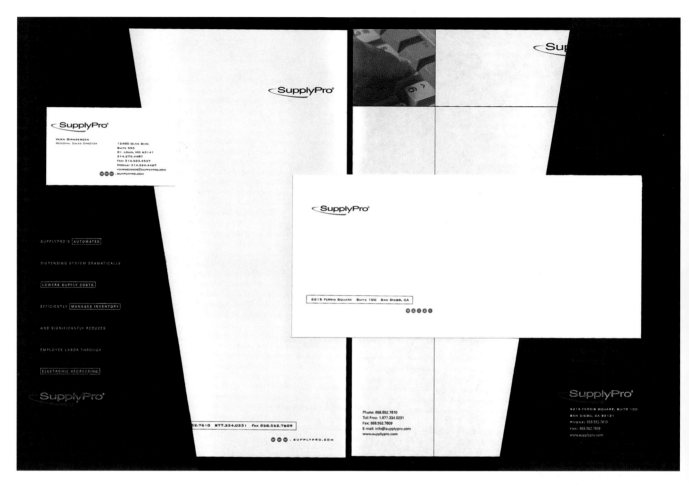

design firm
Laura Coe Design Assoc.
San Diego, California
creative director
Laura Coe Wright
designers
Tracy Castle, Luke Stotler,
Leanne Leveillee, Ryoichi Yotsumoto,
Tom Richman
illustrator
Ryoichi Yotsumoto
client
SupplyPro
(electronic storage cabinets)

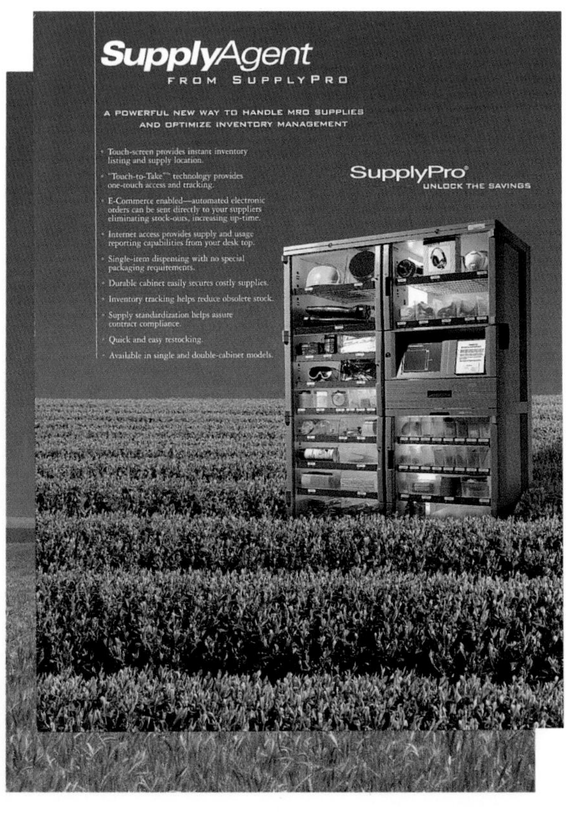

SupplyAgent
FROM SUPPLYPRO
A POWERFUL NEW WAY TO HANDLE MRO SUPPLIES AND OPTIMIZE INVENTORY MANAGEMENT
• Touch-screen provides instant inventory listing and supply location.
• "Touch-to-Take"™ technology provides one-touch access and tracking.
• E-Commerce enabled—automated electronic orders can be sent directly to your suppliers eliminating stock-outs, increasing up-time.
• Internet access provides supply and usage reporting capabilities from your desk top.
• Single-item dispensing with no special packaging requirements.
• Durable cabinet easily secures costly supplies.
• Inventory tracking helps reduce obsolete stock.
• Supply standardization helps assure contract compliance.
• Quick and easy restocking.
• Available in single and double-cabinet models.
SupplyPro®
UNLOCK THE SAVINGS

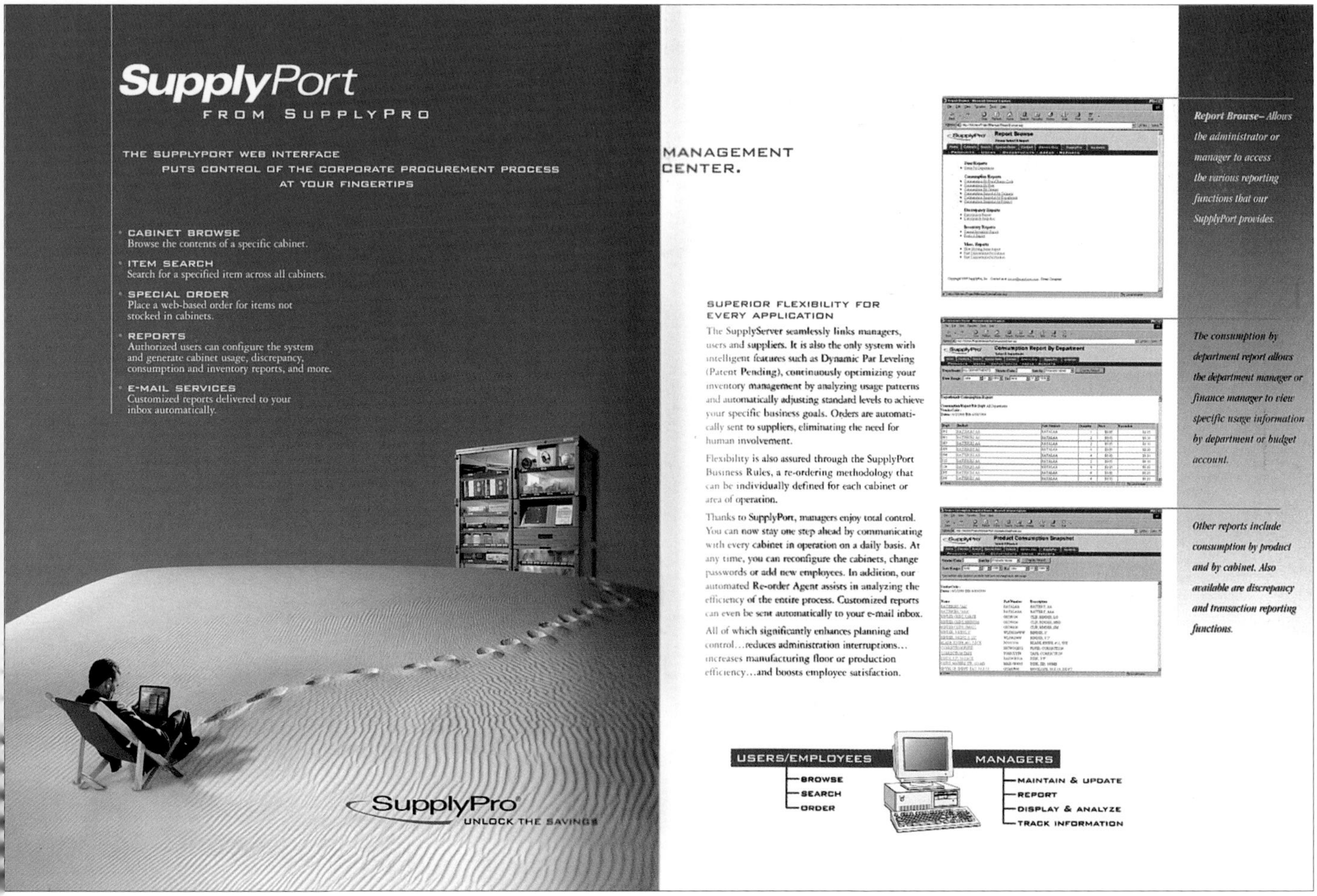

SupplyPort

FROM SUPPLYPRO

THE SUPPLYPORT WEB INTERFACE PUTS CONTROL OF THE CORPORATE PROCUREMENT PROCESS AT YOUR FINGERTIPS

- **CABINET BROWSE** Browse the contents of a specific cabinet.
- **ITEM SEARCH** Search for a specified item across all cabinets.
- **SPECIAL ORDER** Place a web-based order for items not stocked in cabinets.
- **REPORTS** Authorized users can configure the system and generate cabinet usage, discrepancy, consumption and inventory reports, and more.
- **E-MAIL SERVICES** Customized reports delivered to your inbox automatically.

SupplyPro®
UNLOCK THE SAVINGS

MANAGEMENT CENTER.

SUPERIOR FLEXIBILITY FOR EVERY APPLICATION

The SupplyServer seamlessly links managers, users and suppliers. It is also the only system with intelligent features such as Dynamic Par Leveling (Patent Pending), continuously optimizing your inventory management by analyzing usage patterns and automatically adjusting standard levels to achieve your specific business goals. Orders are automatically sent to suppliers, eliminating the need for human involvement.

Flexibility is also assured through the SupplyPort Business Rules, a re-ordering methodology that can be individually defined for each cabinet or area of operation.

Thanks to SupplyPort, managers enjoy total control. You can now stay one step ahead by communicating with every cabinet in operation on a daily basis. At any time, you can reconfigure the cabinets, change passwords or add new employees. In addition, our automated Re-order Agent assists in analyzing the efficiency of the entire process. Customized reports can even be sent automatically to your e-mail inbox.

All of which significantly enhances planning and control…reduces administration interruptions…increases manufacturing floor or production efficiency…and boosts employee satisfaction.

Report Browse– Allows the administrator or manager to access the various reporting functions that our SupplyPort provides.

The consumption by department report allows the department manager or finance manager to view specific usage information by department or budget account.

Other reports include consumption by product and by cabinet. Also available are discrepancy and transaction reporting functions.

USERS/EMPLOYEES
- BROWSE
- SEARCH
- ORDER

MANAGERS
- MAINTAIN & UPDATE
- REPORT
- DISPLAY & ANALYZE
- TRACK INFORMATION

design firm
Gardner Design
Wichita, Kansas
designers
Bill Gardner, Brian Miller
illustrator
Brian Miller
client
Doskocil
(meat promotion)

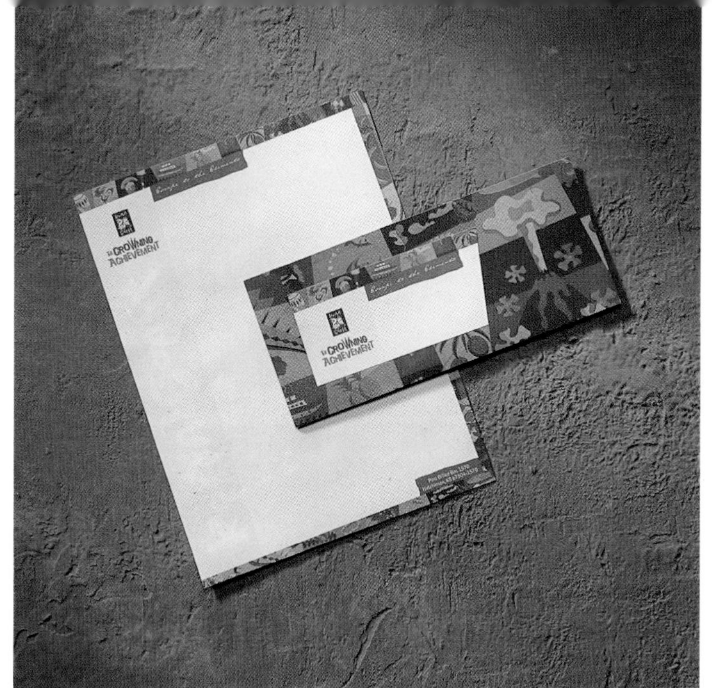

The CROWNING ACHIEVEMENT

THE CROWNING ACHIEVEMENT
KONA COAST

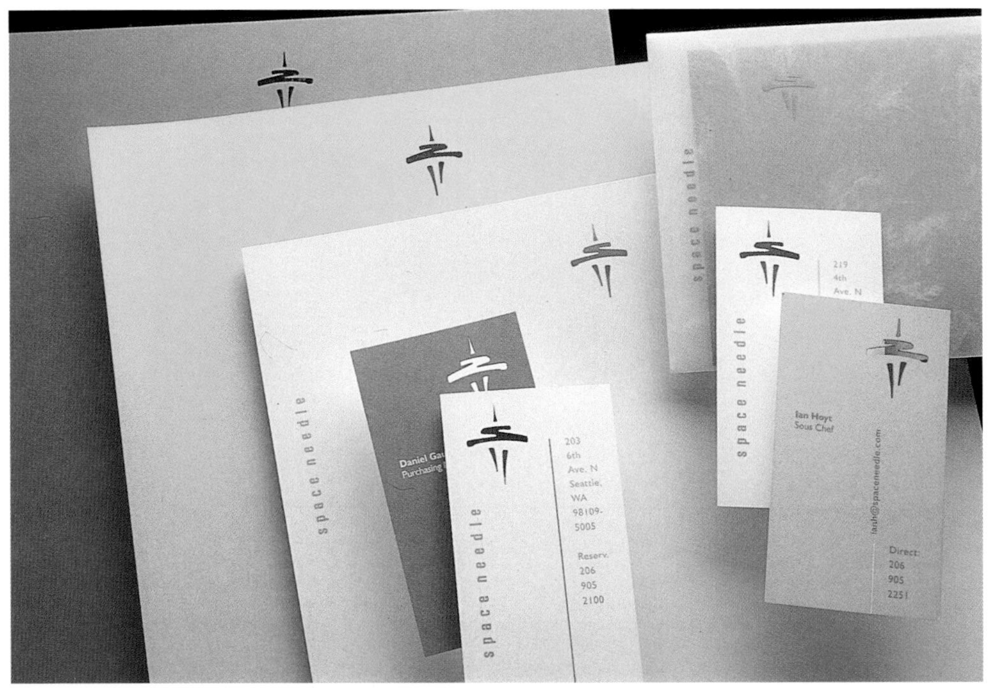

design firm
Hornall Anderson Design Works, Inc.
Seattle, Washington
designers
Jack Anderson, Mary Hermes,
Gretchen Cook, Andrew Smith,
Alan Florsheim, Cliff Chung
client
Space Needle
(destination restaurant and viewdeck
located in downtown Seattle)

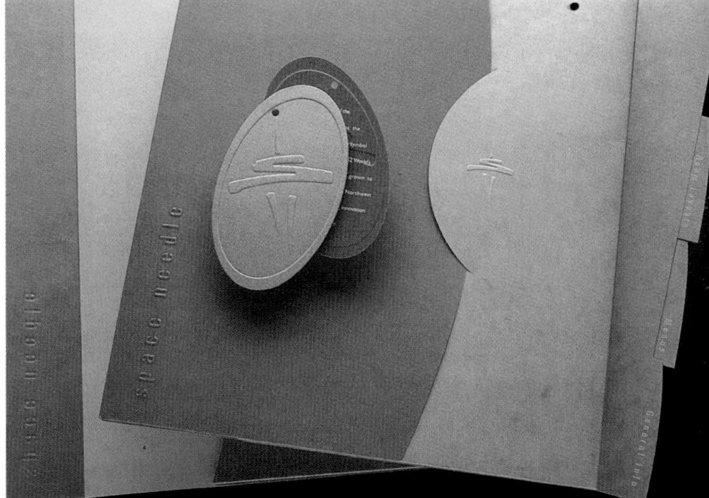

space needle.
space needle.
space needle.

space needle.
space needle.

space
needle.

Luminate™

design firm
Michael Patrick Partners
Palo Alto, California
design director
Darice Scarborough

designer
Connie Hwang
client
Luminate
(management service provider)

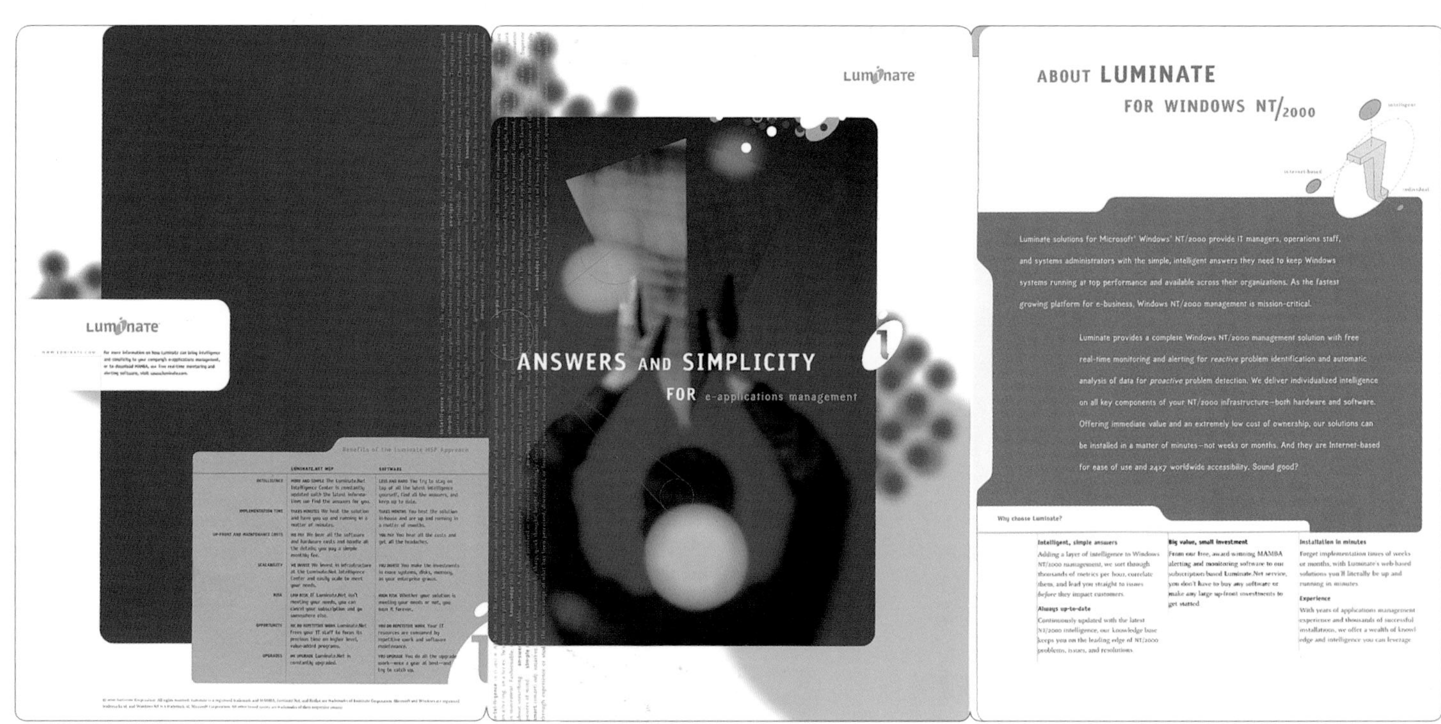

VIZIWORX

design firm
Gardner Design
Wichita, Kansas
art director
Bill Gardner
designers
Chris Parks, Chaney Kimball
client
Viziworx
(enhanced television software)

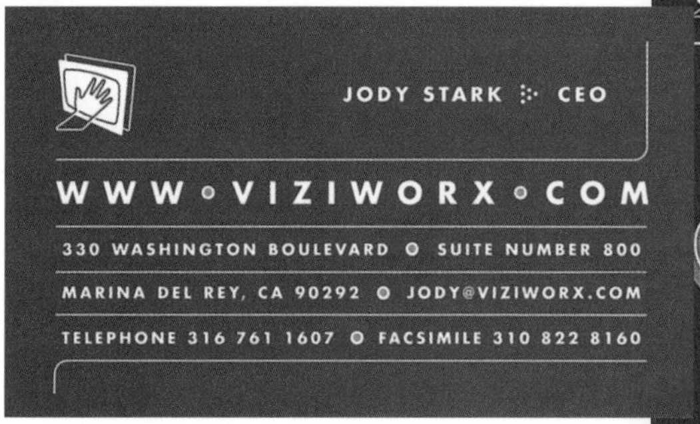

JODY STARK :: CEO
WWW • VIZIWORX • COM
330 WASHINGTON BOULEVARD • SUITE NUMBER 800
MARINA DEL REY, CA 90292 • JODY@VIZIWORX.COM
TELEPHONE 316 761 1607 • FACSIMILE 310 822 8160

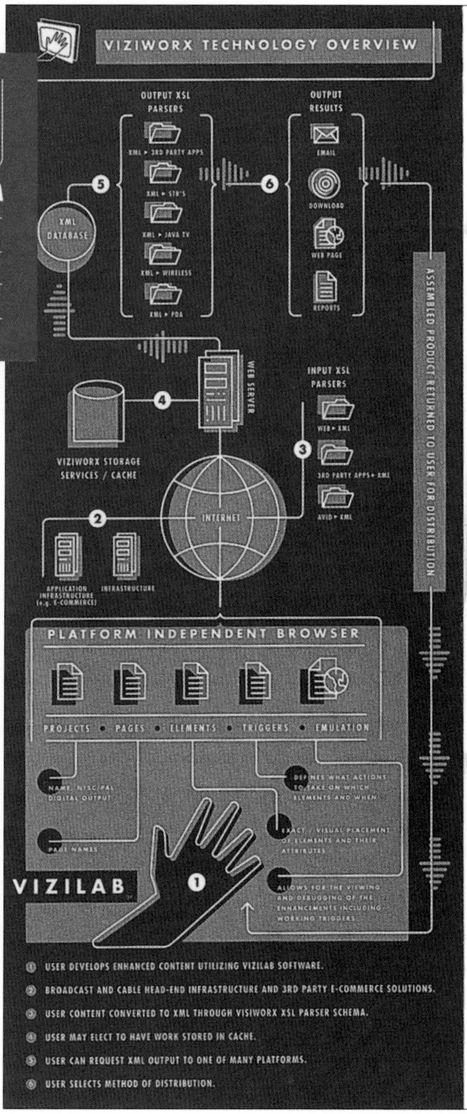

VIZIWORX TECHNOLOGY OVERVIEW

OUTPUT XSL PARSERS
OUTPUT RESULTS
XML DATABASE
WEB SERVER
VIZIWORX STORAGE SERVICES / CACHE
INPUT XSL PARSERS
INTERNET
ASSEMBLED PRODUCT RETURNED TO USER FOR DISTRIBUTION
PLATFORM INDEPENDENT BROWSER
PROJECTS • PAGES • ELEMENTS • TRIGGERS • EMULATION
VIZILAB

1. USER DEVELOPS ENHANCED CONTENT UTILIZING VIZILAB SOFTWARE.
2. BROADCAST AND CABLE HEAD-END INFRASTRUCTURE AND 3RD PARTY E-COMMERCE SOLUTIONS.
3. USER CONTENT CONVERTED TO XML THROUGH VISIWORX XSL PARSER SCHEMA.
4. USER MAY ELECT TO HAVE WORK STORED IN CACHE.
5. USER CAN REQUEST XML OUTPUT TO ONE OF MANY PLATFORMS.
6. USER SELECTS METHOD OF DISTRIBUTION.

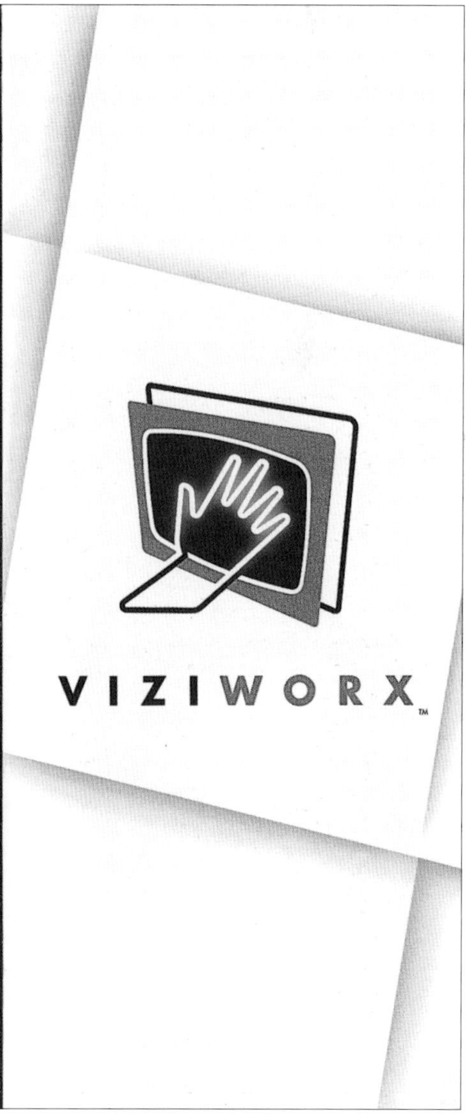

VIZIWORX™

avenue a™

design firm
Hornall Anderson Design Works, Inc.
Seattle, Washington
designers
Jack Anderson, Debra McCloskey, Tobi Brown, Henry Yiu, James Tee, Gretchen Cook, Cliff Chung, Alan Florsheim, Margaret Long, Rick Miller
client
Avenue A
(online advertising)

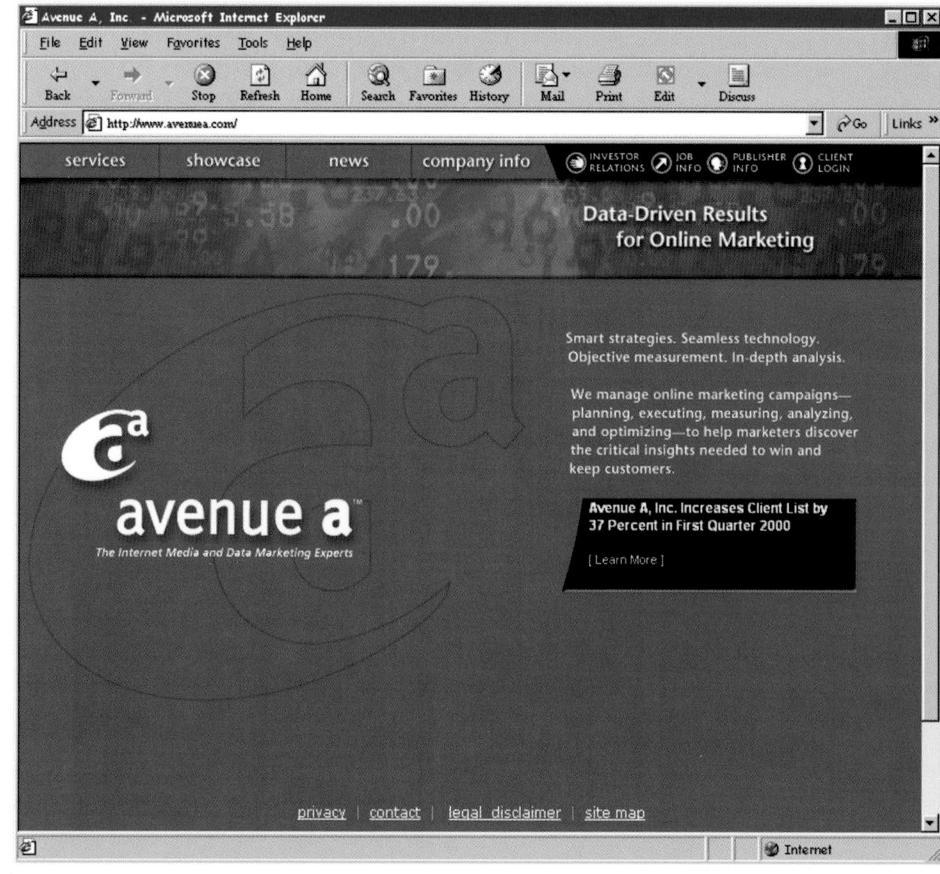

avenue a
avenue a
"They have great people,
technology and expertise,
and they're passionate
about creating a campaign
that meets our needs."

506 Second Avenue
Seattle, WA 98104
206.521.8800
206.521.8808 fax
avenue a
506 Second Avenue
Seattle, WA 98104
206.521.8808 fax
www.avenuea.com
avenue a
www.avenuea.com
506 Second Avenue
Seattle, WA 98104
avenue a
avenue a

avenue a
Data-Driven
Results
from on-line
marketing

WE WANT TO SHOW YOU HOW WE WORK, AND WHAT DRIVES CLARIFY. SO WE'VE CHOSEN THE WORD "FLEX" TO TELL OUR STORY. IT'S ABOUT HAVING GOOD REFLEXES, BEING FLEXIBLE, AND EVEN FLEXING OUR MUSCLES A BIT. BUT THIS ISN'T SIMPLY CLARIFY'S STORY–IT'S OUR CUSTOMERS' STORY.

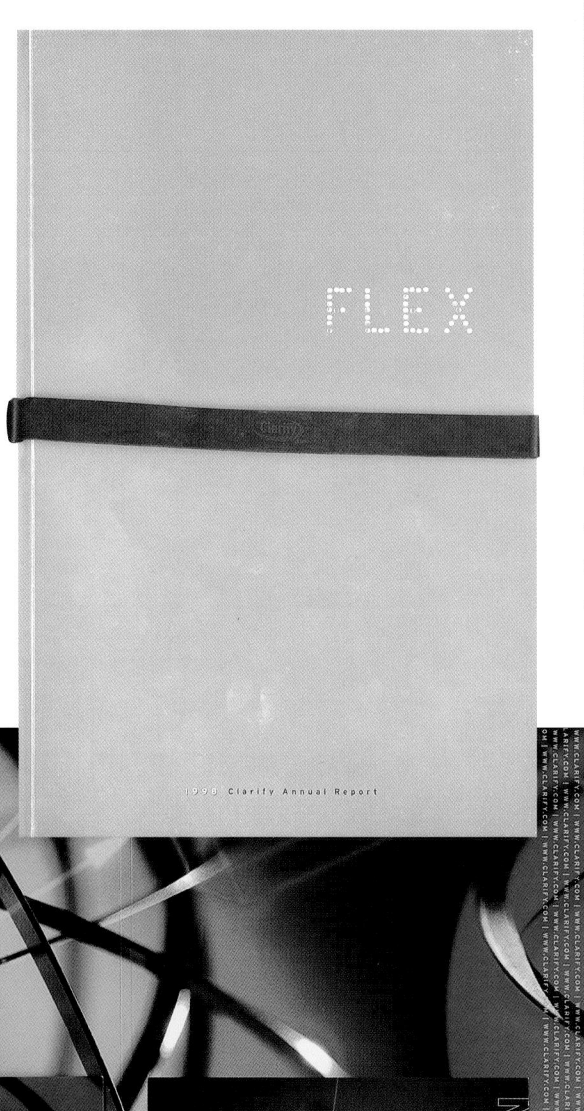

design firm
Michael Patrick Partners
Palo Alto, California
design director
Darice Scarborough
designers
Brooks Beisch, Victoria Pohlmann, Connie Hwang
client
Clarify
(software)

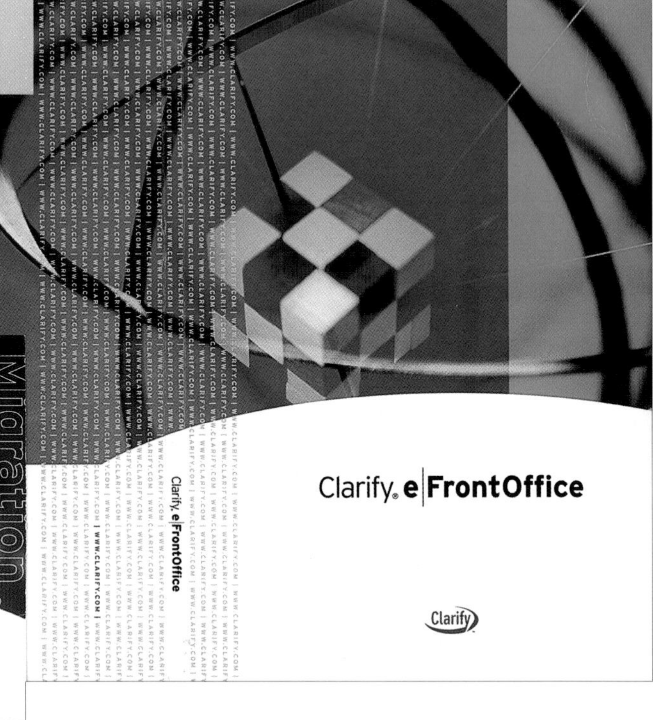

Clarify e|FrontOffice
DEMONSTRATION DISK
Clarify

Clarify e|FrontOffice
Migration Services

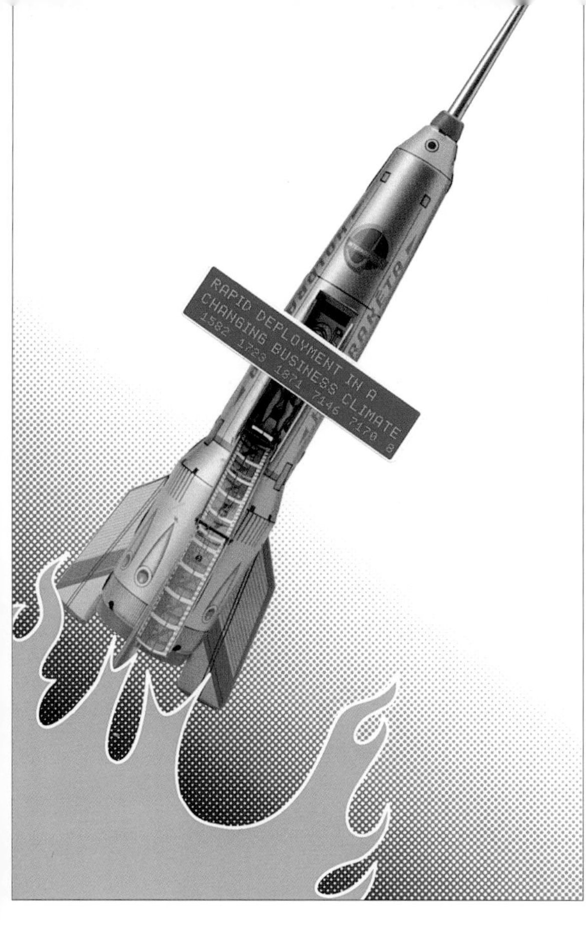

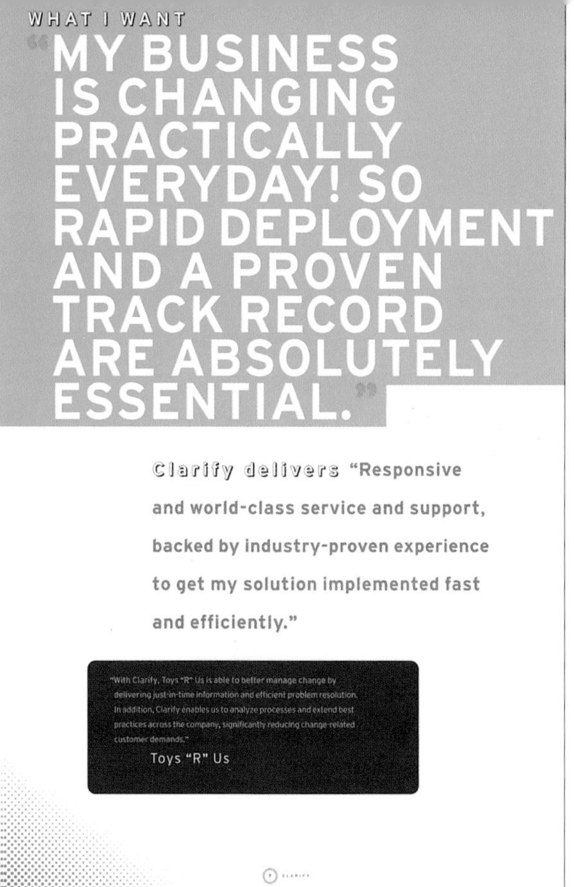

WHAT I WANT
"MY BUSINESS IS CHANGING PRACTICALLY EVERYDAY! SO RAPID DEPLOYMENT AND A PROVEN TRACK RECORD ARE ABSOLUTELY ESSENTIAL."
Clarify delivers "Responsive and world-class service and support, backed by industry-proven experience to get my solution implemented fast and efficiently."
Toys "R" Us

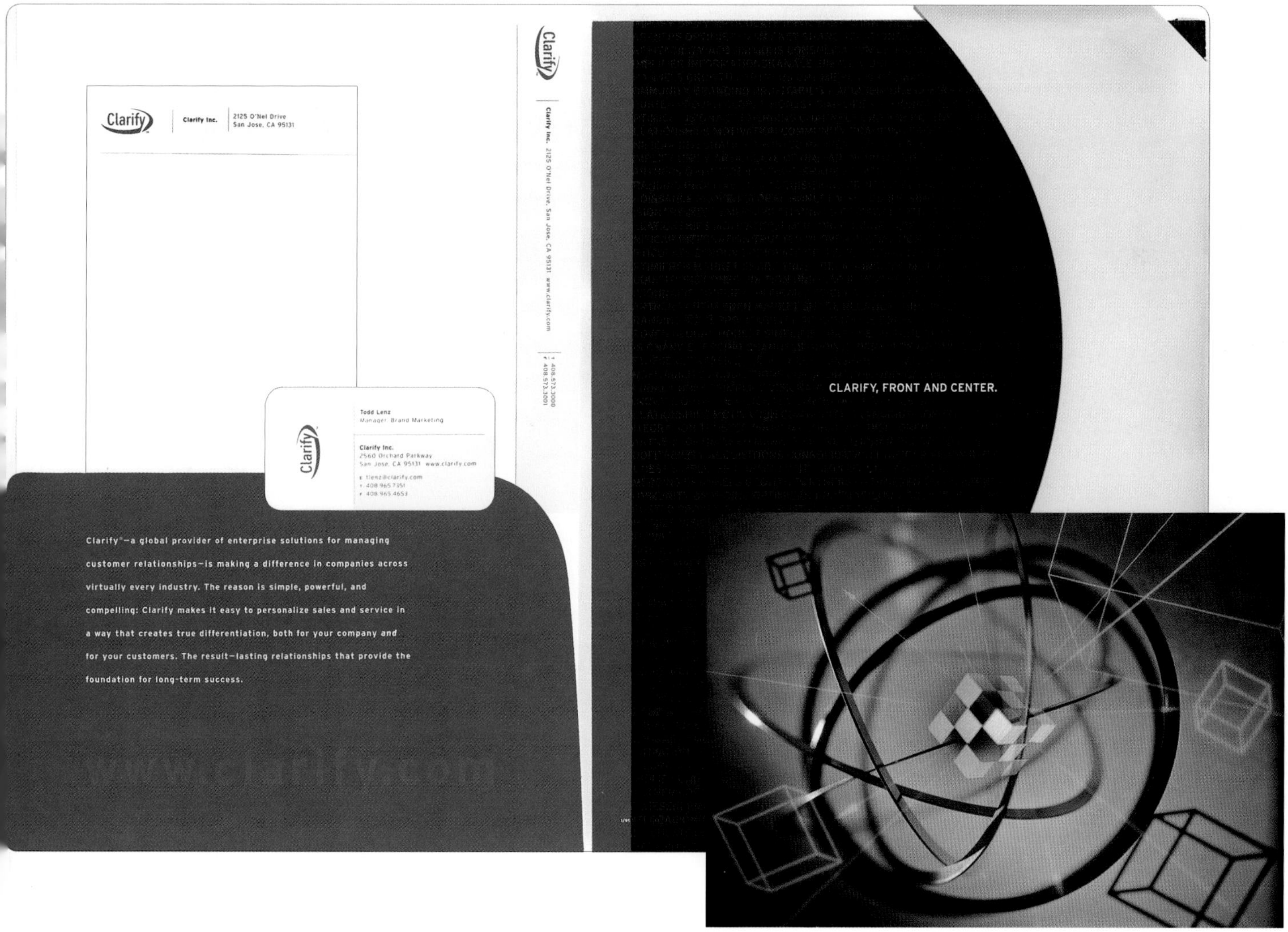

Clarify

Clarify Inc. 2125 O'Nel Drive San Jose, CA 95131

Clarify Inc. 2125 O'Nel Drive, San Jose, CA 95131 www.clarify.com

Todd Lenz
Manager, Brand Marketing

Clarify Inc.
2560 Orchard Parkway
San Jose, CA 95131 www.clarify.com

Clarify®—a global provider of enterprise solutions for managing customer relationships—is making a difference in companies across virtually every industry. The reason is simple, powerful, and compelling: Clarify makes it easy to personalize sales and service in a way that creates true differentiation, both for your company and for your customers. The result—lasting relationships that provide the foundation for long-term success.

www.clarify.com

CLARIFY, FRONT AND CENTER.

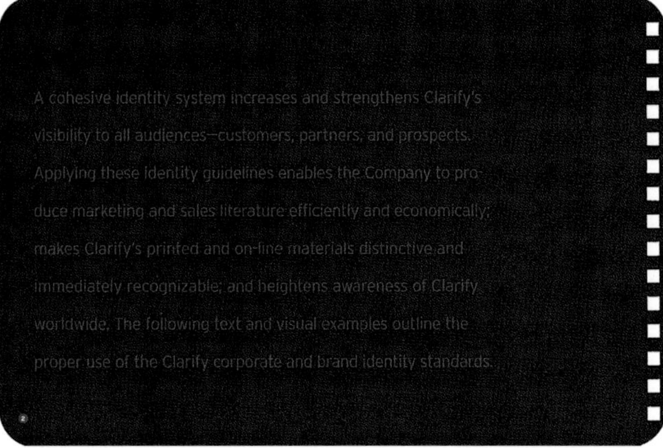
A cohesive identity system increases and strengthens Clarify's visibility to all audiences—customers, partners, and prospects. Applying these identity guidelines enables the Company to produce marketing and sales literature efficiently and economically; makes Clarify's printed and on-line materials distinctive and immediately recognizable; and heightens awareness of Clarify worldwide. The following text and visual examples outline the proper use of the Clarify corporate and brand identity standards.

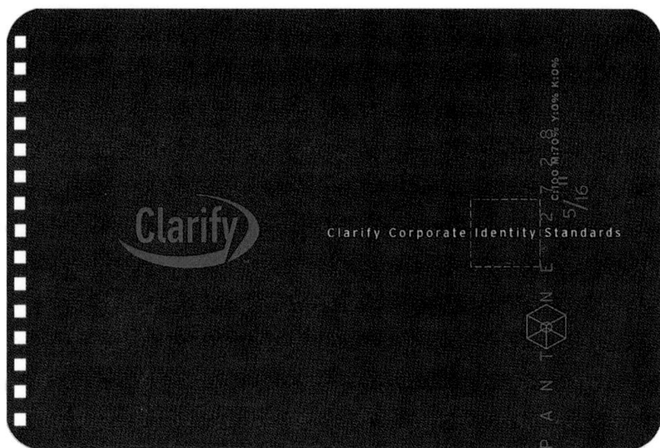
Clarify
Clarify Corporate Identity Standards
PANTONE

Design Elements

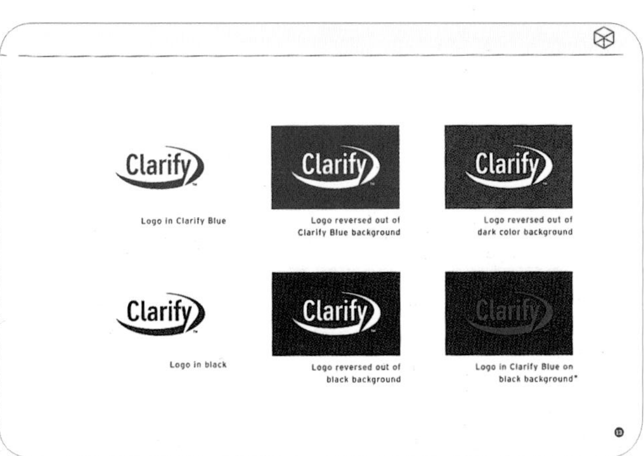
Clarify
Logo in Clarify Blue
Logo reversed out of Clarify Blue background
Logo reversed out of dark color background
Logo in black
Logo reversed out of black background
Logo in Clarify Blue on black background*

Clarify Solutions Alliance
CONSULTING PARTNER PROGRAM
CLARIFY SOLUTIONS ALLIANCE
Clarify Services
CERTIFIED PROFESSIONAL PROGRAM
CLARIFY PROFESSIONAL SERVICES
SOFTWARE PARTNER PROGRAM
CLARIFY SOLUTIONS ALLIANCE
CUSTOMERCARE CUSTOMFIT OPTIONS
CLARIFY CUSTOMER SERVICE
A companion offering to CustomerCARE, CustomFit is a portfolio of service options that allow you to personalize CustomerCARE to your specific requirements. These add-on services give you ultimate flexibility: design a service package that is just right for your company's needs.
This program includes:
Integrated telephone, web, and email service and support
Full access to Clarify's knowledgebase and troubleshooting guidelines
Four standard service level agreements
Four primary contacts, unlimited communication contacts
Site specific reports on service quality
New releases, maintenance releases
Proactive and emergency patches
We understand that your business may require additional support. That's why we offer CustomFit—a menu of services that you can choose from to enhance your CustomerCARE support program. These add-on services give you ultimate flexibility—you can purchase them now or later, you can select just the services right for you, and you can customize a support program to fit your company's needs.
CustomFit Options at a Glance
Extended Hours Support - 7x24x365 or 5x24
Advanced Developer Support
Custom Escalation Management Service
Single Point of Contact
Continued Care for Older Releases
Custom Service Level Agreement
On-site Support - Emergency or Permanent
Add More Contacts
CustomerCARE CustomFit Options

(continued)
design firm
Michael Patrick Partners
Palo Alto, California

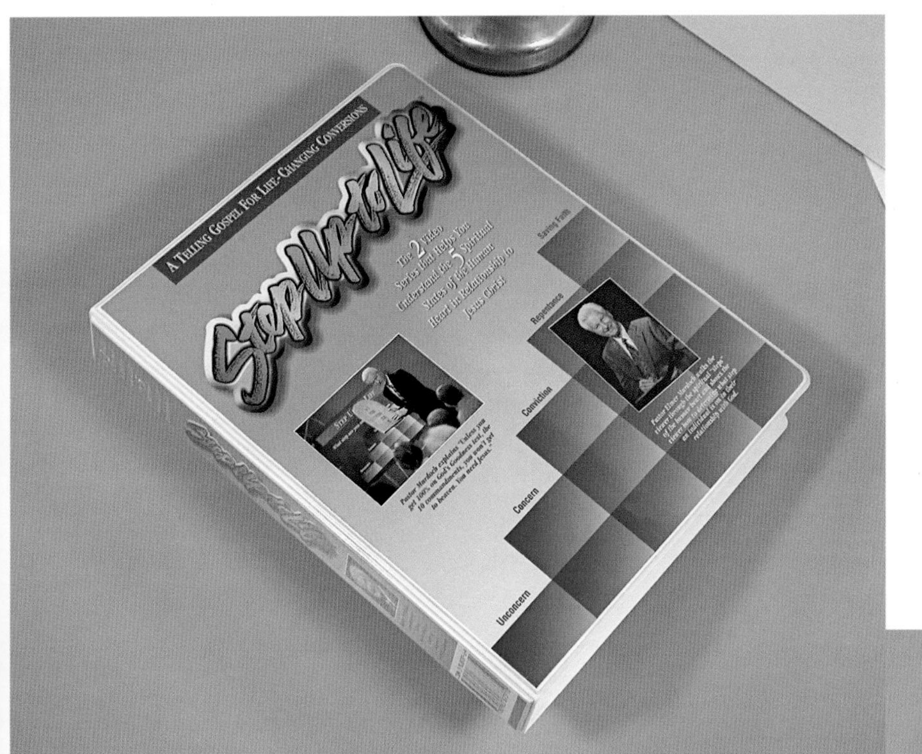

design firm
Dotzler Creative Arts
Omaha, Nebraska
client
Step Up To Life
(Christian ministry)

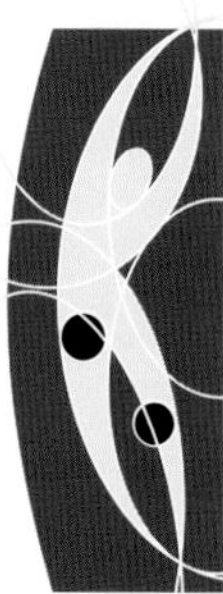

Kansas Joint Replacement Institute

design firm
Gardner Design
Wichita, Kansas
art director
Brian Miller
designers
Bill Gardner, Travis Brown, Brian Miller
client
Kansas Joint Replacement Institute
(joint replacement hospital)

A New Joint Announcement

Ely Bartal, M.D.

Kansas Surgery and Recovery Center

2770 North Webb Road

Wichita, KS 67226

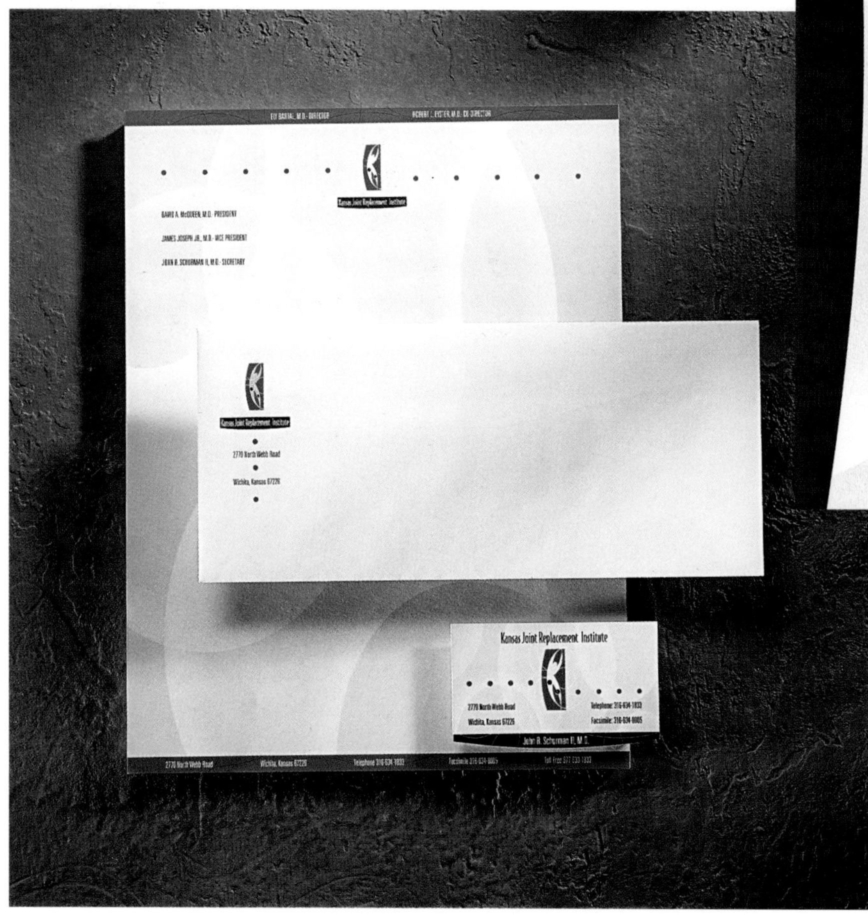

FLEXIBILITY
KANSAS JOINT REPLACEMENT INSTITUTE
Toll Free: 877-633-1833
LIVING
To offer a comprehensive approach to the care of the arthritic patient, the Kansas Joint Replacement Institute provides education as a resource for the greater Wichita area and Kansas community. An important aspect of retaining freedom of movement is an awareness of current treatment options. The physicians and staff of Kansas Joint Replacement Institute offer free information seminars to answer your questions and concerns. Call toll-free 877-633-1833 for times and dates.
PATIENT CARE
EDUCATION
RESEARCH
Another important aspect of education is to pass on the torch to new physicians entering the field. In fact, Kansas Joint Replacement Institute and the University of Kansas School of Medicine - Wichita cooperatively offer an Adult Reconstructive Fellowship in the field of Total Joint Replacement. The position includes a year of intensive study in the clinical field of total joint replacement for orthopaedic physicians.
WHY KANSAS JOINT REPLACEMENT INSTITUTE?
freeDOM
is WHY.
DANCE-OFF
29
CONTESTANT
Kansas Joint Replacement Institute
LIVE LIFE AGAIN

Tenet

Two color reverse version
One color reverse version
Tenet
Stationery
Marketing Collateral

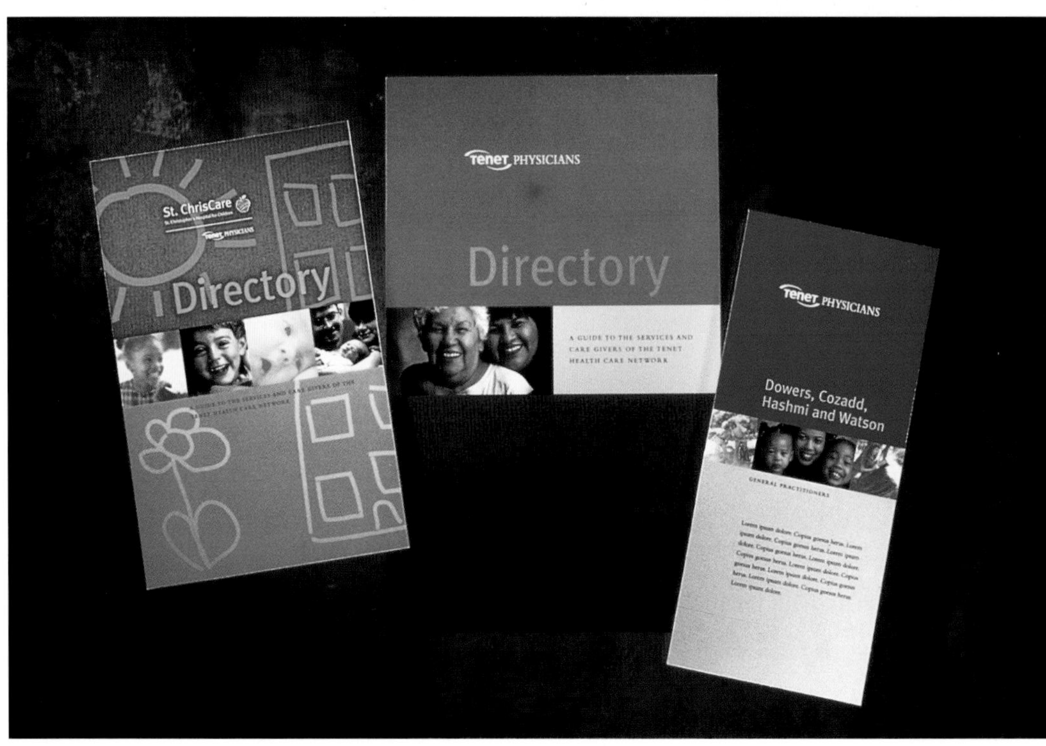
St. ChrisCare
Tenet Physicians
Directory
Tenet Physicians
Directory
A guide to the services and care givers of the Tenet health care network
Tenet Physicians
Dowers, Cozadd, Hashmi and Watson
General Practitioners

design firm
Baker Designed Communications
Santa Monica, California
art director
Gary Baker
designers
Chukyee Cheng, Brian Keenan,
Ron Spohn
client
Tenet Health Care

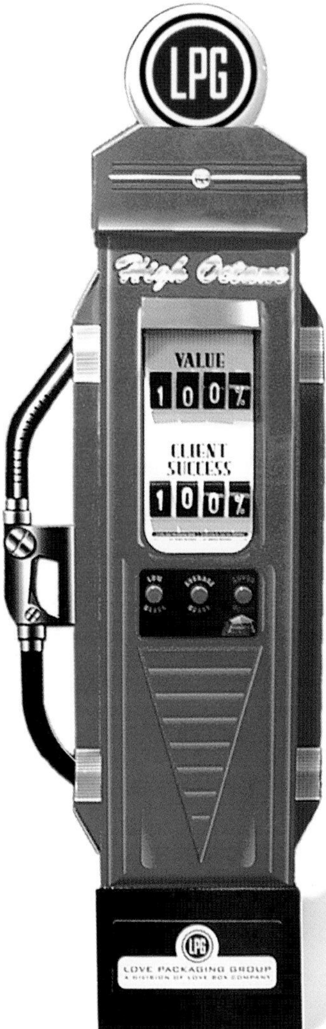

design firm
Love Packaging Group
Wichita, Kansas
designers
Chris West, Rick Gimlin,
Lorna West, Dustin Commer
client
Love Packaging Design
(design firm)

LPG
PREMO
Packaging Design
LOVE PACKAGING GROUP
A DIVISION OF LOVE BOX COMPANY

PERFORMANCE TESTED GRAPHICS
LPG
PREMO
AUTO RAGS
Design Refiners
"Will maintain correct packaging at any temperature"

PERFORMANCE
TESTED
Graphics
LPG
Enjoy
FREE PARKING
HIGH PERFORMANCE
POWER ADDITIVE
Hank
PHONE
AREA CODE (316)
832-3229
DAY OR NIGHT!
Visit LPG. You'll be glad you did!

LPG
LOVE PACKAGING GROUP
A DIVISION OF LOVE BOX COMPANY

ACTIVE MOTIF

design firm
Laura Coe Design Assoc
San Diego, California
creative director
Laura Coe Wright
designers
Ryoichi Yotsumoto, Luke Stotler, Tom Richman
client
Active Motif
(gene analysis and DNA research)

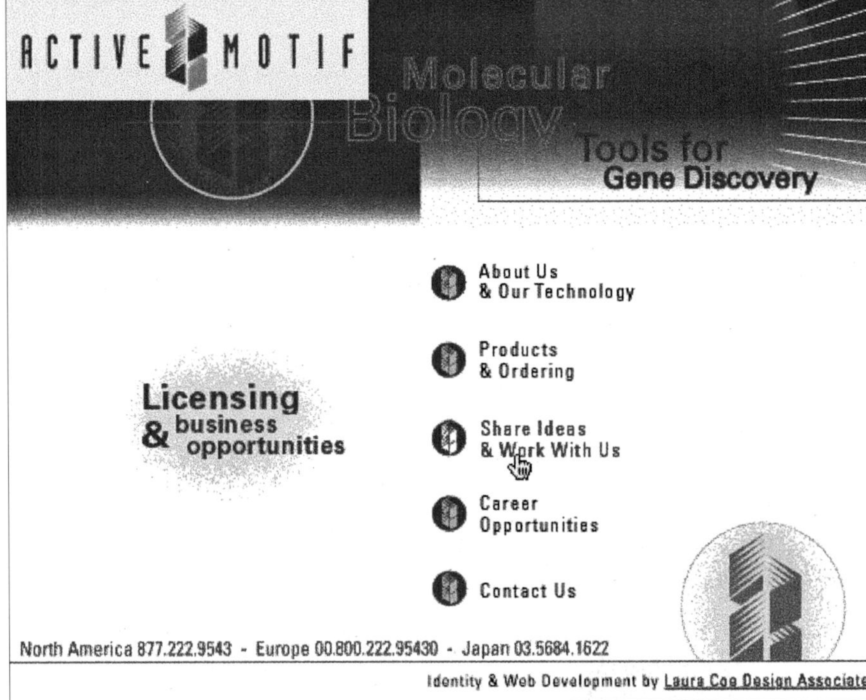

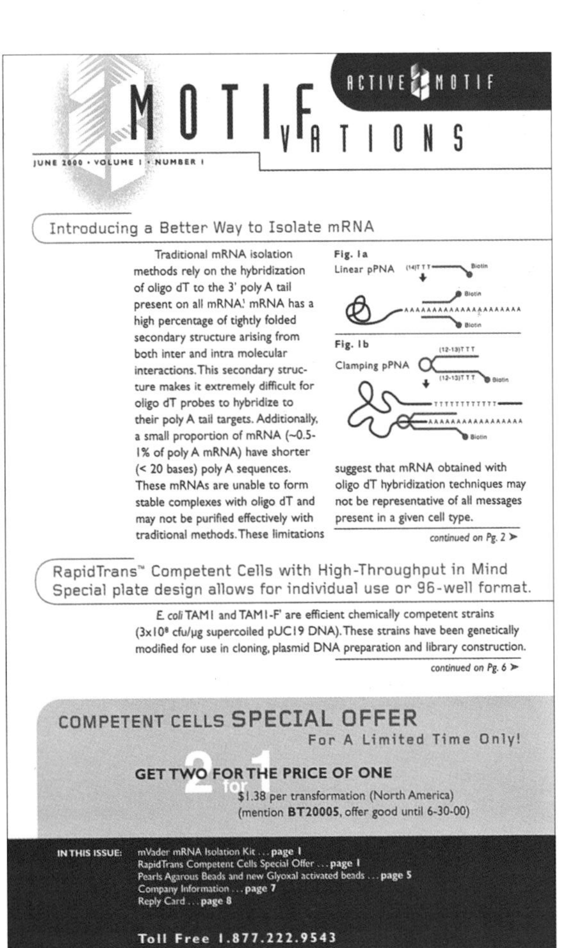

ACTIVE MOTIF

MOTIVATIONS

JUNE 2000 • VOLUME 1 • NUMBER 1

Introducing a Better Way to Isolate mRNA

Traditional mRNA isolation methods rely on the hybridization of oligo dT to the 3' poly A tail present on all mRNA! mRNA has a high percentage of tightly folded secondary structure arising from both inter and intra molecular interactions. This secondary structure makes it extremely difficult for oligo dT probes to hybridize to their poly A tail targets. Additionally, a small proportion of mRNA (~0.5-1% of poly A mRNA) have shorter (< 20 bases) poly A sequences. These mRNAs are unable to form stable complexes with oligo dT and may not be purified effectively with traditional methods. These limitations suggest that mRNA obtained with oligo dT hybridization techniques may not be representative of all messages present in a given cell type.

Fig. 1a
Linear pPNA

Fig. 1b
Clamping pPNA

continued on Pg. 2 ➤

RapidTrans™ Competent Cells with High-Throughput in Mind
Special plate design allows for individual use or 96-well format.

E. coli TAM1 and TAM1-F' are efficient chemically competent strains ($3x10^8$ cfu/µg supercoiled pUC19 DNA). These strains have been genetically modified for use in cloning, plasmid DNA preparation and library construction.

continued on Pg. 6 ➤

COMPETENT CELLS SPECIAL OFFER
For A Limited Time Only!

2 for 1
GET TWO FOR THE PRICE OF ONE
$1.38 per transformation (North America)
(mention **BT20005**, offer good until 6-30-00)

IN THIS ISSUE:

mVader mRNA Isolation Kit . . . page 1
RapidTrans Competent Cells Special Offer . . . page 1
Pearls Agarous Beads and new Glyoxal activated beads . . . page 5
Company Information . . . page 7
Reply Card . . . page 8

Toll Free 1.877.222.9543

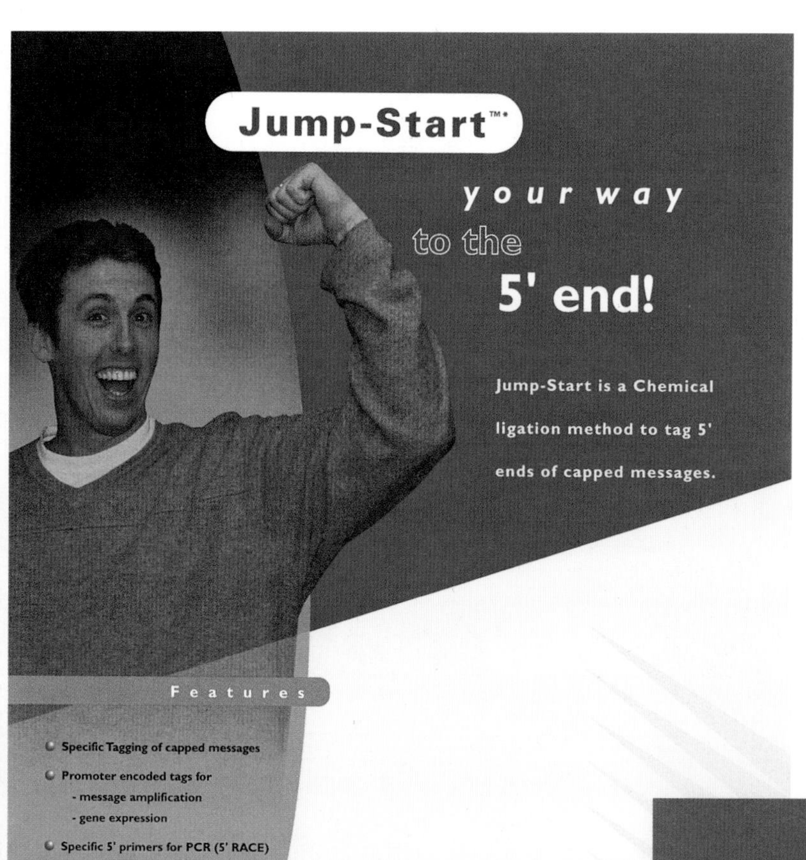
Jump-Start™*
your way
to the
5' end!
Jump-Start is a Chemical
ligation method to tag 5'
ends of capped messages.
Features
Specific Tagging of capped messages
Promoter encoded tags for
- message amplification
- gene expression
Specific 5' primers for PCR (5' RACE)
A rapid two step reaction
ACTIVE MOTIF Molecular Biolog
Tools for

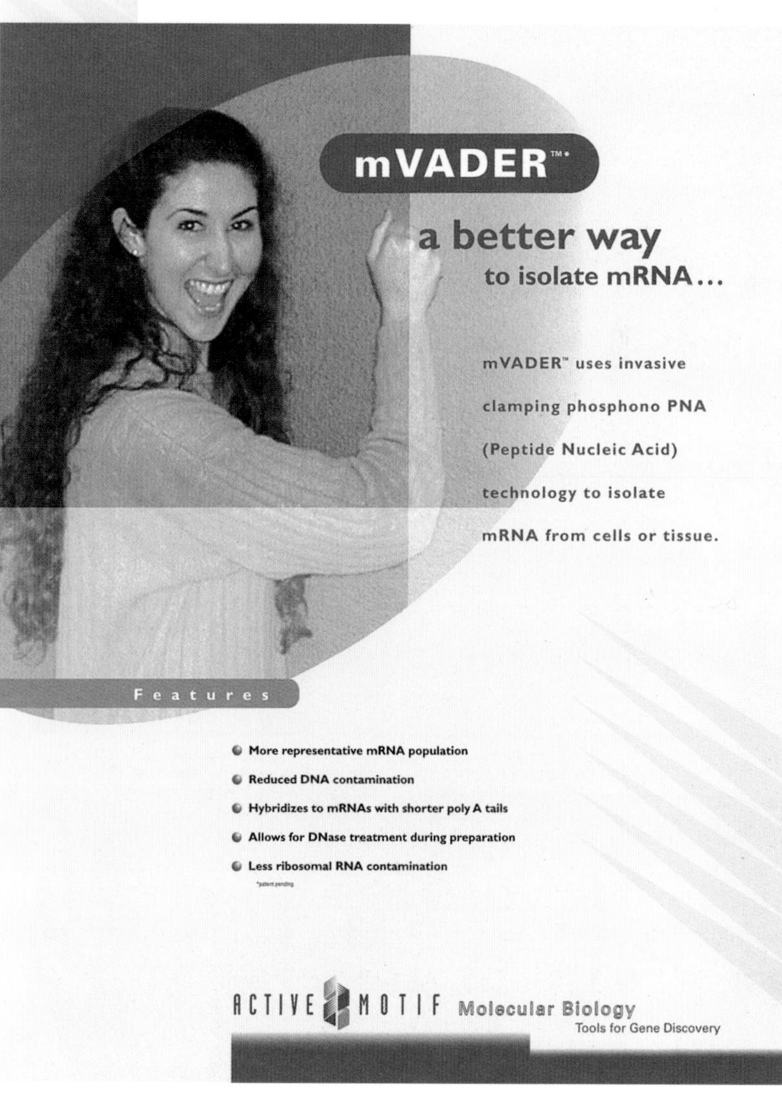
mVADER™*
a better way
to isolate mRNA...
mVADER™ uses invasive
clamping phosphono PNA
(Peptide Nucleic Acid)
technology to isolate
mRNA from cells or tissue.
Features
More representative mRNA population
Reduced DNA contamination
Hybridizes to mRNAs with shorter poly A tails
Allows for DNase treatment during preparation
Less ribosomal RNA contamination
ACTIVE MOTIF Molecular Biology
Tools for Gene Discovery

SCRIPMASTER

OUR COMMITMENT is to provide the most comprehensive software and service in the industry. OUR DILIGENCE to be at the forefront of technology and provide superior customer support ASSURES YOU of our capability to be competitive and successful. –MISSION STATEMENT

toll free	800-444-8486	
PHO	316	262-2231
FAX		262-5115

www.scripmaster.com

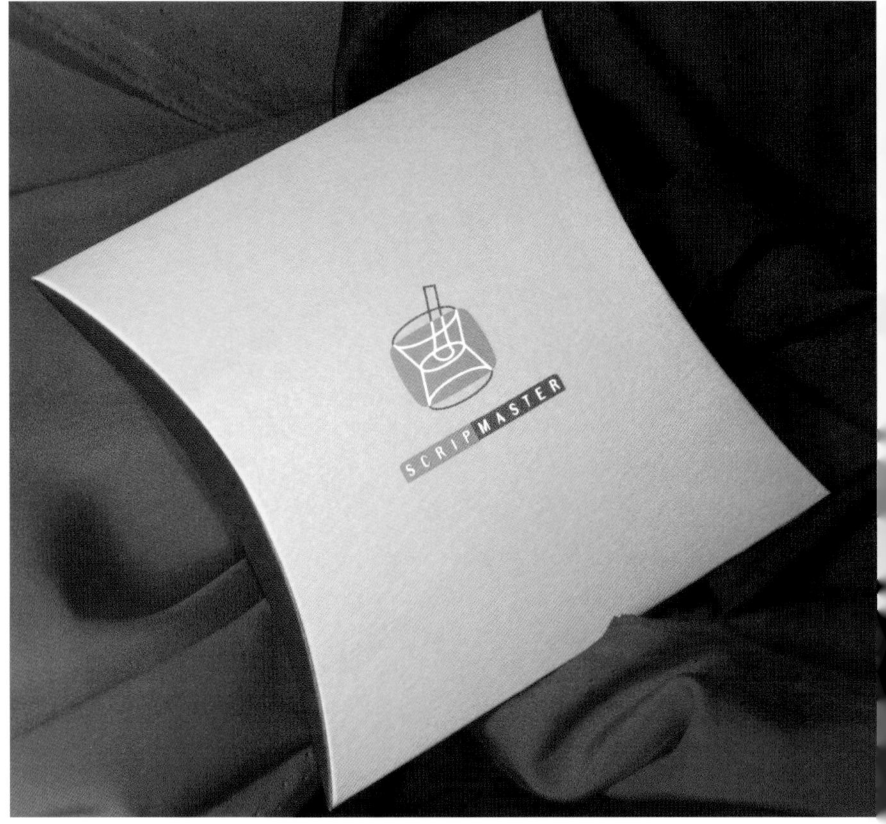

design firm
Gardner Design
Wichita, Kansas
art director
Brian Miller
designers
Brian Miller, Chaney Kimball, Travis Brown
client
Scripmaster
(pharmacy management systems)

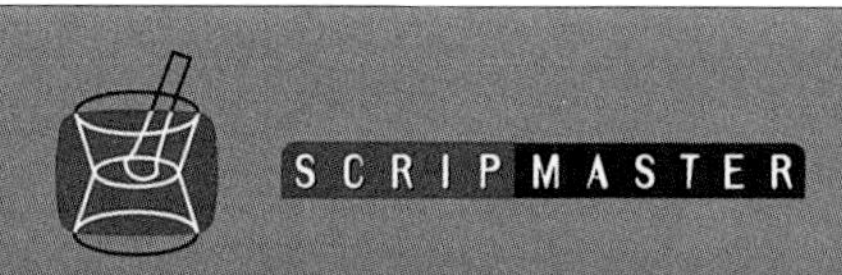

toll free 800-444-8486		
PHO	316	262-2231
FAX		262-5115

245 N. Waco, STE. 100
Wichita, Kansas 67202

PHARMACY
MANAGEMENT
SYSTEMS

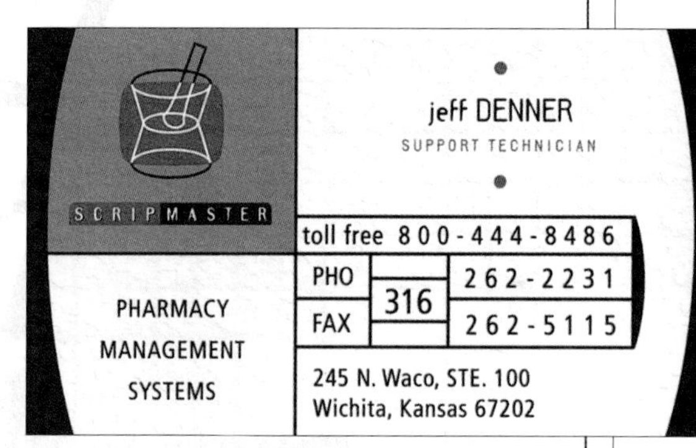

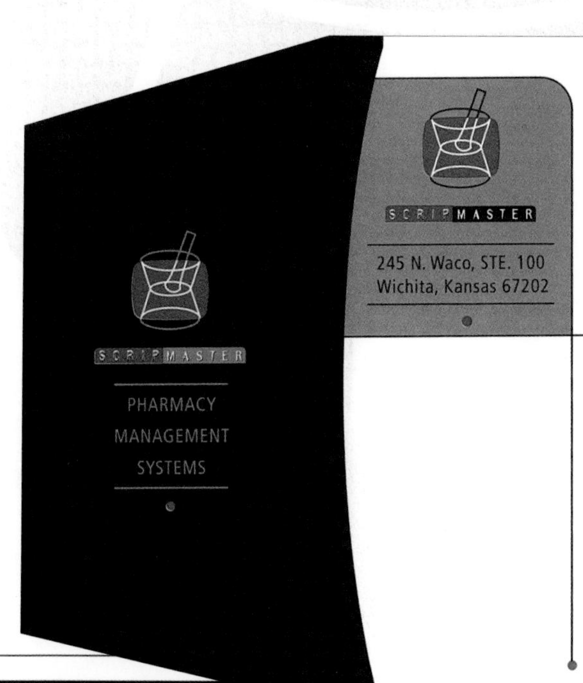

design firm
Sayles Graphic Design
Des Moines, Iowa
designers
John Sayles
client
Schaffer's Bridal Shop
(bridal store)

Schaffer's
Schaffer's
Schaffer's

Schaffer's
Schaffer's
Schaffer's
Schaffer's
Schaffer's

Schaffer's
Schaffer's

design firm
BBK Studio
Grand Rapids, Michigan
designer
Yang Kim
client
BBK Studio
(design firm)

bbkstudio/5242 Plainfield NE/Grand Rapids MI 49525-1047/

bbkstudio/tel 616 447-1460/fax 616 447-1461/www.bbkstudio.com/5242 Plainfield NE/Grand Rapids MI 49525-1047/

bbkstudio/with compliments/

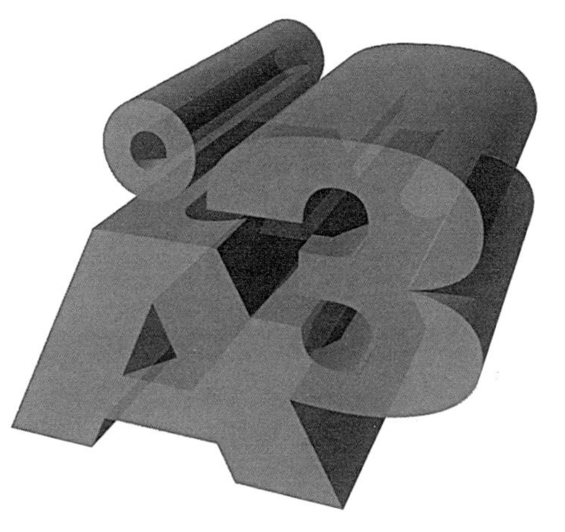

vertical reality

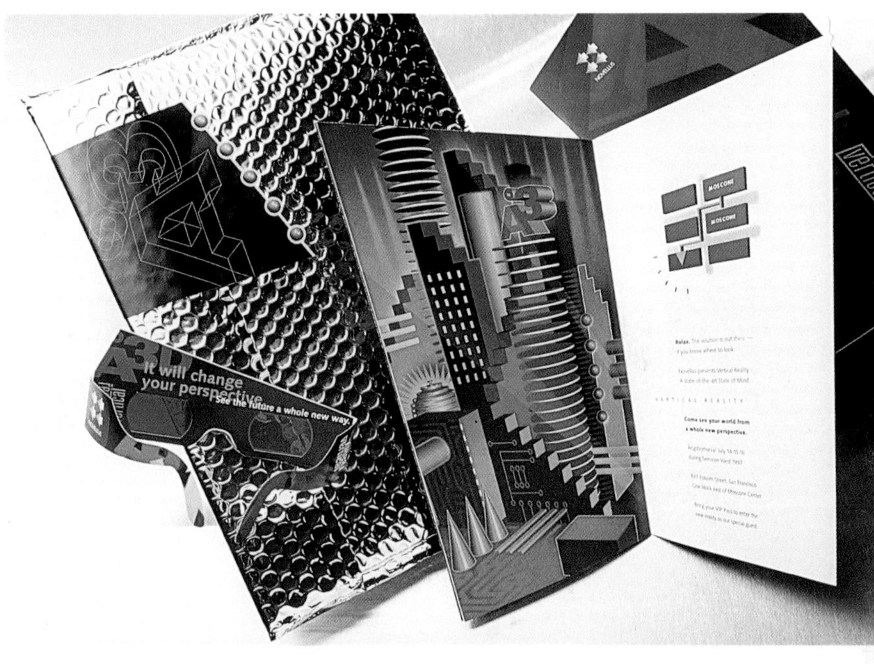

design firm
Larsen Design + Interactive
Minneapolis, Minnesota
creative director
Donna Root

project coordinator
Julie Fortman
designers
David Shultz, John Ferris, Wendy Ruyle, Chad Amon

client
Novellus Systems

design firm
Hans Flink Design Inc.
New York, New York
designer
Chang-Mei Lin
client
Pfizer Inc. (Bengay SPA)

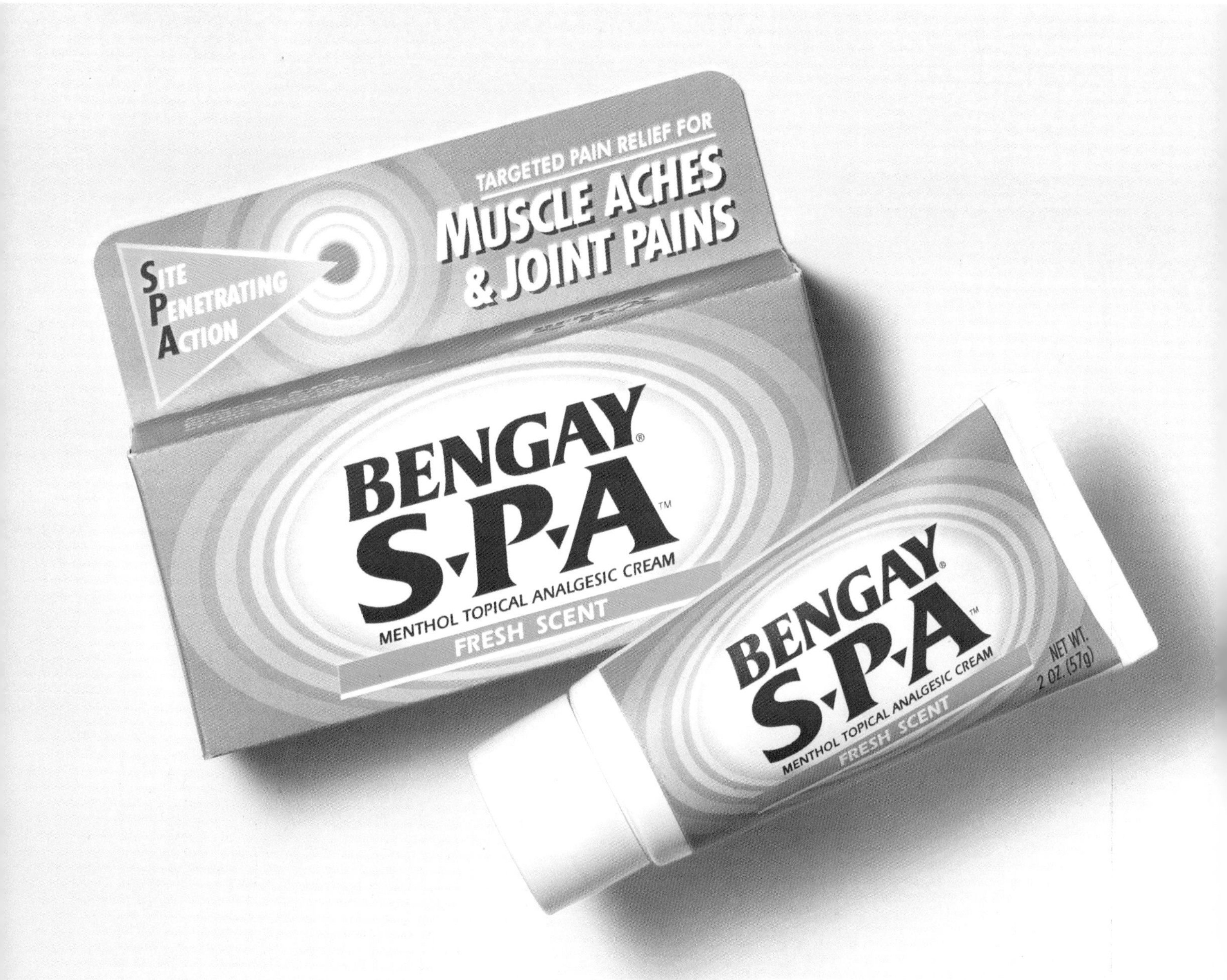

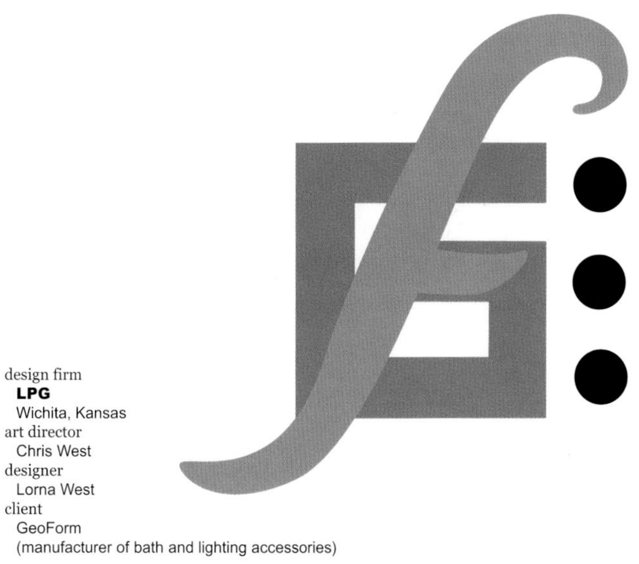

design firm
LPG
Wichita, Kansas
art director
Chris West
designer
Lorna West
client
GeoForm
(manufacturer of bath and lighting accessories)

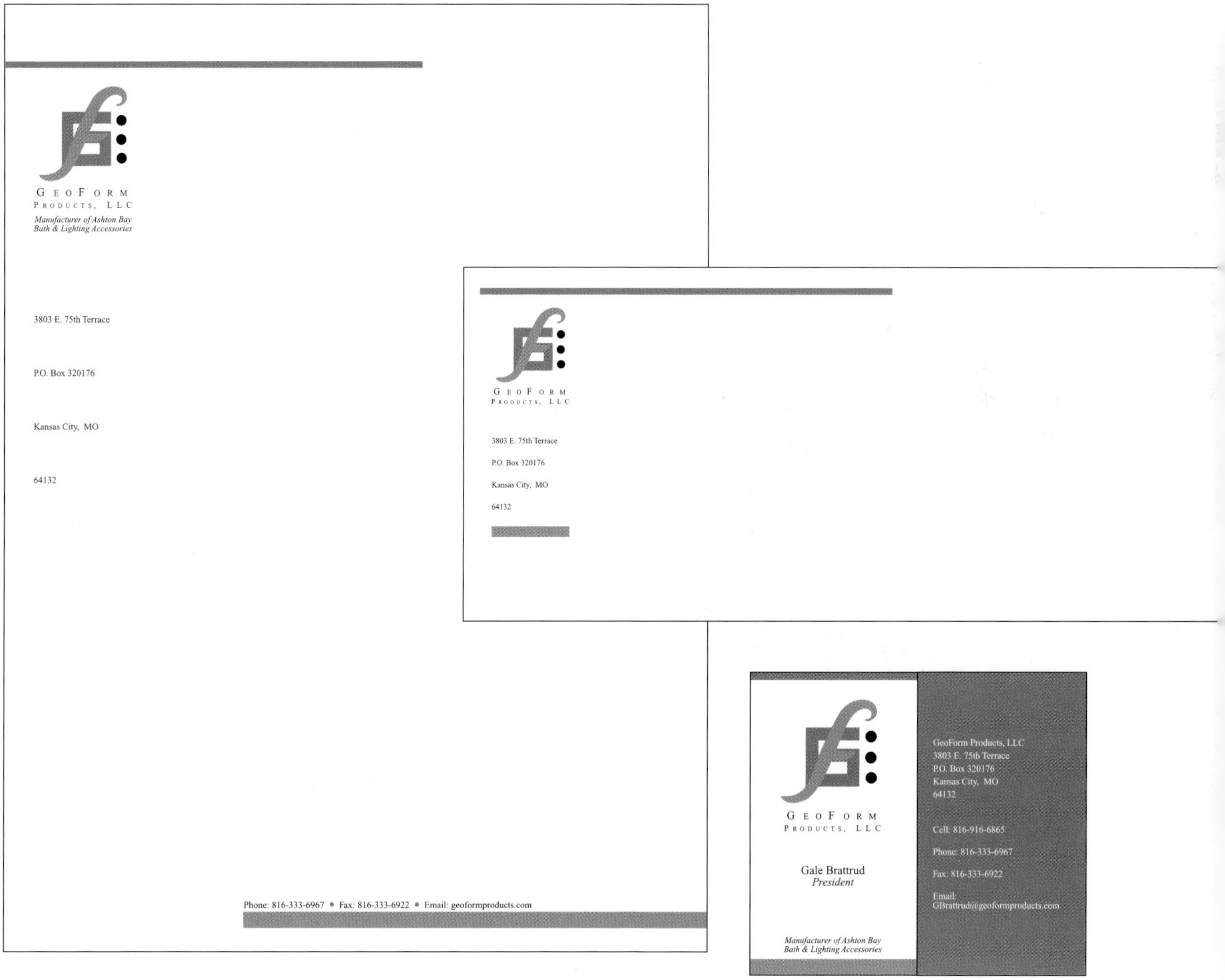

GeoForm
Products, LLC
Manufacturer of Ashton Bay
Bath & Lighting Accessories

3803 E. 75th Terrace

P.O. Box 320176

Kansas City, MO

64132

Phone: 816-333-6967 • Fax: 816-333-6922 • Email: geoformproducts.com

GeoForm
Products, LLC

3803 E. 75th Terrace
P.O. Box 320176
Kansas City, MO
64132

GeoForm
Products, LLC

Gale Brattrud
President

Manufacturer of Ashton Bay
Bath & Lighting Accessories

GeoForm Products, LLC
3803 E. 75th Terrace
P.O. Box 320176
Kansas City, MO
64132

Cell: 816-916-6865

Phone: 816-333-6967

Fax: 816-333-6922

Email:
GBrattrud@geoformproducts.com

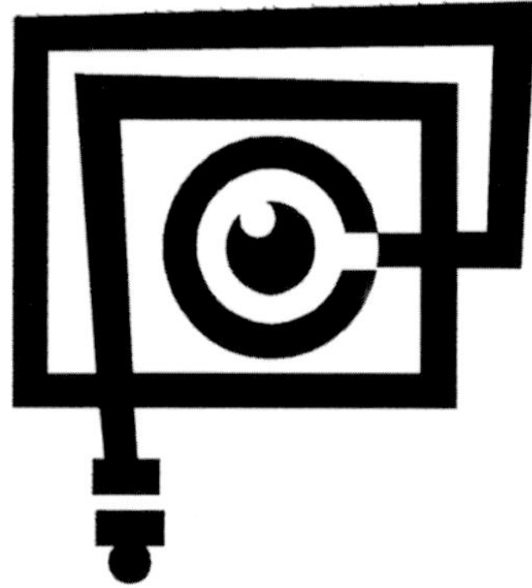

design firm
Gardner Design
Wichita, Kansas
art directors
Bill Gardner, Brian Miller
designers
Bill Gardner, Brian Miller, Travis Brown
client
Paul Chauncey Photography (photographer)

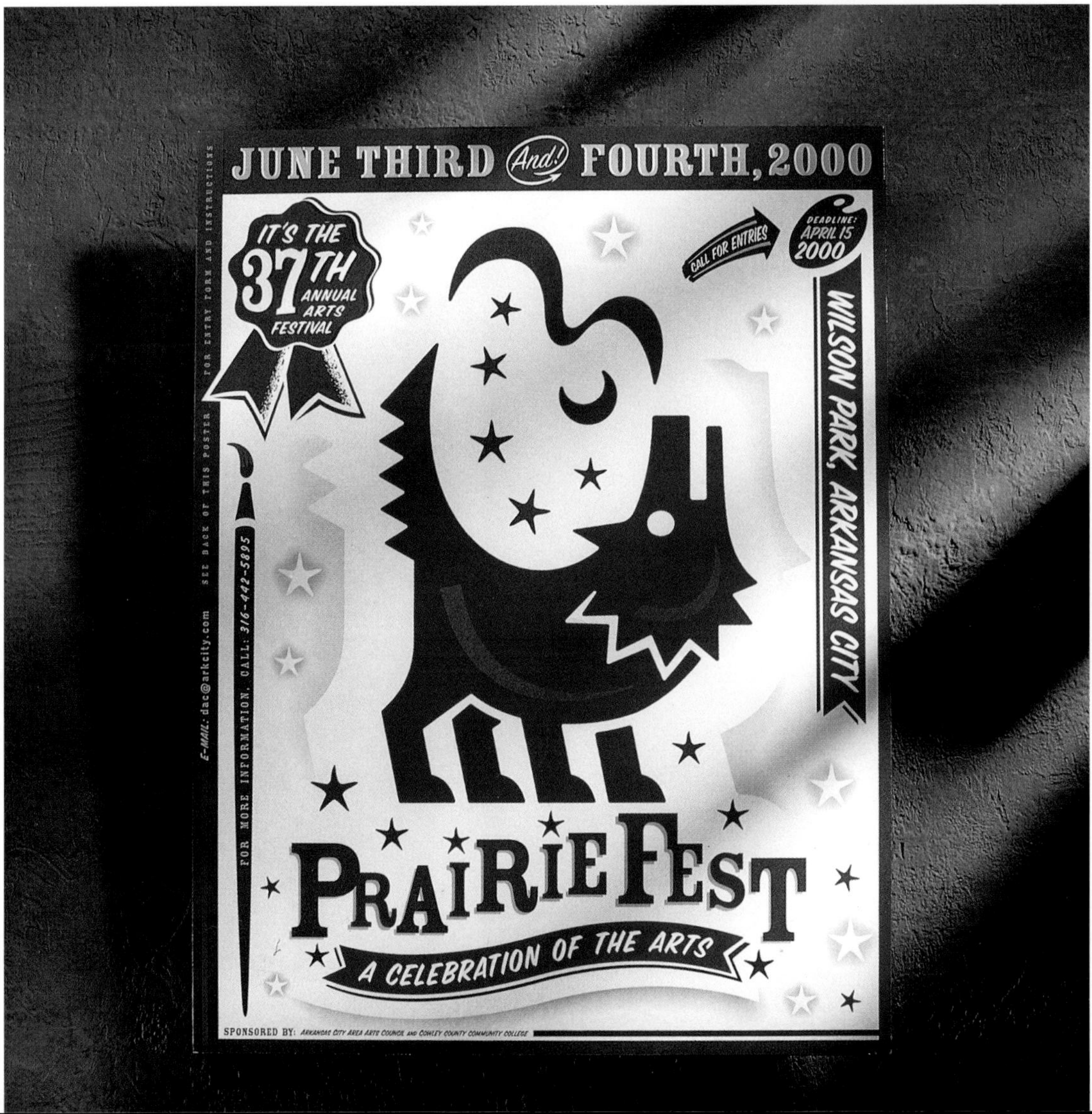

design firm
Gardner Design
Wichita, Kansas
designer
Brian Miller
client
Cowley County Community College
(school festival for community)

Taylor Made®

FIND YOUR GAME™

design firm
Laura Coe Design Assoc
San Diego, California
creative director
Laura Coe Wright
designers
Neville Brody, Leanne Leveillee, Ryoichi Yotsumoto, Jenny Goddard, Tom Richman, Denise Heisey, Lauren Bruhn

photographer
Carl Vanderschuit
client
Taylor Made Golf Co.
(golf equipment and accessories)

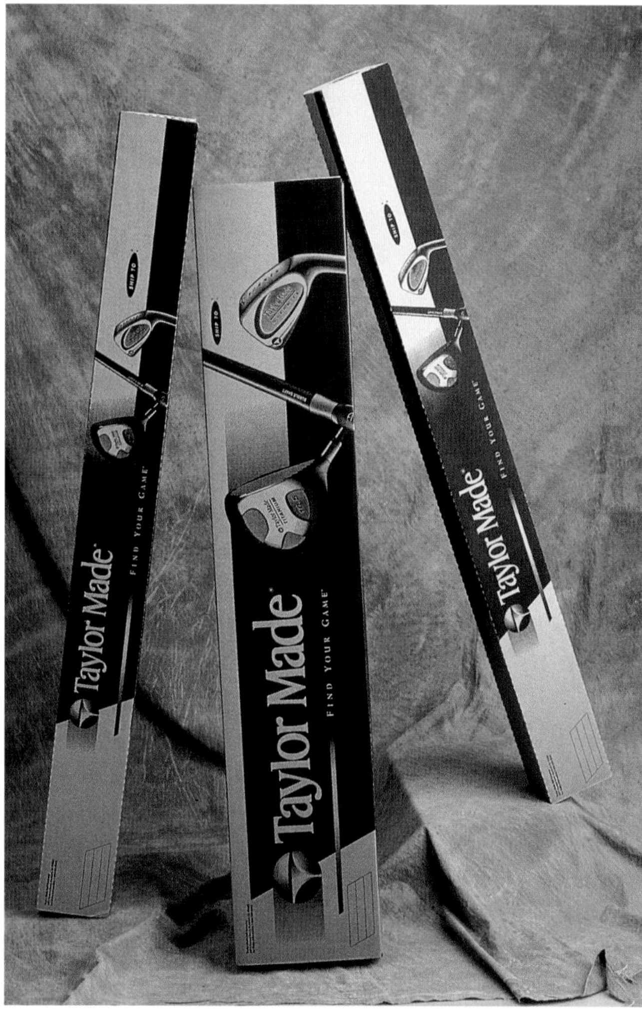

BURNER BUBBLE
BUBBLE SHAFT
BUBBLE SHAFT
US PAT 5,316,299
CAPTURE THE
POWER!
more accurate
longer drives

play it where it lies
Durango
Golf is an Adventure...
TAYLOR MADE

APPAREL & HEADWEAR
FALL 1999 COLLECTION
Taylor Made

GERMAIN
GERMAIN
GERMAIN

Taylor Made
1
1998 A VERY GOOD YEAR!
LEE JANZEN
MARK O'MEARA
FIND YOUR GAME

(continued)
design firm
Laura Coe Design Assoc
San Diego, California

Taylor Made
Taylor Made

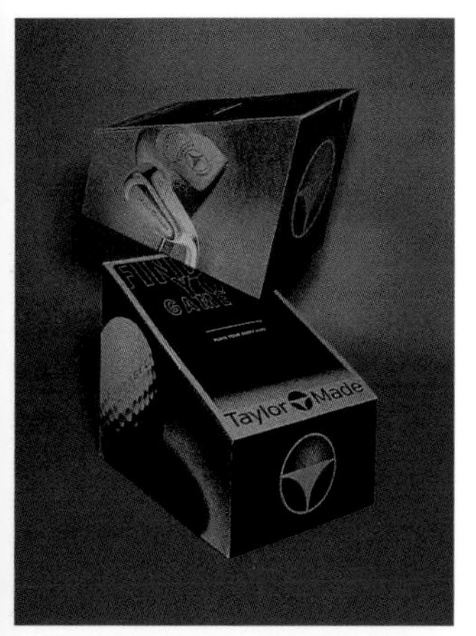
Taylor Made

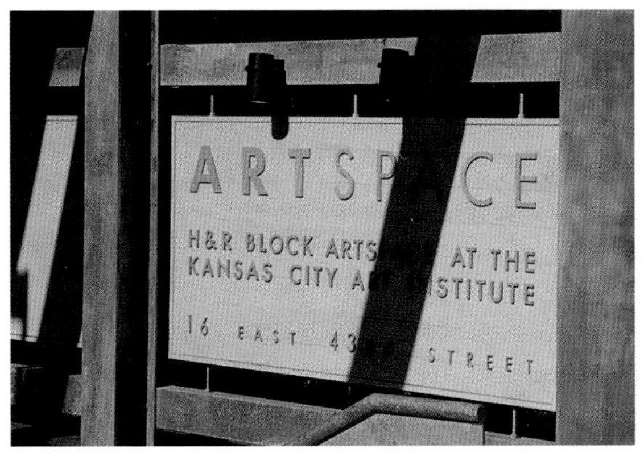

KANSAS CITY ART INSTITUTE IS PLEASED TO ANNOUNCE THE OPENING OF ITS H&R BLOCK ARTSPACE AND THE INAUGURAL EXHIBITION AND PROJECT WALL

H&R BLOCK ARTSPACE AT THE KANSAS CITY ART INSTITUTE

ARTSPACE

H&R BLOCK ARTSPACE AT THE KANSAS CITY ART INSTITUTE

ARTSPACE

H&R BLOCK ARTSPACE
AT THE KANSAS CITY ART INSTITUTE

EXHIBITION SCHEDULE FOR 1999–2000

NOVEMBER 13–AUGUST 2000
Project Wall
Vik Muniz

NOVEMBER 13–DECEMBER 18, 1999
The Viewing Room
Janine Antoni, Lucy Gunning,
Pipilotti Rist and Gillian Wearing

JANUARY 14–FEBRUARY 26, 2000
The 1999 Charlotte Street Fund
Nate Fors, Kee-Sook Lee, Wilbur Niewald,
Michael Rees, Michael Sinclair and Bridget Stewart

MARCH 3–APRIL 22, 2000
Flora and Fauna
Adrian Arleo, Neil Forrest, Ovidio C. Giberga, Marilyn Lysohir,
Keisuke Mizuno, Adelaide Paul and Chris Weaver

APRIL 28–MAY 13, 2000
2000 Annual BFA Exhibition

MAY 26–JULY 7, 2000
Measure for Measure
Guest Jurors: Ann Sutton and Ana Lisa Hedstrom
(in conjunction with the Surface Design Conference)

AUGUST 11–SEPTEMBER 8, 2000
Kansas City Art Institute Faculty Exhibition

H&R BLOCK ARTSPACE
at the Kansas City Art Institute
16 East 43rd Street
Kansas City, Missouri 64111
816.561.5563

Public hours are Tuesday through Saturday from Noon to 6:00 pm. Admission to the gallery is free and open to the public. The H&R Block Artspace is closed December 20th through January 14th, March 15,16,17 and July 10th–August 11th 2000.

PLEASE JOIN US FOR A GRAND OPENING CELEBRATION
SATURDAY NOVEMBER 13TH
7:00 TO 10:00PM
16 EAST 43RD STREET (ONE BLOCK EAST OF MAIN STREET)
Parking is available on 43rd and Walnut Streets
and the H&R Block Tax Office at 43rd and Main Street.
The Viewing Room
Antoni, Gunning, Rist and Wearing (through December 18th)
Project Wall
Vik Muniz (through August 2000)
INFORMATION: 816.802.3483

ARTSPACE

MEASURE FOR MEASURE AND
THE CONTEMPLATIVE STITCH

MAY 27-JULY 8, 2000

RECEPTION AND KC 150 ARTS CRAWL:
JUNE 2, 2000
6:00-9:00 PM

Gallery hours: Tuesday-Saturday, 12:00-6:00 p.m.

Measure for Measure and The Contemplative Stitch are presented by the 11th International Surface Design Conference.

H&R BLOCK ARTSPACE
AT THE KANSAS CITY ART INSTITUTE
16 East 43rd Street
Kansas City, MO 64111
816.561.5563

Non-Profit Org.
US Postage
PAID
Kansas City, MO
Permit No. 1071

design firm
EAT Advertising & Design
Kansas City, Missouri
designers
Patrice Eilts-Jobe, DeAnne Dodd, Jeremy Shellhorn
client
Kansas City Art Institute-Artspace (museum/college)

Atlanta 1996

design firm
Malcolm Grear Designers
Providence, Rhode Island
client
Atlanta Committee for the Olympic Games
(centennial olympic games)

Atlanta 1996
CENTENNIAL OLYMPIC GAMES
LES JEUX OLYMPIQUES DU CENTENAIRE

Atlanta 1996
Atlanta 1996
100

Atlanta 1996
Exit

Atlanta 1996

Atlanta 1996
100

(continued)
design firm
Malcolm Grear Designers
Providence, Rhode Island

Atlanta 1996

Atlanta1996
1996

design firm
Gardner Design
Wichita, Kansas
art director
Brian Miller
designers
Bill Gardner, Travis Brown, Brian Miller, Chris Parks
client
Aspen Traders
(women's clothing store)

Aspen Traders
4724 E. Douglas
Wichita, KS 67208
316-682-6784
ADDRESS SERVICE REQUESTED
ASPEN TRADERS
BULK RATE
U.S. Postage
PAID
Permit #1610
Wichita, KS
ASPEN TRADERS
Mother's Day Sale
Spring 2000
A. T.

4724 East Douglas at Oliver
Wichita, Kansas / 682-6784
M.-TH. 10 AM-7 PM
FRI.-SAT. 10 AM-6 PM
ASPEN TRADERS
Nourish Your Soul
Clothing,
Jewelry
and the Elements
of a
Comfortable
Life
Made from
Nature's Materials

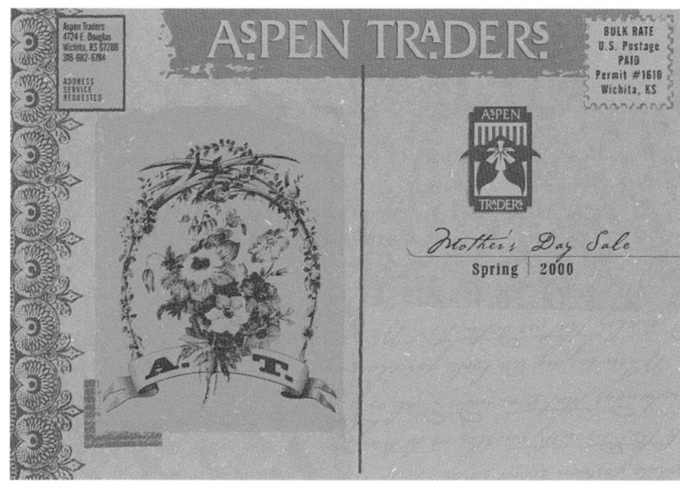
Aspen Traders
4724 E. Douglas
Wichita, KS 67208
316-682-6784
ADDRESS SERVICE REQUESTED
ASPEN TRADERS
BULK RATE
U.S. Postage
PAID
Permit #1610
Wichita, KS
ASPEN TRADERS
Mother's Day Sale
Spring 2000
A. T.

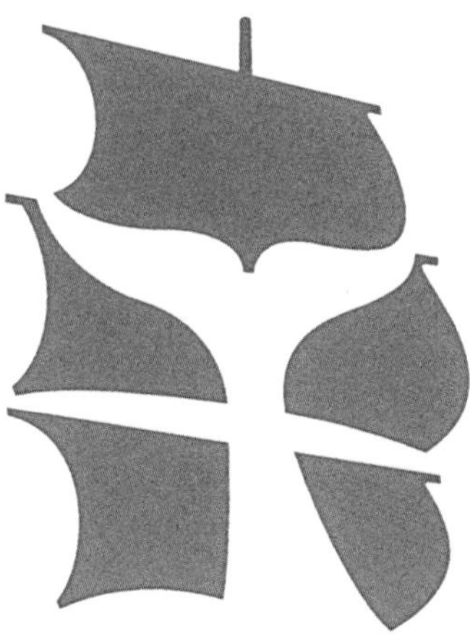

NEW BEDFORD
WHALING
MUSEUM

design firm
Malcolm Grear Designers
Providence, Rhode Island
client
New Bedford Whaling Museum
(whaling museum)

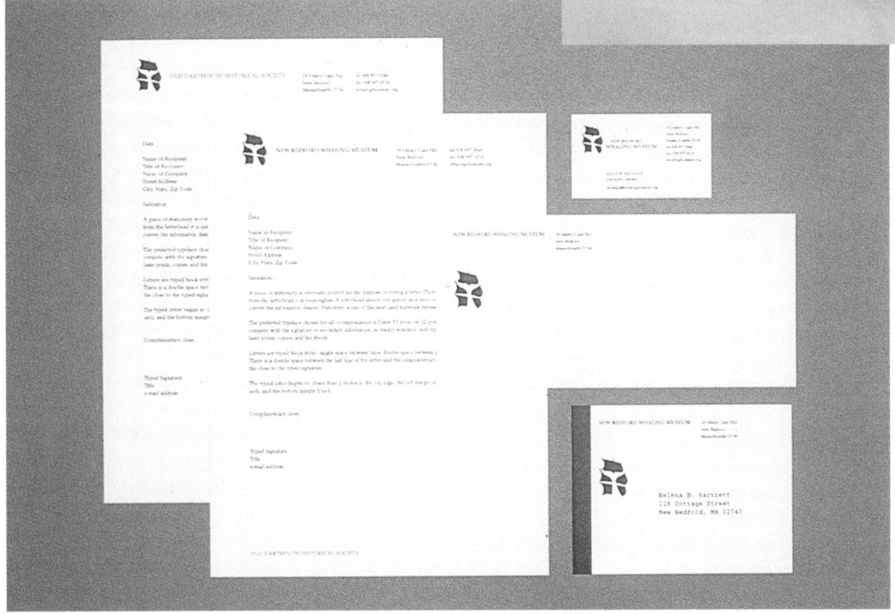

design firm
Hans Flink Design Inc.
New York, New York
designers
Chang-Mei Lin, Susan Kunschaft, Michael Troian
client
Unilever HPC USA (Pond's Clear Solutions)

design firm
Malcolm Grear Designers
Providence, Rhode Island
client
Museum of Art, Rhode Island School of Design
(museum)

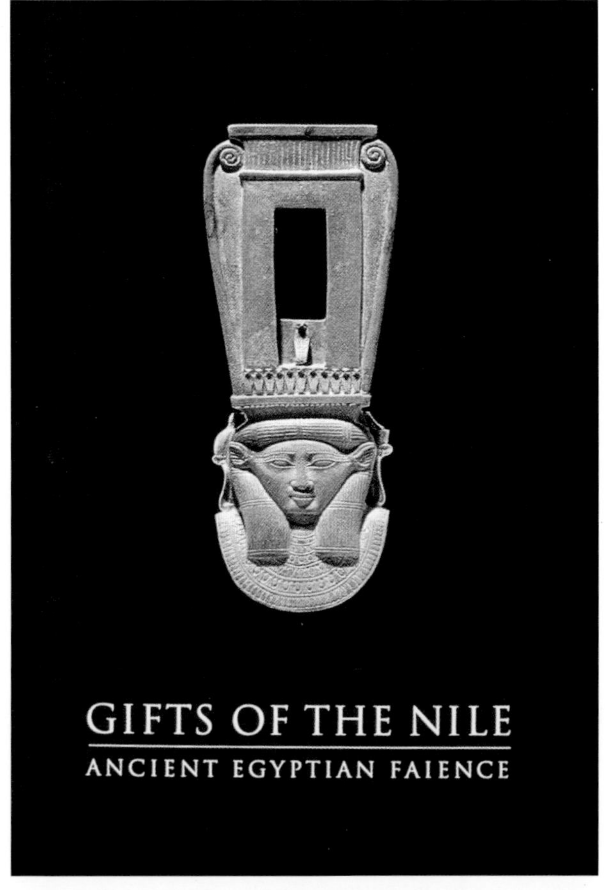
GIFTS OF THE NILE
ANCIENT EGYPTIAN FAIENCE

GIFTS
OF THE
NILE
ANCIENT
EGYPTIAN
FAIENCE

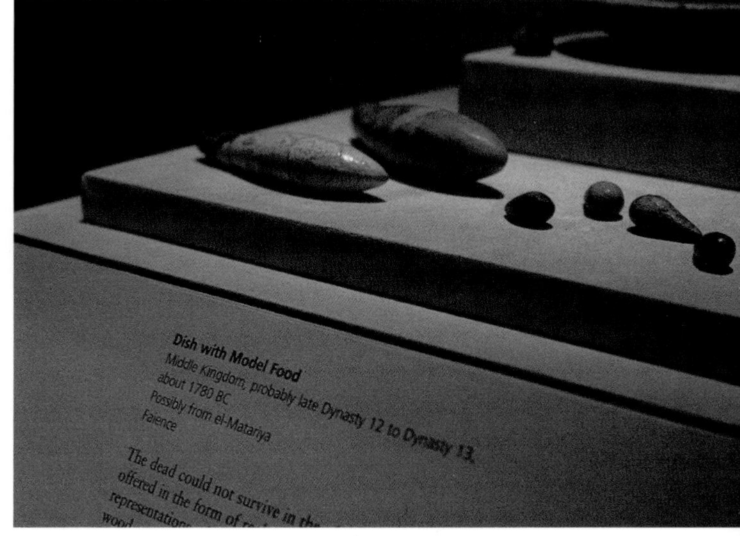
Dish with Model Food
Middle Kingdom, probably late Dynasty 12 to Dynasty 13,
about 1780 BC
Possibly from el-Matariya
Faience

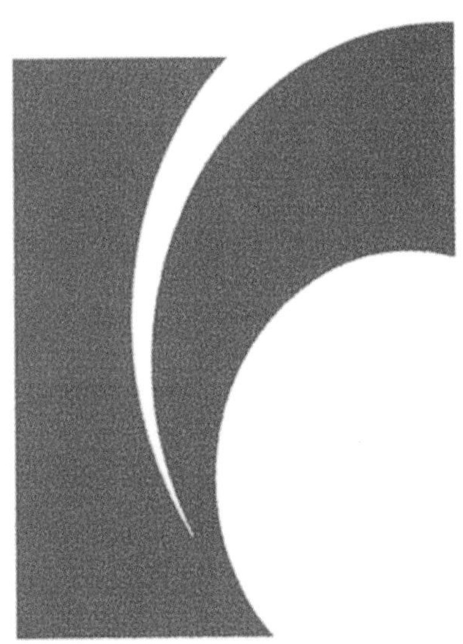

redley™

design firm
The Traver Company
Seattle, Washington
designer
Dale Hart
client
Redley
(Brazilian surf company)

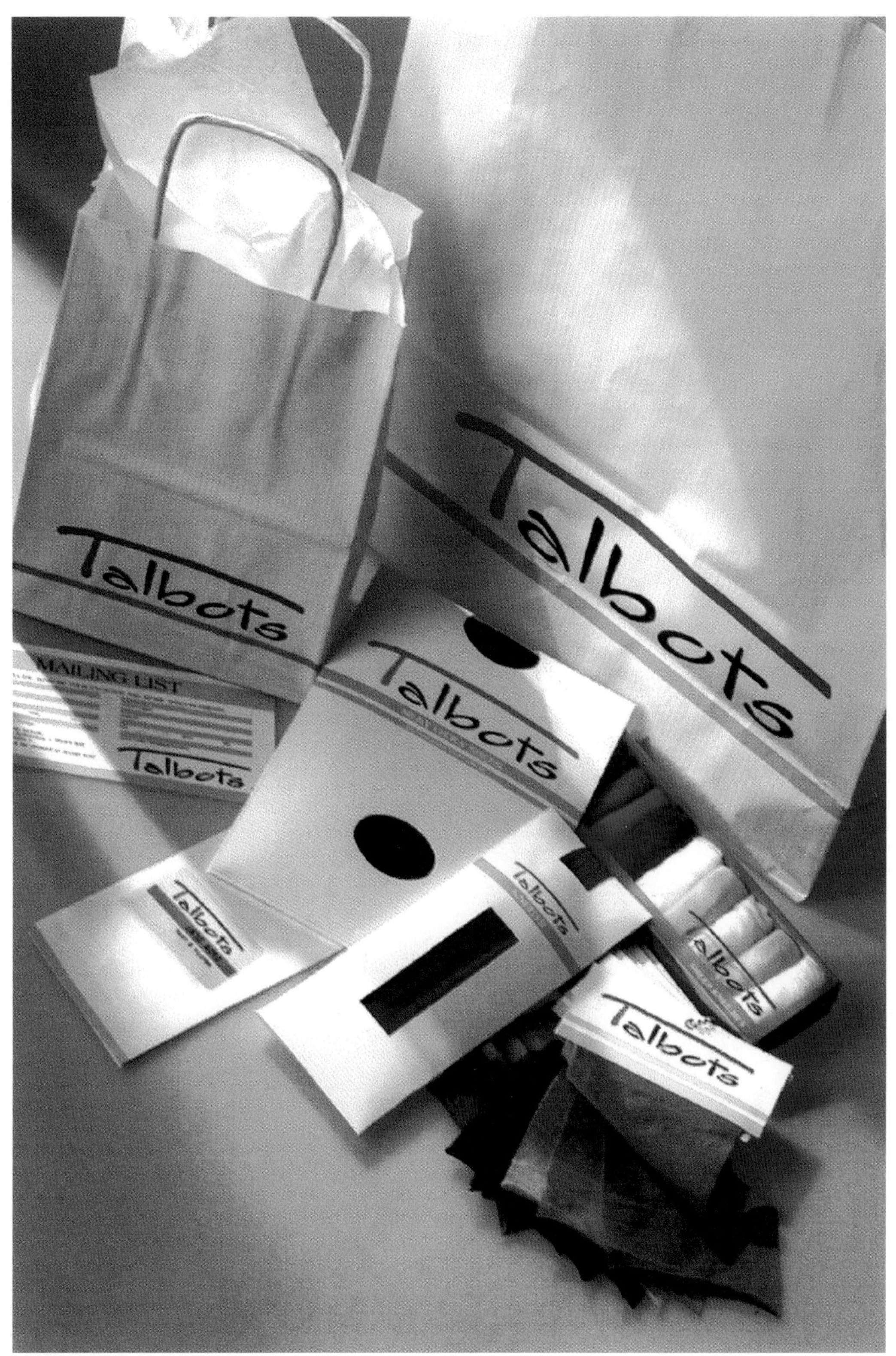

design firm
Studio Izbickas
Boston, Massachusetts
designers
Ed Izbickas, Tom Penn
client
Talbots
(women's clothing)

CHUGACH℠

HERITAGE CENTER

design firm
Walsh & Associates, Inc.
Seattle, Washington
designers
Miriam Lisco, Darrell Peterson
client
Chugach Heritage Center
(cultural tourism)

Kathy Cline
General Manager
Post Office Box 2388
501 Railway Avenue
Seward, Alaska 99664
Phone: (907) 224-5065
Fax: (907) 224-5075

Kathy Cline
General Manager
Post Office Box 2388
501 Railway Avenue
Seward, Alaska 99664
Phone: (907) 224-5065
Fax: (907) 224-5075

Kathy Cline
General Manager
Post Office Box 2388
501 Railway Avenue
Seward, Alaska 99664
Phone: (907) 224-5065
Fax: (907) 224-5075

CHUGACH™
HERITAGE CENTER

JOURNEY
BEYOND
THE
LEGENDS™

CHUGACH℠
HERITAGE CENTER

501 Railway Avenue, Seward, Alaska 99664 • 800.947.5065 • Fax 907.224.5075

design firm
Hans Flink Design Inc.
New York, New York
designers
Mark Krukonis, Susan Kunschaft, Chang-Mei Lin, Michael Troian
client
Unilever HPC USA (Lever 2000)

design firm
The Wyant Simboli Group, Inc.
Norwalk, Connecticut
art directors, designers
Deborah Davis, Julia Wyant
client
GE Capital Services,
Center for Learning and Organizational Excellence

Gillette
MACH3
Razor Pack
Packaging
6.1
The Design Concept
The Visual Identity
2.1

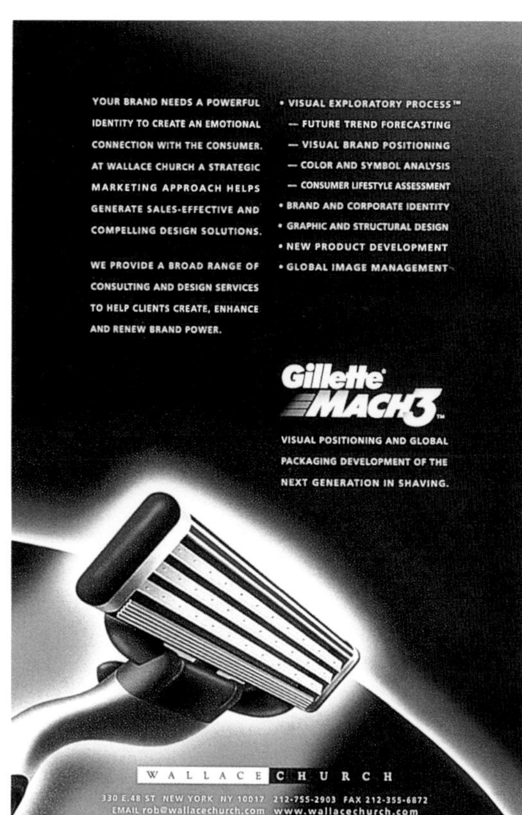

design firm
Wallace Church ass., inc.
New York, New York
designers
Stan Church, David Minkley
client
The Gillette Co.

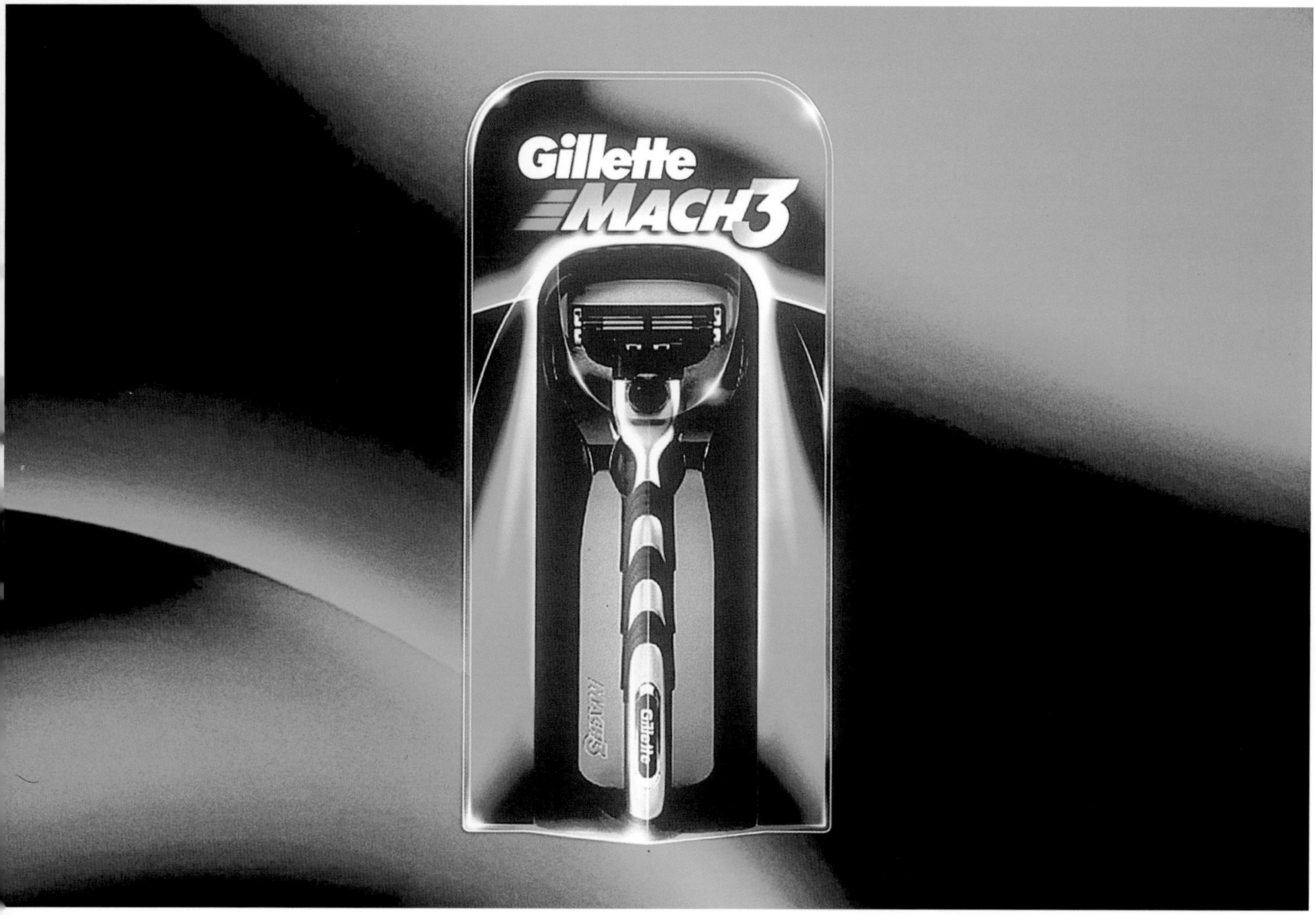

a natural day spa

design firm
LPG
Wichita, Kansas
designer
Lorna West
client
beau monde

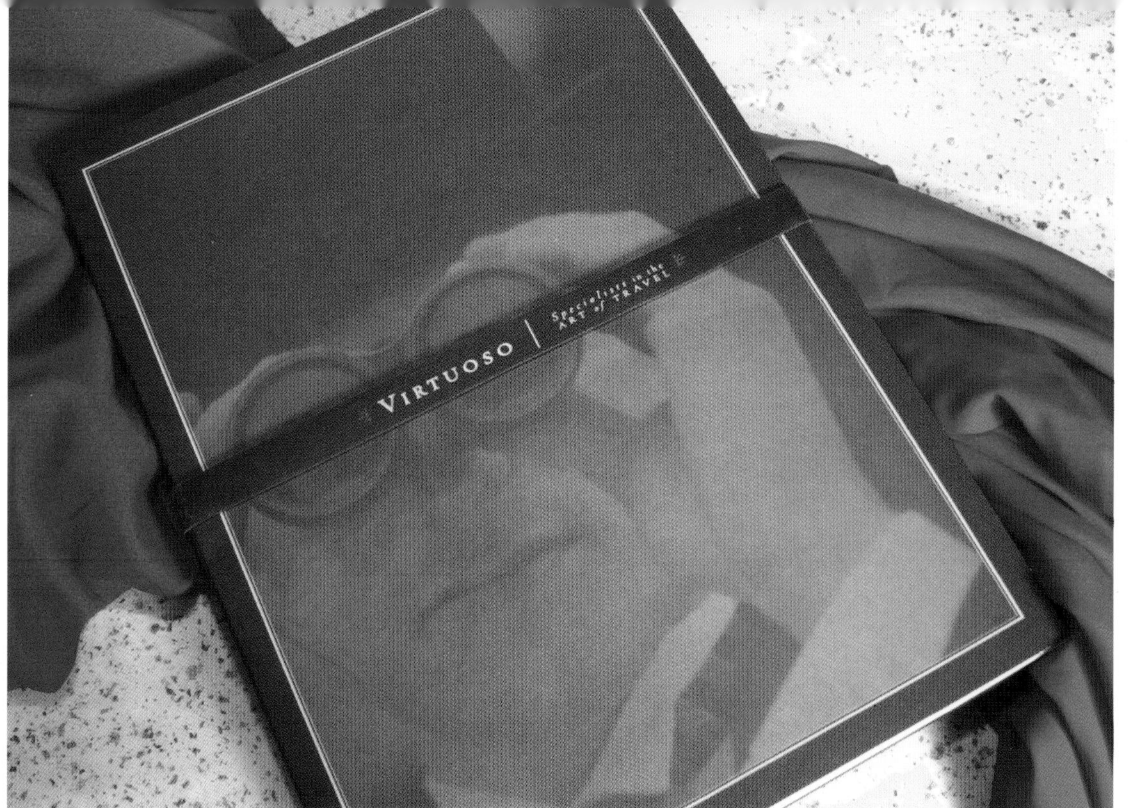

design firm
David Carter Design Assoc.
Dallas, Texas
designers
David Kampa, Ashley Barron,
Tabitha Bogard, Melissa Pattison
client
Virtuoso

VIRTUOSO
SPECIALISTS IN THE ART OF TRAVEL

500 Main Street, Suite 400 | Fort Worth, Texas 76102-3941
information@virtuoso.com www.virtuoso.com
817-870-0300 Telephone 817-870-1050 Facsimile

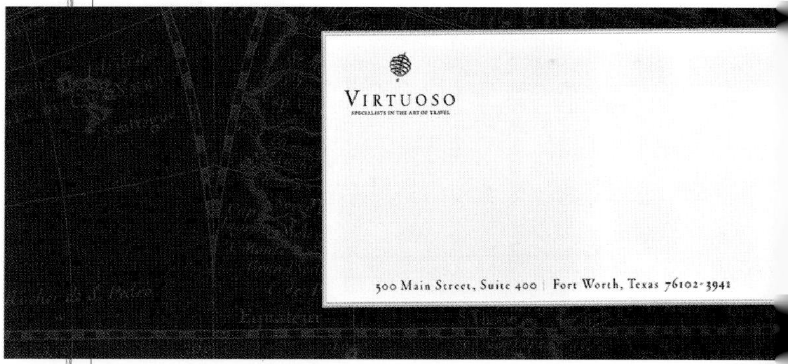

VIRTUOSO
SPECIALISTS IN THE ART OF TRAVEL

500 Main Street, Suite 400 | Fort Worth, Texas 76102-3941

Covington Square
InMotion Pictures
IN MOTION
BORED TO TEARS?
RENT A MOVIE
NEED A BABYSITTER?
RENT A MOVIE
GOLD
A PRESENTATION OF CREATIVE SAMPLES OF GOLD & ASSOCIATES, INC.

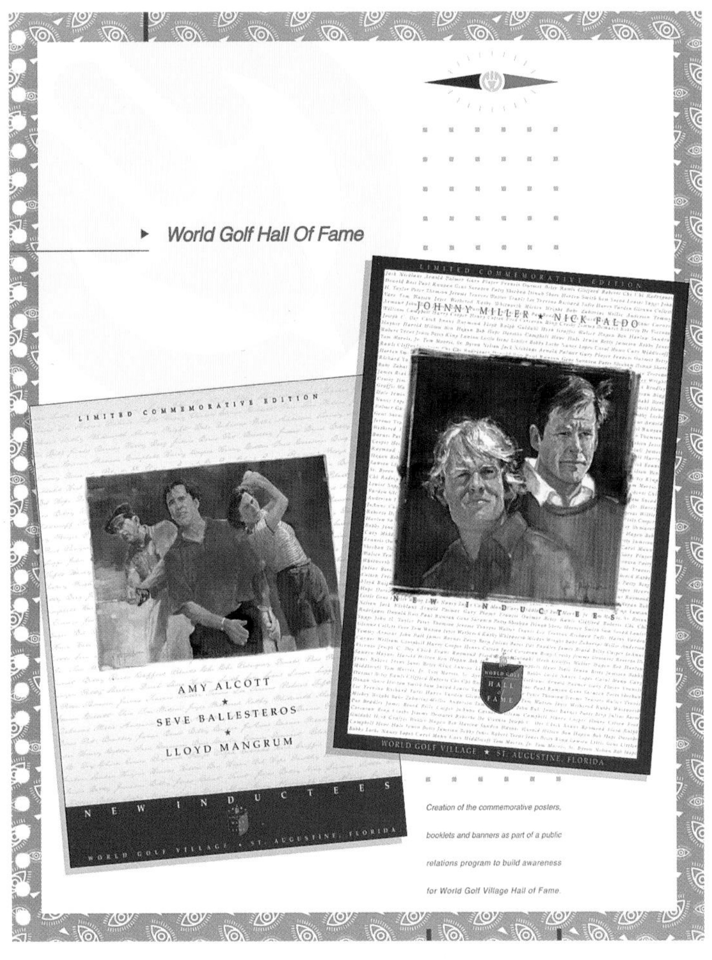
World Golf Hall Of Fame
LIMITED COMMEMORATIVE EDITION
JOHNNY MILLER ★ NICK FALDO
HALL OF FAME
WORLD GOLF VILLAGE ★ ST. AUGUSTINE, FLORIDA
LIMITED COMMEMORATIVE EDITION
AMY ALCOTT
SEVE BALLESTEROS
LLOYD MANGRUM
NEW INDUCTEES
WORLD GOLF VILLAGE ★ ST. AUGUSTINE, FLORIDA
Creation of the commemorative posters,
booklets and banners as part of a public
relations program to build awareness
for World Golf Village Hall of Fame.

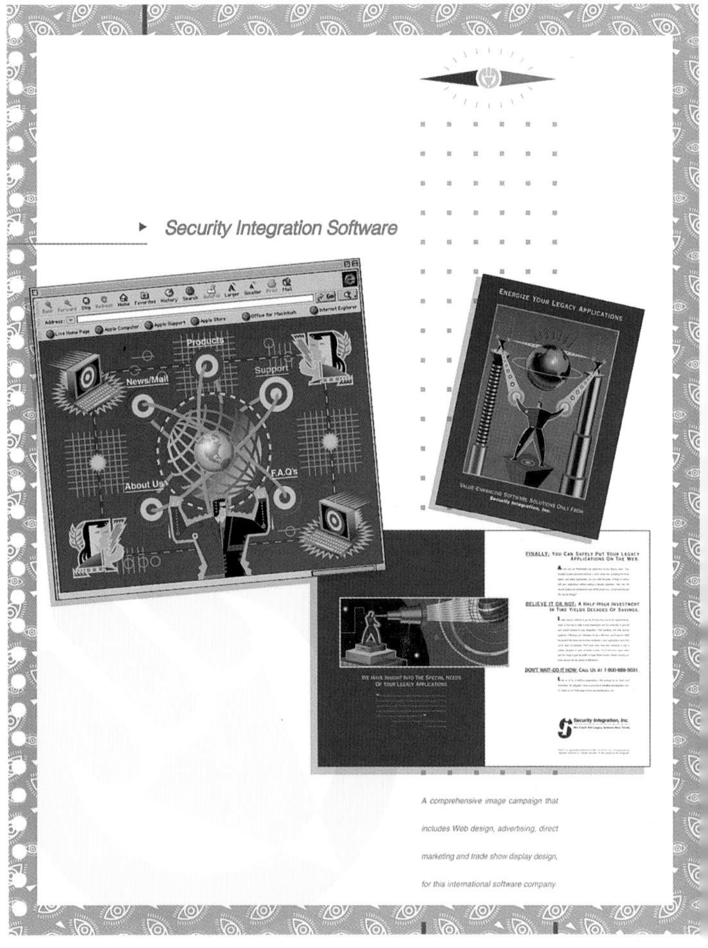
Security Integration Software
Products
Support
News/Mail
About Us
F.A.Q's
Energize Your Legacy Applications
Security Integration, Inc.
We Have Insight Into The Special Needs Of Your Legacy Applications
A comprehensive image campaign that
includes Web design, advertising, direct
marketing and trade show display design,
for this international software company.

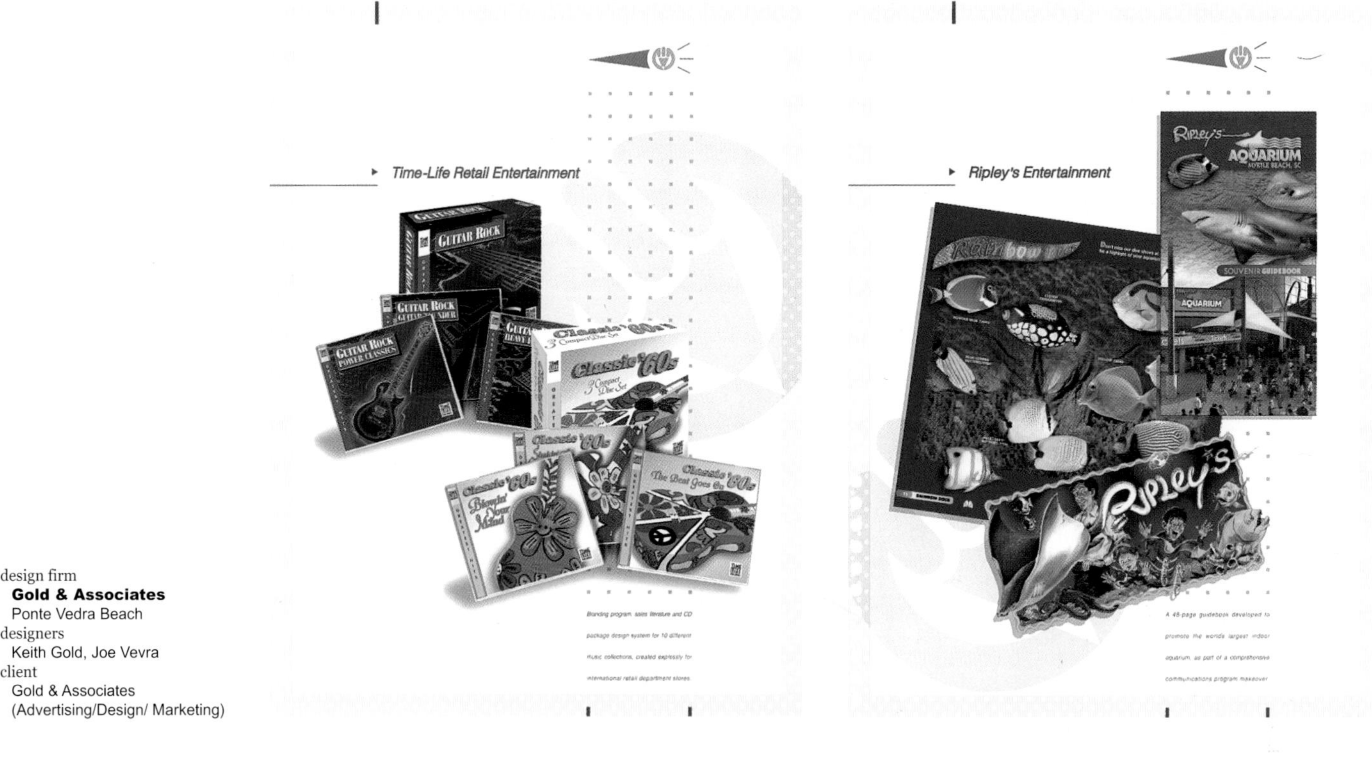

design firm
Gold & Associates
Ponte Vedra Beach
designers
Keith Gold, Joe Vevra
client
Gold & Associates
(Advertising/Design/ Marketing)

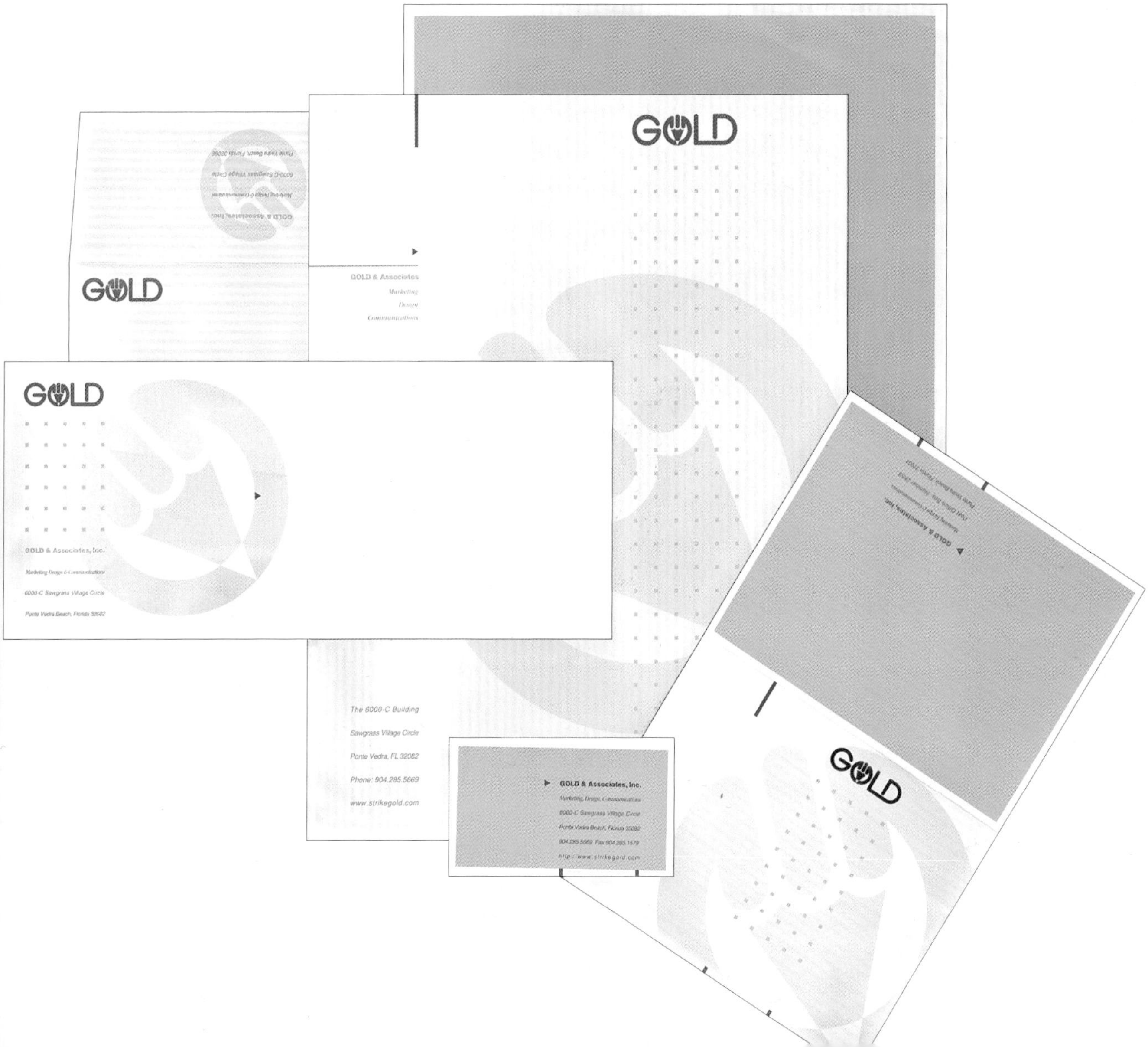

GOLD

The 6000-C Building
Sawgrass Village Circle
Ponte Vedra, FL 32082
Phone: 904.285.5669
www.strikegold.com

GOLD & Associates, Inc.

design firm
Paprika Communications
Montreal, Canada
art director
Louis Gagnon
designer
Francis Turgeon
client
Développements Germain-des-Prés

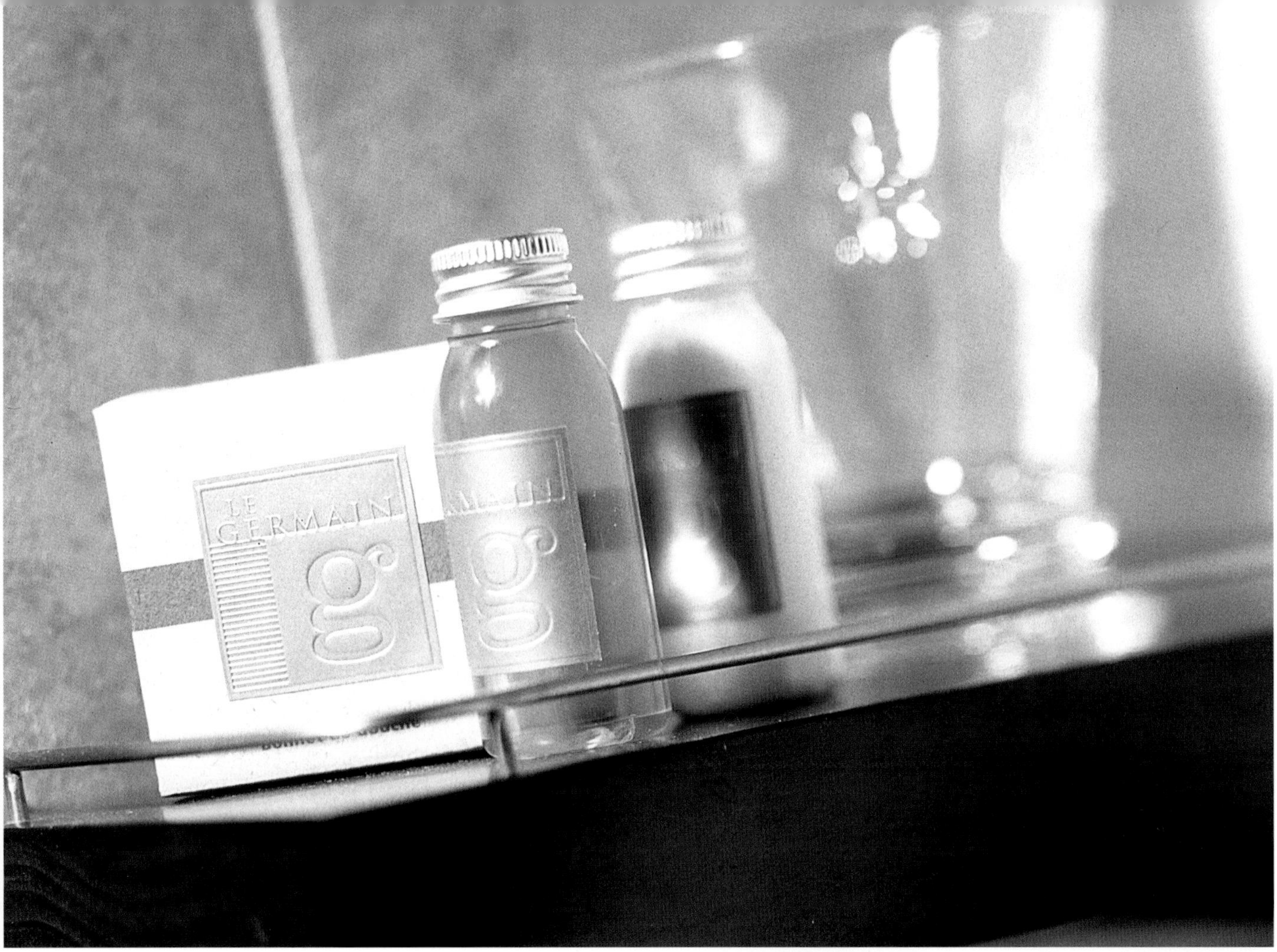

FOR YOUR COMFORT

g
LE GERMAIN

Henry Ford Museum Store

Henry Ford Museum Store

Henry Ford Museum Store

24"

94"

IMAX®

A Spine Tingling Experience

MUSEUM

Automobile In American Life

Experience Our Favorite Exhibit

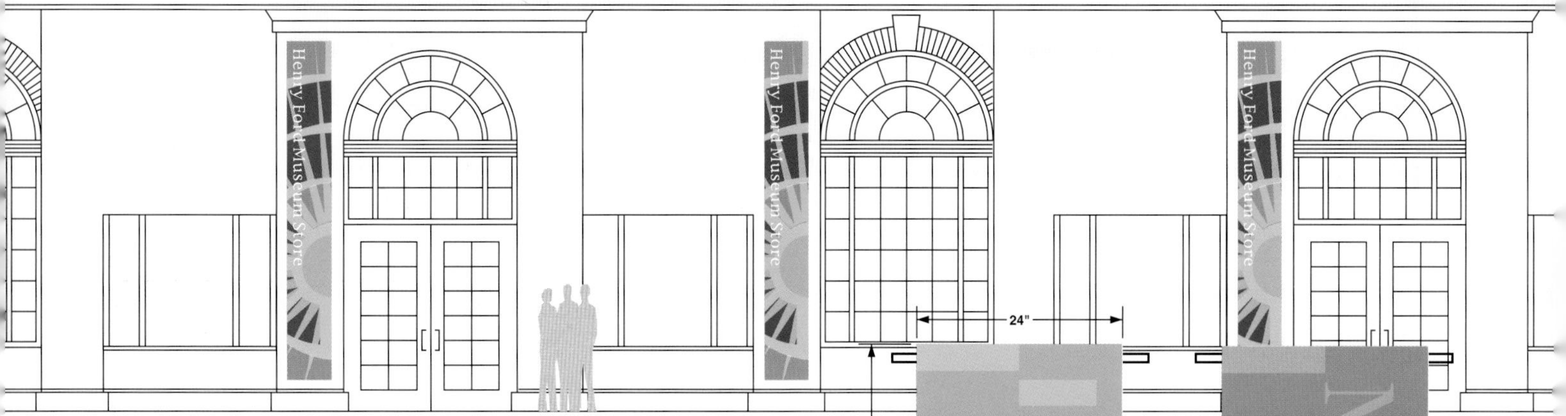

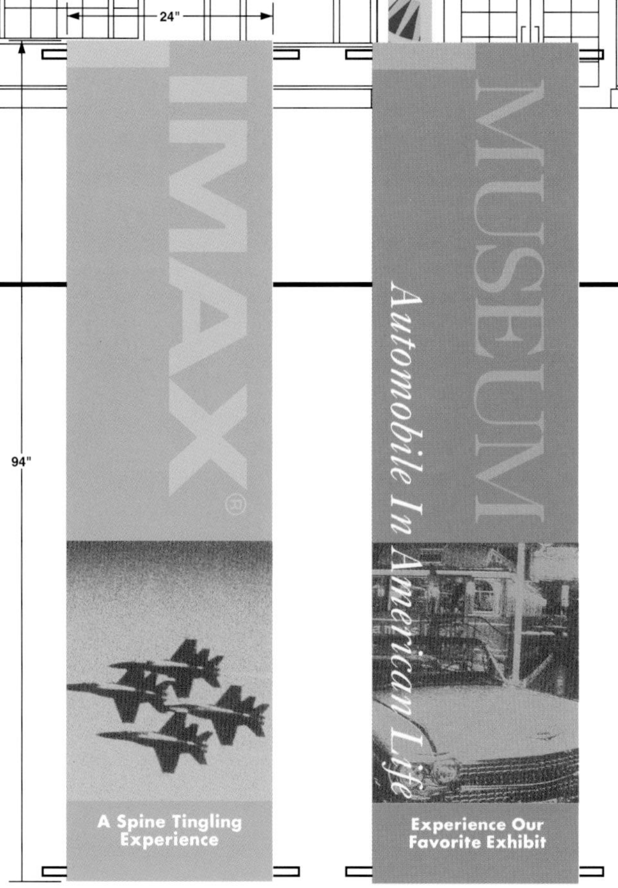

design firm
JGA, Inc.
Southfield, Michigan
senior vice president
Tony Camilletti
director of graphic design
Brian Eastman
client
Henry Ford Museum and Greenfield Village (attraction retail)

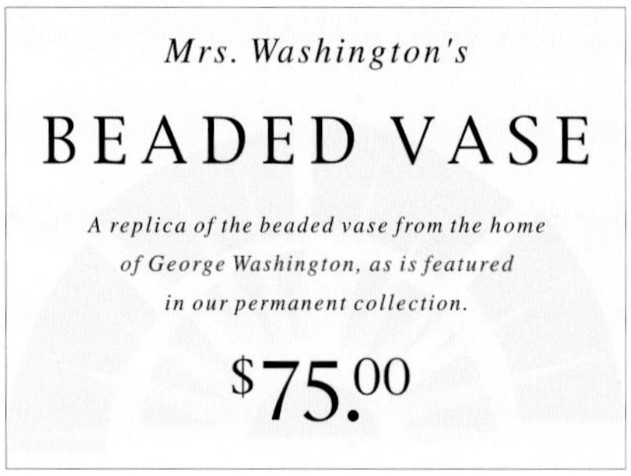

Mrs. Washington's

BEADED VASE

A replica of the beaded vase from the home of George Washington, as is featured in our permanent collection.

$75.00

96"
Experience HENRY FORD MUSEUM
48"
2'-0"
Henry Ford Museum Store
15'-0"
96"
Experience THE IMAX® THEATRE
48"
22"
IMAX® Theatre
Exit To Parking Lot
Museum Entrance
ATM
Phone
Restrooms
Concessions
Museum Store
Clocktower Entrance
Group Entrance
Greenfield Village
Michigan Cafe
28"

TABACALERA
1636 1636
DE ESPAÑA

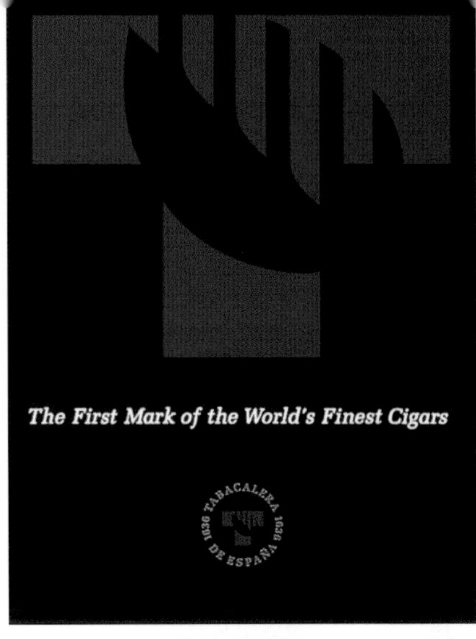

design firm
Malcolm Grear Designers
Providence, Rhode Island
client
Tabacalera de Espana
(cigar manufacturer)

1636 TABACALERA 1636
DE ESPAÑA

1636 TABACALERA 1636
DE ESPAÑA

QUINTERO
VEGAFINA
VEGAFINA

CLAIREMONT
Town Square

design firm
Graphic Solutions
San Diego, California
designers
Frank Mando, Dan Adams, Mike Wosika
client
Landgrant

design firm
Hans Flink Design Inc.
New York, New York
designers
Chang-Mei Lin, Susan Kunschaft
client
Whitehall-Robins (Centrum Performance)
(pharmaceutical)

design firm
Sayles Graphic Design
Des Moines, Iowa
designer
John Sayles
client
Gianna Rose
(cosmetic company)

PARFUM VOYAGE
DESTINATION

GYPSY
BALM
PARFUM VOYAGE
PARFUM VOYAGE
DESTINATION
Nº 3
GYPSY BALM
DESTINATION
Nº 3
lost in a dense
aromatic paradise
sweet and pungent
spices lie in bowls
their colors glowing
like an artist's palette
wander intoxicated with
the scent of dreams

GYPSY
BALM
PARFUM VOYAGE
PARFUM VOYAGE
DESTINATION
Nº 4
GYPSY BALM
Nº 4
secret gardens and
fragrant courtyards
the scented air

BALM
PARFUM VOYAGE
PARFUM VOYAGE
DESTINATION
Nº 5
GYPSY BALM

design firm
Mires Design
San Diego, California
art directors
Scott Mires, Neill Archer Roan, Laura Hull
designers
Miguel Perez, Deborah Hom
illustrators
Jody Hewgill, Wilson McLean, Mark Ulriksen
copywriters
Neill Archer Roan, Laura Hull
client
Arena Stage
(regional theater)

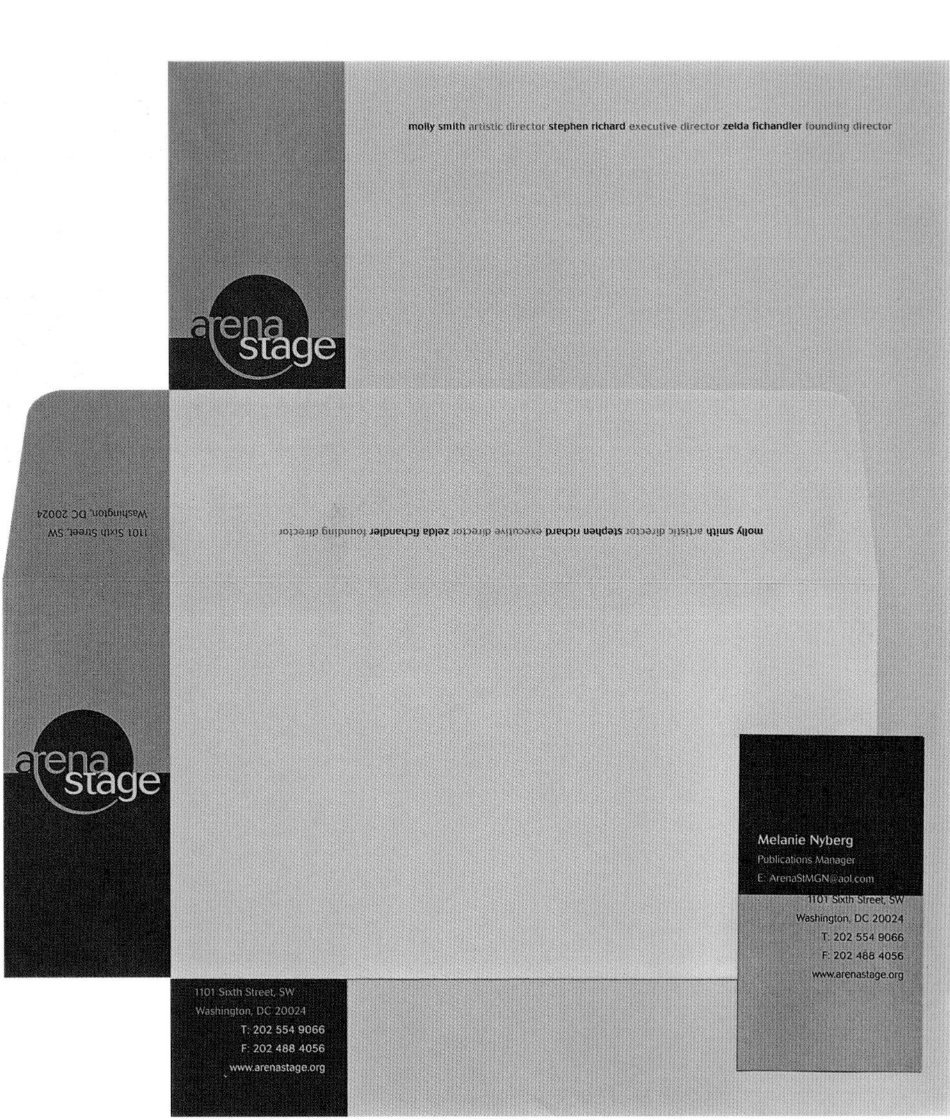

This gut-wrenching story of two heroic climbers, told against the backdrop of Ming Cho Lee's towering wall of snow and ice, created a sensation at Arena in 1982 for its great acting, forceful direction and incomparable design. Whether you remember the original or you're seeing it for the first time, I guarantee our celebratory revival of *K2* will keep you on the edge of your seat. —molly

K2

K2
by Patrick Meyers
directed by Wendy C. Goldberg
December 8, 2000 through
January 28, 2001
in the Kreeger

Sponsored by Helga and Paul Tarver, Farmington Asset Management, Ltd. and Strategic Investment Group

K2: the most dangerous mountain in the world. It beckons to the daring, cloaking incredible menace in a magnificent façade. In this exhilarating drama, two audacious climbers—friends for life—risk everything to answer the peak's alluring call. As their lives hang in the balance on an unyielding wall of ice, one implores the other, "You entertain me. Tell me stories you've never told before, big entertaining lies about your life..." Out of the "stories and lies" come moving, joyful and triumphant truths about friendship, life and love—and the strength it takes to climb all the mountains in our lives.

xclusive
iamond
3-play
ubscriber
enefits

Aaking a commitment to
full season subscription
neans a lot to us. Diamond
-play subscribers receive
hese additional benefits:

IP Parking
pre-paid, pre-reserved)
n the Arena lot, steps
way from the Fichandler
nd Kreeger Lobbies.
48 for the year. Spaces
re limited, so subscribe
arly to take advantage
f this incredible offer!

p to 50% Discount
t Gallery Sales Booth
n sale items.

ree Backstage Tours
cheduled four times
luring the season.

estaurant and
Aerchant Discounts
Vith Diamond
ubscriber Card.

ne Free Ticket
nd one 50% discount
oupon per
ubscription.

isit our website at
ww.arenastage.org

Illustrations: *Jody Hewgill (For The Pleasure of Seeing Her Again, Tom Walker, Coyote Builds North America, A Streetcar Named Desire) and Gary Kelley (The Great White Hope, Play On!, K2, Constant Star)* **Photography:** *Joan Marcus and Stan Barouh* **Design:** *Mires Design Inc.*

perks

Don't be left out. Thousands of people were turned away from our sold-out productions during the 1999/2000 season—but not Arena Stage subscribers.

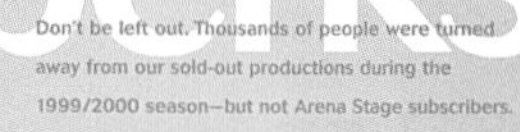

Ottawa, I was completely bowled over. I knew Michel Tremblay as one of Montreal's finest playwrights, but I was absolutely swept away by this warm and funny reverie. Tremblay's portrait of his mother evokes memories of doting mothers everywhere and shows us just how extraordinary an ordinary life can be. —molly

for the pleasure of seeing her again

For the Pleasure of Seeing Her Again
by Michel Tremblay
translated by Linda Gaboriau
directed by Gordon McCall
a production of Canadian Stage Company/
Centaur Theatre Company
September 15 through October 29, 2000
in the Kreeger

How do you pay tribute to your mother, especially if she is exasperating, given to reckless hyperbole, extravagant with her emotions but, most of all, utterly wonderful? This exquisitely funny and poignant U.S. premiere does just that: it's a portrait of one remarkable mother—story-teller, homemaker, everywoman—that offers us an opportunity to revisit all the extraordinary women who have shaped our lives. Canadian critics hailed this play as "a warm and loving gift to anyone who cherishes rich characterization...and the kind of emotional intensity—laughter and tears—that has always been at the center of great-hearted drama."

car
ed
re

streetcar at
ment, she is
he squalor
s of Stella's
rately clings
d, faintly lit
er's tragic
t is haunting,
f the truly
, a master-
s at his best.

any times, I urge you
Janós Szász. On a
ector's work in a spell-
binding production of *Mother Courage*. Janós is one of those artists who works beautifully in both theater and film. He's received numerous international honors and was saluted in 1998 by *Daily Variety* as a "Director to Watch." I think we're in for a rare treat. —molly

Laura Coe Design Associates

design firm
Laura Coe Design Assoc
San Diego, California
creative director
Laura Coe Wright
designers
Laura Coe Wright, Lauren Bruhn, Ryoichi Yotsumoto, Luke Stotler, Leanne Leveillee, Tracy Castle, Jenny Goddard, Tom Richman, Carey Jones
client
Laura Coe Design Assoc

Laura Coe Design Associates
Laura Coe Wright
Principal
Laura Coe Design Associates
4918 N. Harbor Drive Suite 206A
San Diego, CA 92106
Fax: 619/223-0939
619/223-0909
Laura Coe Design Associates

PEACE ON EARTH
PEACE ON EARTH
PEACE ON EARTH
PEACE ON EARTH

the
Magic of
Giving

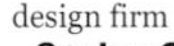

design firm
Sayles Graphic Design
Des Moines, Iowa
designer
John Sayles
client
Buena Vista College
(private college)

BUENA VISTA COLLEGE
BUENA VISTA COLLEGE
NEW VISTAS

BUENA VISTA COLLEGE
1891
1991
NEW VISTAS

BUENA VISTA COLLEGE
1891
1991
NEW VISTAS

BUENA VISTA COLLEGE

design firm
Hornall Anderson Design Works, Inc.
Seattle, Washington
designers
Lisa Cerveny, Michael Brugman, Mary Hermes, John Anicker, Robb Anderson, Rick Miller, Naomi Davidson, Don Kenoyer, Denise Bouvet, Merran Kubalak, Hallie Bowker, Roel Nava, Steve Apel, James Moriarity, Joseph Collas
client
Hardware.com

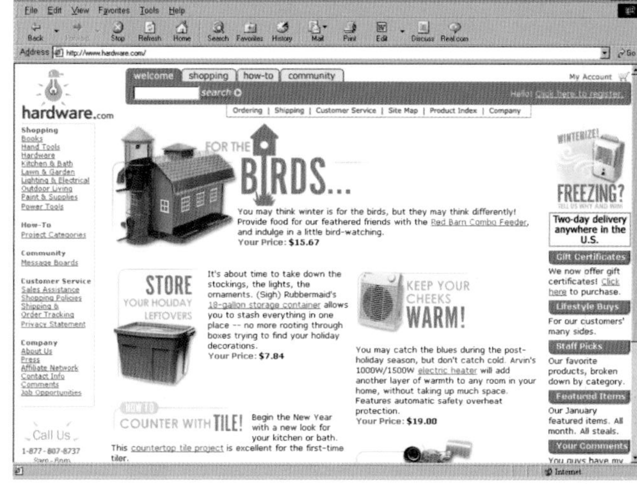

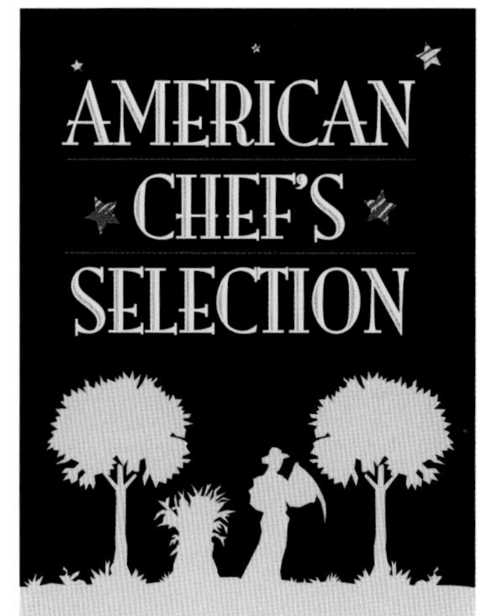

design firm
Gardner Design
Wichita, Kansas
designers
Bill Gardner, Travis Brown
illustrator
Tracy Sabin
client
Excel

design firm
Hans Flink Design Inc.
New York, New York
designers
Michael Troian, Harry Bertschmann
client
Unilever HPC USA (Sunlight)

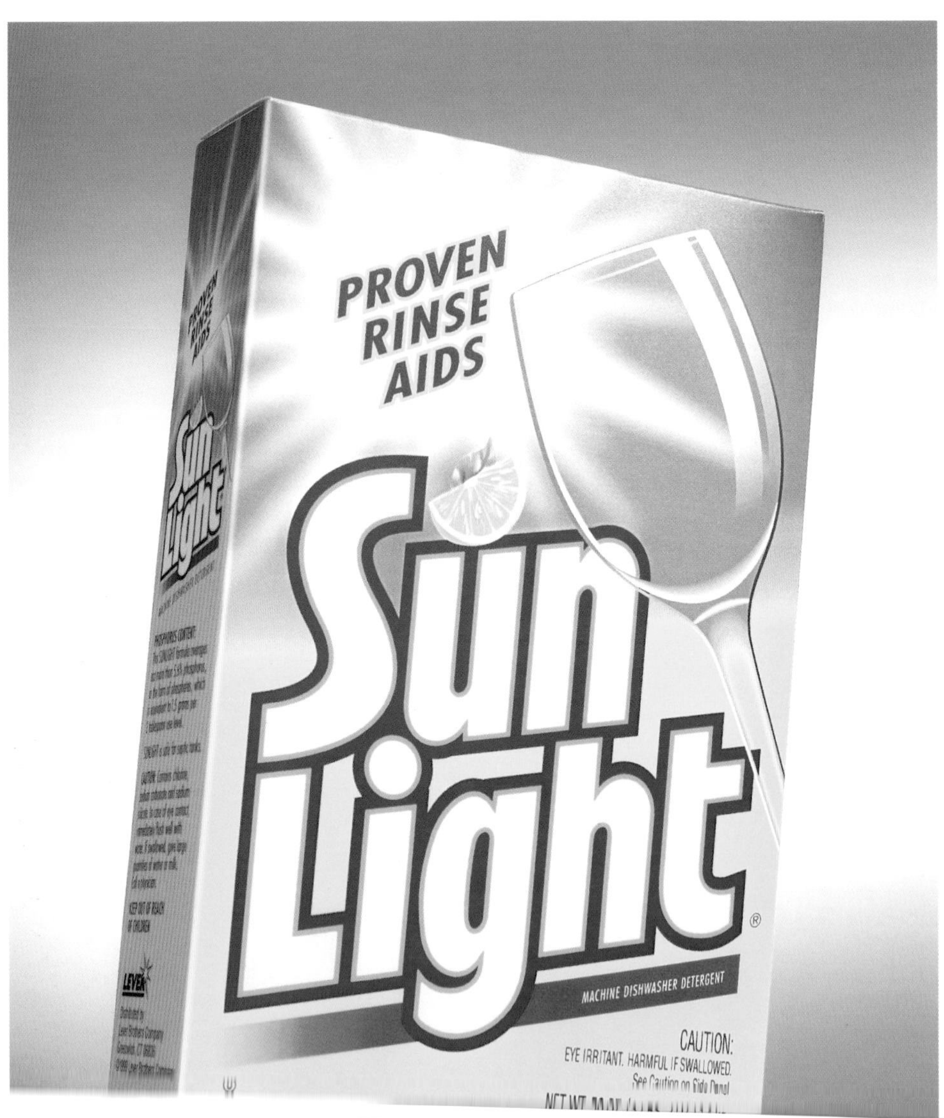

design firm
Jensen Design Associates
Long Beach, California
designer
Pil Ho Lee
client
Robeks Juice

design firm
Hornall Anderson Design Works, Inc.
Seattle, Washington
designers
John Hornall, Julie Lock, Mary Hermes,
Mary Chin Hutchison, David Bates, Cliff Chung,
Alan Florsheim, John Anicker, Naomi Davidson,
Margaret Long, James Moriarity, Merran Kubalak
client
NextRx Corporation
(pharmaceutical)

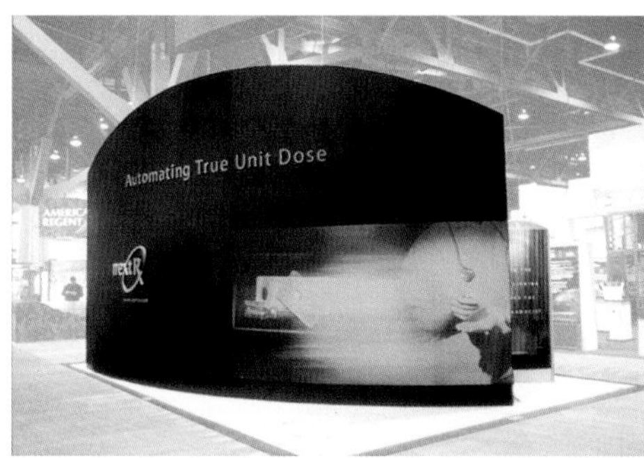

NEXT:
Automated Distribution
NEXT:
Modified Unit Dose
Pharmacist as distribution manager
Floor Stock
True Access
True Freedom
True Control
IN THE BEGINNING WAS THE PHARMACIST

nextRx

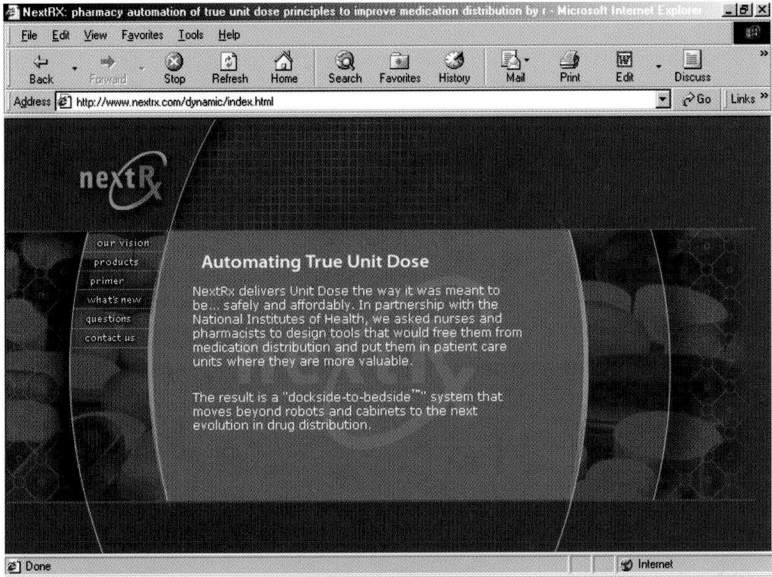
NextRX: pharmacy automation of true unit dose principles to improve medication distribution by r - Microsoft Internet Explorer
File Edit View Favorites Tools Help
Back Forward Stop Refresh Home Search Favorites History Mail Print Edit Discuss
Address http://www.nextrx.com/dynamic/index.html
Go Links
nextRx
our vision
products
primer
what's new
questions
contact us
Automating True Unit Dose
NextRx delivers Unit Dose the way it was meant to be... safely and affordably. In partnership with the National Institutes of Health, we asked nurses and pharmacists to design tools that would free them from medication distribution and put them in patient care units where they are more valuable.
The result is a "dockside-to-bedside™" system that moves beyond robots and cabinets to the next evolution in drug distribution.
Done
Internet

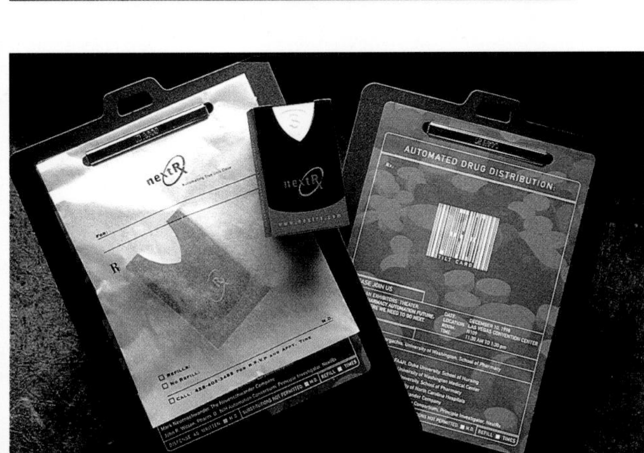
nextRx
AUTOMATED DRUG DISTRIBUTION

nextRx
IN THE BEGINNING WAS THE PHARMACIST

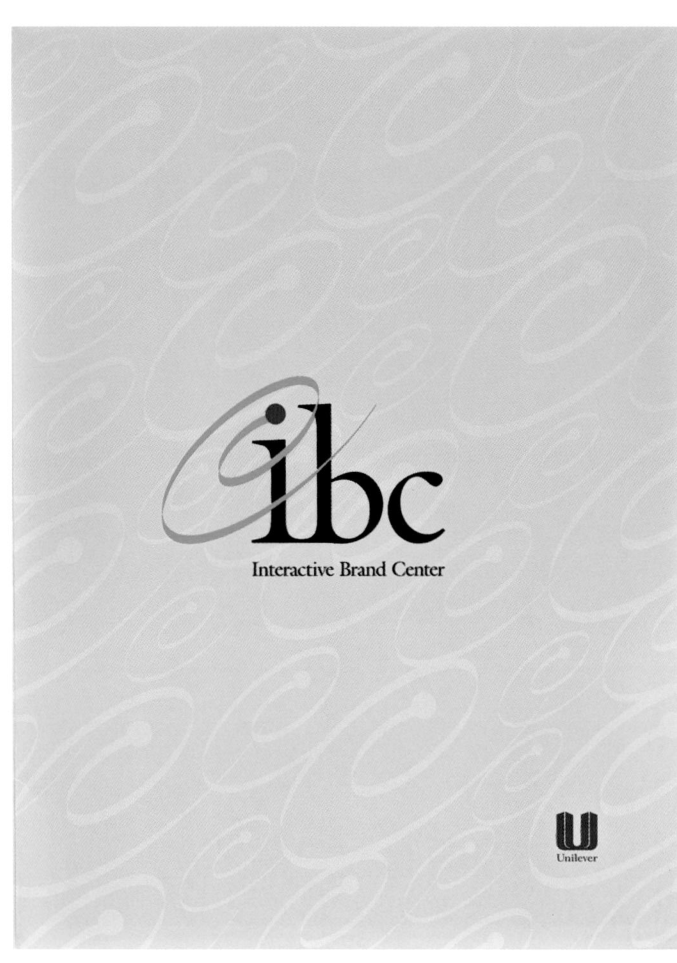

design firm
Tom Fowler, Inc.
Norwalk, Connecticut
designer
Elizabeth P. Ball
client
IBC Creative Services of Unilever HPC

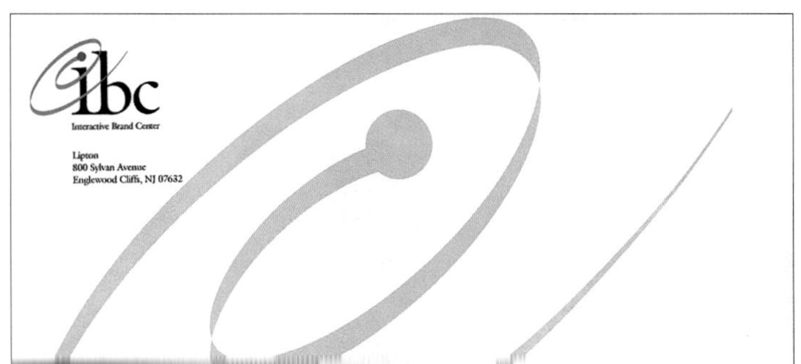

FISHER

design firm
The Leonhardt Group
Seattle, Washington
designers
Steve Watson, Ray Ueno
client
Fisher Companies Inc.

design firm
Sussman/Prejza & Co., Inc.
Culver City, California
designers
Deborah Sussman, Yuki Nishinaka, Paula Loh,
Debra Valencia, Maureen Nishikawa
client
City of Santa Monica

City of
Santa Monica℠

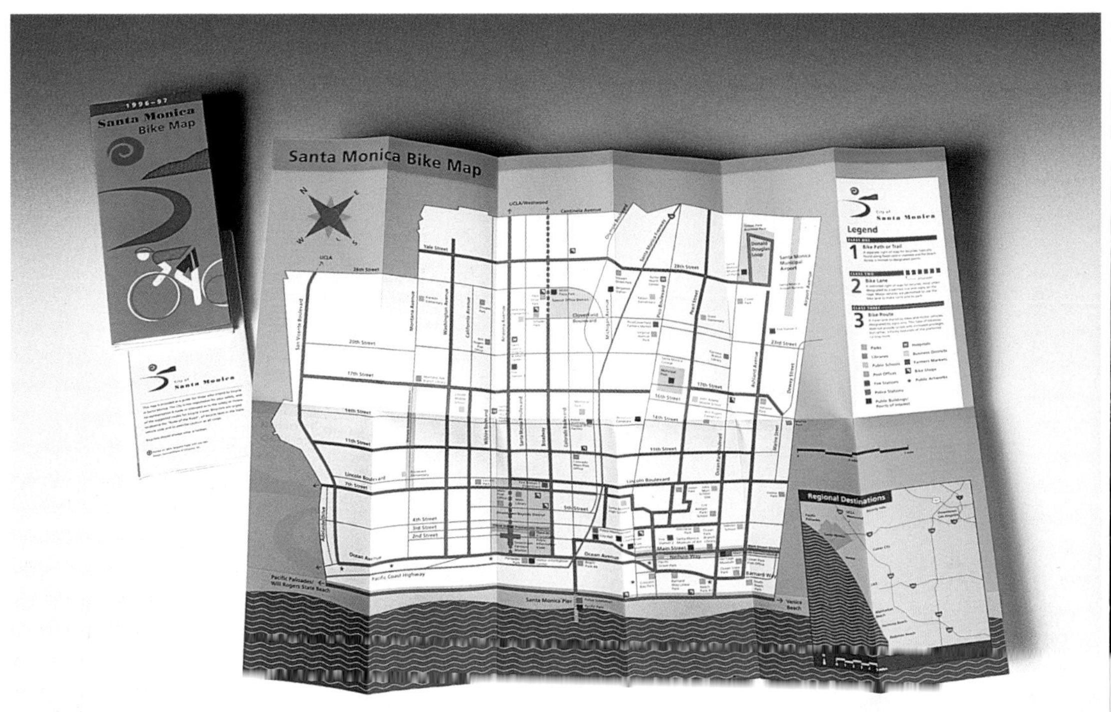

Marine

City of Santa Monica
blue
big
bus
Carnival

style 134

design firm
Design Guys
Minneapolis, Minnesota
designers
Steven Sikora, Dawn Selg, John Moes, Jerry Stenback
client
Target Stores
(retail)

HAIR CARE
Shampoo
Hair Treatment
Hair Coloring
HARNETTS
HARNETTS
HARNETTS
Gotu Kola
Joint Ease
STRESS PAK
gift certificate

design firm
Hans Flink Design Inc.
New York, New York
designers
Susan Kunschaft, Mark Krukonis
client
Mead Johnson Nutritionals (Alacta Formula)

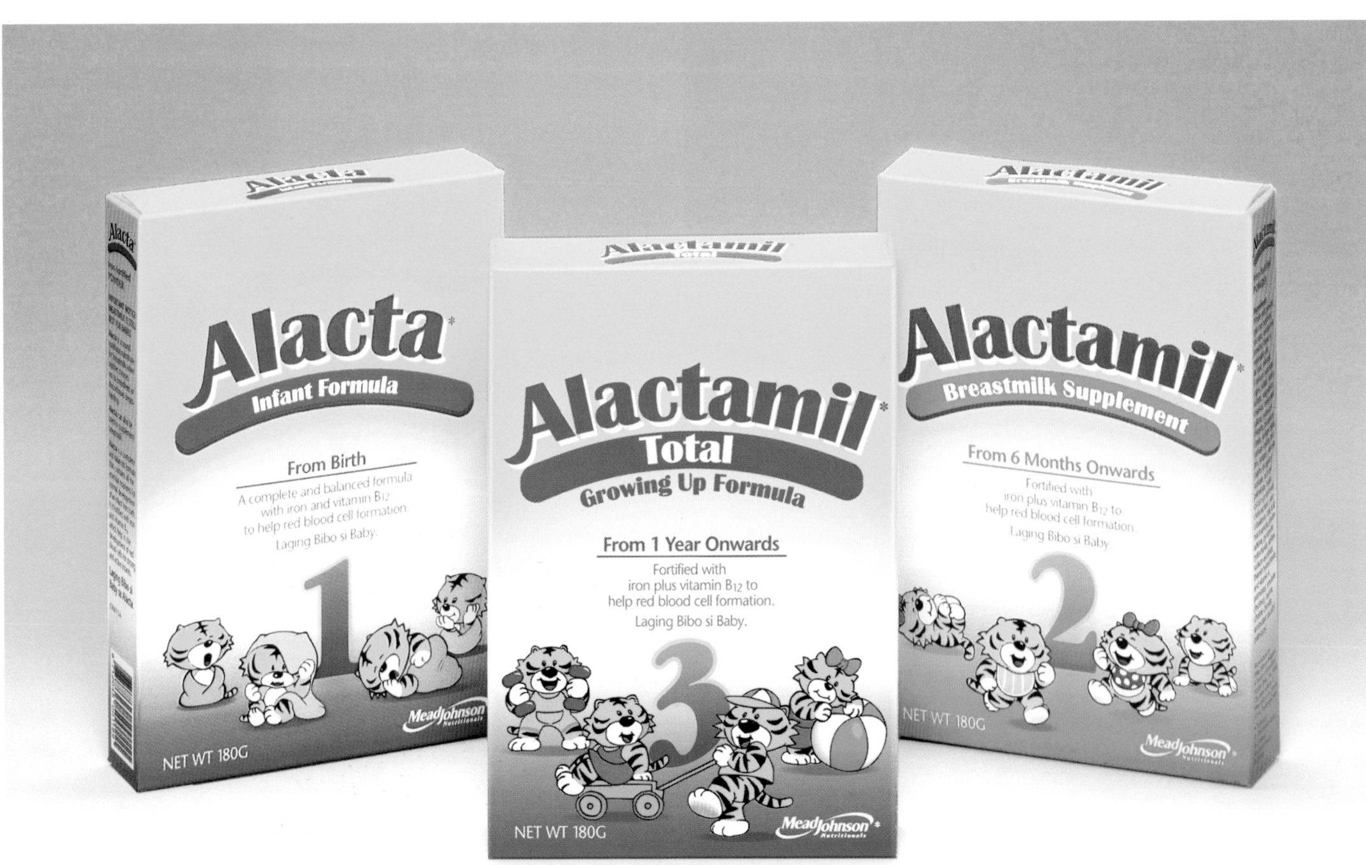

design firm
Gardner Design
Wichita, Kansas
designers
Bill Gardner, Brian Miller
client
Somnograph
(sleep diagnostic services)

FreemanWhite

design firm
Malcolm Grear Designers
Providence, Rhode Island
client
FreemanWhite, Inc.
(a multi-disciplined planning, architectural, and engineering firm)

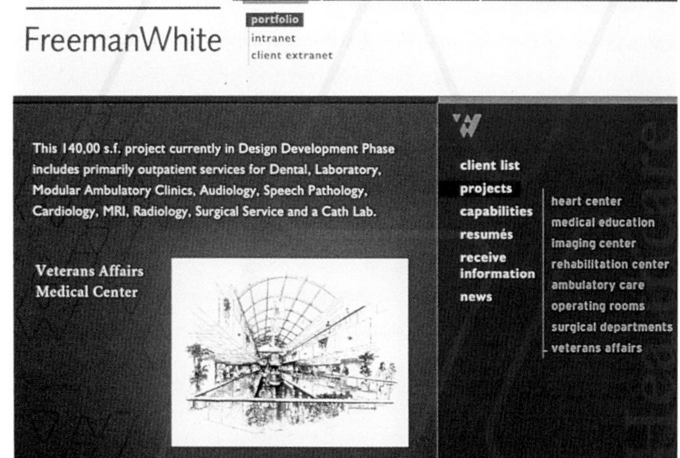

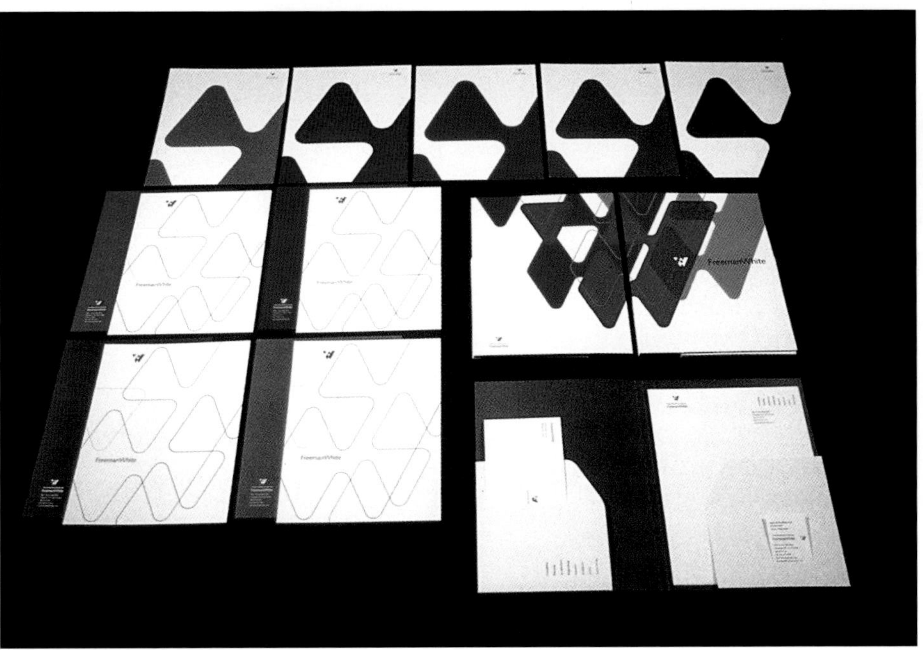

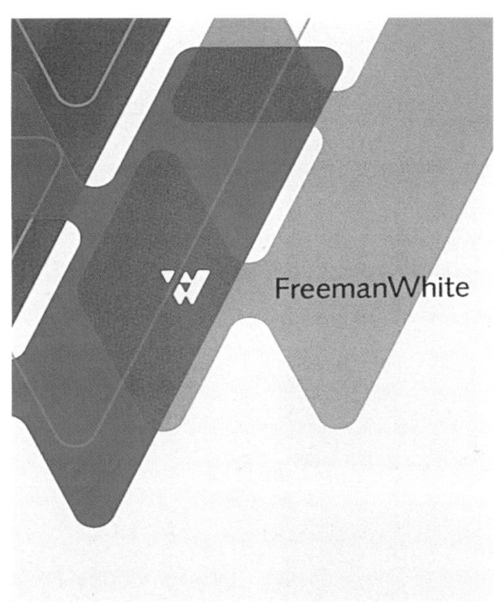

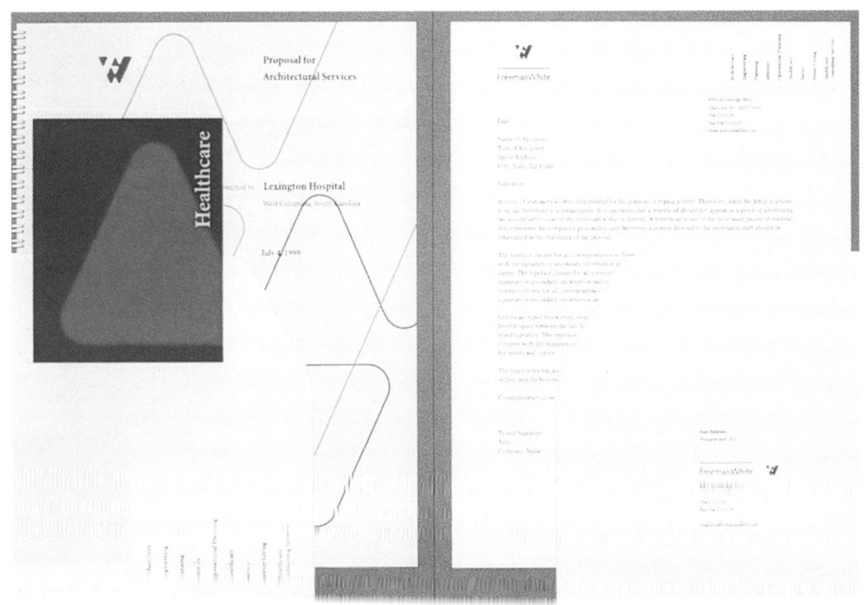

Healthcare
Senior Living
Justice
Healthcare Consulting Services
FreemanWhite
portfolio
intranet
client extranet

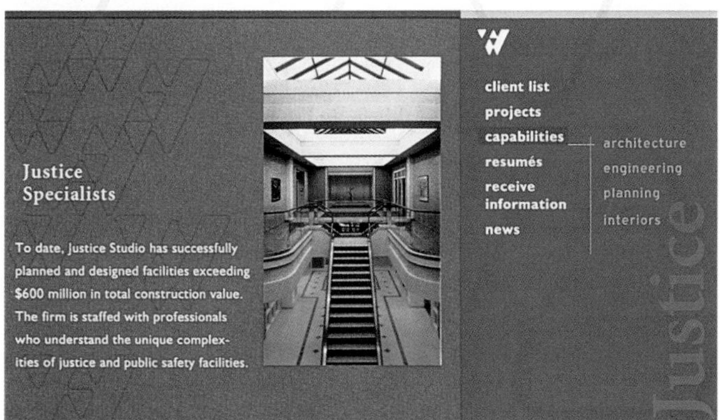
Justice Specialists
To date, Justice Studio has successfully planned and designed facilities exceeding $600 million in total construction value. The firm is staffed with professionals who understand the unique complexities of justice and public safety facilities.
client list
projects
capabilities
resumés
receive information
news
architecture
engineering
planning
interiors
Justice

Proposed Team
Joseph W. Smith, AIA

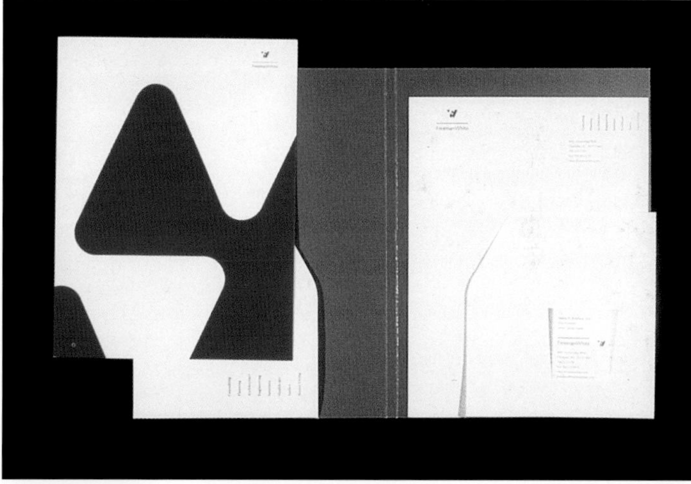

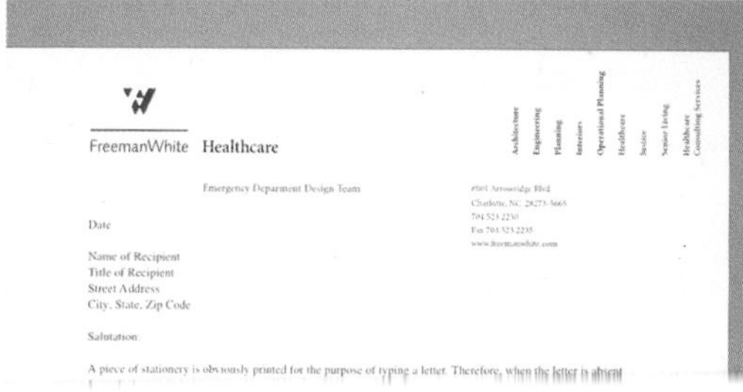
FreemanWhite Healthcare
Emergency Department Design Team
Date
Name of Recipient
Title of Recipient
Street Address
City, State, Zip Code
Salutation

design firm
EAT Advertising & Design
Kansas City, Missouri
designers
Patrice Eilts-Jobe, Peggy Reilly, Jeremy Shellhorn
client
Organized Living
(retail)

tie it up!
Organized Living
Organized Living
box it up!

design firm
Hans Flink Design Inc.
New York, New York
designers
Chang-Mei Lin
client
Unilever HPC USA (Mentadent)

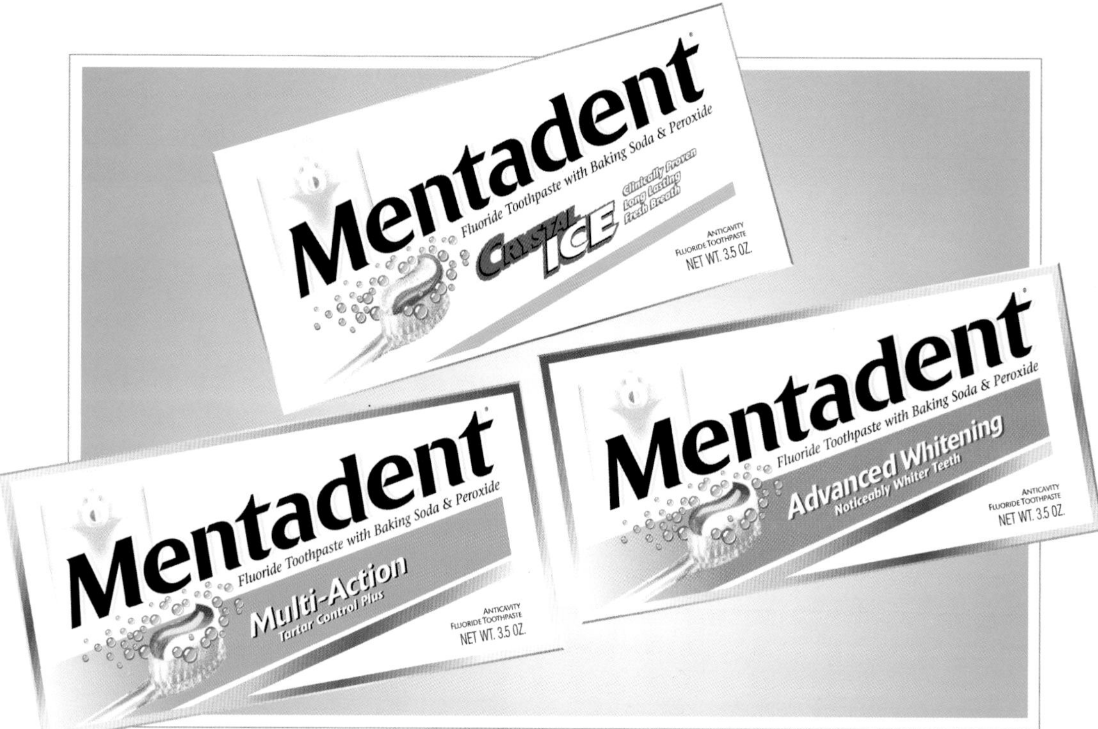

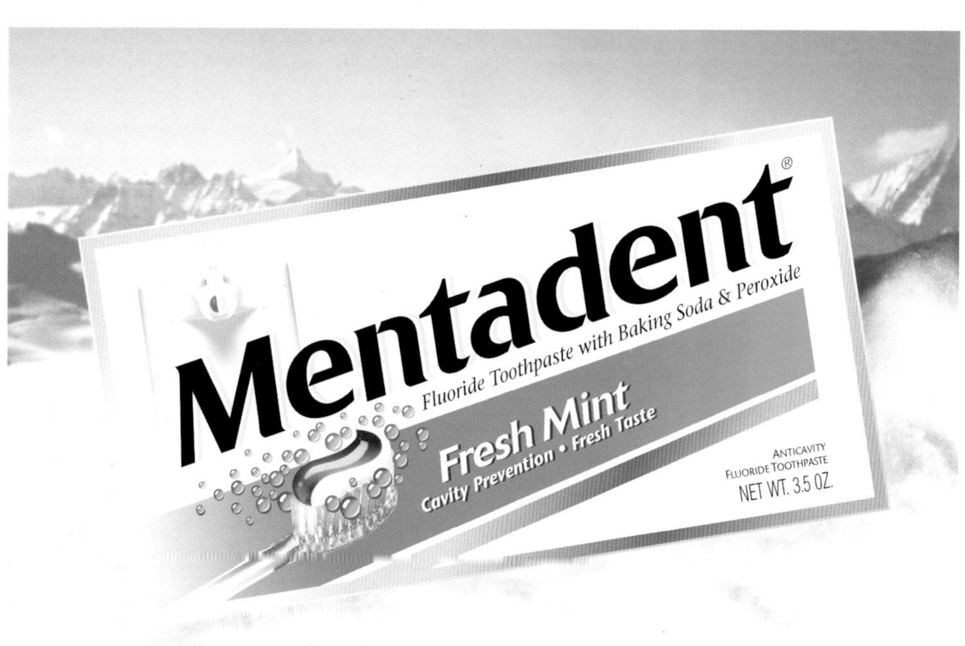

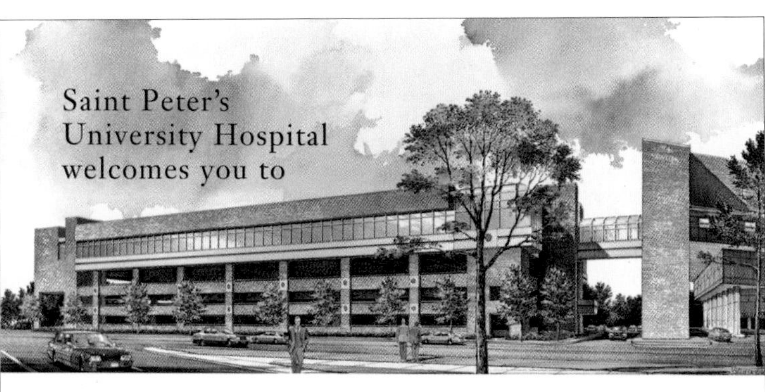

CARES

The Center for Ambulatory Resources

Ambulatory Surgery

Health Center for Women

Sports Physical Therapy Institute

Pediatric Specialty Group

CENTER FOR AMBULATORY RESOURCES

Saint Peter's University Hospital

CARES

The Center for Ambulatory Resources

Health Center For Women

Women's Breast and Imaging Center

Comprehensive Care Just for Women

design firm
Pink Coyote Design, Inc.
New York, New York
designer
Joel Ponzan
client
St. Peter's University Hospital
(surgical medicine)

Saint Peter's University Hospital

CARES

The Center for Ambulatory Resources

Sports Physical Therapy Institute

Saint Peter's University Hospital

CARES

The Center for Ambulatory Resources

Ambulatory Surgery

State-of-the-Art Healthcare for your Whole Family

Saint Peter's University Hospital

CARES

The Center for Ambulatory Resources

The Program for Female Urinary Incontinence and Pelvic Organ Prolapse

A Program Created Just for Women

KNOWLEDG≡XCHANGE

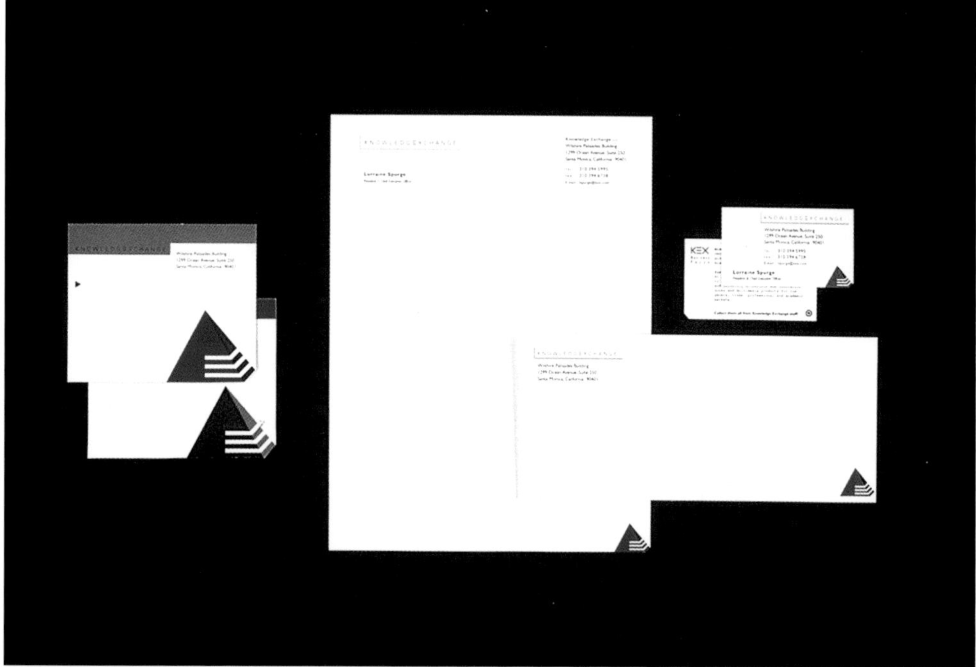

design firm
Sussman/Prejza & Co., Inc.
Culver City, California
designers
Deborah Sussman, Paula Loh, Hsin Hsien Tsai, Debra Valencia, Natalie Rosbottom
client
Knowledge Exhange

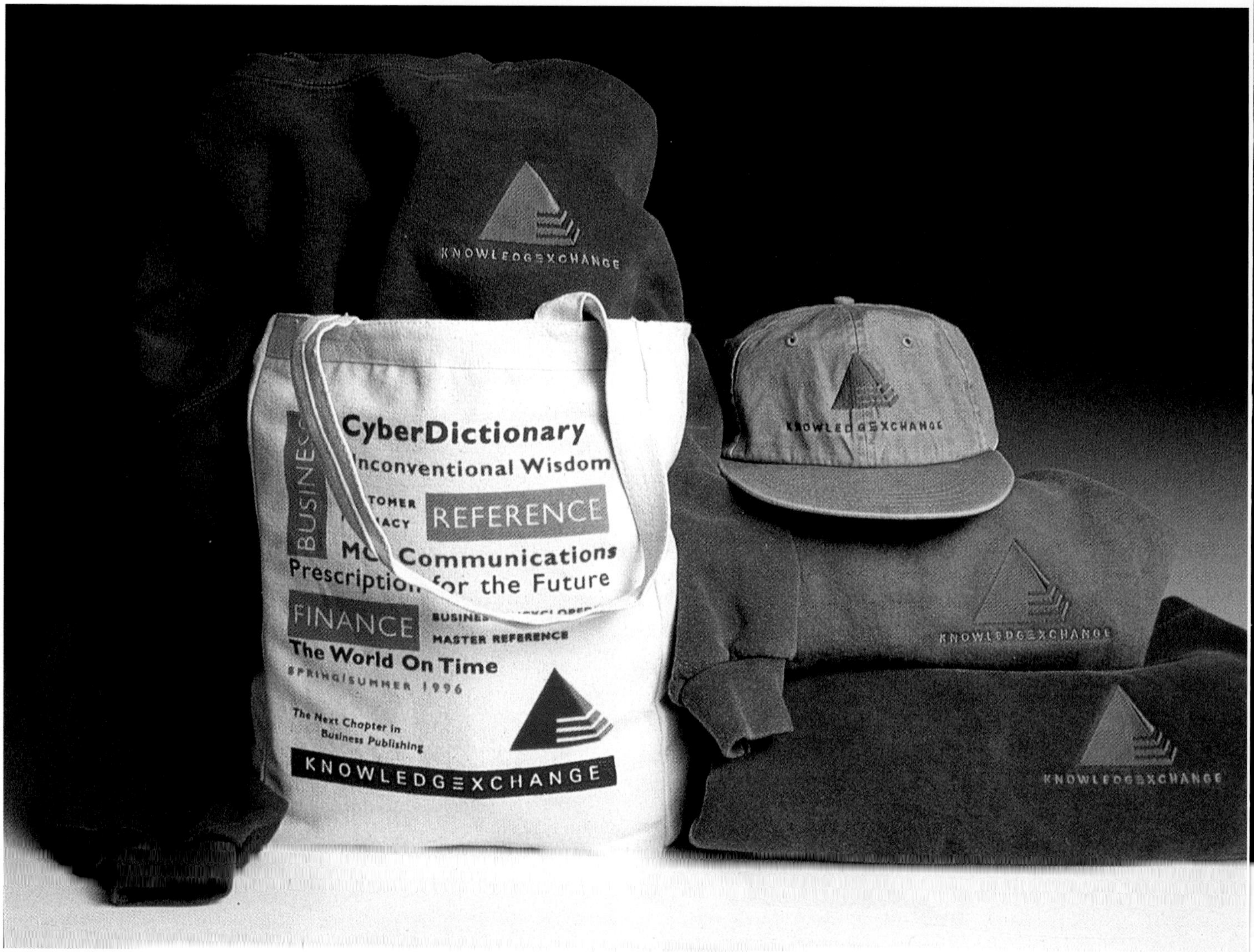

Unisom®

design firm
Hans Flink Design Inc.
New York, New York
designers
Michael Troian, Harry Bertschmann
client
Pfizer Inc. (Unisom sleep aid)

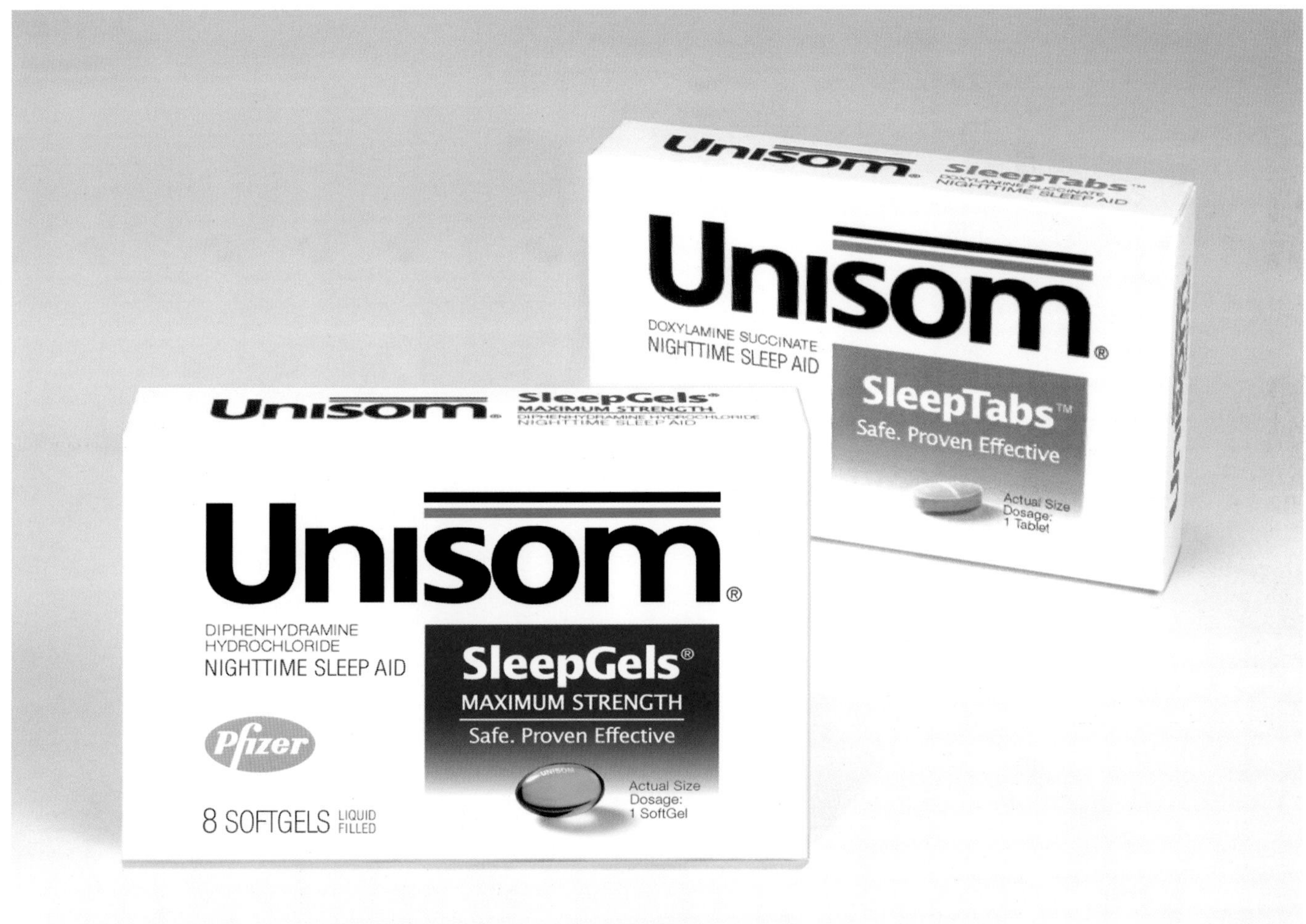

design firm
Sayles Graphic Design
Des Moines, Iowa
designer
John Sayles
client
American Cancer Society
(non-profit organization)

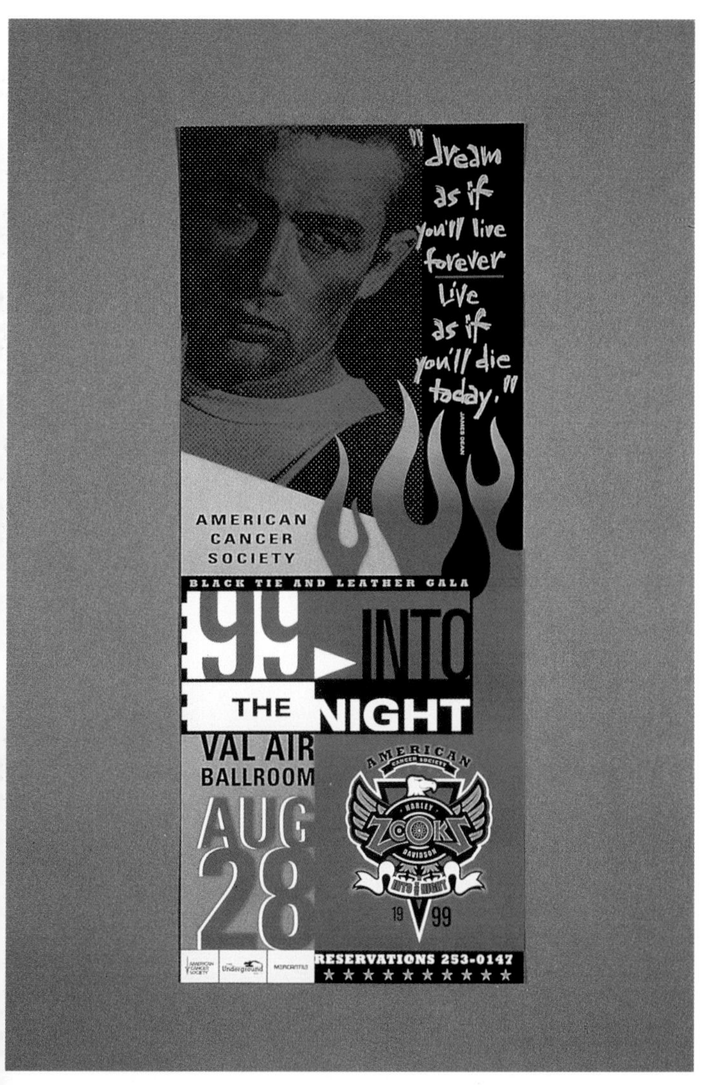
"dream as if you'll live forever
Live as if you'll die today."
JAMES DEAN
AMERICAN CANCER SOCIETY
BLACK TIE AND LEATHER GALA
99 INTO THE NIGHT
VAL AIR BALLROOM
AUG 28
AMERICAN CANCER SOCIETY
HARLEY DAVIDSON
19 99
RESERVATIONS 253-0147

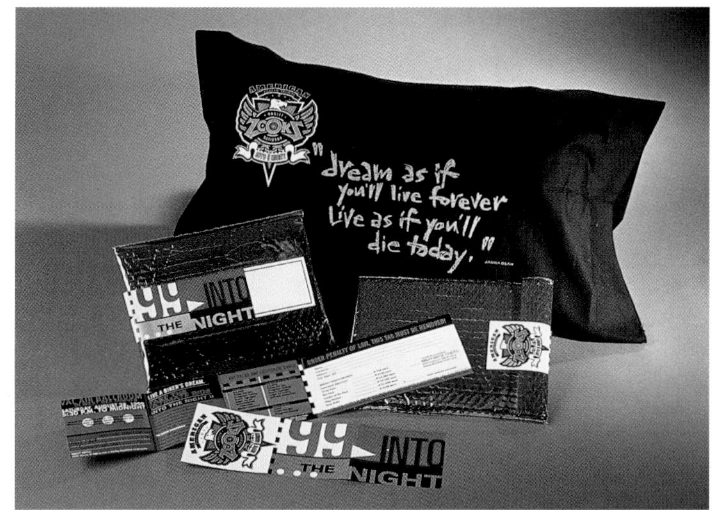
"dream as if you'll live forever
Live as if you'll die today."
99 INTO THE NIGHT

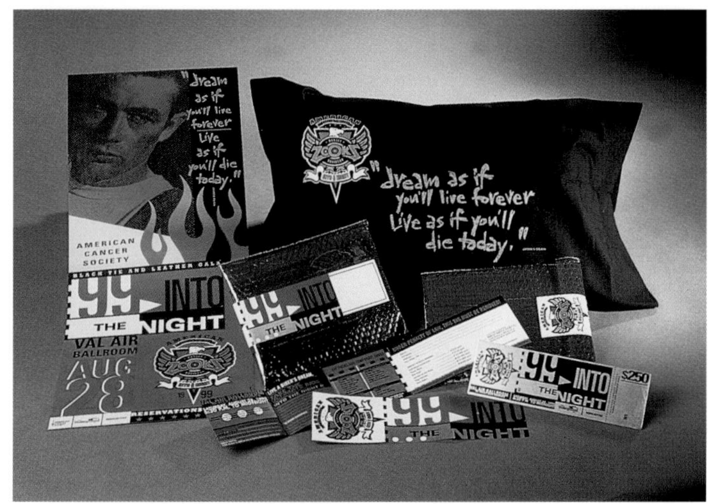
"dream as if you'll live forever
Live as if you'll die today."
AMERICAN CANCER SOCIETY
99 INTO THE NIGHT
VAL AIR BALLROOM
AUG 28

AMERICAN
CANCER SOCIETY
HARLEY
DAVIDSON
AMERICAN CANCER SOCIETY
BLACK TIE AND LEATHER GALA
RESERVATIONS 253-0147
VAL AIR BALLROOM
AUG. 28
99 INTO ... THE NIGHT
ELLER

design firm
Gardner Design
Wichita, Kansas
designers
Bill Gardner, Brian Miller
client
Avalanche Popcorn
(popcorn company)

design firm
Sibley Peteet
Dallas, Texas
designers
Don Sibley, Tom Hough, David Beck
client
Bellagio Hotel & Casino

BELLAGIO
RELAXING
FOAM BATH
200 ML

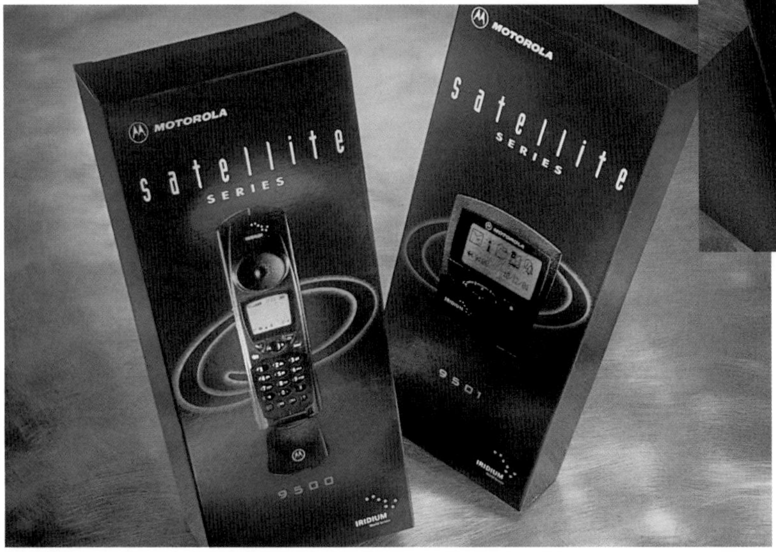

design firm
Lipson Alport Glass & Assoc.
Northbrook, Illinois
designer
Sue Cole
digital imaging
Dave Stoken
client
Motorola, Inc.
(consumer electronics)

design firm
Lipson Alport Glass & Assoc.
Northbrook, Illinois
creative director
Sam Ciulla
designer
Lisa Maraldi
client
Pritzker Realty Group LLC
(transportation)

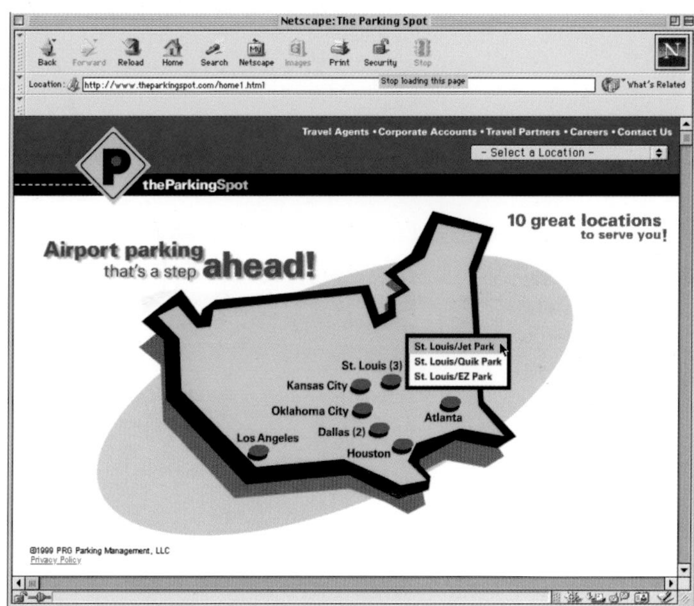

design firm
Mires Design
San Diego, California
art director
John Ball
designers
Miguel Perez, John Ball, Deborah Hom
client
Nike, Inc.

MARTHA
STEWART
everyday™

design firm
Doyle Partners
New York, New York
creative director
Stephen Doyle
client
Kmart

jumpstart

Get financing.

Hire great people.

Create alliances.

Go global.

thinkresu

goulston&storrs
counsellors at law

Goulston & Storrs, A Professional Corporation • Boston, MA • 617-482-1776 • www.goulstonstorrs.com

goulston&storrs
counsellors at law

buildempires

Structure the venture.
Close the financing.
Lease it up.
Break ground.

think*results*

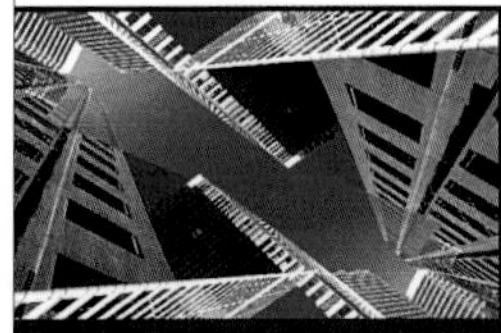

goulston&storrs
counsellors at law

Goulston & Storrs, A Professional Corporation • Boston, MA • 617-482-1776 • www.goulstonstorrs.com

rulemarkets

Scale the idea.
Find strategic partners.
License the product.
Take it global.

think*results*

goulston&storrs
counsellors at law

Goulston & Storrs, A Professional Corporation • Boston, MA • 617-482-1776 • www.goulstonstorrs.com

caseclosed

Show a strong hand.
Control the dialogue.
Prove your point.
Get back to business.

think*results*

goulston&storrs
counsellors at law

Goulston & Storrs, A Professional Corporation • Boston, MA • 617-482-1776 • www.goulstonstorrs.com

design firm
Greenfield/Belser Ltd.
Washington, DC
art director
Burkey Belser
designer
Tom Cameron
client
Goulston & Storrs
(legal)

P.S. the letter / 5122 camp bowie blvd. / fort worth, texas 76107 / (817)731-2032 fax (817)377-9238
P.S. the letter / 5122 camp bowie blvd. / fort worth, texas 76107
P.S. the letter
5122 camp bowie blvd.
fort worth, texas 76107
(817)731-2032
fax (817)377-9238

design firm
Michael Niblett Design
Fort Worth, Texas
designer
Michael Niblett
client
P.S. the Letter
(retail, gifts, stationery)

the P.S. letter
the P.S. letter

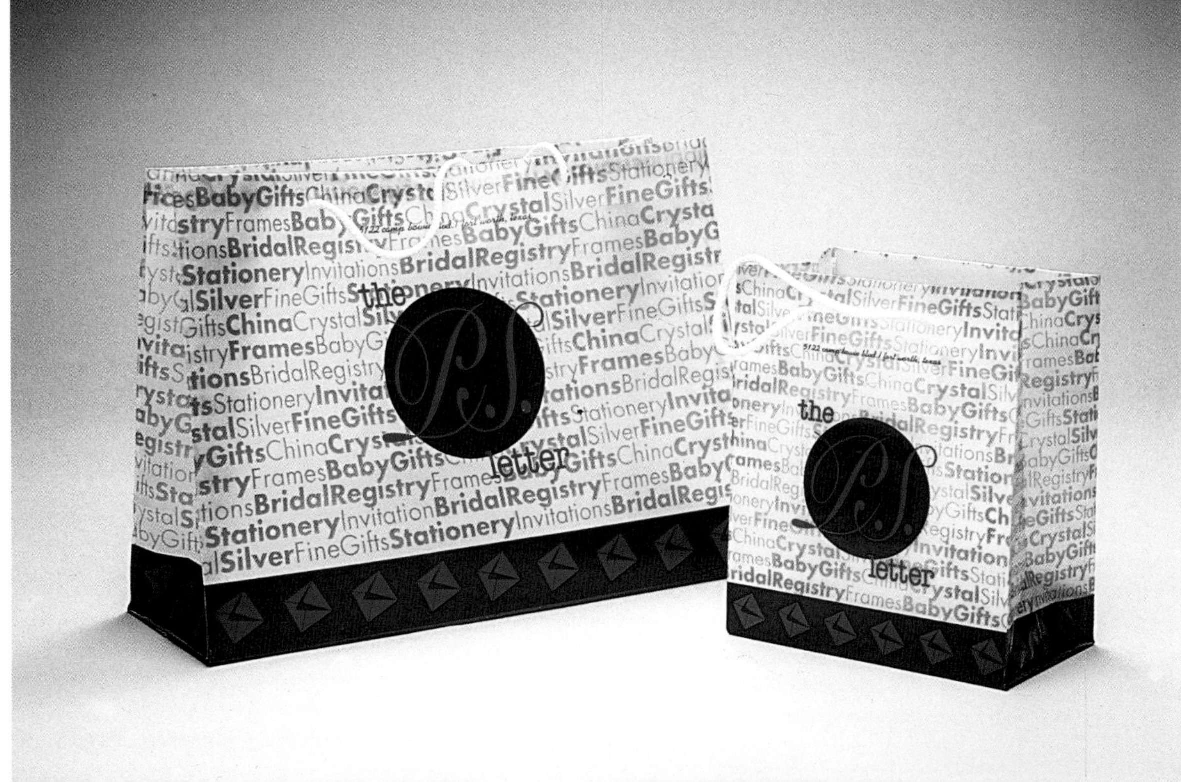

design firm
Sayles Graphic Design
Des Moines, Iowa
designer
John Sayles
client
Glazed Expressions
(do-it yourself pottery store)

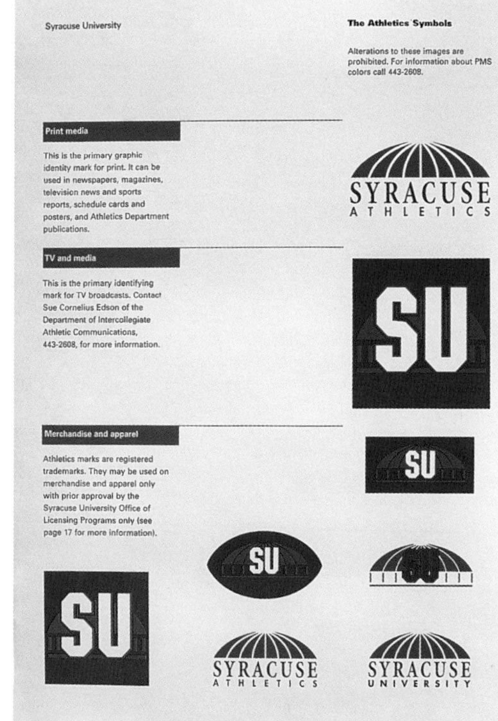
Syracuse University

The Athletics Symbols

Alterations to these images are prohibited. For information about PMS colors call 443-2608.

Print media

This is the primary graphic identity mark for print. It can be used in newspapers, magazines, television news and sports reports, schedule cards and posters, and Athletics Department publications.

TV and media

This is the primary identifying mark for TV broadcasts. Contact Sue Cornelius Edson of the Department of Intercollegiate Athletic Communications, 443-2608, for more information.

Merchandise and apparel

Athletics marks are registered trademarks. They may be used on merchandise and apparel only with prior approval by the Syracuse University Office of Licensing Programs only (see page 17 for more information).

SYRACUSE ATHLETICS

SYRACUSE UNIVERSITY

15

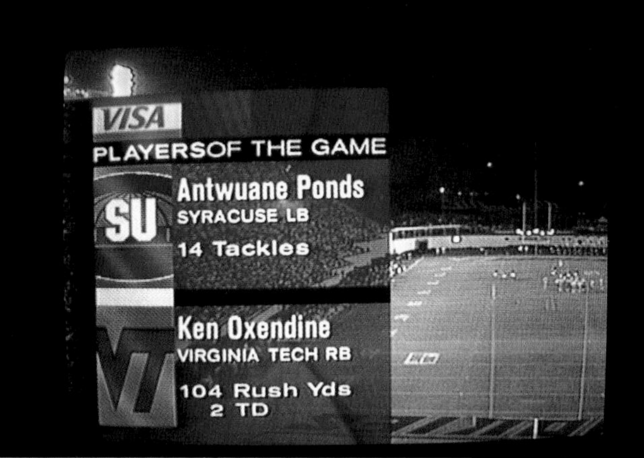

design firm
John Milligan Design
Largo, Florida
designers
John Milligan, Michael Milligan
client
Syracuse University Athletic Department

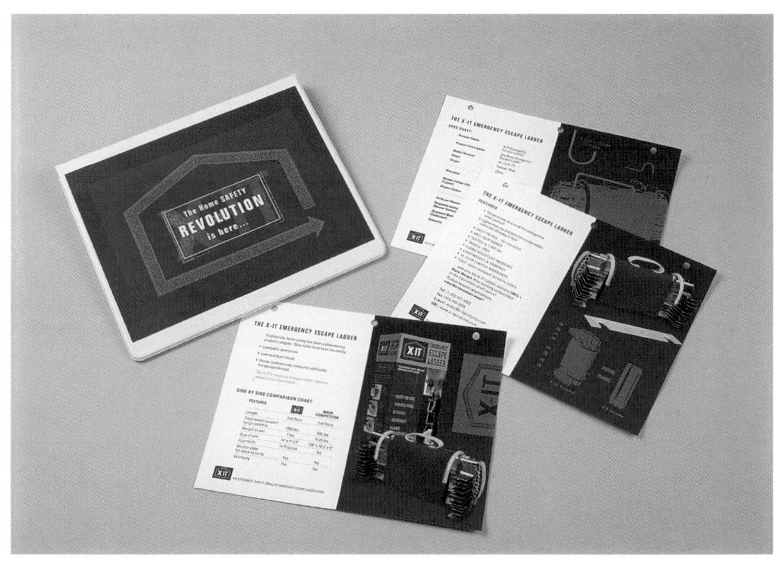

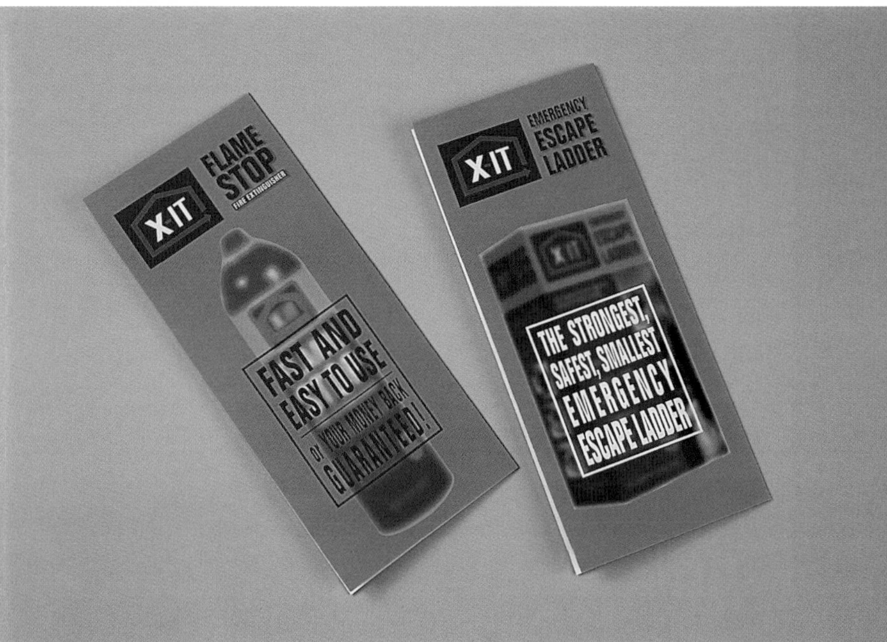

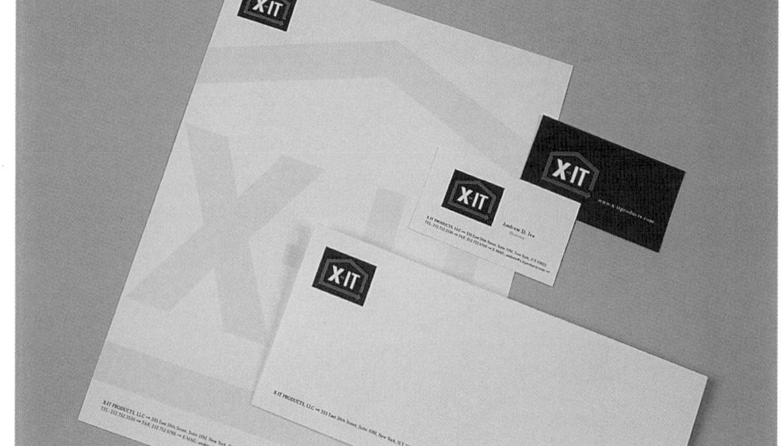

design firm
Maffini & Bearce
New York, New York
designer
Philippe Maffini
client
X-IT Products LLC

BROWN SHOE

design firm
Kiku Obata + Company
St. Louis, Missouri
designers
Scott Gericke, Amy Knopf, Joe Floresca, Jennifer Baldwin, Carole Jerome
client
Brown Shoe Company
(manufacturer + distributer of footwear worldwide)

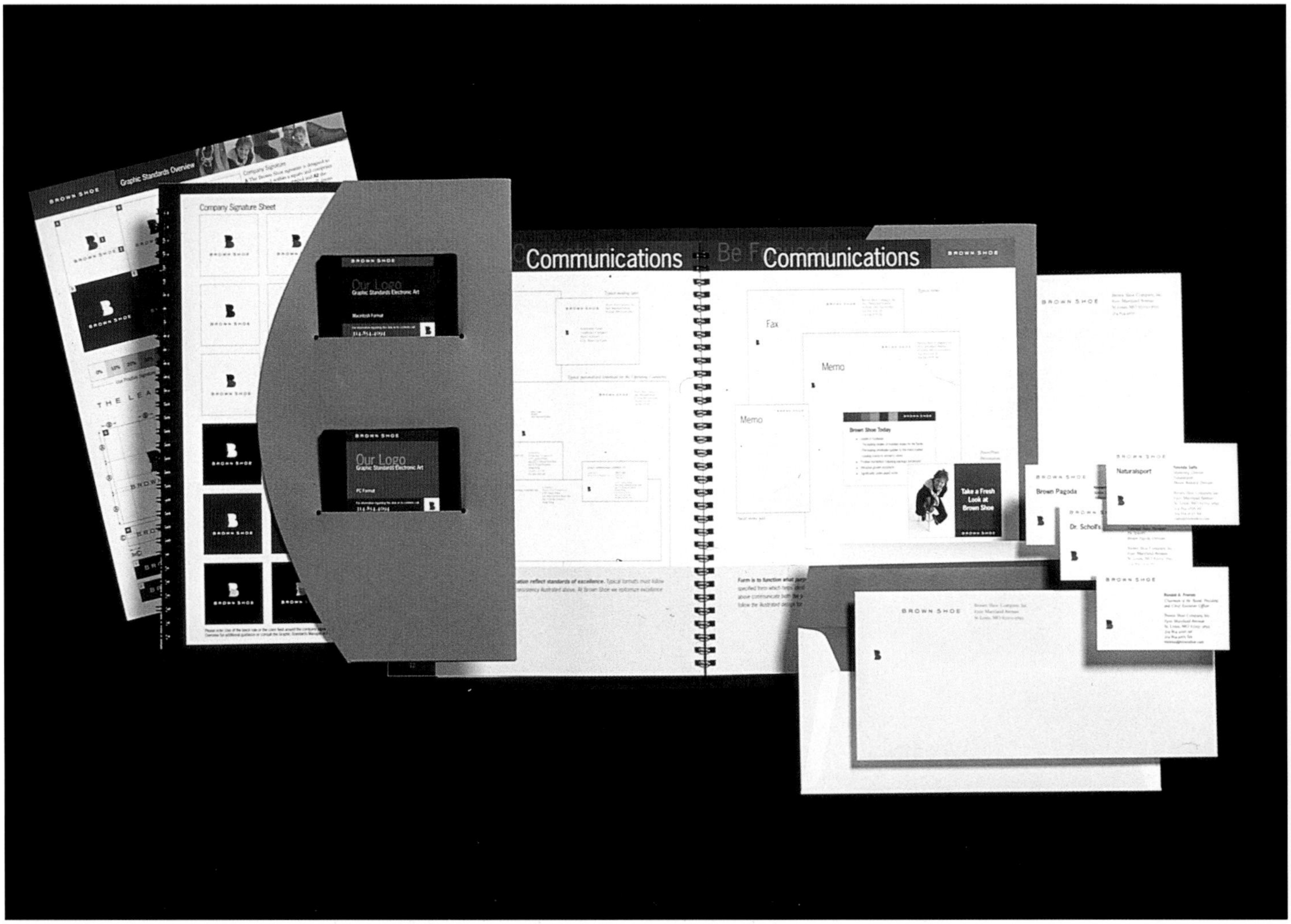

BROWN SHOE

Be Real. Be Together. Be Ready.
BROWN SHOE
Be Real. Be Together. Be Ready.
BROWN SHOE
THE LEADER IN FOOTWEAR.
BROWN SHOE

Looking Good. Feeling Good.
Be Real. Be Together. Be Ready.
BROWN SHOE
Be Smart.
information about our new identity
Be Together.
Be Cool.
Be Real.
Be Happy.
Be Ready.
Looking Good.
Feeling Good.
BROWN SHOE
Looking Good. Feeling Good.
BROWN SHOE The Leader in Footwear.
Looking Good. Feeling Good.
WE ARE ONE INTEGRATED, BRAND-DRIVEN FOOTWEAR COMPANY. Brown Shoe has always been the leader in family footwear. From our retail operations – Famous Footwear and Naturalizer – to our Brown Branded, Brown Pagoda and Brown Canada footwear portfolios, combined with the worldwide capabilities of our Brown Shoe Sourcing division, we have what it takes to exceed the expectation of today's footwear consumers. We're Brown Shoe – we're bold, we're the best of class, and we're only just begun.
BROWN SHOE

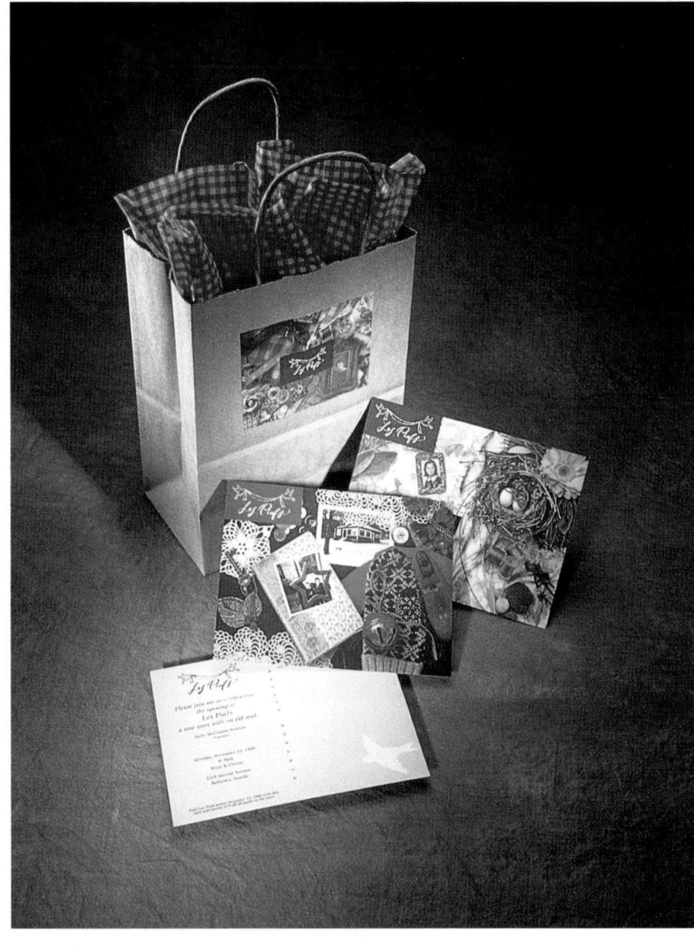

design firm
Belyea
Seattle, Washington
creative director
Patricia Belyea
designer
Christian Salas
client
Les Piafs
(retail store)

CruiseWest

design firm
Belyea
Seattle, Washington
creative director
Patricia Belyea
designer
Ron Lars Hansen
client
Cruise West
(small ship cruise line)

design firm
CommArts
Boulder, Colorado
designers
Traci Jones, Dave Tweed, Karl Hirshmann
client
Go Boulder
(Boulder's transit authority)

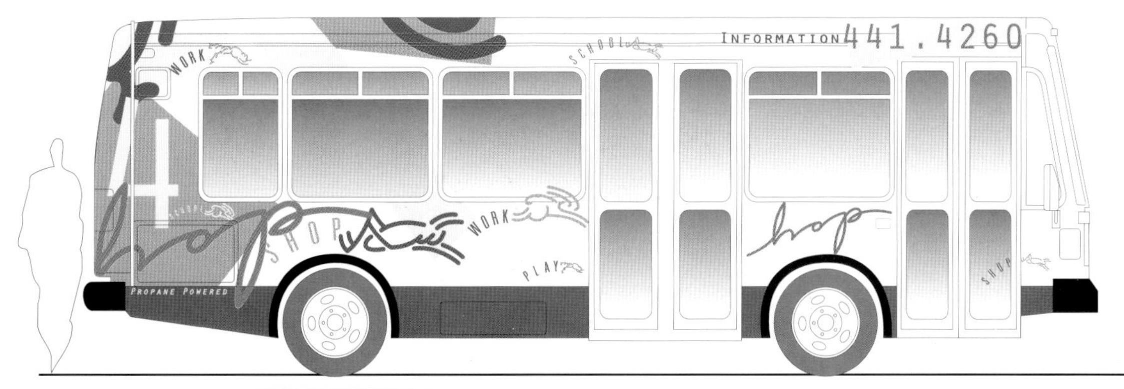
INFORMATION 441.4260
WORK
SCHOOL
SHOP
WORK
PLAY
SHOP
PROPANE POWERED

441.4260 INFORMATION
SCHOOL
SHOP
WORK
WORK
PLAY
SHOP
SCHOOL
PROPANE POWERED

303.299.6000 INFORMATION
JUST FOR YOU
THE ONLY WAY TO TRAVEL!
RTD 1010
10
Leap
TRY IT!
DID I SAY
EASY
ALONG
PEARL
55th
ELECTRONIC DIESEL
ARE YOU READY?

RTD 1010
INFORMATION 303.299.6000
Leap
ELECTRONIC DIESEL

relax
RTD 1010
Leap

33!
...30TH
STREET IN A
SINGLE...
BOUND

20
JUMP
along
Arapahoe
...BOULDER
TO LAFAYETTE...
"GOOD FOR YOU"
OATMEAL
ELECTRONIC DIESEL

RTD 3815
INFORMATION 303.299.6000
UP AND DOWN
Sk'p
BROADWAY
15
ELECTRONIC DIESEL

303.299.6000 INFORMATION
RTD 3815
15
Sk'p
UP AND DOWN
BROADWAY
ELECTRONIC DIESEL

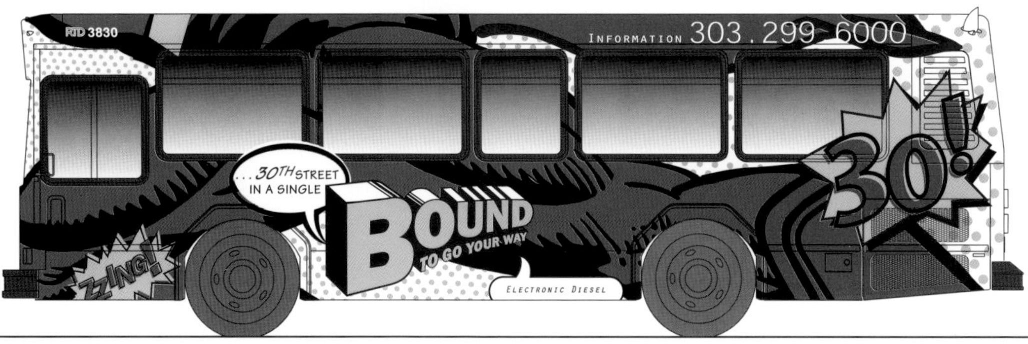

design firm
CommArts
Boulder, Colorado
designers
Traci Jones, Dave Tweed, Karl Hirshmann
client
Go Boulder
(Boulder's transit authority)

veenendaal**cave**

design firm
Belyea
Seattle, Washington
creative director
Patricia Belyea
designer
Anne Dougherty
client
Veenendaal Cave
(interior design firm)

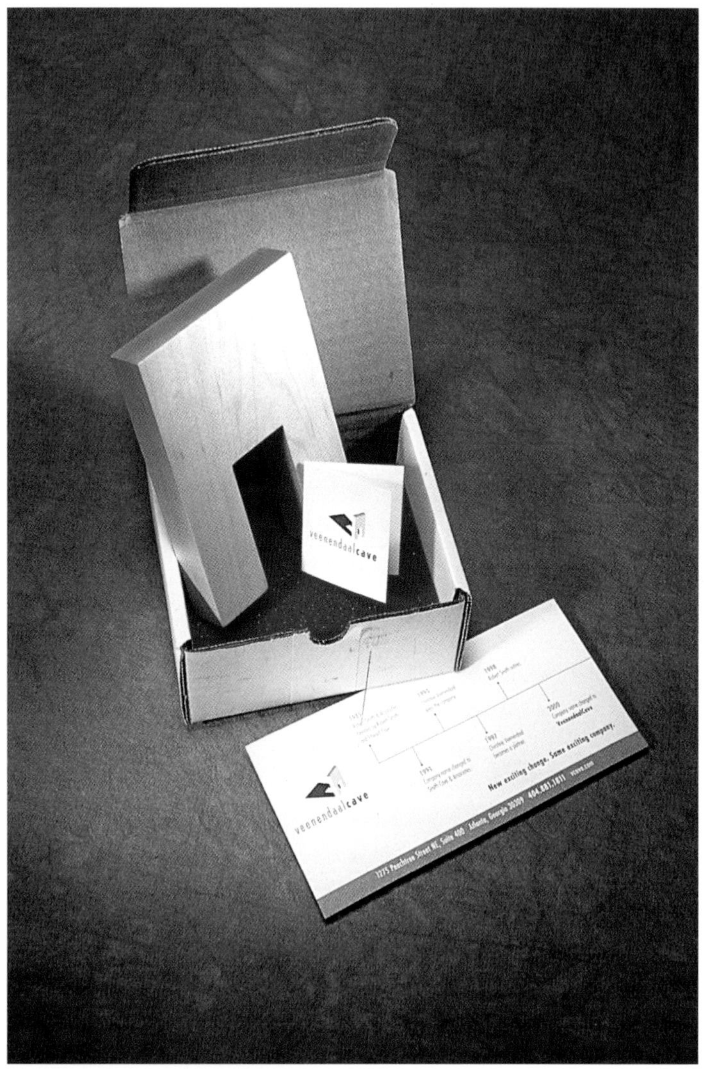

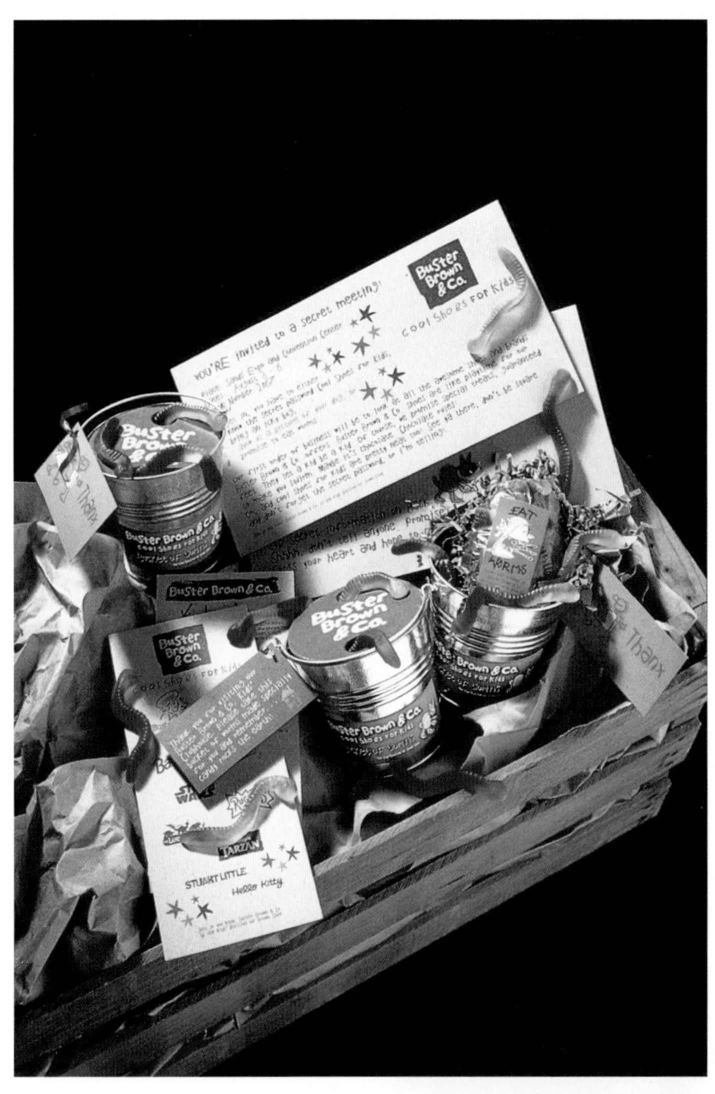

design firm
Kiku Obata + Company
St. Louis, Missouri
designers
Scott Gericke, Carole Jerome
client
Buster Brown + Co.
(manufacturer + distributer
of children's footwear)

The **Speed** Art Museum

design firm
Malcolm Grear Designers
Providence, Rhode Island
client
The Speed Art Museum

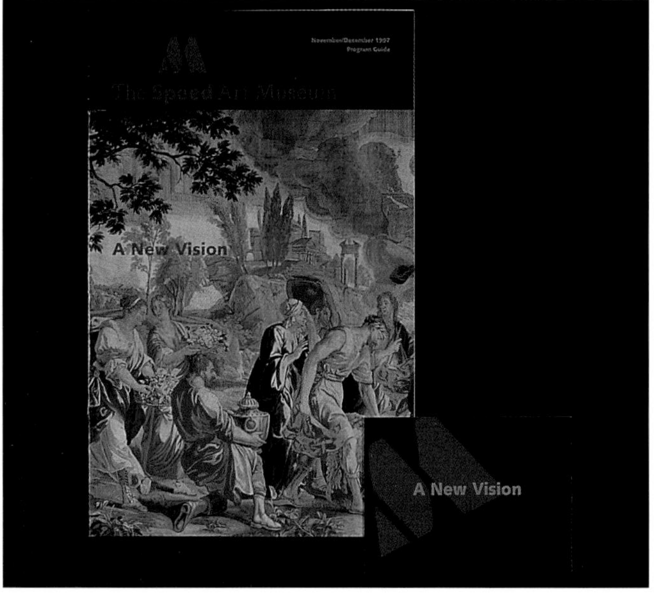

SafeGuard

design firm
Baker Design Associates
Santa Monica, California
creative director
Gary Baker
designer
Louis D'Esposito
client
SafeGuard Health Enterprises, Inc.

95 Enterprise
Aliso Viejo, California 92656
714.778.1005

John E. Cox
President and
Chief Operating Officer
SafeGuard Health Enterprises, Inc.

direct 714.758.4376
fax 714.758.4383
e-mail me at johnc@safeguard.net

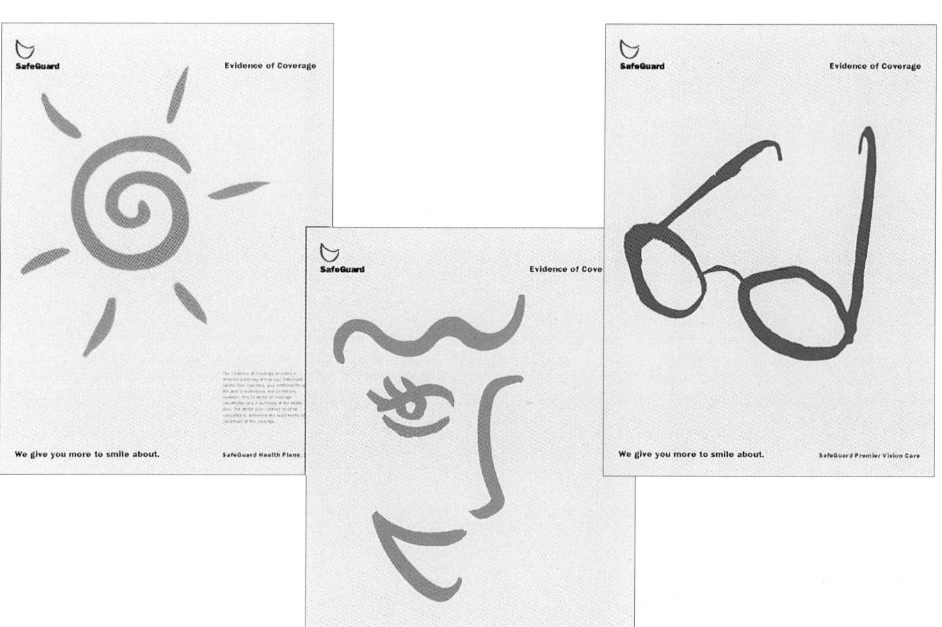

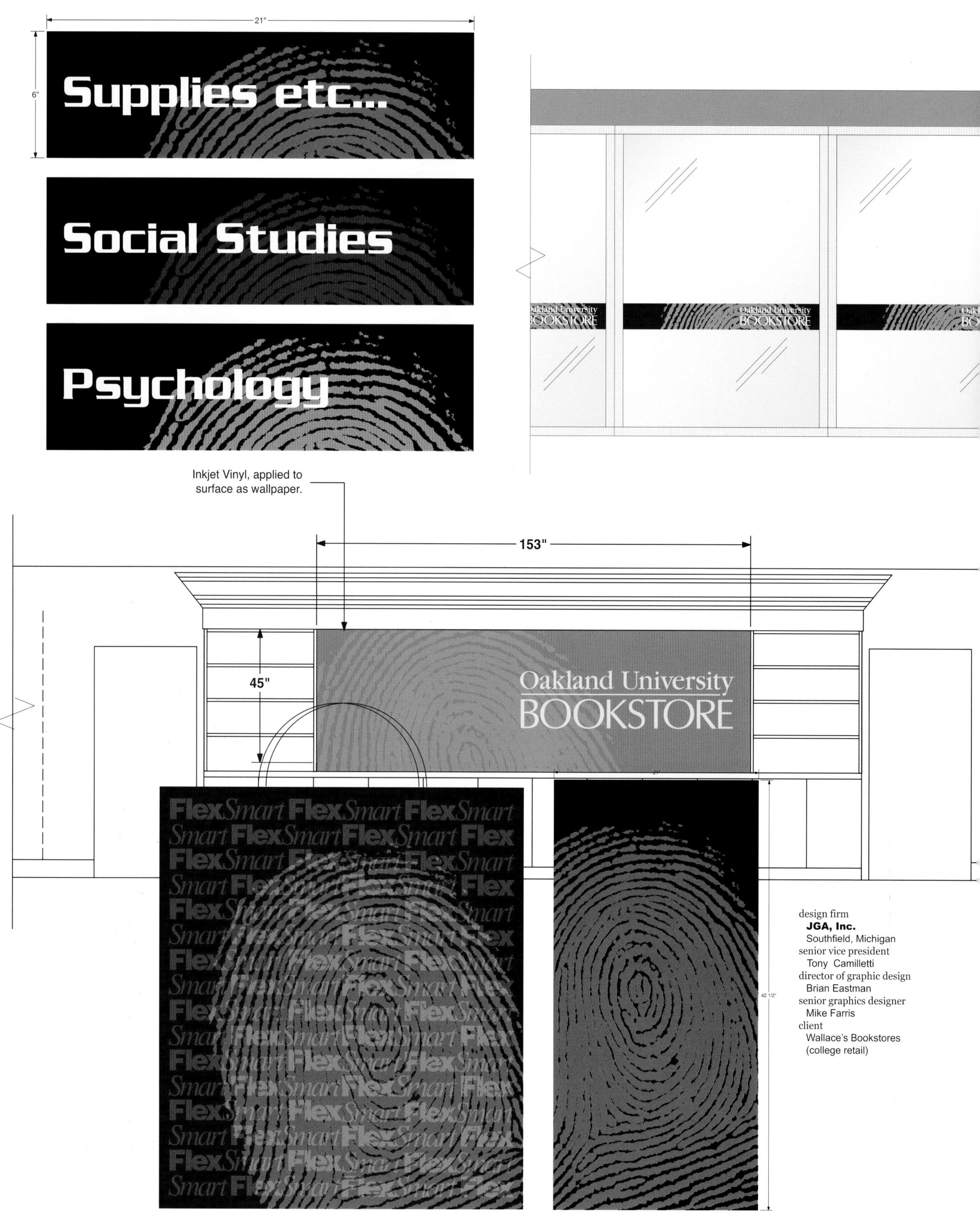

design firm
JGA, Inc.
Southfield, Michigan
senior vice president
Tony Camilletti
director of graphic design
Brian Eastman
senior graphics designer
Mike Farris
client
Wallace's Bookstores
(college retail)

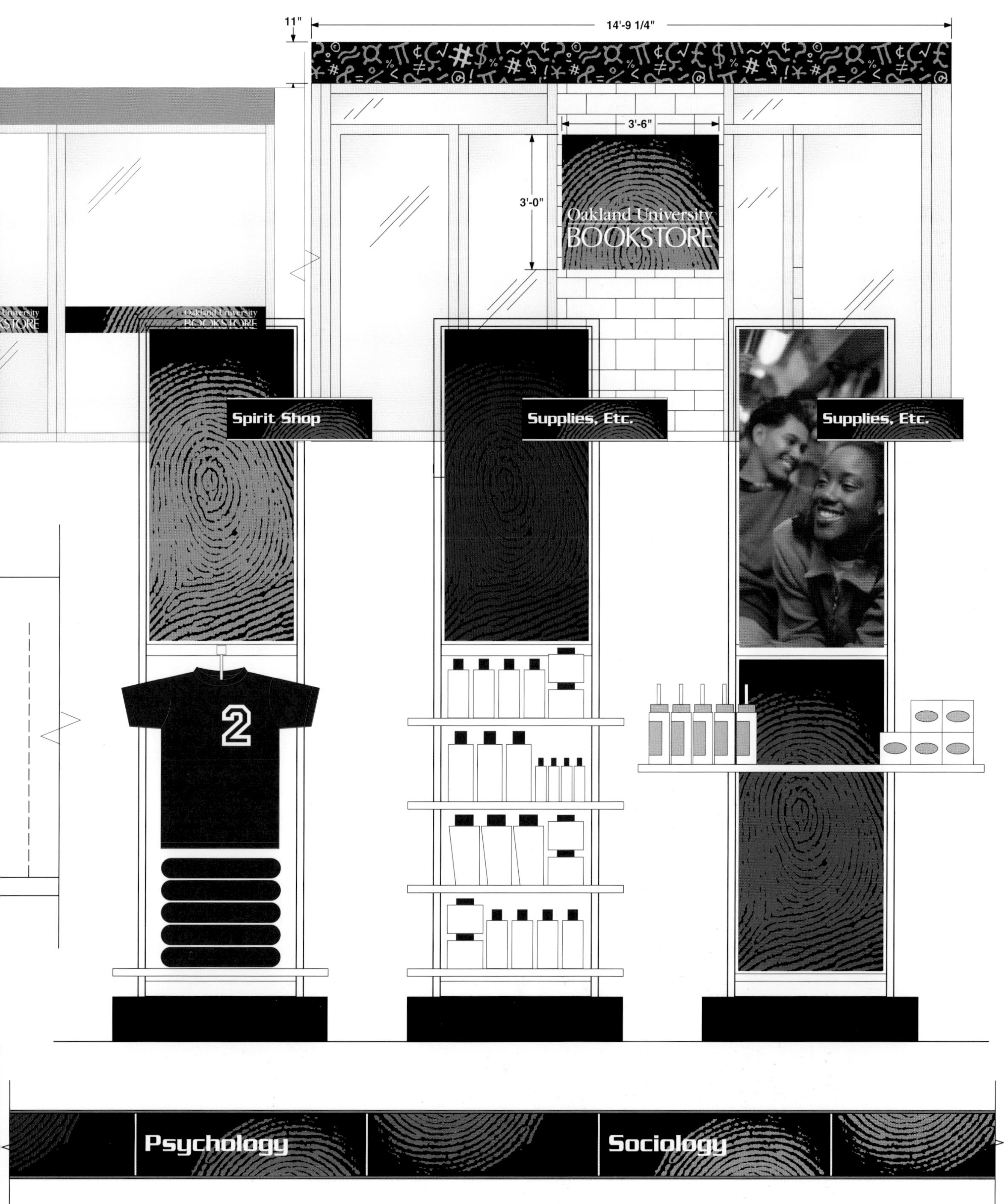
11"
14'-9 1/4"
3'-6"
3'-0"
Oakland University
BOOKSTORE
Spirit Shop
Supplies, Etc.
Supplies, Etc.
2
Psychology
Sociology

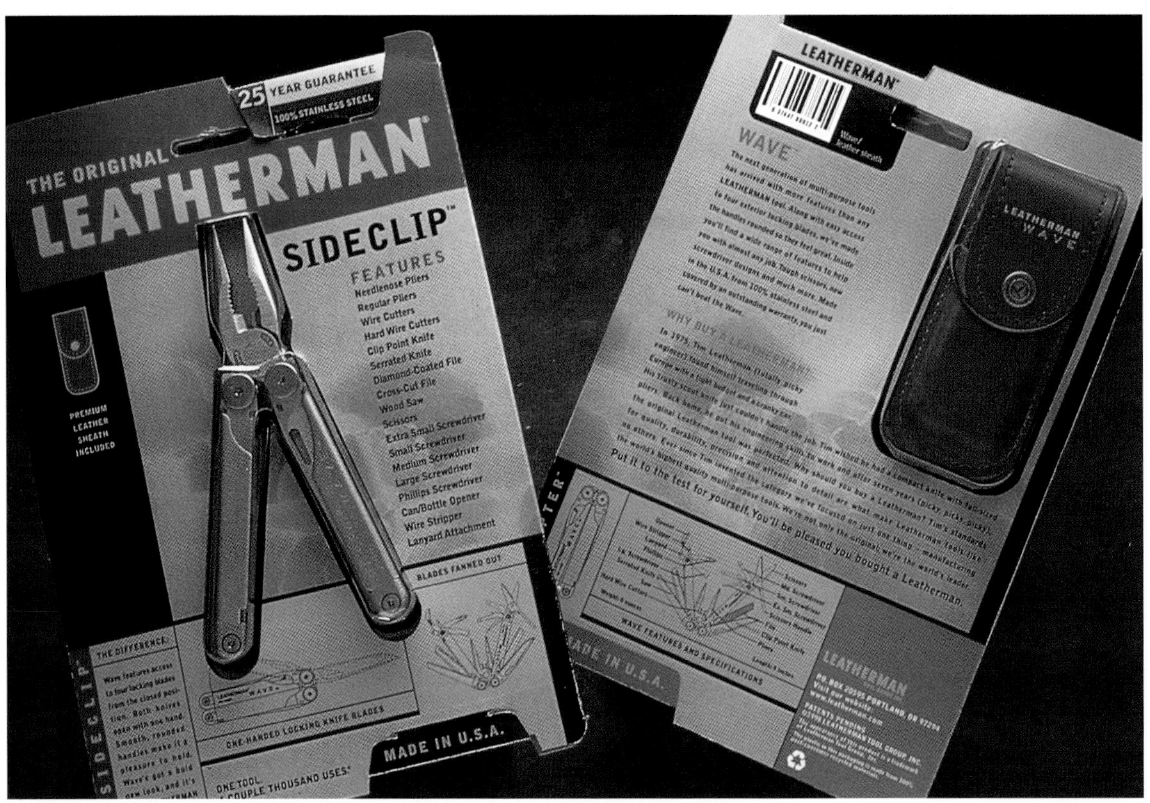

design firm
Hornall Anderson Design Works, Inc.
Seattle, Washington
designers
Jack Anderson, Lisa Cerveny, David Bates, Alan Florsheim
client
Leatherman Tool Group
(all-purpose tool manufacturer)

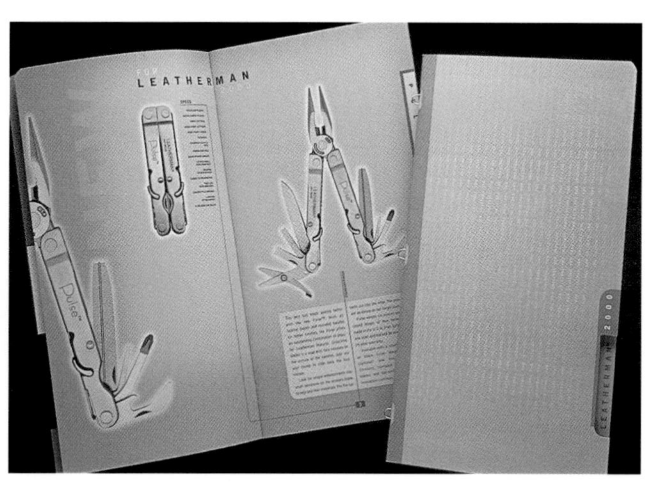
FOR
LEATHERMAN
LEATHERMAN 2000

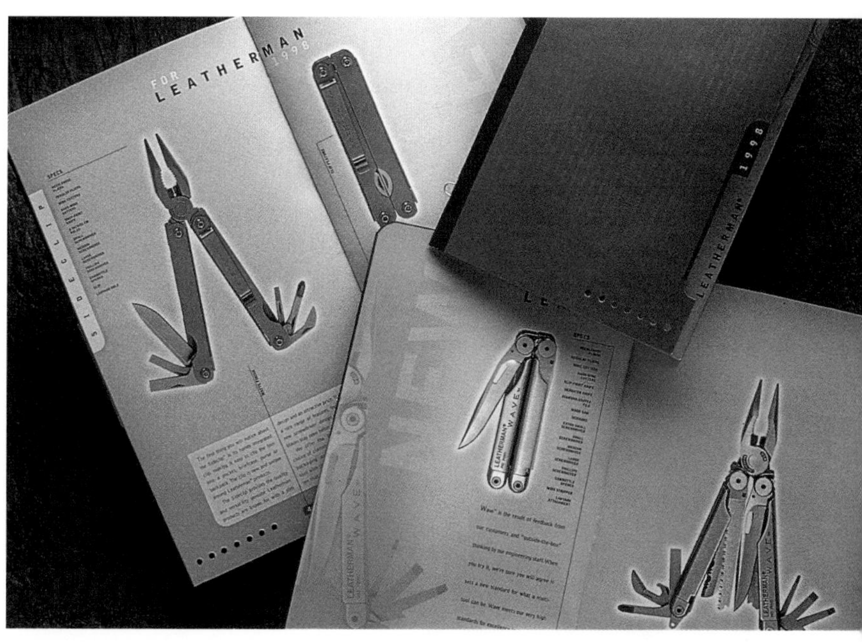
FOR
LEATHERMAN
1998
SPECS
SIDECLIP
LEATHERMAN 1998
WAVE

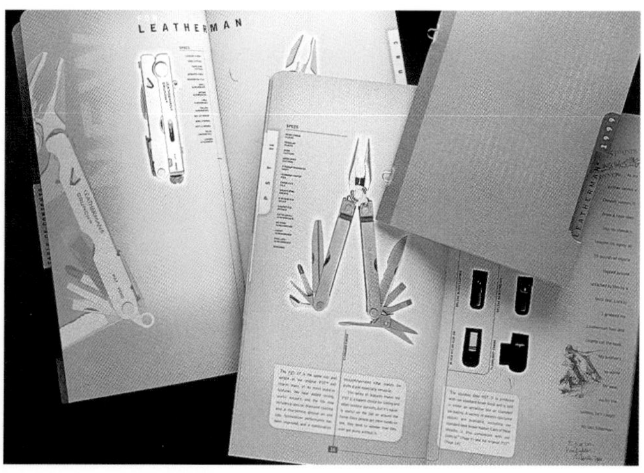
LEATHERMAN
SPECS
PST
LEATHERMAN 1999

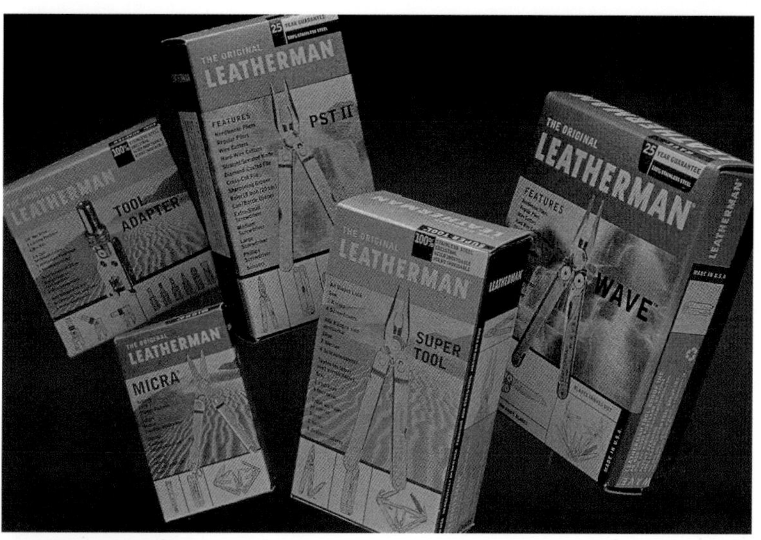
THE ORIGINAL
LEATHERMAN
TOOL ADAPTER
25 YEAR GUARANTEE
FEATURES
PST II
MICRA
SUPER TOOL
WAVE

25 YEAR GUARANTEE
100% STAINLESS STEEL
WARRANTY SERVICE
STEEL CHARACTERISTICS
MINI-TOOL SPECS
TOOL ADAPTER SPECS
PST SPECS
PST II SPECS
SIDECLIP SPECS
FLAIR SPECS
CRUNCH SPECS
WAVE SPECS
SUPER TOOL
SIDECLIP
LEATHERMAN

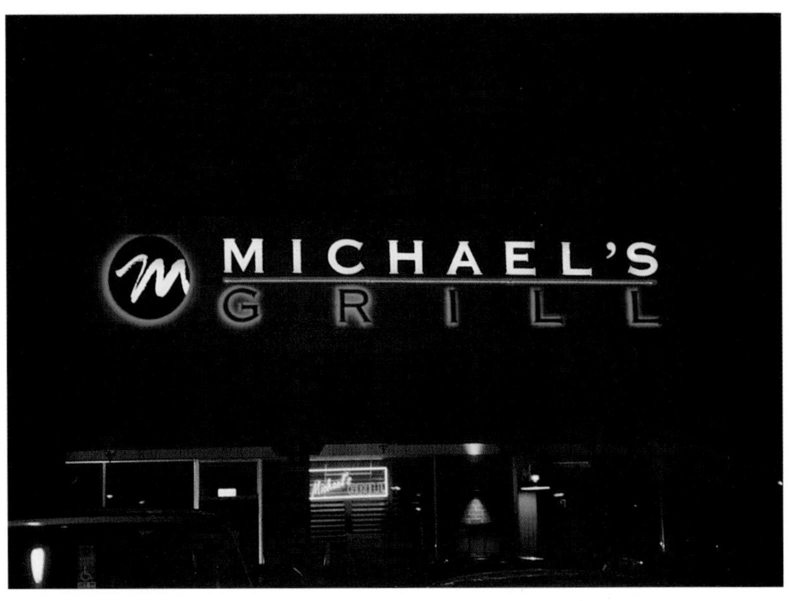

design firm
EAT Advertising & Design
Kansas City, Missouri
designers
Patrice Eilts-Jobe, DeAnne Dodd, Jeremy Shellhorn
client
Michael's Grill
(restaurant)

MICHAEL'S GRILL GREAT BUFFET LUNCH
ENJOY SOUP TO DESSERT,
AND STILL GET BACK TO WORK ON TIME.

Enough of the brown-bagging already.
Michael's Grill invites you to enjoy a more meaningful lunch break that's as fast as any fast food joint (although you'll be tempted to stay much longer). Our Great Buffet Lunch features Michael's famous pasta creations and fried catfish, as well as seasonal favorites, carved meats, homemade soups and plenty of fresh salads & fruit.

Plus, just in time for summer, we're offering Strawberry Shortcake to complete your buffet meal. Come on, take an hour and treat yourself to some delicious food, not to mention some great people ready to wait on your every need (kind of like you at work, but in reverse).

Michael's Grill Great Buffet Lunch.
It'll be the best hour of your work day.

BRING A FRIEND FOR LUNCH AND SAVE!

BUY ONE BUFFET LUNCH
GET THE SECOND FOR
50% OFF

MICHAEL'S
GRILL

THE NICE PLACE TO EAT
JUST DOWN THE STREET

7539 WORNALL IN WALDO
(816) 444-5445

NOT GOOD WITH ANY OTHER OFFERS OR HOLIDAYS. EXPIRES 10/31/00

MICHAEL'S
GRILL
7539 WORNALL
KANSAS CITY, MO 64114

BULK RATE
US POSTAGE
PAID
KANSAS CITY, MO
PERMIT #1396

YOUR SUMMER
HOT
SPOT

INTRODUCING THE NEW MICHAEL'S GRILL
WE'VE CHANGED EVERYTHING FOR
THE BETTER, INCLUDING OUR NAME.

Our location's been a fixture in Waldo for years, but now there's a new cozy little spot in its place. It's called, simply, Michael's Grill.

We've remodeled inside and out, and made some fresh improvements to the menu we know you're going to love. We now serve a wonderful lunch buffet, a fabulous Sunday brunch and a full menu from soups to sandwiches to entrees.

If you were a regular before—or if you've been meaning to stop in for lunch or dinner, we look forward to serving you a memorable meal at Michael's Grill. Try us soon, and see why our neighbors are calling us "the nice place to eat just down the street."

JOIN US FOR LUNCH OR DINNER AND RECEIVE
$10 OFF
YOUR MEAL
WHEN YOUR BILL TOTALS $25 OR MORE.

MICHAEL'S
GRILL

7539 WORNALL IN WALDO
(816)444-5445
OFFER GOOD MONDAY-THURSDAY
OFFER EXPIRES 1/27/2000

design firm
Tilka Design
Minneapolis, Minnesota
designers
Jane Tilka, Mark Mularz
client
Setter Leach & Lindstrom

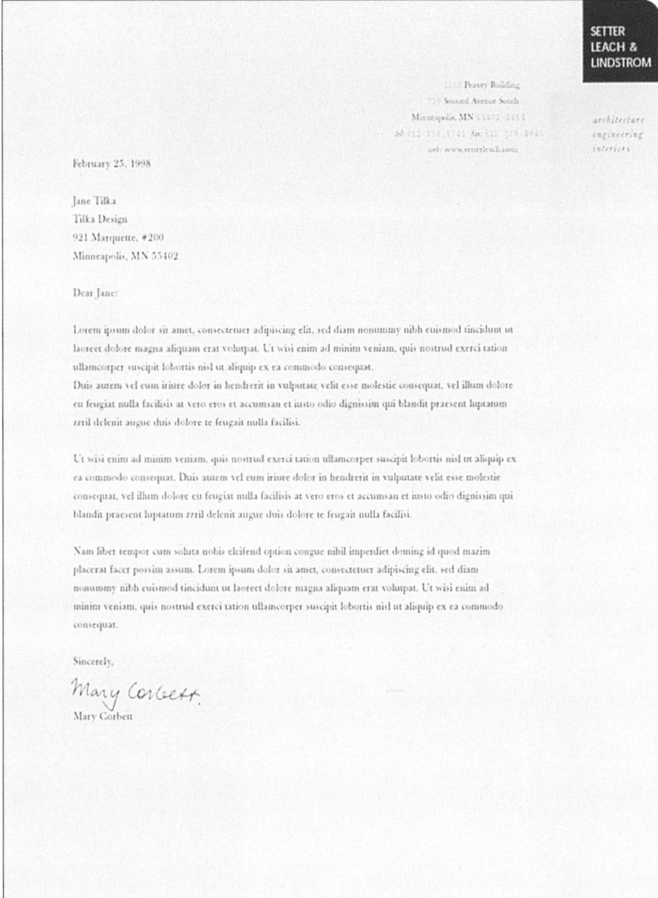

February 25, 1998

Jane Tilka
Tilka Design
921 Marquette, #200
Minneapolis, MN 55402

Dear Jane:

Lorem ipsum dolor sit amet, consectetuer adipiscing elit, sed diam nonummy nibh euismod tincidunt ut laoreet dolore magna aliquam erat volutpat. Ut wisi enim ad minim veniam, quis nostrud exerci tation ullamcorper suscipit lobortis nisl ut aliquip ex ea commodo consequat.
Duis autem vel eum iriure dolor in hendrerit in vulputate velit esse molestie consequat, vel illum dolore eu feugiat nulla facilisis at vero eros et accumsan et iusto odio dignissim qui blandit praesent luptatum zzril delenit augue duis dolore te feugait nulla facilisi.

Ut wisi enim ad minim veniam, quis nostrud exerci tation ullamcorper suscipit lobortis nisl ut aliquip ex ea commodo consequat. Duis autem vel eum iriure dolor in hendrerit in vulputate velit esse molestie consequat, vel illum dolore eu feugiat nulla facilisis at vero eros et accumsan et iusto odio dignissim qui blandit praesent luptatum zzril delenit augue duis dolore te feugait nulla facilisi.

Nam liber tempor cum soluta nobis eleifend option congue nihil imperdiet doming id quod mazim placerat facer possim assum. Lorem ipsum dolor sit amet, consectetuer adipiscing elit, sed diam nonummy nibh euismod tincidunt ut laoreet dolore magna aliquam erat volutpat. Ut wisi enim ad minim veniam, quis nostrud exerci tation ullamcorper suscipit lobortis nisl ut aliquip ex ea commodo consequat.

Sincerely,

Mary Corbett

Mary Corbett

design firm
Tim Girvin Design, Inc.
Seattle, Washington
designers
Laurie Vette, Jeff Haack
client
Stockpot Soups

design firm
Lipson Alport Glass & Assoc.
Northbrook, Illinois
art director
Tracy Bacilek
creative director
Sam Ciulla
designers
Lori Cerwin, Jon Shapiro
client
The Coca-Cola Company
(beverages/soft drinks)

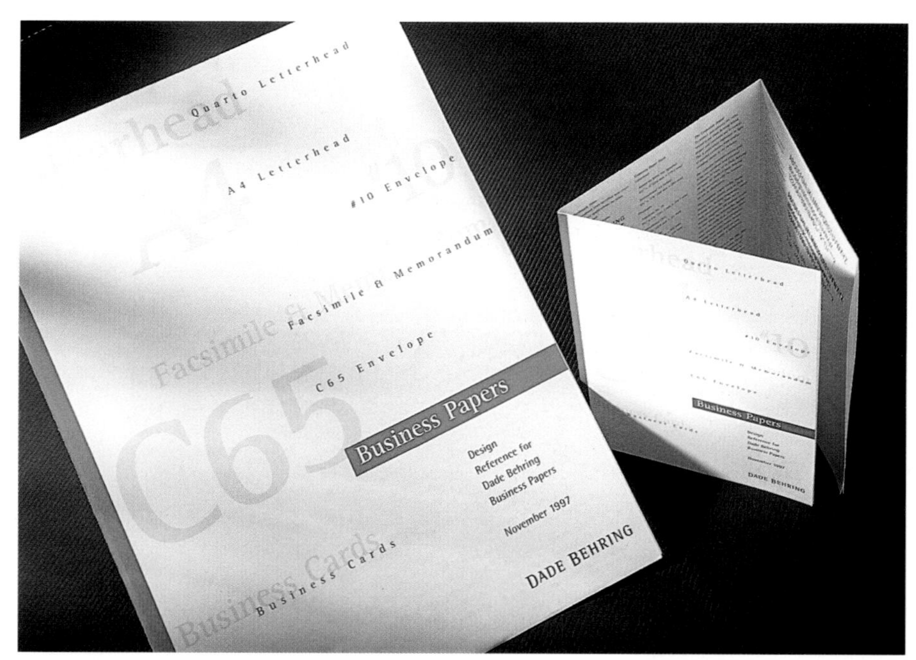

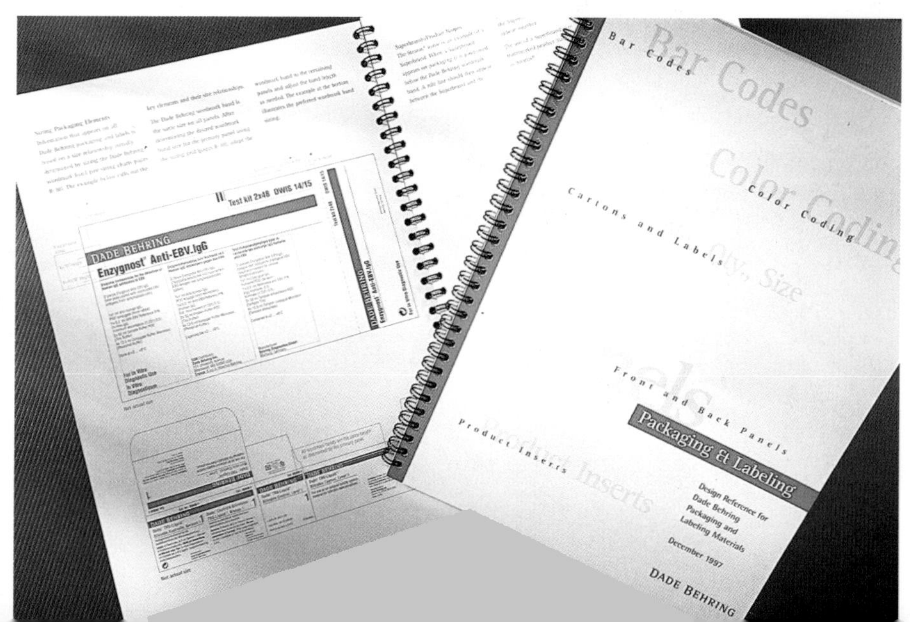

design firm
Lipson Alport Glass & Assoc.
Northbrook, Illinois
designers
Katherine Holaereid, Tracy Bacilek
client
Dade Behring
(medical equipment)

BAPTIST
HEALTH CARE

design firm
BrandEquity International
Newton, Massachusetts
designers
Anne McCuen, Todd Moxcey
client
Baptist Health Care

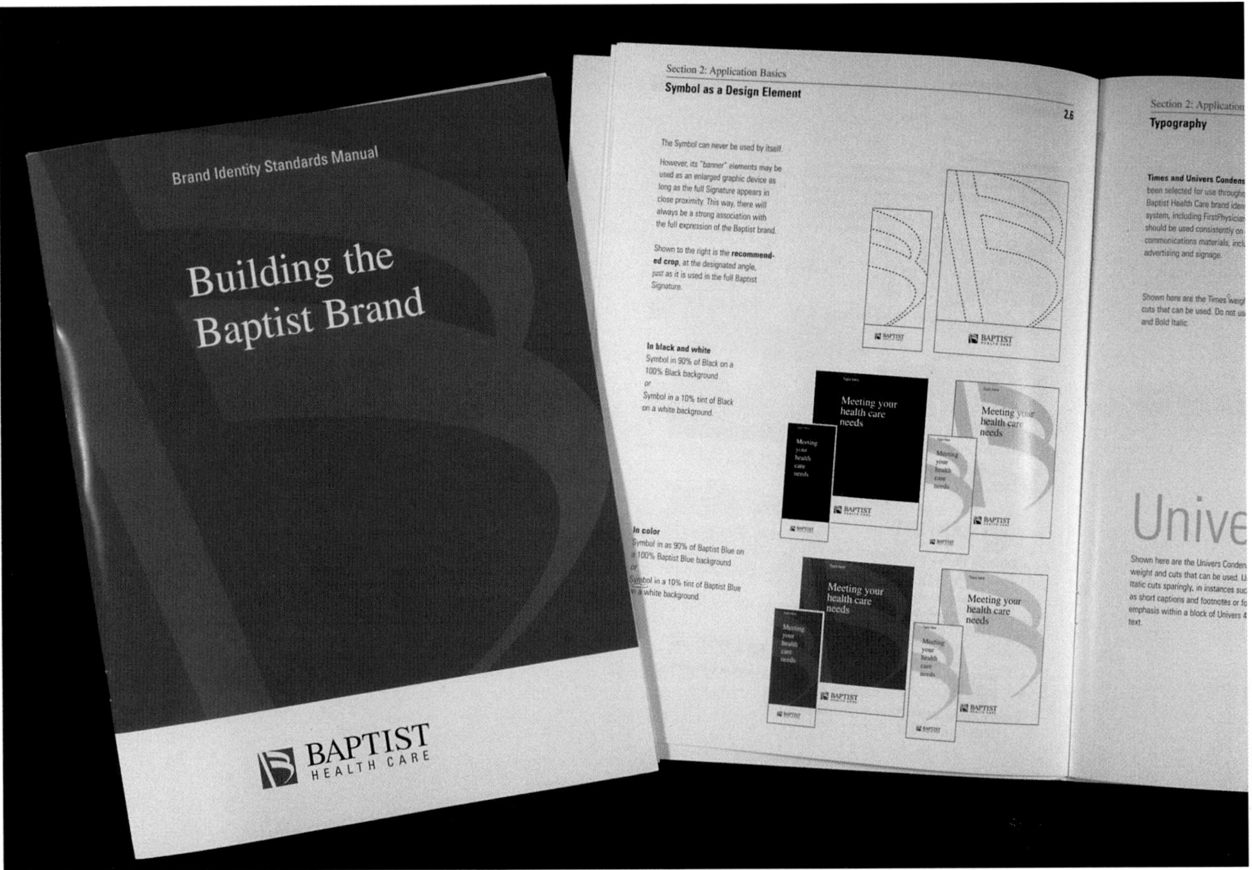

design firm
Herip Associates
Peninsula, Ohio
designers
Walter Herip, John Menter
client
The Cleveland Indians

design firm
Sayles Graphic Design
Des Moines, Iowa
designer
John Sayles
client
1998 Iowa State Fair
(state fair)

iowa state fair
august
13 ★ 23
1998
Way Too much FUN!
Moines Register
The Register Brings Even More Fun to Fair
Way Too much FUN!

iowa state fair
Way Too much FUN!
aug. 13 - 23

iowa state fair
Way Too much FUN!

UNIVERSAL
Way Too much FUN!
iowa state fair
august
13 ★ 23

Way Too much FUN!
iowa state fair
august
13 - 23
1998

iowa state fair
august
13 ★ 23
1998
Way Too much FUN!

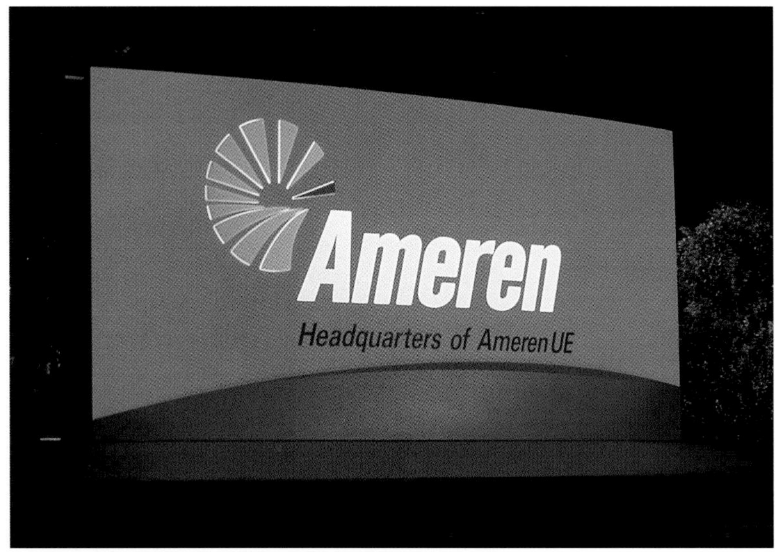

design firm
Kiku Obata + Company
St. Louis, Missouri
designers
Scott Gericke, Jim Datema, Carole Jerome, Eleanor Safe, Tim Wheeler, Chris Mueller, Todd Mayberry
client
Ameren Corporation

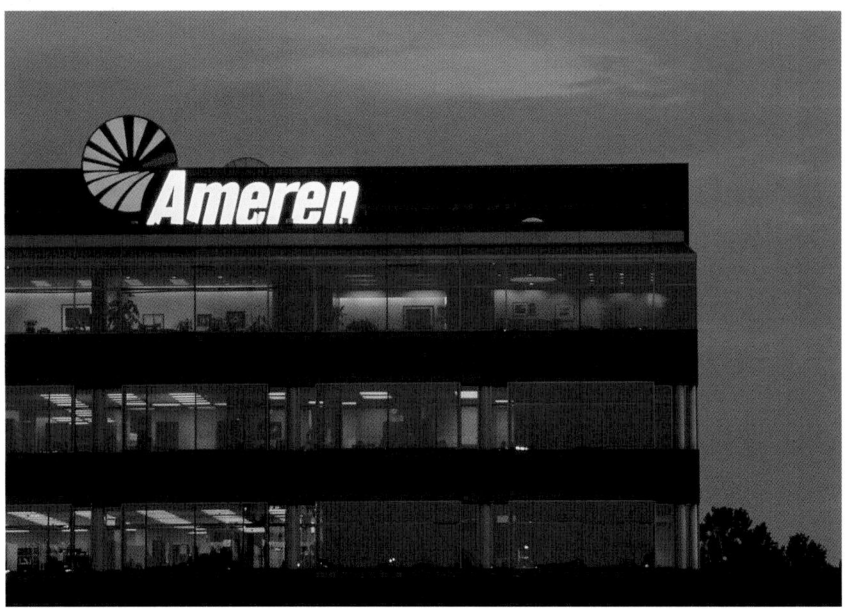

SHURGARD®

design firm
Tim Girvin Design, Inc.
Seattle, Washington
designers
Aki Morino, Brian Boram
client
Shurgard

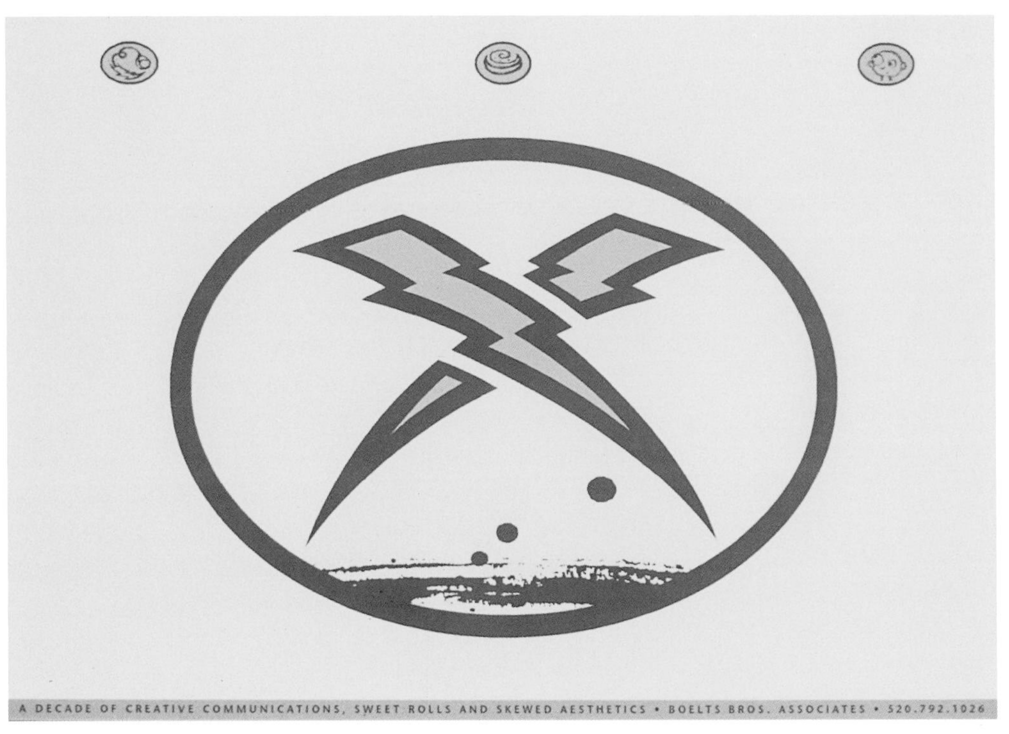

design firm
Boelts Bros Associates
Tucson, Arizona
designers
E. Boelts, J. Boelts, K. Stratford, D. Perry, E. Taylor, N. Daly, S. Norris, W. Andrews
client
Boelts Bros Associates: 10th Anniversary ID

edible aRT 97

design firm
Flanders + Associates
Boston, Massachusetts
project principal
MB Flanders
designer
Chris DiMarzo
client
The Art Institute of Boston, Edible Art 1997

SINCE 1921
Lascco
BRAND

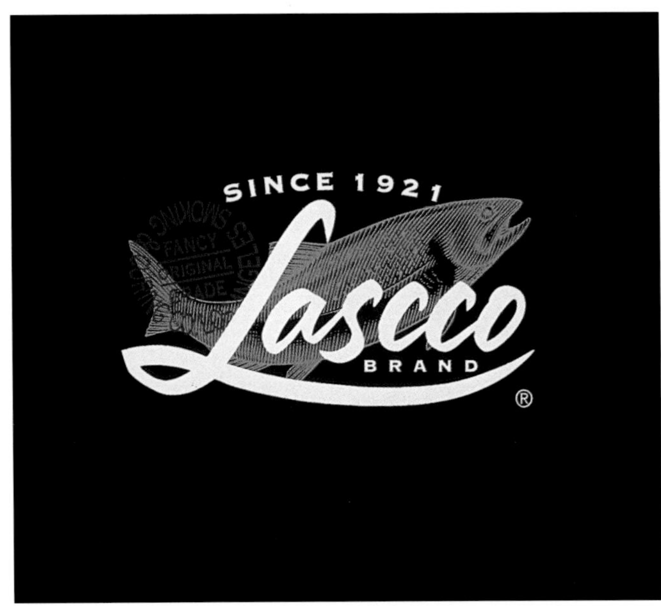

design firm
Mark Oliver, Inc.
Santa Barbara, California
designers
Mark Oliver, Patty Devlin-Driskel
calligrapher
Holly Dickens
client
Lascco
(seafood manufacturer)

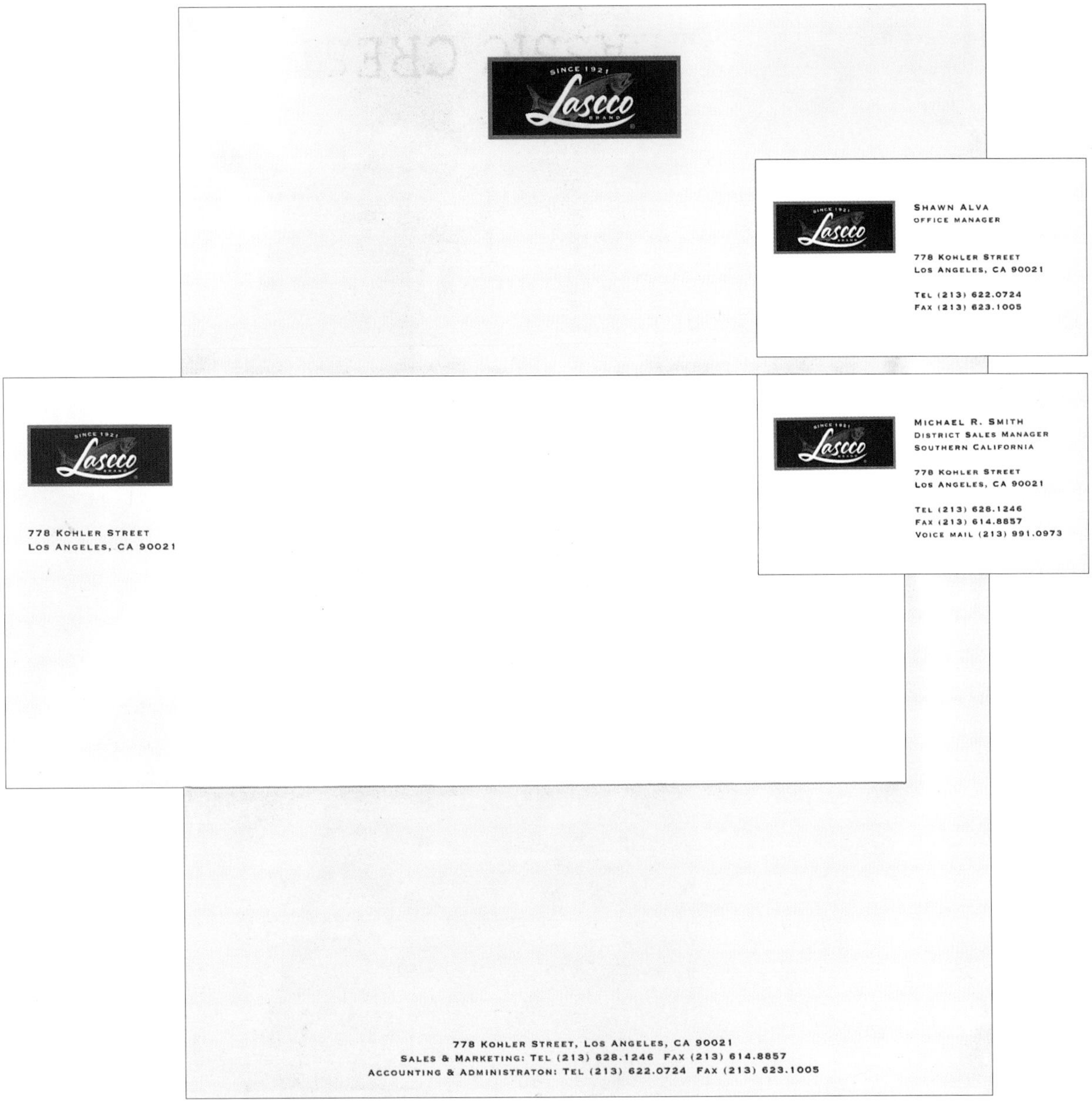

Shawn Alva
Office Manager
778 Kohler Street
Los Angeles, CA 90021
Tel (213) 622.0724
Fax (213) 623.1005
Michael R. Smith
District Sales Manager
Southern California
778 Kohler Street
Los Angeles, CA 90021
Tel (213) 628.1246
Fax (213) 614.8857
Voice Mail (213) 991.0973
778 Kohler Street
Los Angeles, CA 90021
778 Kohler Street, Los Angeles, CA 90021
Sales & Marketing: Tel (213) 628.1246 Fax (213) 614.8857
Accounting & Administraton: Tel (213) 622.0724 Fax (213) 623.1005

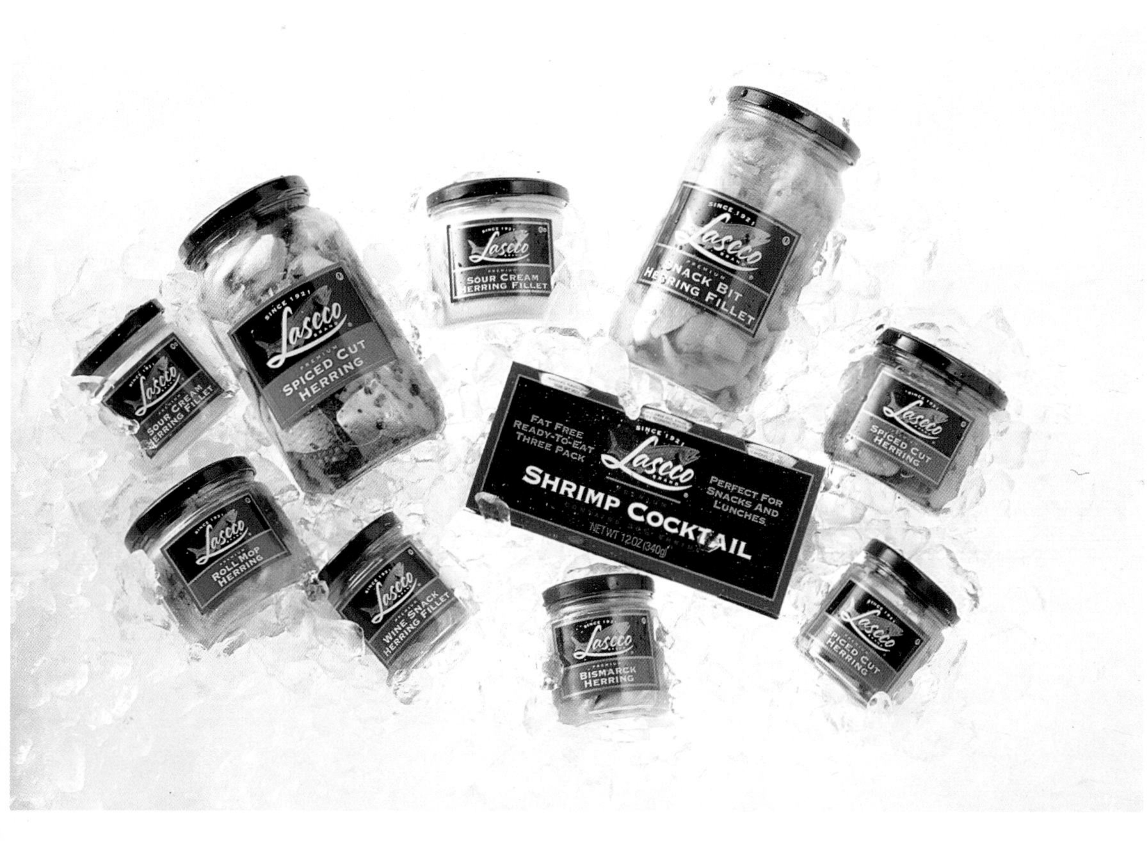

Since 1921
Lascco
Sour Cream Herring Fillet
Spiced Cut Herring
Snack Bit Herring Fillet
Fat Free Ready-To-Eat Three Pack
Shrimp Cocktail
Perfect For Snacks And Lunches.
Net Wt 12 Oz (340g)
Roll Mop Herring
Wine Snack Herring Fillet
Bismarck Herring

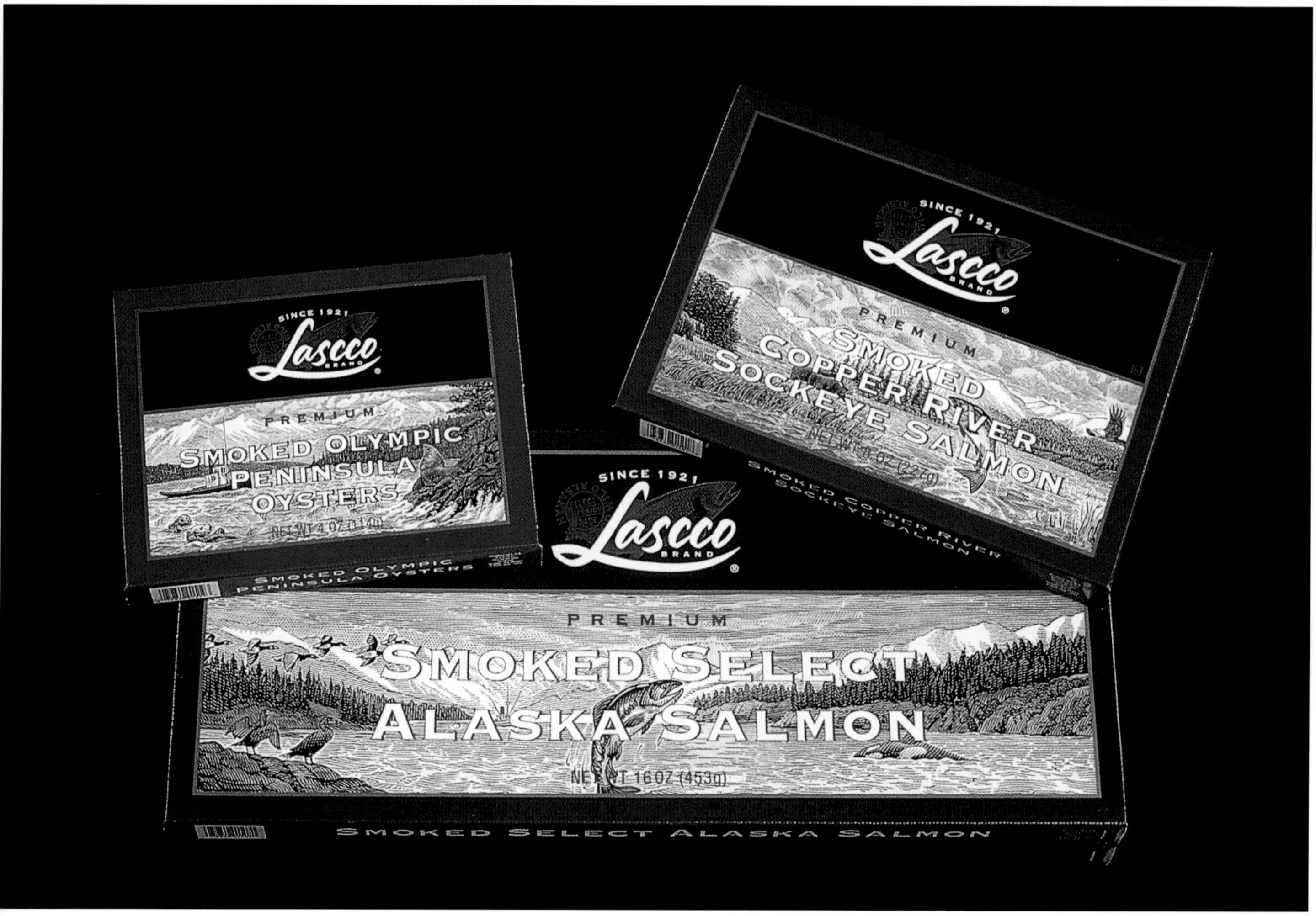

Since 1921
Lascco
Brand
Premium
Smoked Copper River Sockeye Salmon
Premium
Smoked Olympic Peninsula Oysters
Smoked Olympic Peninsula Oysters
Smoked Copper River Sockeye Salmon
Premium
Smoked Select Alaska Salmon
Net Wt 16 Oz (453g)
Smoked Select Alaska Salmon

design firm
Larsen Design Office, Inc.
Minneapolis, Minnesota
client
Novellus Systems, Inc.

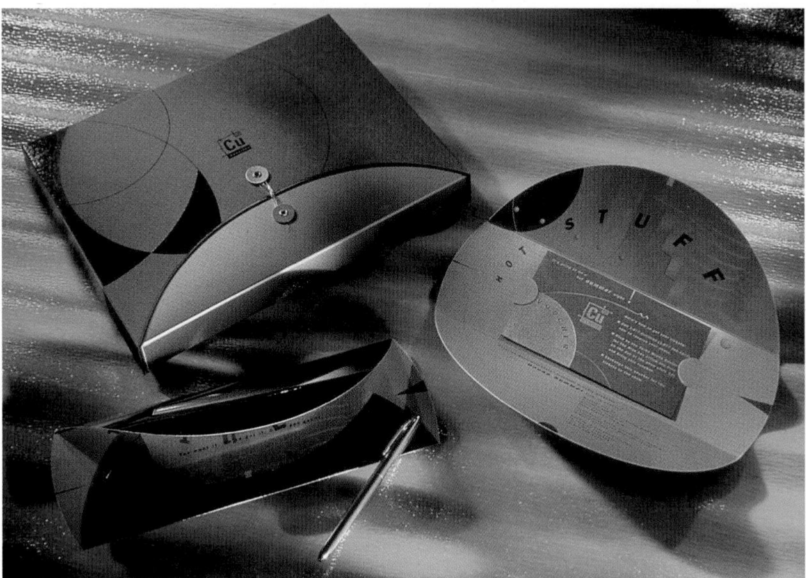

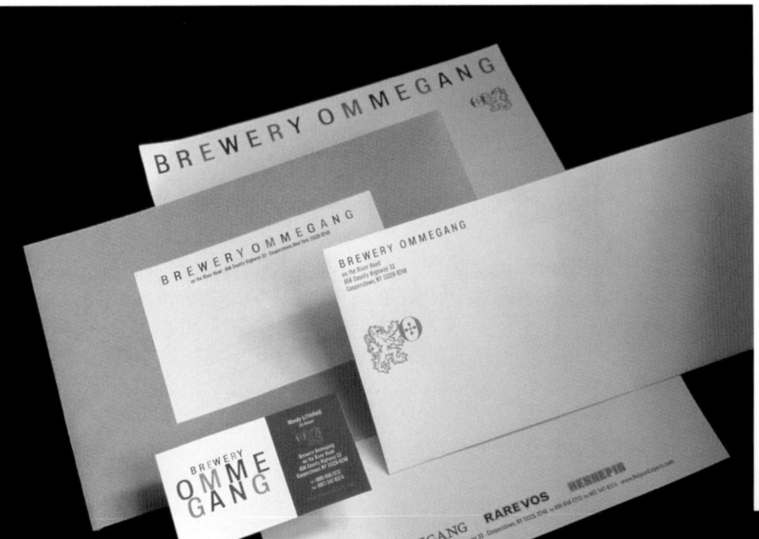

BREWERY
OMME
GANG

design firm
Doyle Partners
New York, New York
designers
Tom Kwepfel, Elizabeth Lee
client
Ommegang Brewery

design firm
Hornall Anderson Design Works, Inc.
Seattle, Washington
designers
Jack Anderson, Lisa Cerveny,
Bruce Branson-Meyer, Alan Florsheim
client
Custom Building Products

design firm
Hornall Anderson Design Works, Inc.
Seattle, Washington
designers
Jack Anderson, Debra Hampton,
Heidi Favour, Jana Wilson,
Nicole Bloss, Larry Anderson
client
Novell, Inc.

design firm
Evenson Design Group
Culver City, California
creative director
Stan Evenson
designer
Ken Loh
client
New England Patriots
(NFL football team)

11

design firm
David Lemley Design
Seattle, Washington
designers
David Lemley, Matt Peloza
client
One Reel

design firm
RKS Design, Inc.
Thousand Oaks, California
client
RKS Design, Inc.

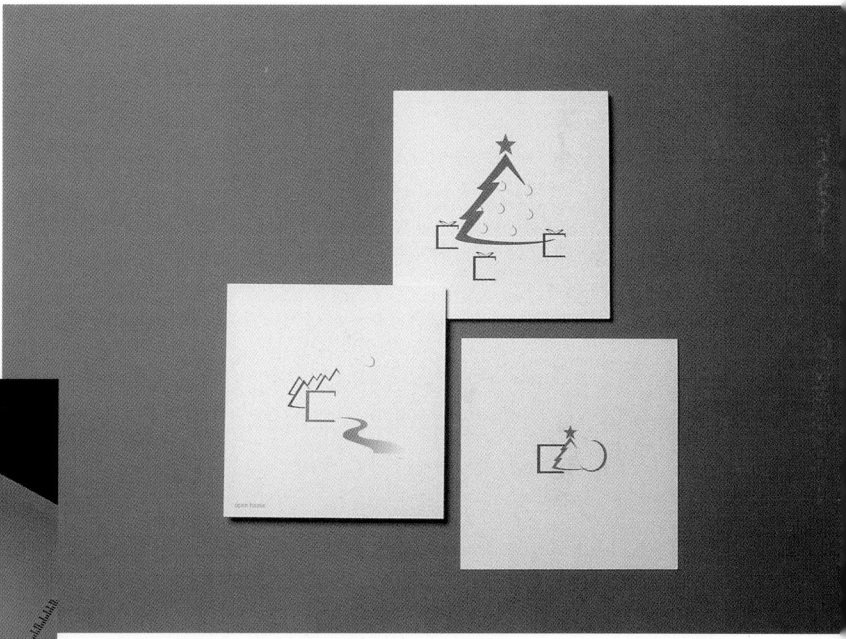

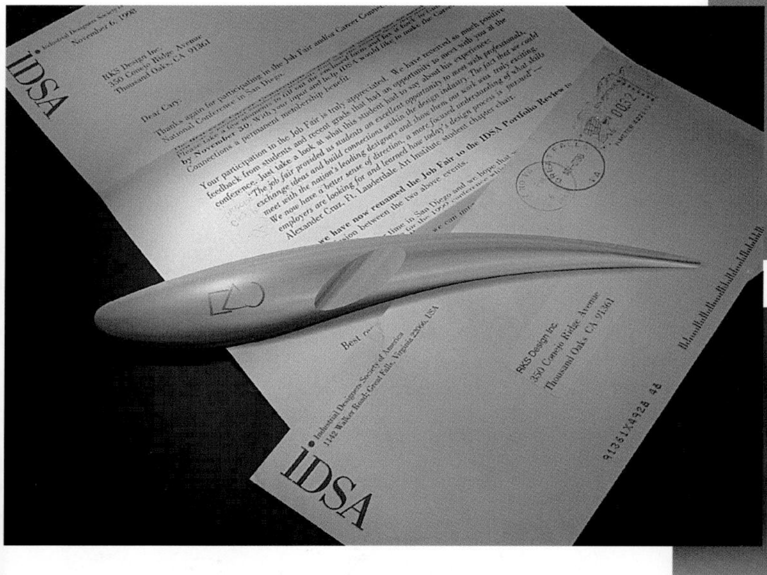

Osool أصول

A Finance Company شركة تمويل

design firm
WalkerGroup/CNI
New York, New York
interior designer
Julio Braga
graphic designer
Michael Ross
client
Mashreq Bank

dream ride

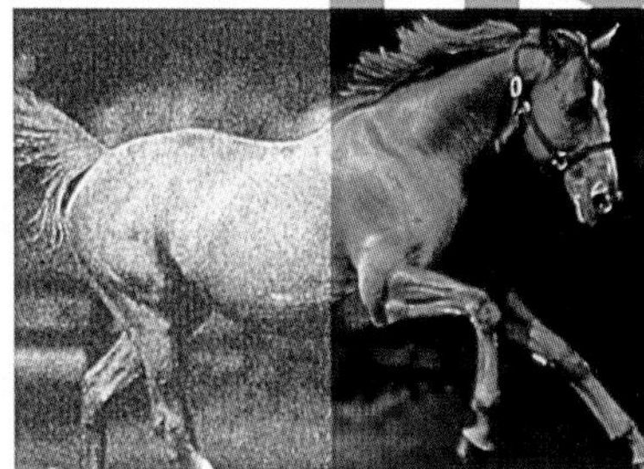

Abdul Rahim has loved horses ever since he was a child. For as long as Abdul can remember, he has always dreamed of owning a race horse. His passion for equestrian sports grew as he did until his childhood hobby became a career. So when the opportunity came to purchase a future champion, Abdul shared his dream with an Osool Relationship Manager. Today Abdul owns one of the finest race horses in the U.A.E.
At Osool, we make the dreams of our customers like Abdul, come true. We offer flexible and convenient payment plans that meet your needs and match your lifestyle.
So whether you're dreaming of owning a horse, a Honda or a house, Osool can make your dream come true.
dream loan

Providing
the means
... to reach your dreams.

Osool أصول
شركة تمويل

design firm
Mires Design
San Diego, California
art director
John Ball
designers
John Ball, Miguel Perez
client
Verde Communications

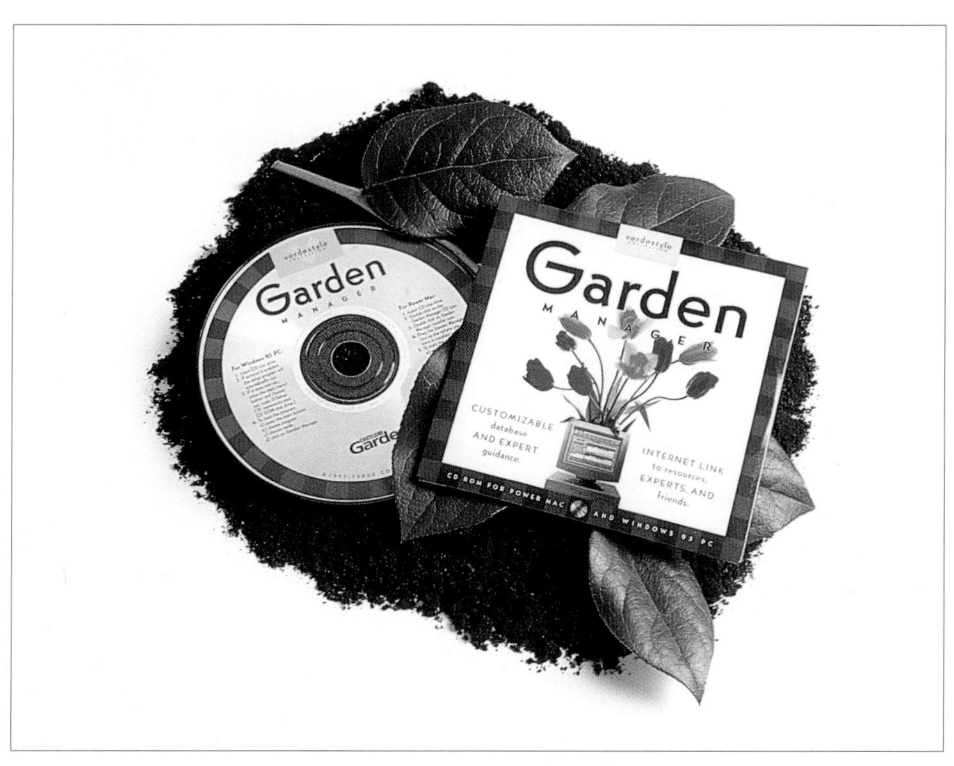

GUESS?

design firm
Desgrippes Gobé & Associates
New York, New York
design director
Lori Yi
client
Guess? Inc.

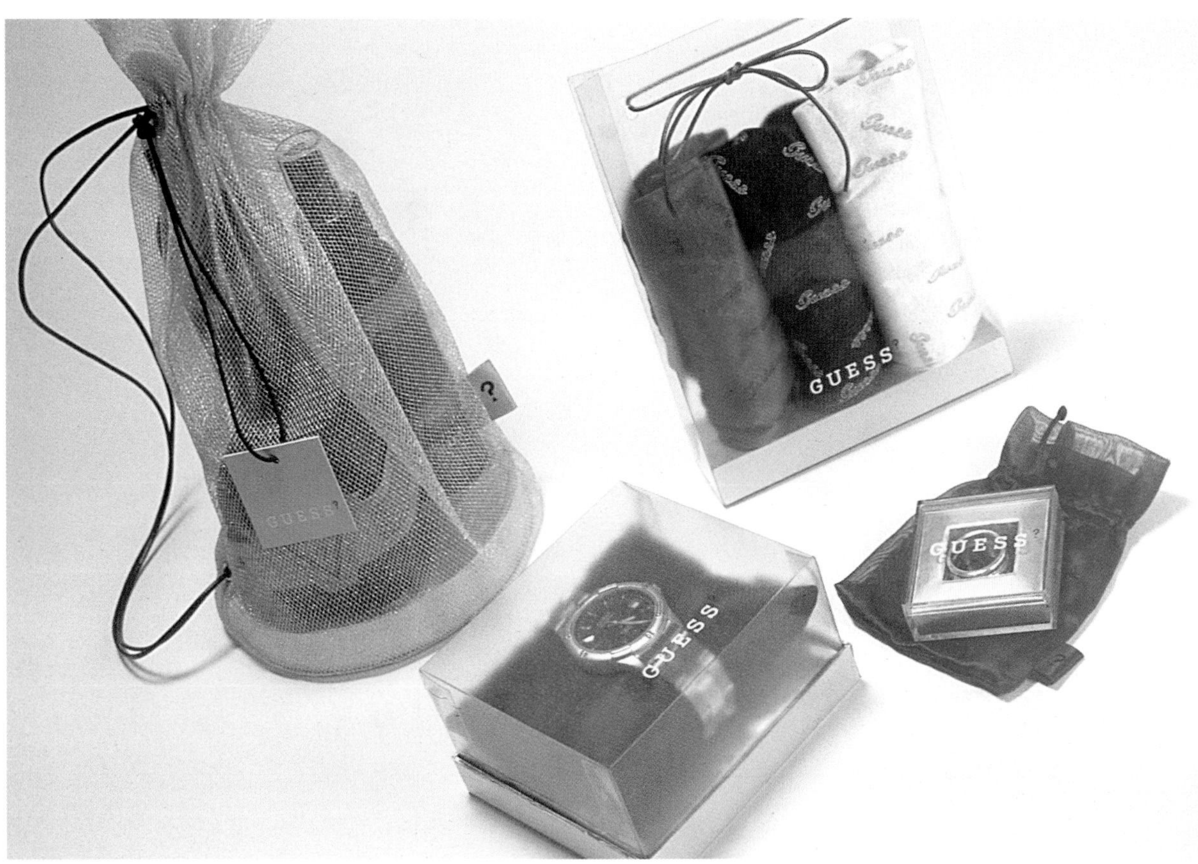

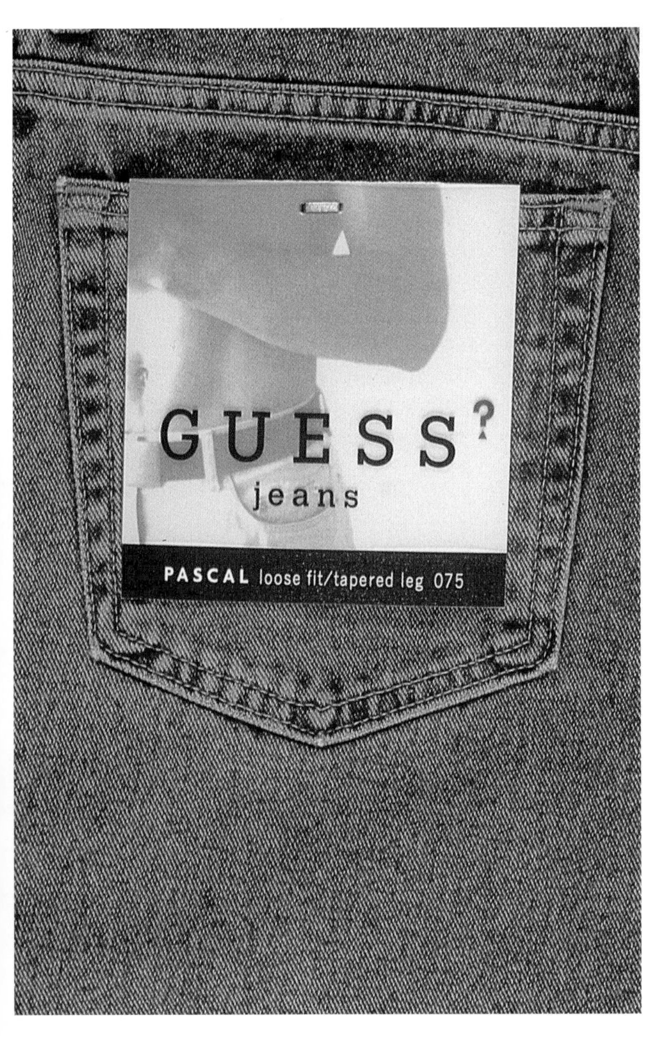
GUESS?
jeans
PASCAL loose fit/tapered leg 075

GUESS?
accessories

rinse denim
GUESS?
jeans

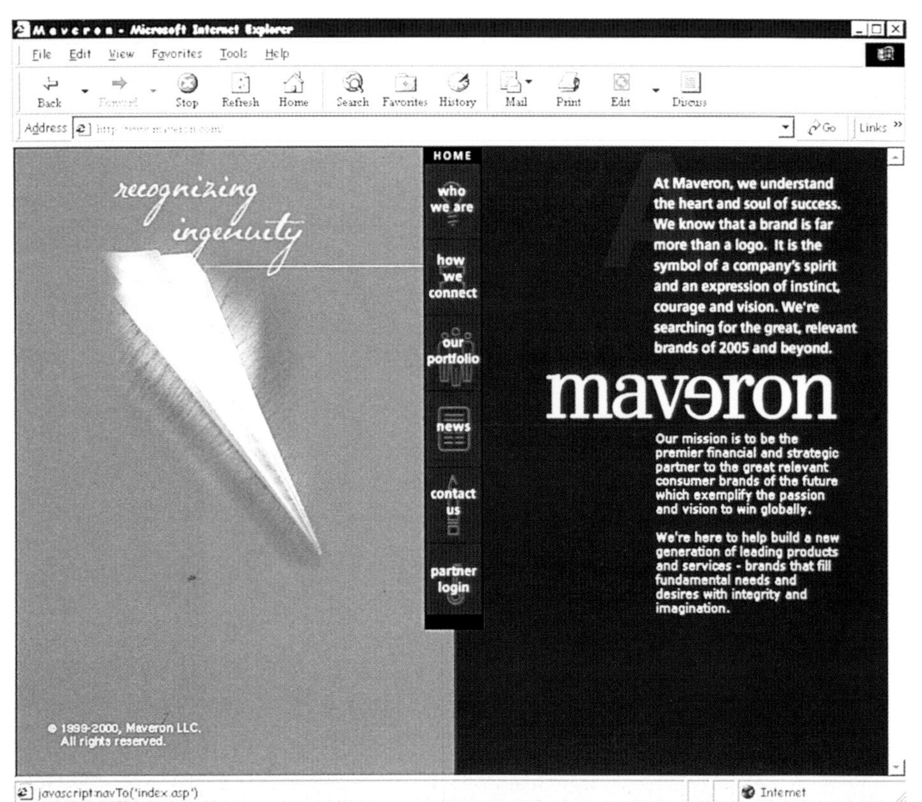
Maveron - Microsoft Internet Explorer
File Edit View Favorites Tools Help
Back Forward Stop Refresh Home Search Favorites History Mail Print Edit Discuss
Address
Go Links
recognizing ingenuity
HOME
who we are
how we connect
our portfolio
news
contact us
partner login
At Maveron, we understand the heart and soul of success. We know that a brand is far more than a logo. It is the symbol of a company's spirit and an expression of instinct, courage and vision. We're searching for the great, relevant brands of 2005 and beyond.
maveron
Our mission is to be the premier financial and strategic partner to the great relevant consumer brands of the future which exemplify the passion and vision to win globally.
We're here to help build a new generation of leading products and services - brands that fill fundamental needs and desires with integrity and imagination.
© 1999-2000, Maveron LLC. All rights reserved.
javascript:navTo('index.asp')
Internet

design firm
Hornall Anderson Design Works, Inc.
Seattle, Washington
designers
Jack Anderson, Margaret Long, John Anicker, Jana Nishi, Merran Kubalak, James Moriarity
client
Maveron
(venture capital company)

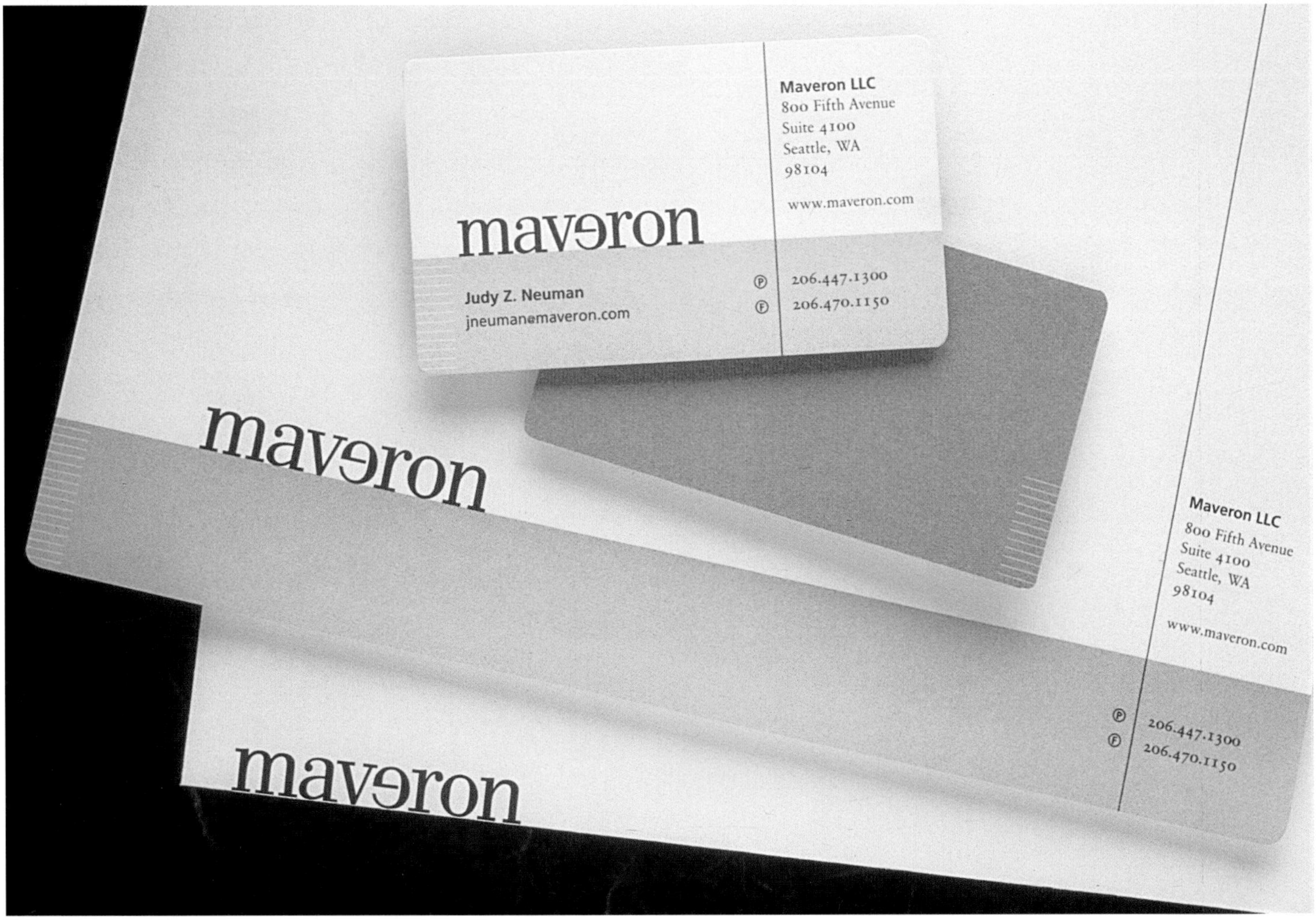

design firm
Hornall Anderson Design Works, Inc.
Seattle, Washington
designers
John Hornall, Katha Dalton,
Nicole Bloss, Julie Keenan
client
Foster Pepper Shefelman

Welcome to MuseumExpo99

Cleveland Convention Center Exhibit Hall A

- Discover unique products and services
- Network with company representatives and museum colleagues
- Meet new friends
- Learn how your colleagues deal with important workplace issues
- Find out more about AAM programs

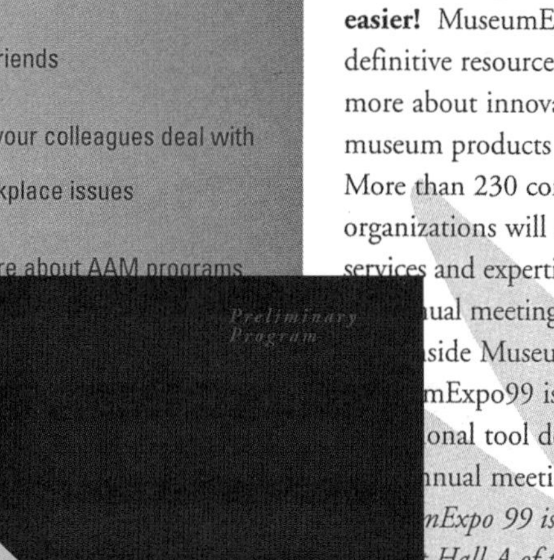

Explore MuseumExpo99 and find the latest information, AAM services, professional trends, and innovative products and services designed to make your job easier! MuseumExpo99 is the definitive resource to help you learn more about innovative and beneficial museum products and services. More than 230 companies and affiliate organizations will showcase their services and expertise. While you're at ...ual meeting, spend some quality ...side MuseumExpo99. After all, ...mExpo99 is an important ...onal tool designed to enhance ...nnual meeting experience. *...nExpo 99 is located in ... Hall A of the Clevelend ...tion Center.*

...UMEXPO99 HOURS

...emember that MuseumExpo99 ...n Wednesday at 2:30 p.m.

...y, April 26

...m. - 5:30 p.m.
...Hall Hours

...m. - 1:30 p.m.
...Reception
...nd Tailgate Party—enjoy a ...of ethnic foods and entertainment

Tuesday, April 27

9:00 a.m. - 5:30 p.m.
Exhibit Hall Hours

9:00 a.m. – 10:45 a.m.
Morning Coffee Break
Sponsored by the American Association of Museums

3:00 - 3:30 p.m.
Ice Cream Break
Sponsored by AAM Affinity Partners. Located at the AAM Resource Center between rows 600 and 700.

Wednesday, April 28

9:00 a.m. – 2:30 p.m.
Exhibit Hall Hours

9:00 a.m. – 10:45 a.m.
Morning Coffee Break
Sponsored by the American Association of Museums

1:30 - 2:30 p.m.
Closing Reception

A variety of foods will be available for purchase during MuseumExpo99 show hours at concession areas located in the front and rear of the exhibit hall.

Grab a cup of coffee from the Gourmet Coffee Cart located near the AAM Resource Center, between aisles 600 and 700.

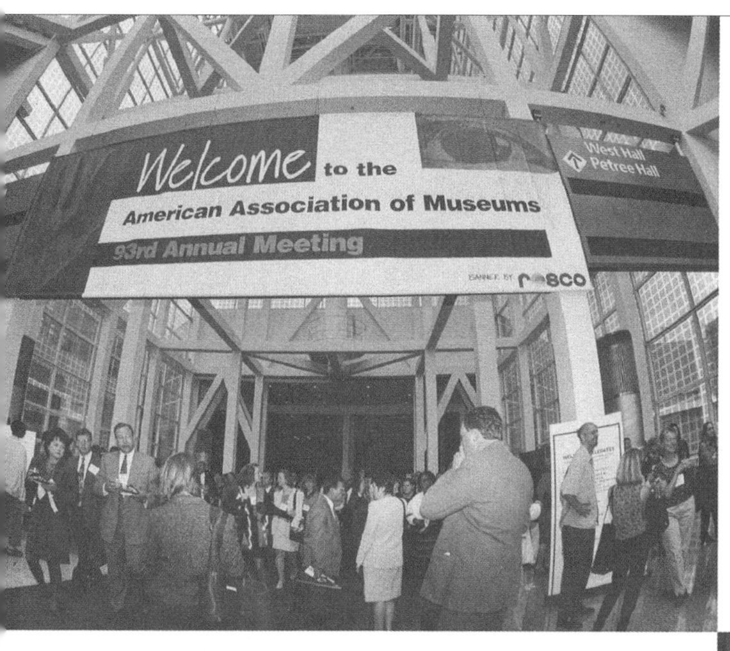

vey Says. . . . Survey Works, ill be randomly surveying annual ng attendees. The electronic will only take a few minutes to ete. By completing the survey, ill receive a $1 off coupon nable at any concession facility d in the convention center.

over 100,000 square feet of space, MuseumExpo will also :

GENERAL

benefits, or pick up the latest copy of *Museum News* or *Aviso*. Visit AAM's Web site and discover the new Museum Marketplace On-line directory.

A special area in the AAM Resource Center invites you to learn more about AIDS in the workplace issues and pick up informative brochures from the Center for Disease Control.

AAM BOOKSTORE FOR MUSEUM PROFESSIONALS

Convention Center–Exhibit Hall A

) and 700

ource Center, ications on field. ilable for legal issues, ting, public museum rams and ff facilities y. Stop in ed by your

kstore
rce Center
.m. - 5:30 p.m.
.m. - 5:30 p.m.
.m. - 2:30 p.m.

Exhibitor's Prospectus

MuseumExpo99

AMERICAN ASSOCIATION OF MUSEUMS
94TH ANNUAL MEETING
AND MUSEUMEXPO99

April 25-29, 1999
Cleveland Convention Center
Cleveland, Ohio

Use the Exhibitor Guide on pages 104-131 to find the products and services you need!

Visit the AAM Resource Center and see Museum Marketplace On-line,™ the new online buyers guide

13

design firm
Dever Designs
Laurel, Maryland
designers
Jeffrey L. Dever, Amy W. Sucherman
client
American Association of Museums
(trade association)

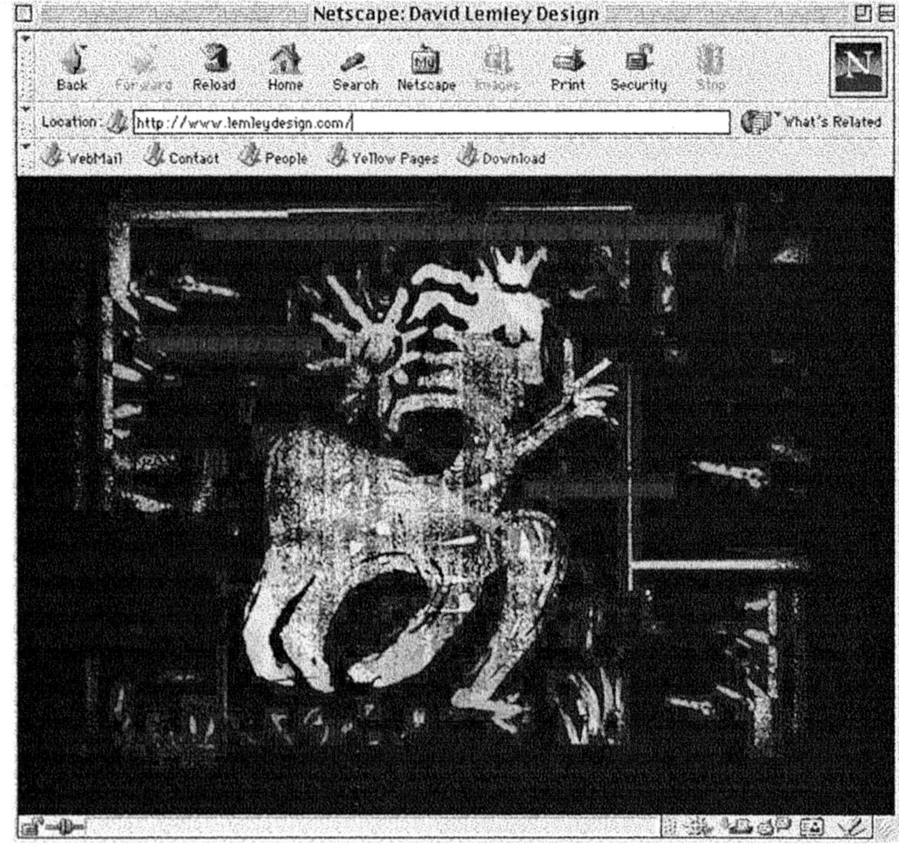

design firm
David Lemley Design
Seattle, Washington
designers
David Lemley, Matt Peloza
client
David Lemley Design

design firm
EAT Advertising & Design, Inc.
Kansas City, Missouri
designers
Patrice Eilts-Jobe, DeAnne Kelly
client
PB&J Restaurants/Yahooz
(comtemporary cowboy cuisine)

design firm
Sayles Graphic Design
Des Moines, Iowa
designer
John Sayles
client
Des Moines "Firstar Nitefall On The River" (jazz festival)

firstar
nitefall
on the
river

anvil
firstar
nitefall
firstar
nitefall
on the
river

firstar
nitefall
on the
river
firstar
nitefall

Firstar
NITE
FALL
on the
river

UNIVERSAL
firstar
nitefall
on the river
STARTS
JUNE 12
CALL 246-5600 x 6151

Firstar
Nitefall
on the river

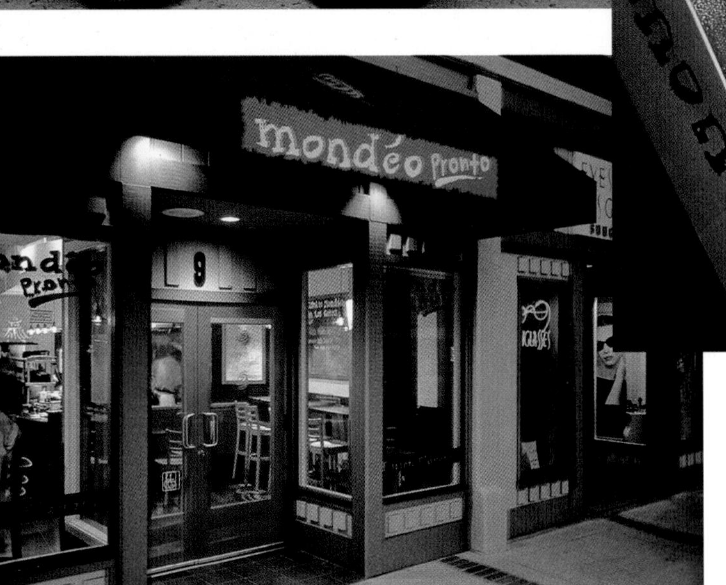

design firm
Hornall Anderson Design Works, Inc.
Seattle, Washington
designers
Jack Anderson, David Bates,
Sonja Max
client
CW Gourmet/Mondeo

design firm
Hornall Anderson Design Works, Inc.
Seattle, Washington
designers
Jack Anderson, David Bates,
Lisa Cerveny, Jana Wilson
client
Best Cellars

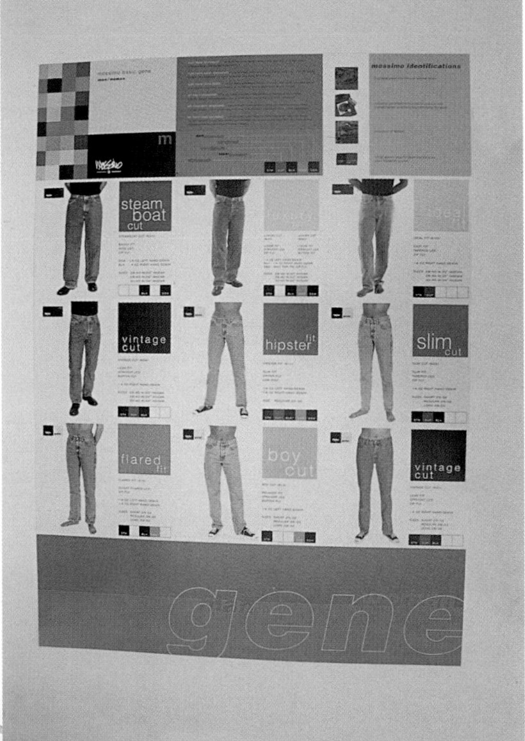

design firm
Mossimo In-House Graphis
Irvine, California
designers
Jonathan Lo, Garrison Smet, Tam Dang
client
Mossimo, Inc.

design firm
Herbst Lazar Bell INC
Chicago, Illinois
designers
Jose Perez, Diana Bush, Elizabeth Dziersk, Ralph Lazar
client
Eric Long (general manager of the Waldorf Astoria Hotel)

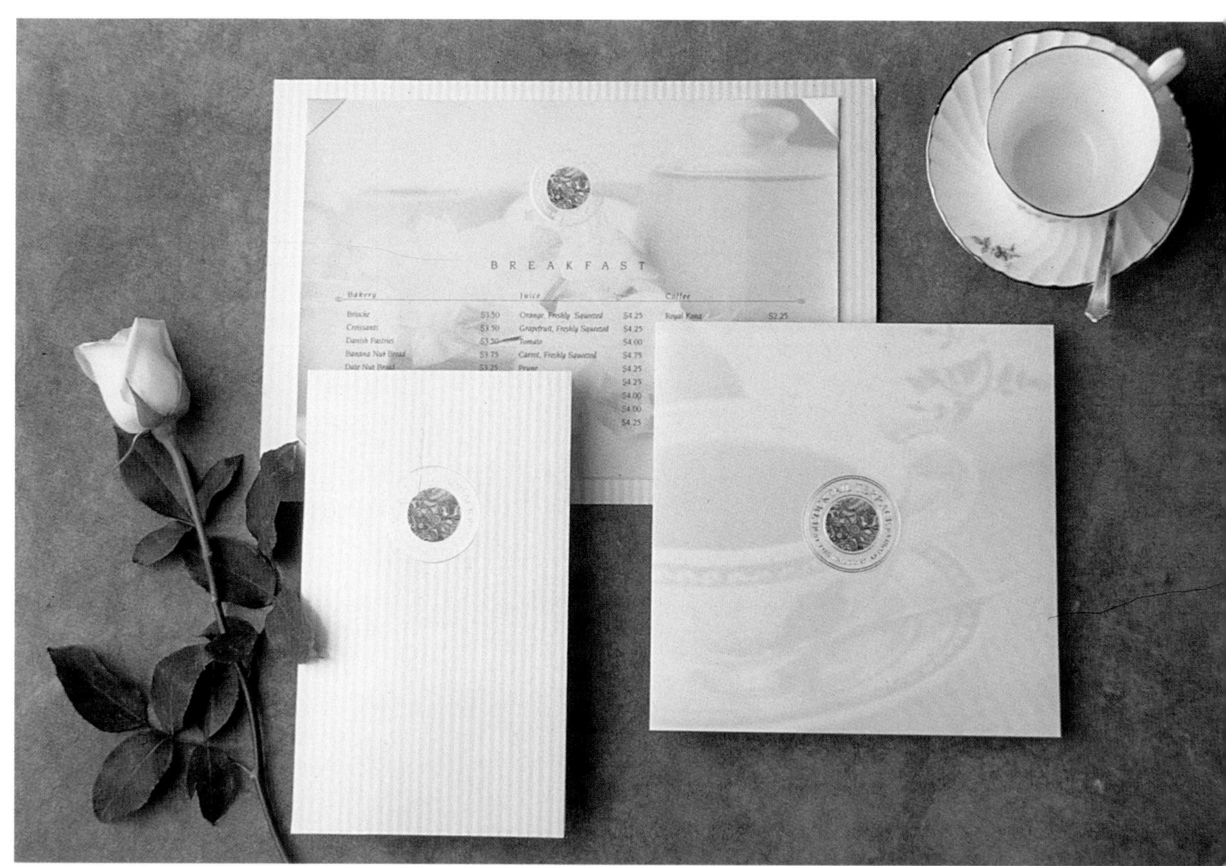

7960 NIWOT ROAD BLDG. B-12
NIWOT, COLORADO 80503
LOST, FOUND...RETURNED!
STUFF
BAK
.com

design firm
CommArts
Boulder, Colorado
designers
Eric Fowles, John Bacus
client
Stuffbak.com
(E-business)

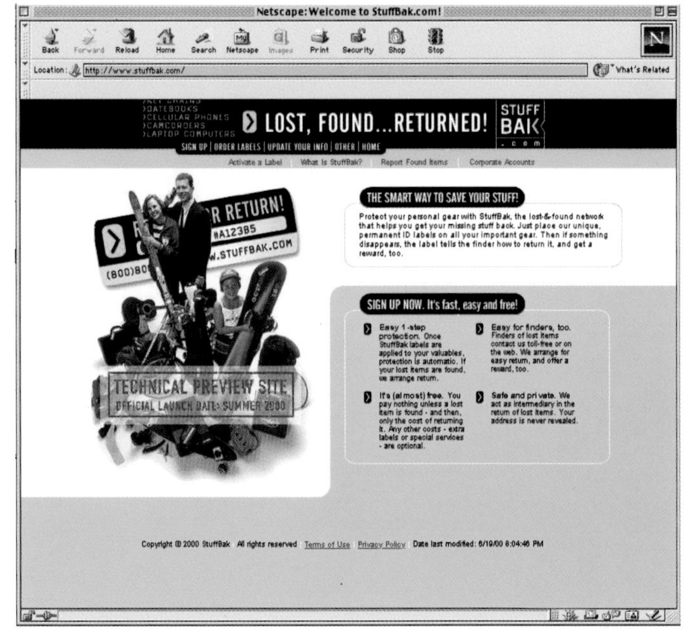

ROUND

STANDARD RECTANGLE

EYEWARE

WRAP-AROUND

NARROW RECTANGLE

REWARD FOR RETURN!
OWNER #A123B5
(800)800-8257 WWW.STUFFBAK.COM

LARGE STANDARD RECTANGLE

IRON-ON

ALUMINUM KEY RING

ALUMINUM BAG TAG

Stuffbak.com - Identity Standard

Color Logo

Black & White Logo

	Web colors	Pantone Uncoated	Pantone Coated	Background colors and applications
	Stuffbak Yellow #FFCC00	Stuffbak Yellow PMS 109u	Stuffbak Yellow PMS 116c	STUFF BAK .com / STUFF BAK .com / STUFF BAK .com
	Black #000000	Black PMS Process Blacku	Black PMS 419c	STUFF BAK .com / STUFF BAK .com / STUFF BAK .com
	White #FFFFFF	White	White	

WWW.STUFFBAK.COM

Optional one line horizontal Logo (Always in One color) - Only used with original logo or in Text applications.

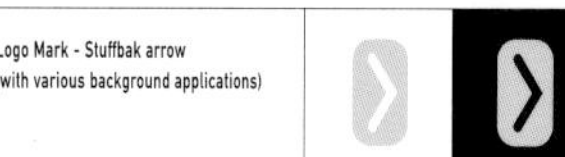

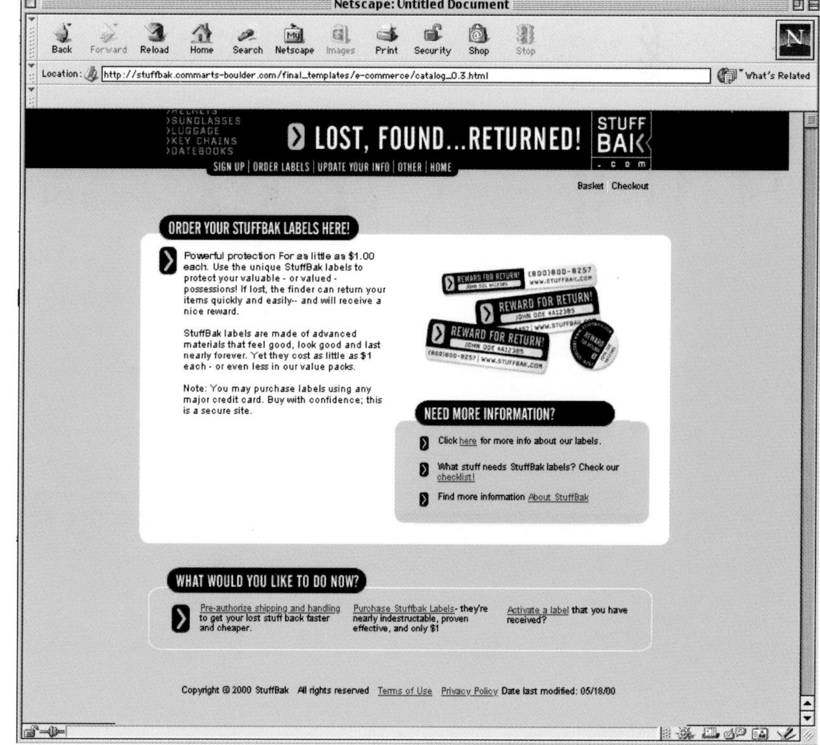

HOT SOX

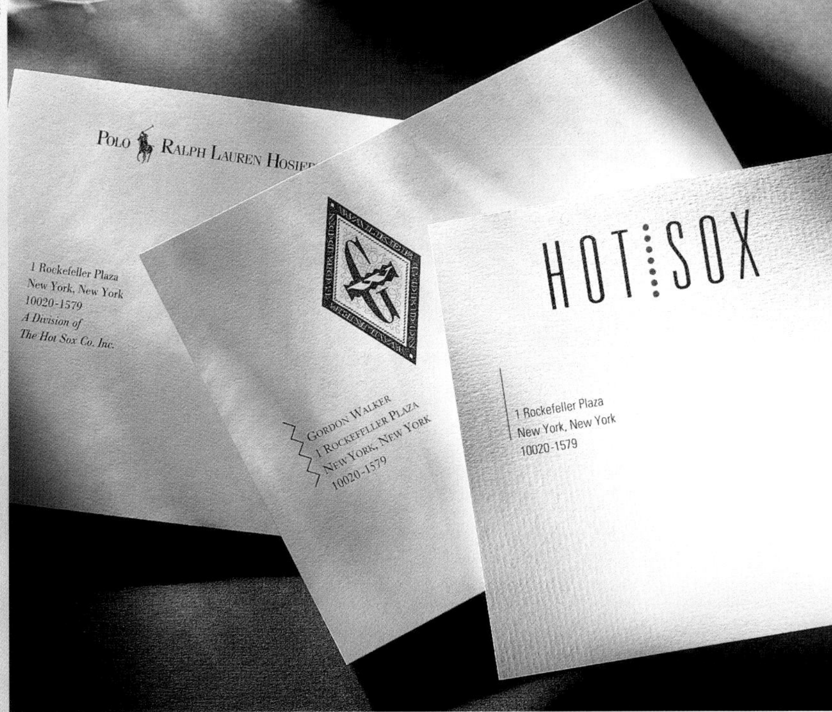

design firm
Studio Morris LA/NY
New York, New York
designer
Jeffrey Morris
client
Hot Sox

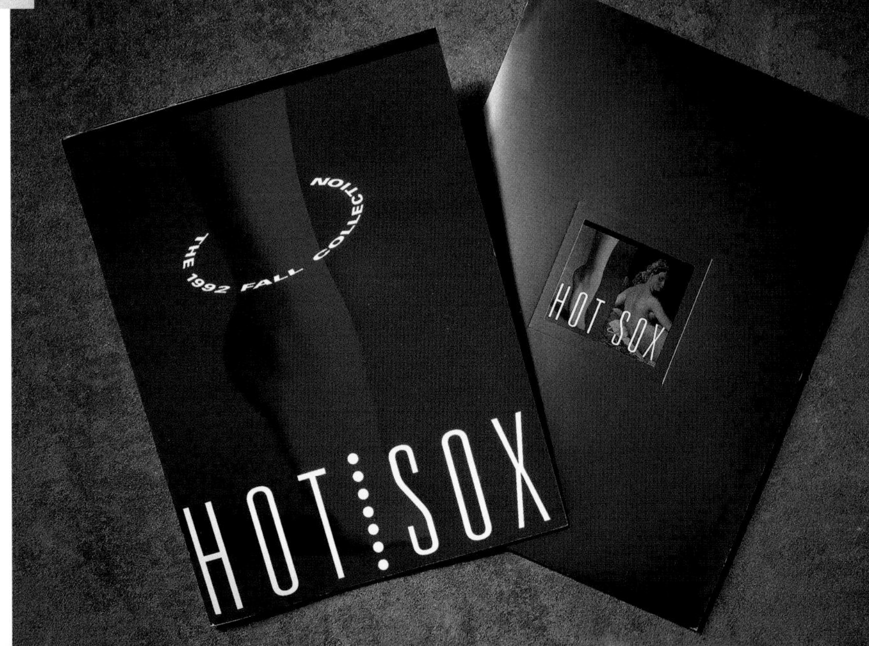

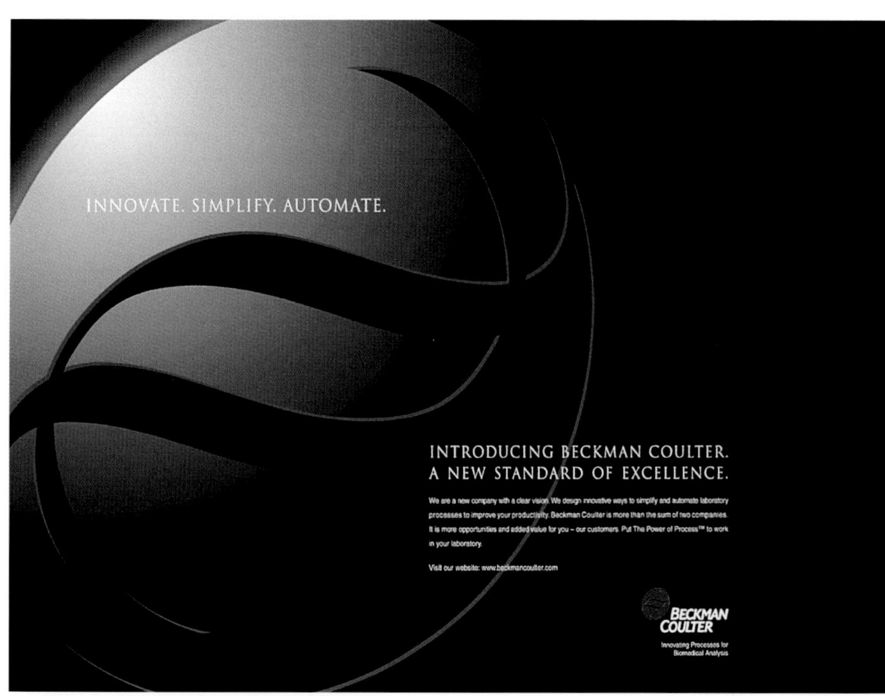

design firm
Bright/Point Zero
Fullerton, California
designer
Gary Hinsche
client
Beckman Coulter, Inc.

design firm
Mires Design
San Diego, California
art director
Jose A. Serrano
designers
Jose A. Serrano, Francoise Lemieux, Miguel Perez, Eric Freedman
illustrators
Nancy Stahl, Tracy Sabin
photographer
Carl Vanderschuit
client
Deleo Clay Tile Company

design firm
Smart Design Inc.
New York, New York
designers
Debbie Hahn, Paul Hamburger, Tom Dair, Tam Thomsen, with Alex Isley & Jessica Simmons (Alexander Isley Design)
client
Polaroid

RESTAURANT.™
COM
WHERE TO EAT.

RESTAURANT.™
COM
WHERE TO EAT.

RESTAURANT.™
COM
WHERE TO EAT.

RESTAURANT.™
COM
WHERE TO EAT.

RESTAURANT.™
COM
WHERE TO EAT.

RESTAURANT.™
COM
WHERE TO EAT.

May 3, 2000 | About Us | Site Map | Help | Feedback

RESTAURANT.™ COM

QUICK SEARCH | FULL SEARCH

State + city or zip required: State / City / Zip — Go
Optional: Restaurant Name — Begins / Contains

MY RESTAURANT.COM | CATERING | GIFT CERTIFICATES | BEHIND THE MENU

BEHIND THE MENU

If you agree with us that dining out is one of the most pleasurable aspects of life, then this section is for you. Go "Behind the Menu" and indulge in a smorgasbord of information. Everything from cocktails to cutlery; bistros to boulangeries is all right here. Bon appetit!

FEATURE STORIES

At The Bar: Rum's New Comeback

Entertaining: Recipes Using Wine

Global Dining: Eating out Ethnic (and Healthy)

also Behind The Menu... At The Bar, The Buzz, Master Chefs, Entertaining, Tipping Guide, Healthy Eating, Restaurant Etiquette, Global Dining, Spice Rack, Recipes

Find an article — Keyword — Go

RESTAURANT. COM — WHERE TO EAT? | FULL SEARCH | NEW SEARCH | SEARCH RESULTS

bistro 2k

NEWS & REVIEWS | TAKE-OUT MENU | MENU | WINE LIST | CHEF BIO | COUPONS | GIFT CERTIFICATES | ADD TO FAVORITES | E-MAIL TO A FRIEND

Menu

Select a course from the list below. Main Course

Main Course	Serving Size	$Price
Seared Sea Scallops with Hoisin BBQ Beef Ravioli and Scallion Shrimp	per serving	23.50
Wood Grilled Filet of Beef New Potato Frites & Pernod Butter	per serving	26.50
New England Lobster Steam with Fresh Corn, Fingerling Potatoes & Drawn Butter	per serving	22.50
California sturgeon with yukon gold potato and celery root hash, oxtail jus and pickled red onions braised	per serving	18.00
Roasted Mediterranean Turbot wrapped in buckwheat crepe with black chanterelles, shallots, roasted garlic	per serving	21.00

Return to top

Prices are subject to change without notice.

MAP

Aurelios Pizza
1545 Western Ave
Chicago Heights, IL 60411

Driving Directions — Enter your starting address below: Address, City, State, Zip

Display route as: Text Only / Overview Map with Text / Turn-by-Turn Maps with Text

Calculate Directions

© 1999 MapQuest.com, Inc.; © 1999 Navigation Technologies

May 3, 2000 | About Us | Site Map | Help | Feedback

MY RESTAURANT.COM | CATERING | GIFT CERTIFICATES | BEHIND THE MENU

THE BEST OF THE BEST

The DiRoNA award is given every year to restaurants which excel in service and cuisine. Search for DiRoNA award recipients in your area.

CORPORATE ORDERS

Impress your colleagues and clients with a ready-made meal. Visit Corporate Orders to find out more.

RESTAURANT OWNERS

Already a member? Access your personal web site editor here. Want to become one? Call 1-800-979-8985.

Welcome to the Web's premiere restaurant network. Here you'll find a restaurant to match your ideal dining experience, read about current news and events, and even order your meals online. We're brand new, but growing every day, so visit us often!

HEALTHY EATING

Get tips and tricks for eating (and living) well at Healthy Eating.

bistro 2k

MENU | TAKE-OUT MENU | SPECIALS | WINE LIST | CHEF BIO | COUPONS | GIFT CERTIFICATES | ADD TO FAVORITES | E-MAIL TO A FRIEND

You Have: 3 items in your order $00.00

Bistro 2k
21 East 5th Street
Chicago, IL 60000
Downtown

(312) 555-1212 phone
(312) 555-0000 fax
bistro@y2k.com

Hours:
M 11:00am - 3:30pm
T 11:00am - 3:30pm
W 11:00am - 3:30pm
Th 11:00am - 3:30pm
F 11:00am - 3:30pm
Sa 11:00am - 3:30pm
Su 11:00am - 3:30pm

Payment:
• Cash
• Personal Check
• Discover Card
• Master Card
• Visa

Ammenities:
• Parking available
• Television
• Banquet Facilities
• Full Bar

Description

bistro2K was established at the turn of the millennium, and has been dishing out the latest in modern urban cuisine ever since. The brainchild of Nathan Dunbar, who achieved success with his chain of cyber-cafes, DotCommons, the space-aged eatery has quickly become a Chicago hotspot. The menu is southwestern eclectic, with specialties ranging from the black bean and chipolte salad to the grilled portobello tamale. Drink specials include the "WhyTooKay Martini" and the "Apocalypse Microbrew," a favorite of the hipsters who frequent the upstairs club area. Open late seven days a week, bistro2K celebrates the best in dining that the twenty-first century has to offer.

Specialities

Truffled potato puree, field mushrooms and serano ham.

Related Articles

Finding the perfect wine
Tips for a flawless dinner party

May 4, 2000

Select any additional criteria you would like to search by. Be selective, choosing too many options may limit your chances of finding the perfect restaurant.

Looking For: Carry Out, Catering, Lunch, Late Night; Sit Down, Breakfast, Dinner, Early Bird

Atmosphere: Water Park, Romantic, Live Music, Themed/Costumes, Sports Bar, Resort/Country Club; Dude Ranch, Fireplace, Entertainment, Outdoor Dining, Open-Lively, Quiet-Cozy

Amenities: Billiards / Pool, Casino, Children's Play Area, Cigar Rooms; Dancing, Special Occasions, TV, Darts

Specialties: Early Bird Specials, Continental Breakfast, Home Meal Replace, Senior Discounts; All You Can Eat, Low Cholesterol, Box Lunches, Children's Menu

Special Needs: Smoking Section, Senior Discount, Cigar Friendly; Booster/High Chairs, Non Smoking Area

Banquet Facilities: 10 - 20 People, Over 100 People, Off-Site Catering; 20 - 50 People, Banquet Menu, Event Coordinator; 50 - 100 People, Private Room

Average Price: Under $10, $25 - $35; $10 - $15, $35 - $50; $15 - $25, Over $50

Payment Type: Check, Diners Club, Visa; Cash Only, Mastercard, Debit / Bank; Discover, Amex

Bar: No Bar, Wines; Full Bar, Micro Brews; Beer

Go | Clear

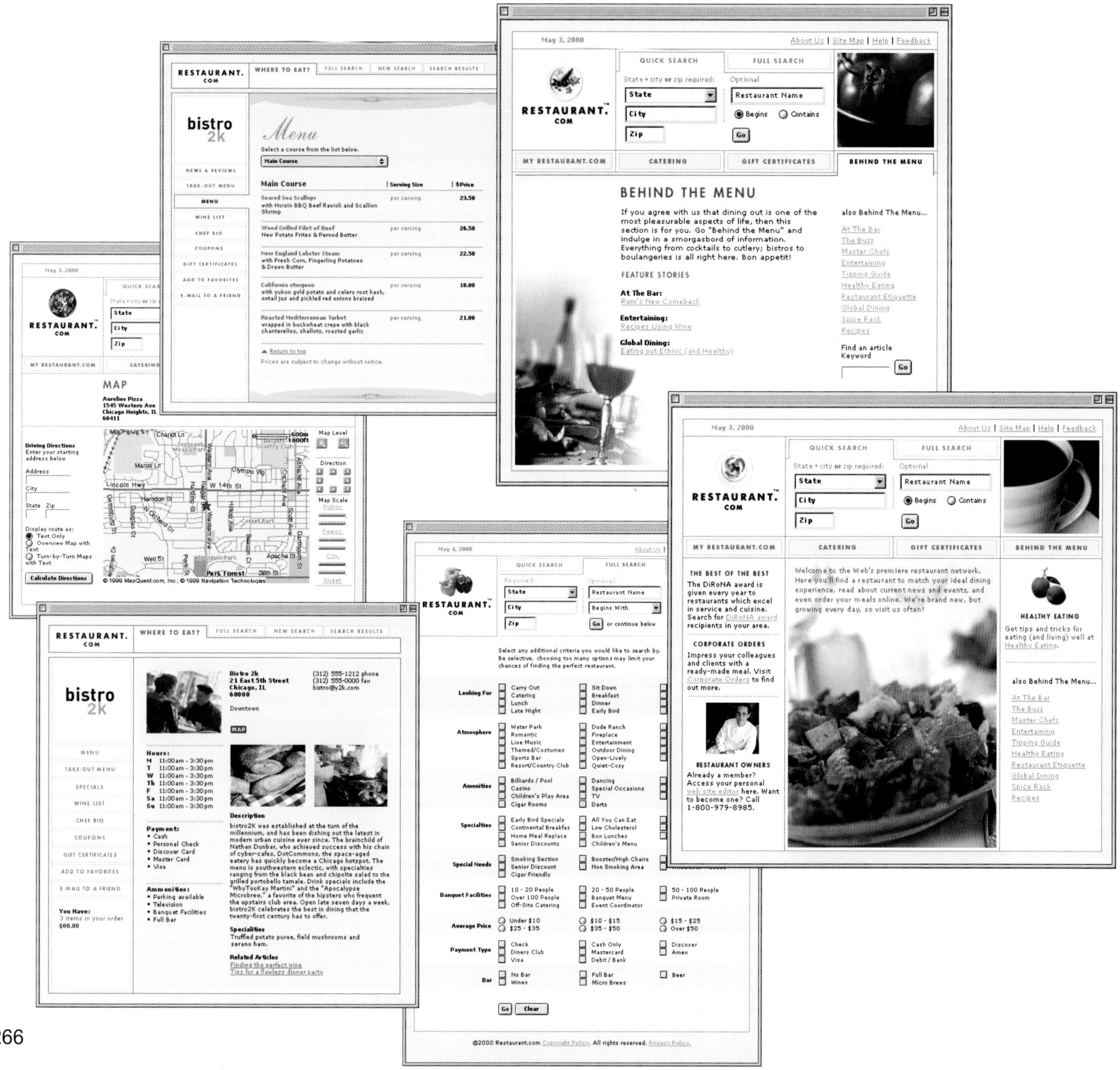

design firm
IXL
Chicago, Illinois
designers
Tim O'Hara, Mark Pelletier, Bob Domenz
client
Restaurant.com

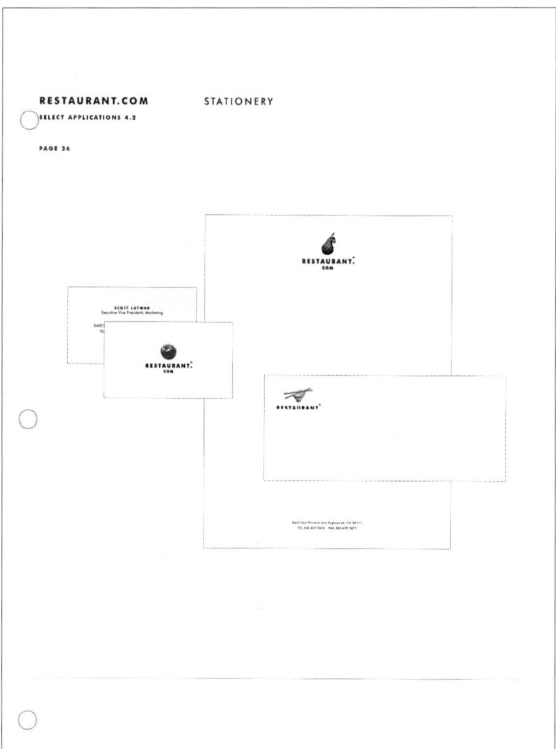

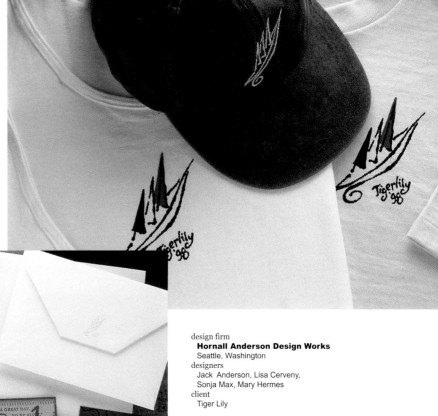

design firm
Hornall Anderson Design Works
Seattle, Washington
designers
Jack Anderson, Lisa Cerveny,
Sonja Max, Mary Hermes
client
Tiger Lily

design firm
Wallace Church ass., inc.
New York, New York
designers
Stan Church, Nin Glaister, John Bruno
client
Polly-O Italian Cheese Co. (Kraft Foods)
(food)

design firm
Stein & Company
Cleveland, Ohio
designer
Sue Lesko
client
Digital Navigation Corporate ID

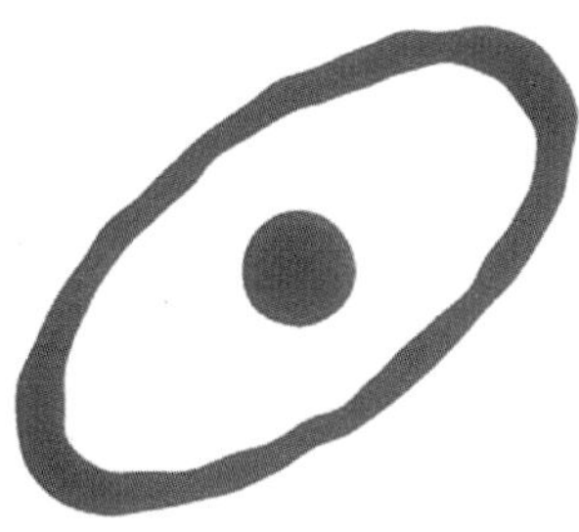

p i t t a r d s u l l i v a n

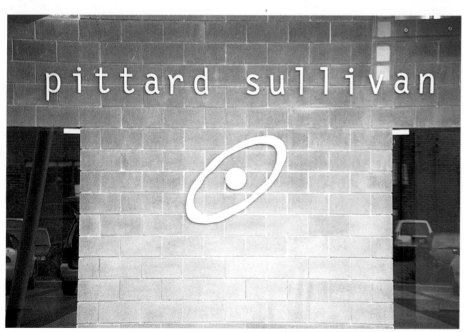

design firm
Pittard Sullivan
Culver City, California
designers
Creative Team at Pittard Sullivan
client
Pittard Sullivan

design firm
Wallace Church ass., inc.
New York, New York
designers
Stan Church, John Waski, Derek Samuel
client
Maxfli
(sporting goods)

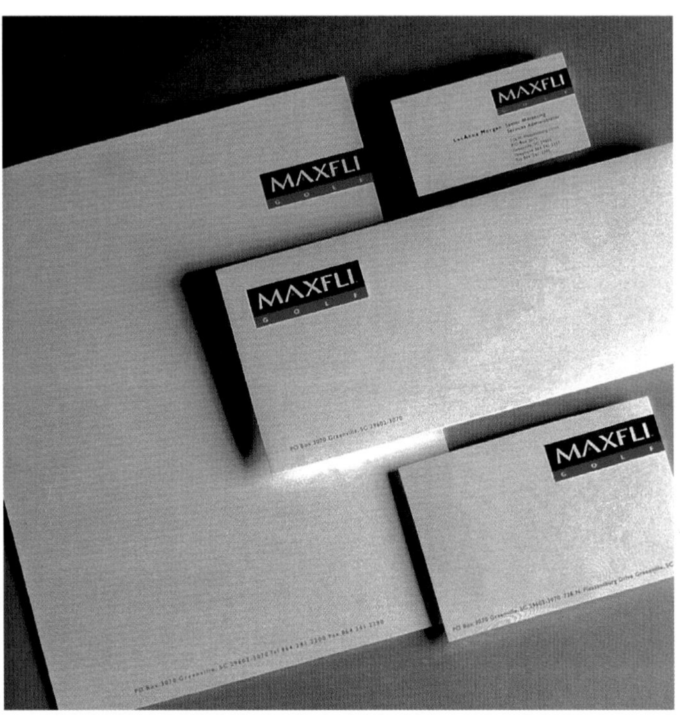

MAXFLI

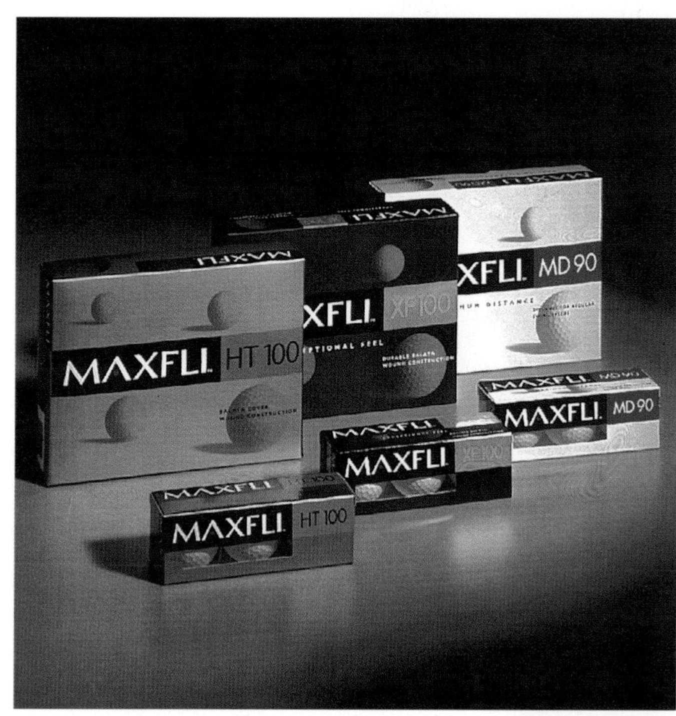
MAXFLI HT 100
MAXFLI MD 90
MAXFLI HT 100
MAXFLI MD 90
MAXFLI

MAXFLI
MAXFLI
MAXFLI
MAXFLI
EXCEPTIONAL DURABILITY
XD
Exclusive long lasting Innofibers™ provide superior fit, weather resistance and wearability
MAXFLI
EXCEPTIONAL FEEL
XF
Genuine leather palm provides maximum feel, grip and touch
MAXFLI
EXCEPTIONAL SOFTNESS
XS
Finest quality leather worn by tour pros worldwide

PANoRAMA®

design firm
Tharp Did It
Los Gatos, California
designers
Mr. Tharp, Nicole Coleman, Dena Holmes
client
PANoRAMA Baking Company
(retail and wholesale breads)

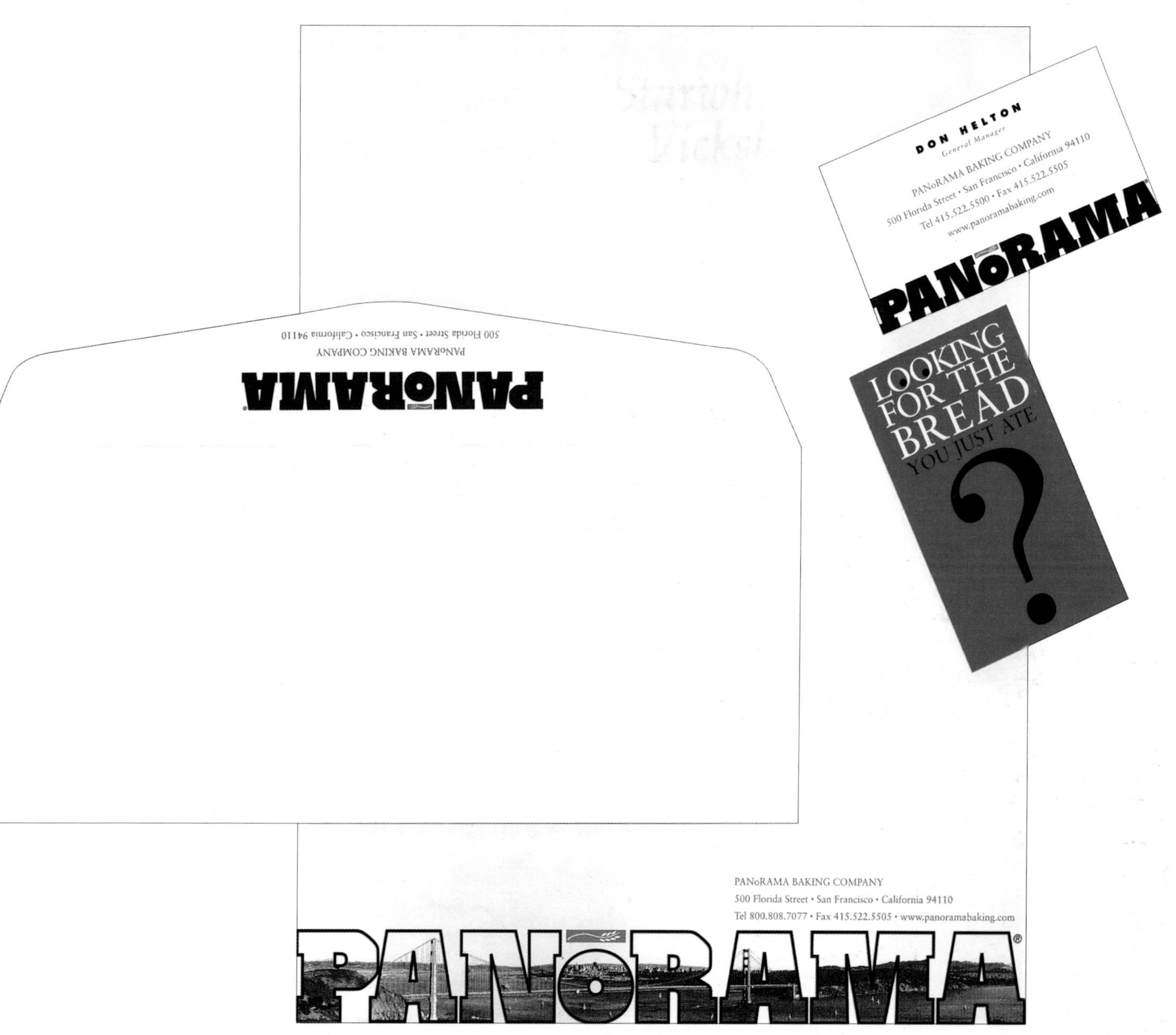
DON HELTON
General Manager
PANoRAMA BAKING COMPANY
500 Florida Street • San Francisco • California 94110
Tel 415.522.5500 • Fax 415.522.5505
www.panoramabaking.com
PANoRAMA
LOOKING FOR THE BREAD YOU JUST ATE ?
PANoRAMA
PANoRAMA BAKING COMPANY
500 Florida Street • San Francisco • California 94110
PANoRAMA BAKING COMPANY
500 Florida Street • San Francisco • California 94110
Tel 800.808.7077 • Fax 415.522.5505 • www.panoramabaking.com
PANoRAMA

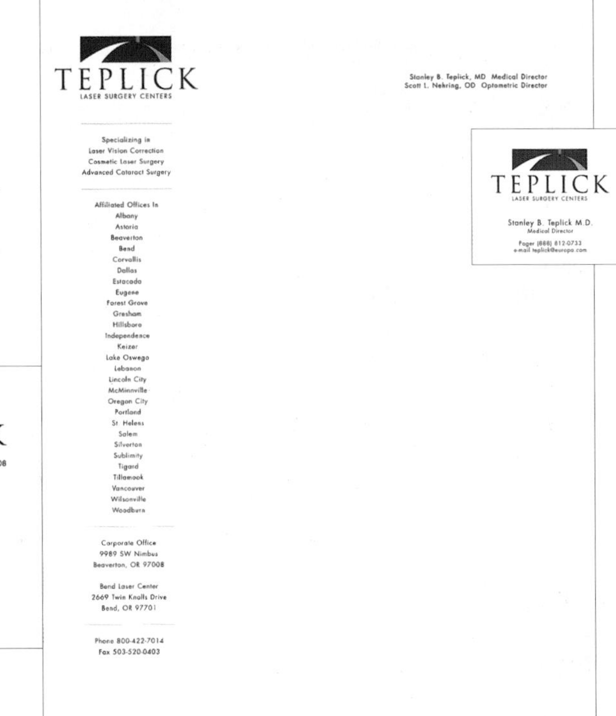

design firm
Woodson & Newroth
Beaverton, Oregon
designer
Ken Steckler
client
Teplik Laser Surgery Centers

design firm
Hanson Associates, Inc.
Philadelphia, Pennsylvania
designers
Tobin Beck, Mary Zook
client
Finlandia Vodka Americas, Inc.

ALPHABET SOUP
LEADING THE WAY
IN GREAT TOYS!

UNIVERSAL
ALPHABET SOUP
LEADING THE WAY
IN GREAT TOYS!

SUMMER FUN FROM BRIO
TOP TEN SUMMER TOYS:
Parade
FOR THE BIRDS...

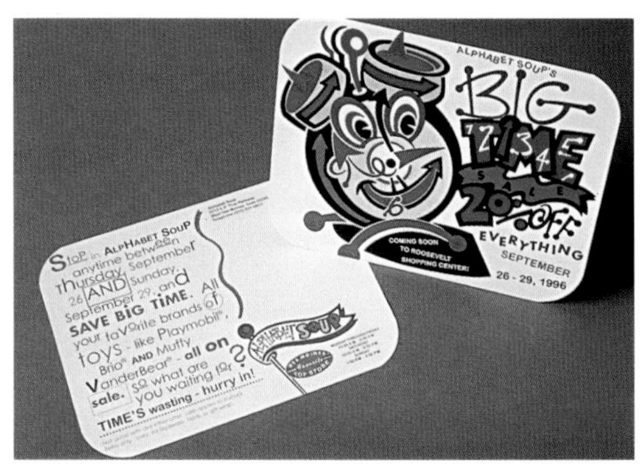
ALPHABET SOUP'S
BIG TIME SALE
20% OFF
EVERYTHING
SEPTEMBER
26 - 29, 1996
COMING SOON TO ROOSEVELT SHOPPING CENTER!
SAVE BIG TIME.
TIME'S wasting - hurry in!

design firm
Sayles Graphic Design
Des Moines, Iowa
designer
John Sayles
client
Alphabet Soup
(children's toy store)

handyvan.com[SM]

Click to install.[SM]

design firm
Tharp Did It
Los Gatos, California
designers
Mr. Tharp, Dena Holmes, Cheryl Layton
client
handyvan
(home installation experts)

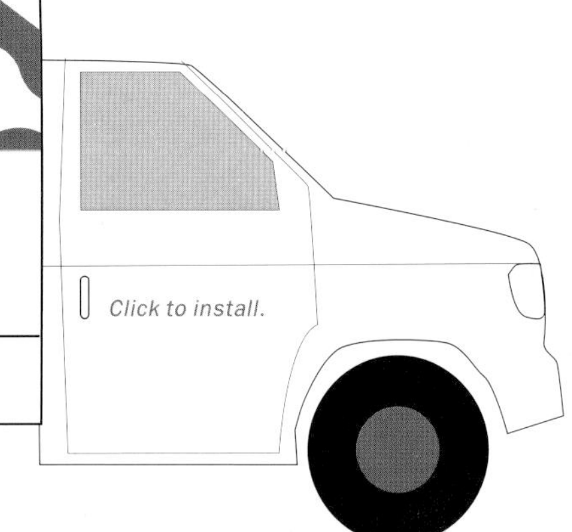

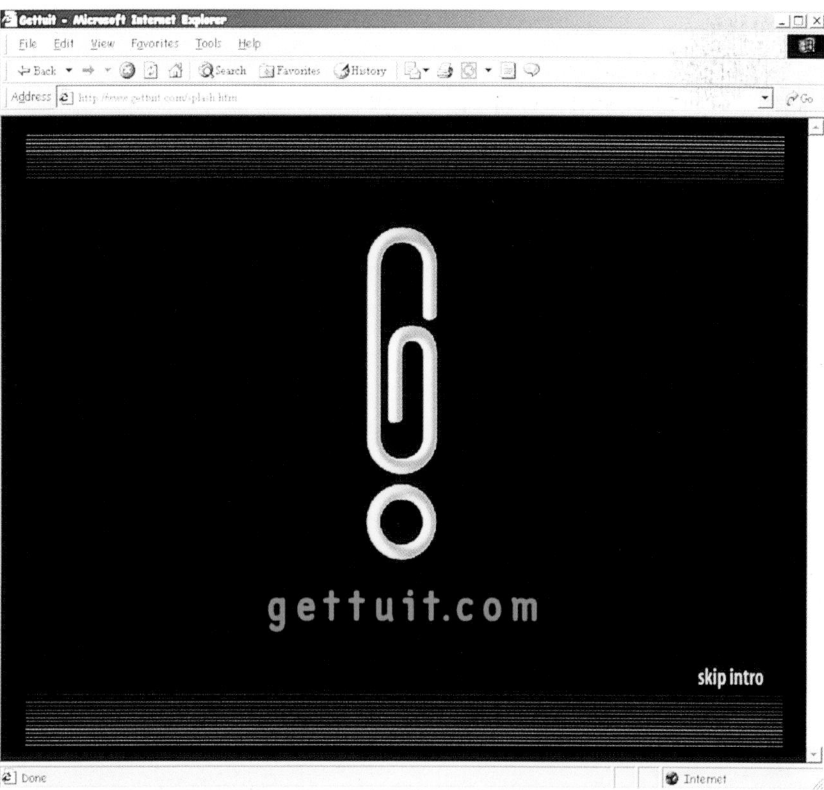

design firm
Hornall Anderson Design Works, Inc.
Seattle, Washington
designers
Jack Anderson, Kathy Saito, Gretchen Cook, James Tee, Julie Lock, Henry Yiu, Sonja Max, Ryan Wilkerson, Alan Copeland, Margaret Long, Jason Hickner
client
Gettuit.com
(service providing customized work engines to businesses for helping them work more efficiently)

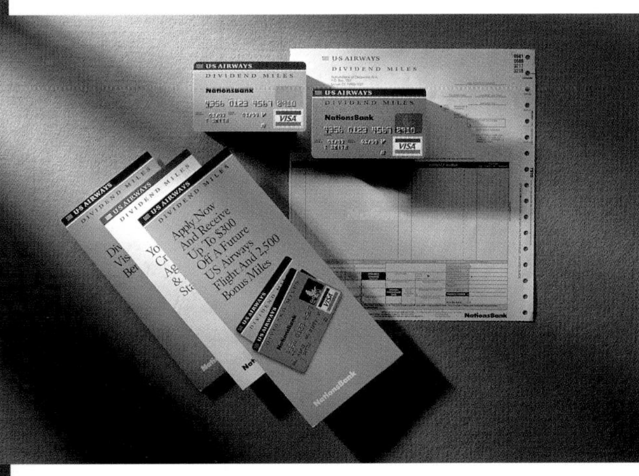

design firm
Deskey Associates
New York, New York
designer
Genie King
client
U.S. Airways

Liechtenstein Global Trust

design firm
Lister Butler Consulting Inc.
New York, New York
client
Liechtenstein Global Trust

LGT Bank in Liechtenstein
A Member of Liechtenstein Global Trust

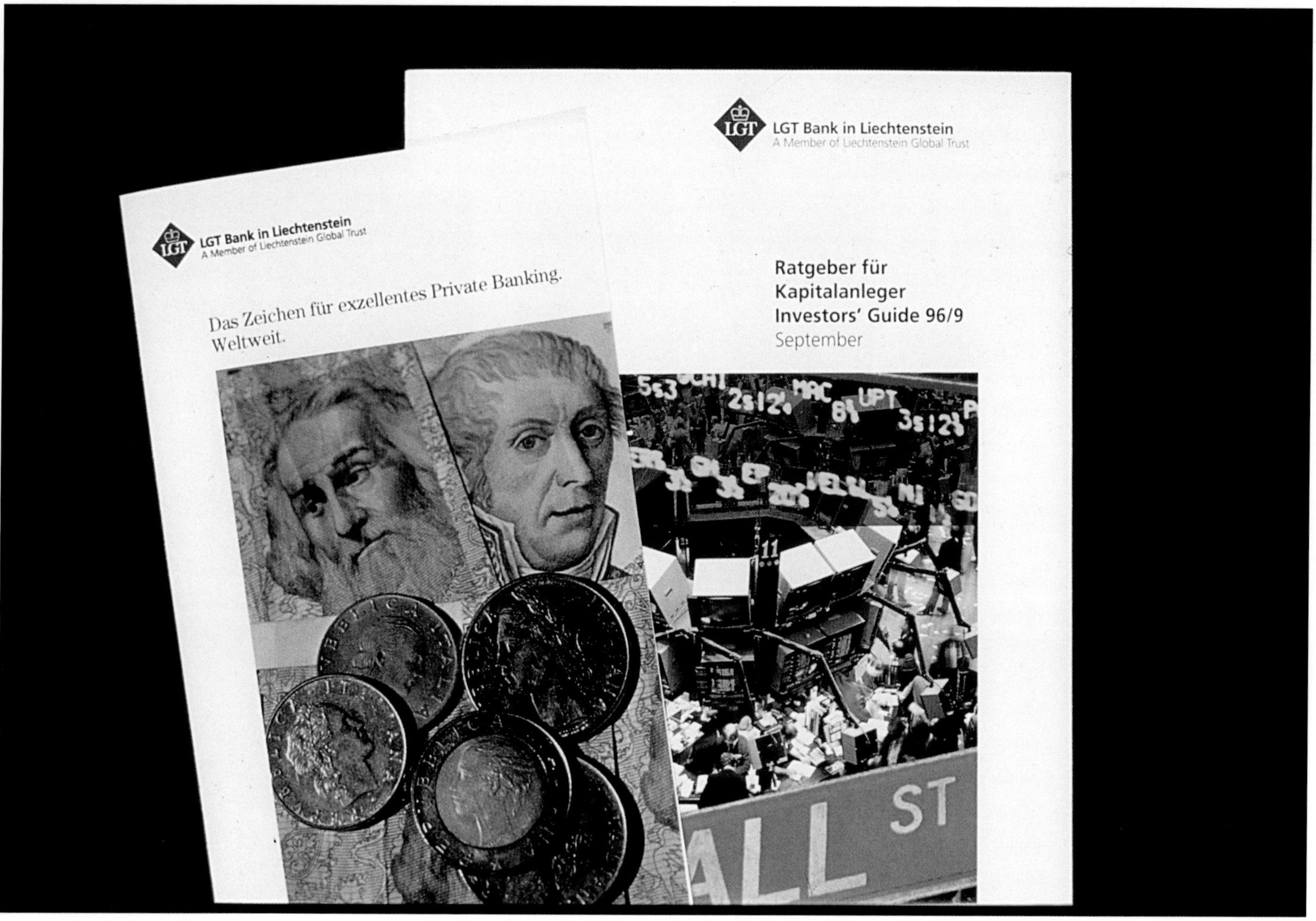

design firm
CommArts
Boulder, Colorado
client
The Alpine World Championships

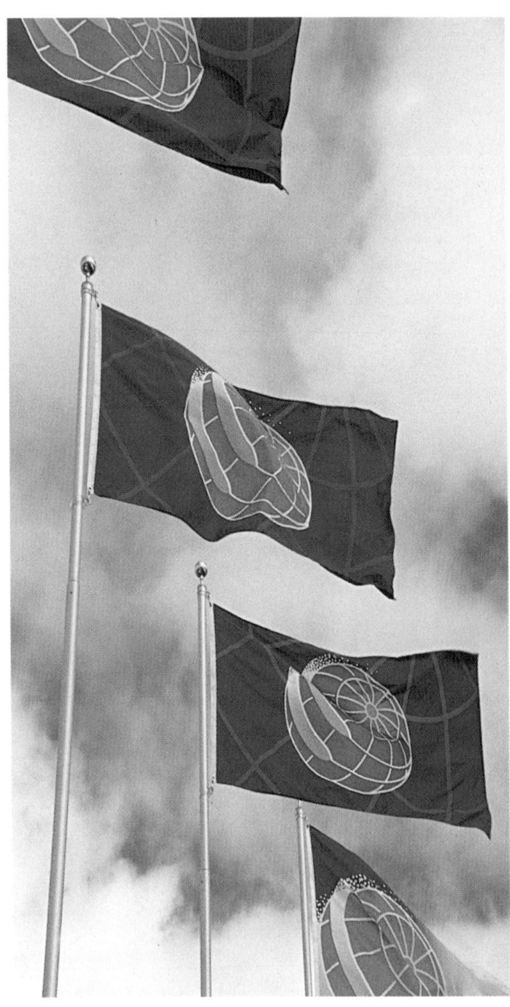

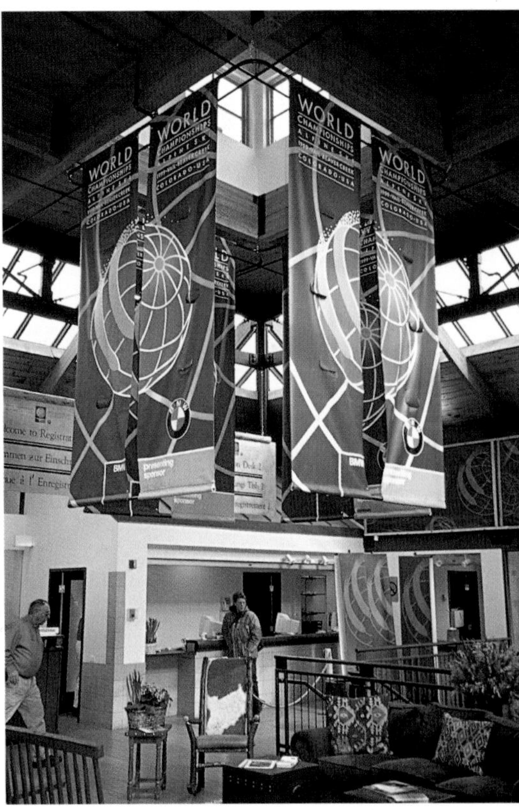

CHAMPIONSHIPS
VAIL·BEAVER CREEK
COLORADO·USA
WORLD
CHAMPIONSHIPS
LOW
CLEARANCE
14' 2"
CONCIERGE
?
INFORMATION

THE

STEVEN KENT

WINERY

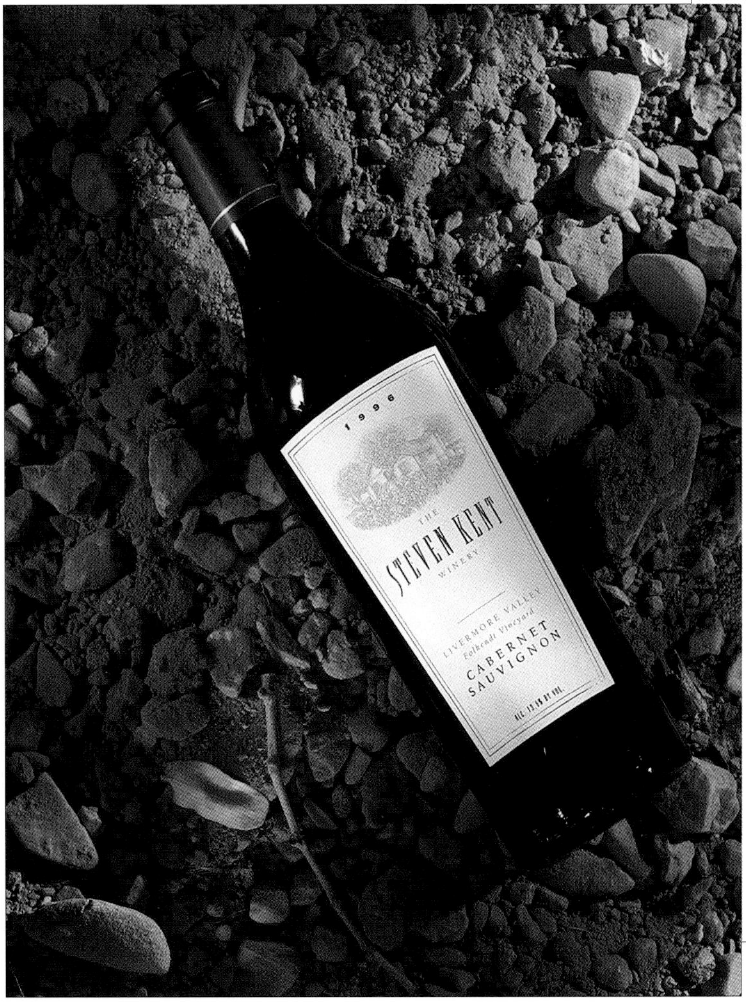

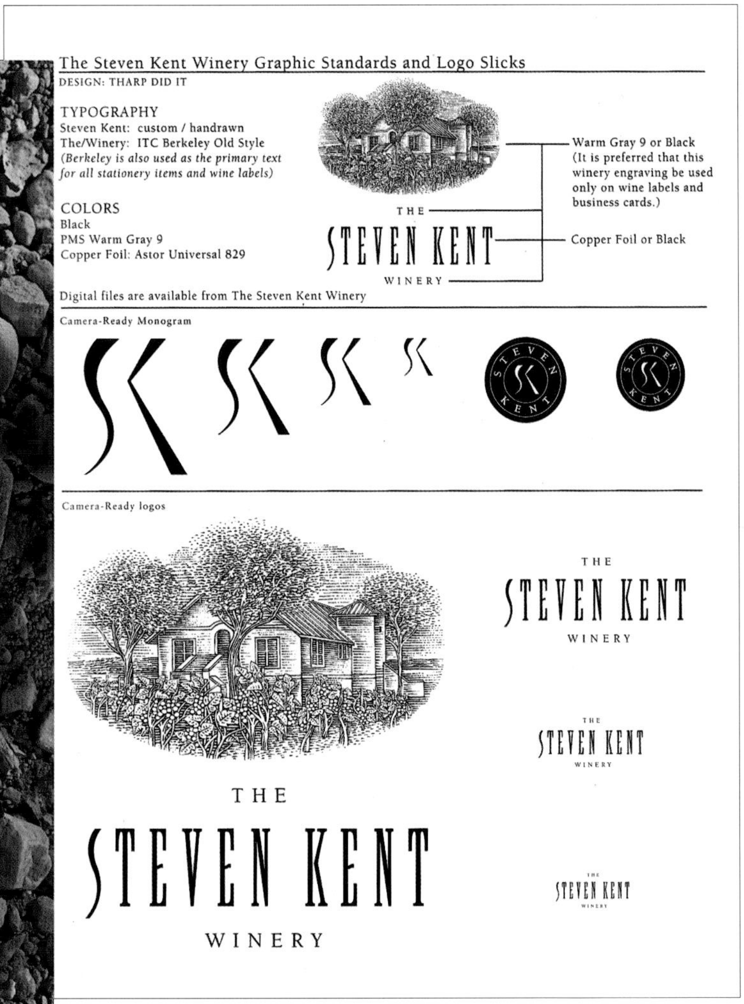

The Steven Kent Winery Graphic Standards and Logo Slicks

DESIGN: THARP DID IT

TYPOGRAPHY
Steven Kent: custom / handrawn
The/Winery: ITC Berkeley Old Style
(Berkeley is also used as the primary text for all stationery items and wine labels)

COLORS
Black
PMS Warm Gray 9
Copper Foil: Astor Universal 829

THE
STEVEN KENT — Copper Foil or Black
WINERY

Warm Gray 9 or Black (It is preferred that this winery engraving be used only on wine labels and business cards.)

Digital files are available from The Steven Kent Winery

Camera-Ready Monogram

STEVEN KENT

Camera-Ready logos

THE
STEVEN KENT
WINERY

design firm
Tharp Did It
Los Gatos, California
designer
Mr. Tharp
client
The Steven Kent Winery
(fine wines)

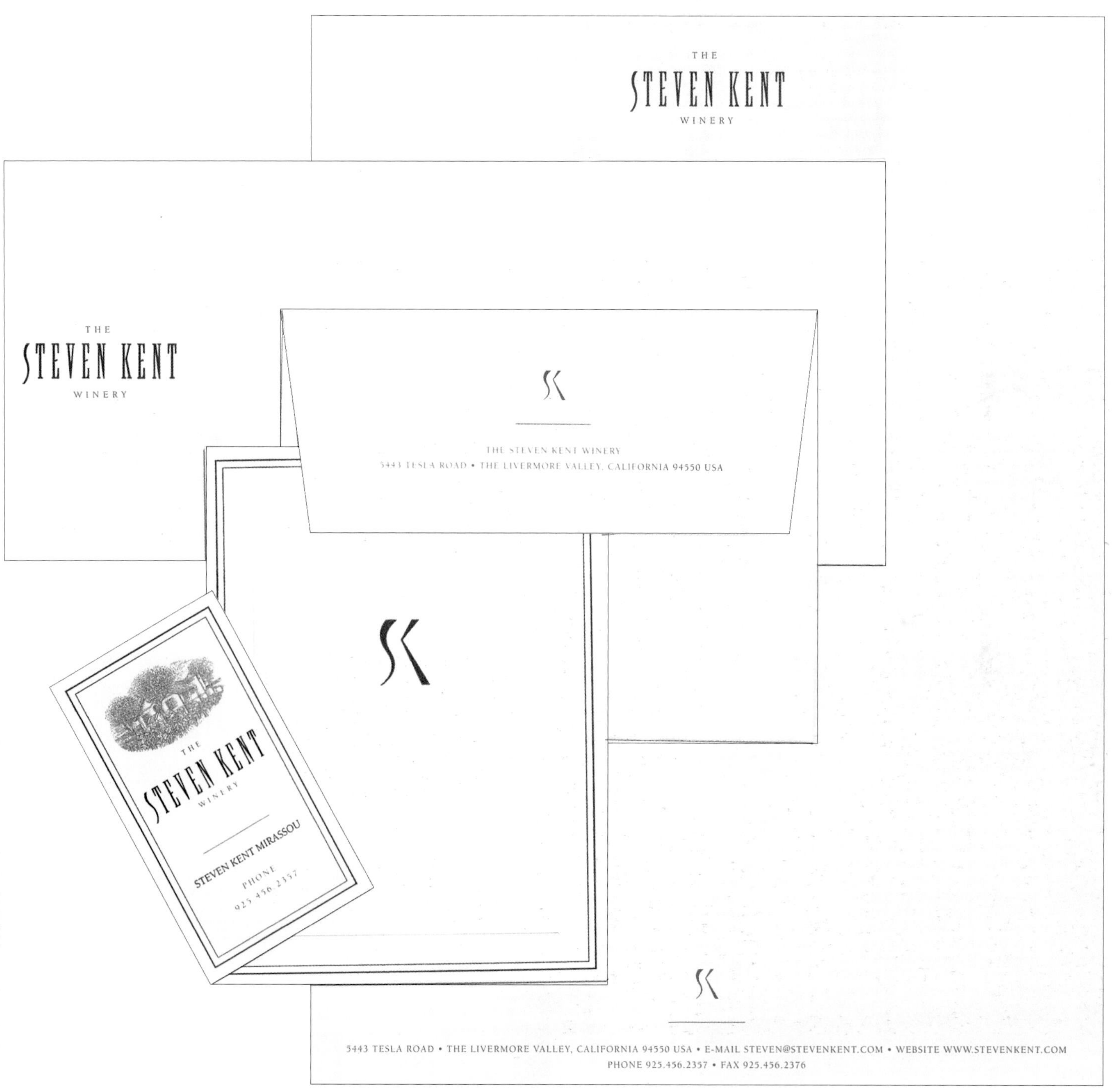
THE
STEVEN KENT
WINERY
THE
STEVEN KENT
WINERY
THE STEVEN KENT WINERY
5443 TESLA ROAD • THE LIVERMORE VALLEY, CALIFORNIA 94550 USA
THE
STEVEN KENT
WINERY
STEVEN KENT MIRASSOU
PHONE
925.456.2357
5443 TESLA ROAD • THE LIVERMORE VALLEY, CALIFORNIA 94550 USA • E-MAIL STEVEN@STEVENKENT.COM • WEBSITE WWW.STEVENKENT.COM
PHONE 925.456.2357 • FAX 925.456.2376

design firm
Hornall Anderson Design Works, Inc.
Seattle, Washington
designers
Jack Anderson, Cliff Chung
client
University Village

SASAKI

design firm
Sasaki Associates
Watertown, Massachusetts
designers
John Barry, Susan Hoy, Kelly Milligan,
Brian Pearce, Boyd Morrison, Kris Waldman
client
Sasaki Associates

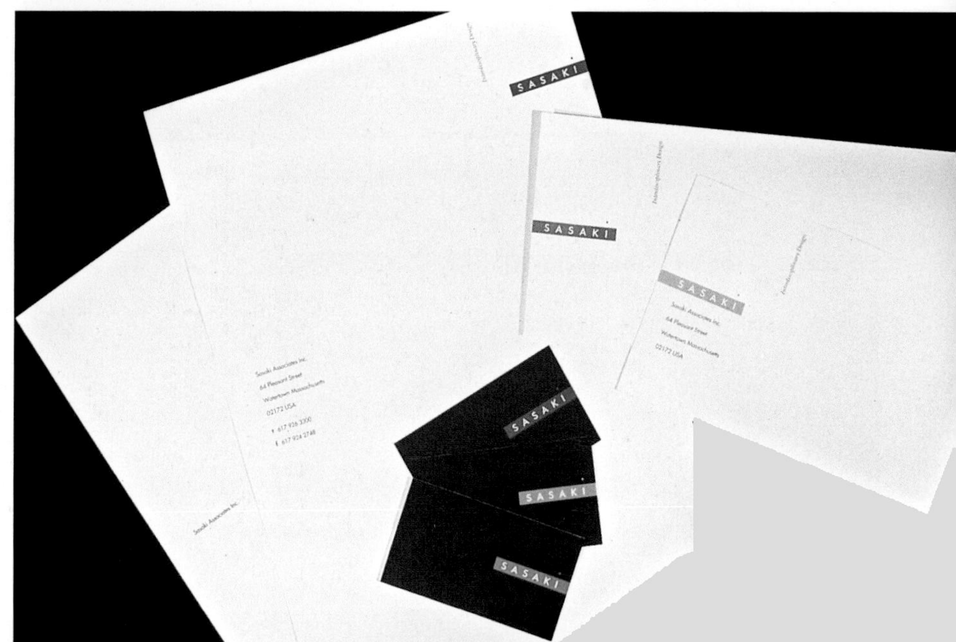

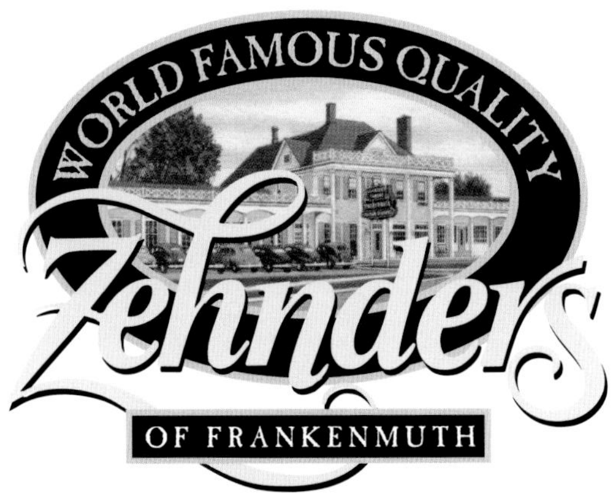

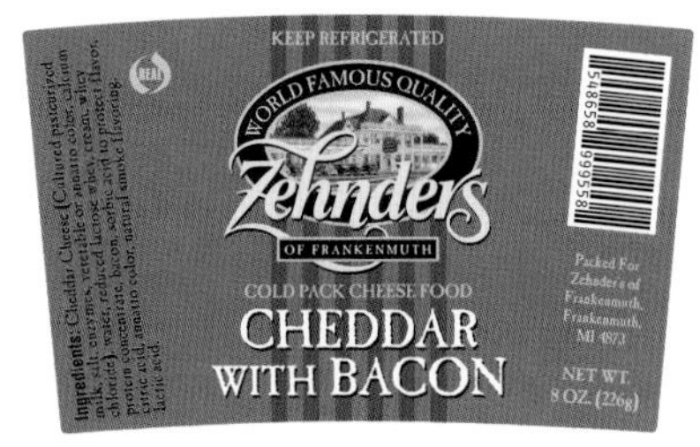

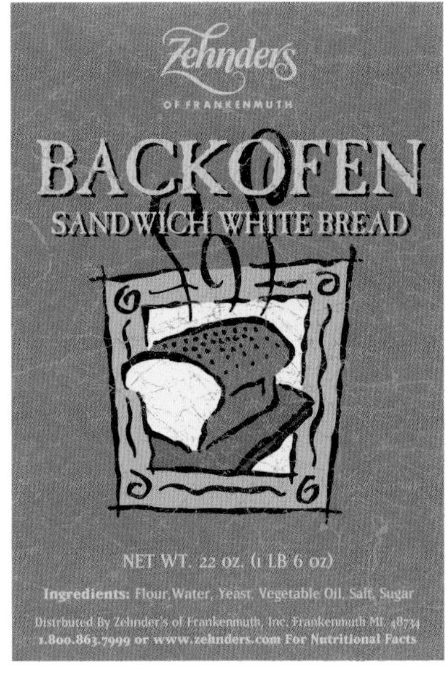

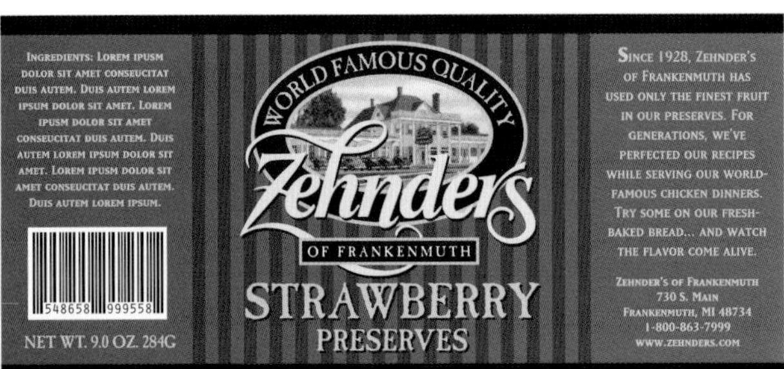

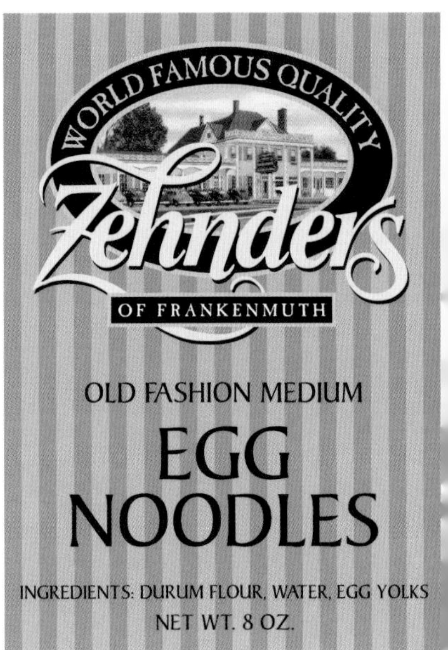

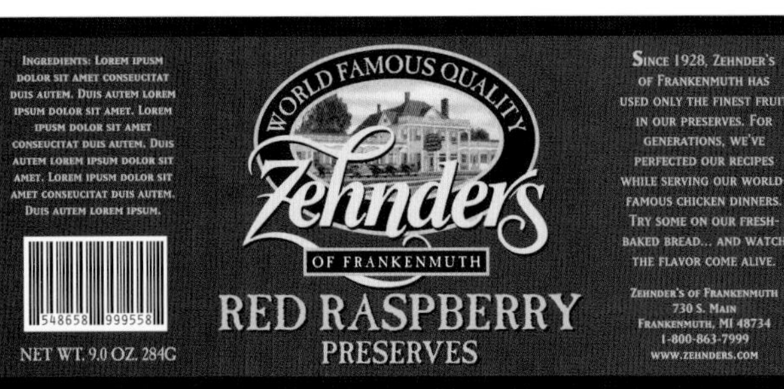

design firm
JGA, Inc.
Southfield, Michigan
director of graphic design
Brian Eastman
client
Zehnders of Frankenmuth
(restaurant and retail)

Zehnder's of Frankenmuth
730 S. Main
Frankenmuth, MI 48734
1.800.863.7999
Produced and Bottled For Zehnder's Of Frankenmuth By Honeywood Inc. Salem, Oregon. Oregon Bonded Winery 26
Contains Sulfites
World Famous Quality
Zehnders
of Frankenmuth
California Chablis
750ml
Lorem ipsum dolor sit amet, consectetuer adipiscing elit, sed diam nonummy nibh euismod tinci dunt ut laoreet dolore magna aliquam erat volutpat. Ut wisi enim ad minim veniam, quis nostrud exerci tation ullamcorper suscipit lobortis nisl ut aliquip ex ea commodo consequat.

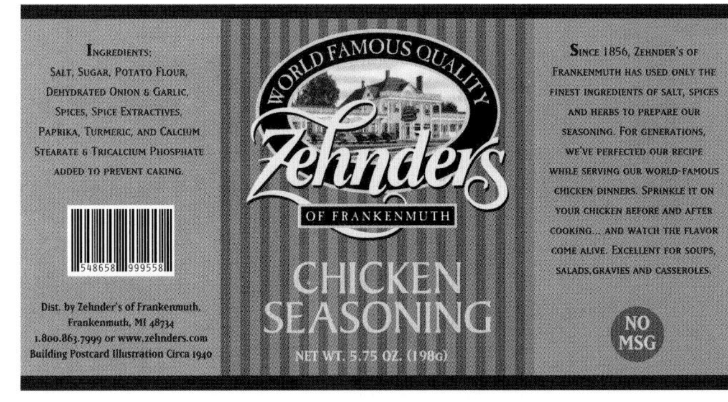
Ingredients:
Salt, Sugar, Potato Flour, Dehydrated Onion & Garlic, Spices, Spice Extractives, Paprika, Turmeric, and Calcium Stearate & Tricalcium Phosphate added to prevent caking.
Dist. by Zehnder's of Frankenmuth, Frankenmuth, MI 48734
1.800.863.7999 or www.zehnders.com
Building Postcard Illustration Circa 1940
World Famous Quality
Zehnders
of Frankenmuth
Chicken Seasoning
Net Wt. 5.75 oz. (198g)
Since 1856, Zehnder's of Frankenmuth has used only the finest ingredients of salt, spices and herbs to prepare our seasoning. For generations, we've perfected our recipe while serving our world-famous chicken dinners. Sprinkle it on your chicken before and after cooking... and watch the flavor come alive. Excellent for soups, salads, gravies and casseroles.
No MSG

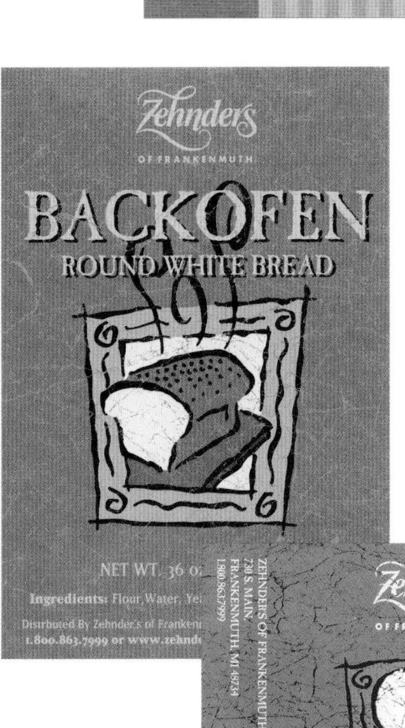
Zehnders
of Frankenmuth
Backofen
Round White Bread
Net Wt. 36 oz
Ingredients: Flour, Water, Ye
Distributed By Zehnder's of Frankenm
1.800.863.7999 or www.zehnd

Zehnders
of Frankenmuth
Potato
Dinner Rolls
ozen
Water, Yeast, Eggs, Salt, Sugar
nmuth, Inc. Frankenmuth MI. 48734
ers.com For Nutritional Facts

Ingredients:
Salt, Sugar, Potato Flour, Dehydrated Onion & Garlic, Spices, Spice Extractives, Paprika, Turmeric, and Calcium Stearate & Tricalcium Phosphate added to prevent caking.
Dist. by Zehnder's of Frankenmuth, Frankenmuth, MI 48734
1.800.863.7999 or www.zehnders.com
Building Postcard Illustration Circa 1940
World Famous Quality
Zehnders
of Frankenmuth
All-Purpose Seasoning
Net Wt. 5.75 oz. (198g)
Since 1928, Zehnder's of Frankenmuth has used only the finest ingredients of salt, spices and herbs to prepare our seasoning. For generations, we've perfected our recipe while serving our world-famous chicken dinners. Sprinkle it on your chicken before and after cooking... and watch the flavor come alive. Excellent for soups, salads, gravies and casseroles.
No MSG

Zehnders of Frankenmuth
730 S. Main
Frankenmuth, MI 48734
1.800.863.7999
Zehnders
of Frankenmuth
Harvest Blend Marinade
Net Wt. 8.0 oz. 266g

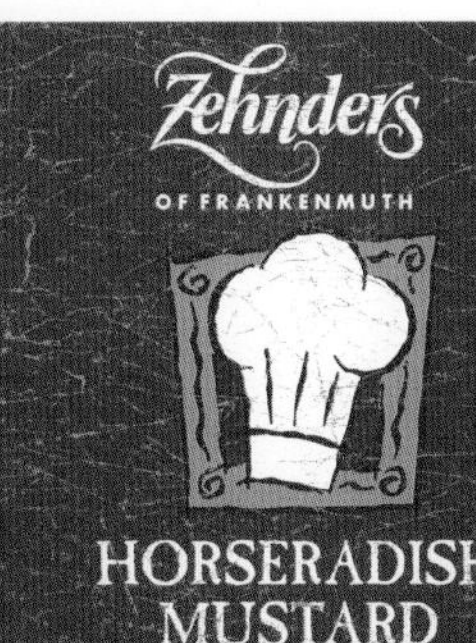
Zehnders of Frankenmuth
730 S. Main
Frankenmuth, MI 48734
1.800.863.7999
Zehnders
of Frankenmuth
Horseradish Mustard
Net Wt. 8 oz. 266g

Zehnders
of Frankenmuth
Vidalia Onion
oney Mustard Dressing
Net Wt. 8.0 oz. 266g

Zehnders of Frankenmuth
730 S. Main
Frankenmuth, MI 48734
1.800.863.7999
Zehnders
of Frankenmuth
Classic Blend Marinade
Net Wt. 8.0 oz. 266g

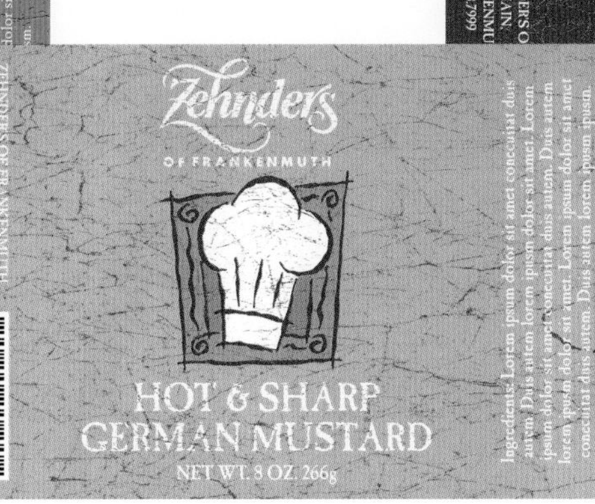
Zehnders of Frankenmuth
730 S. Main
Frankenmuth, MI 48734
1.800.863.7999
Zehnders
of Frankenmuth
Hot & Sharp German Mustard
Net Wt. 8 oz. 266g

Zehnders
of Frankenmuth
Vidalia Onion
Peppercorn Dressing
Net Wt. 8.0 oz. 266g

design firm
LAT Diseño Grafico
San Juan, Puerto Rico
designer
Lydimarie Aponte Tañón
client
Turabo Medical Group

Pharmacia &Upjohn

design firm
Interbrand
New York, New York
designer
Marksteen Adamson
client
Pharmacia + UpJohn

design firm
Mires Design
San Diego, California
art director
John Ball
designer
Jeff Samaripa
illustrator
Neil Shigley
client
Southern Comfort
(alcoholic beverage sales)

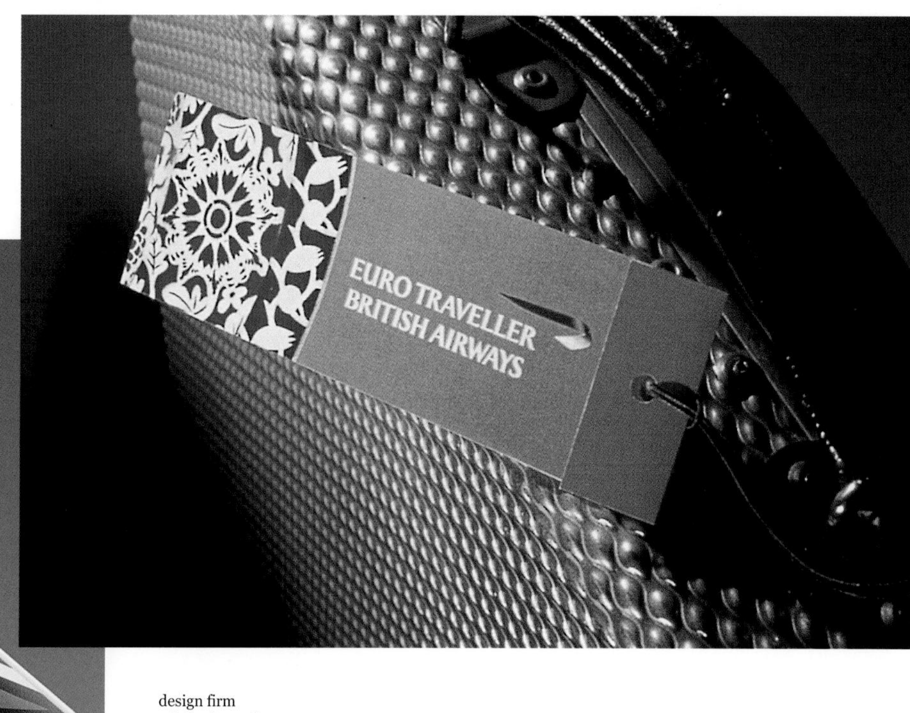

design firm
Interbrand
New York, New York
designers
John Sorrel, Francis Newell
client
British Airways

CONCORD MILLS℠

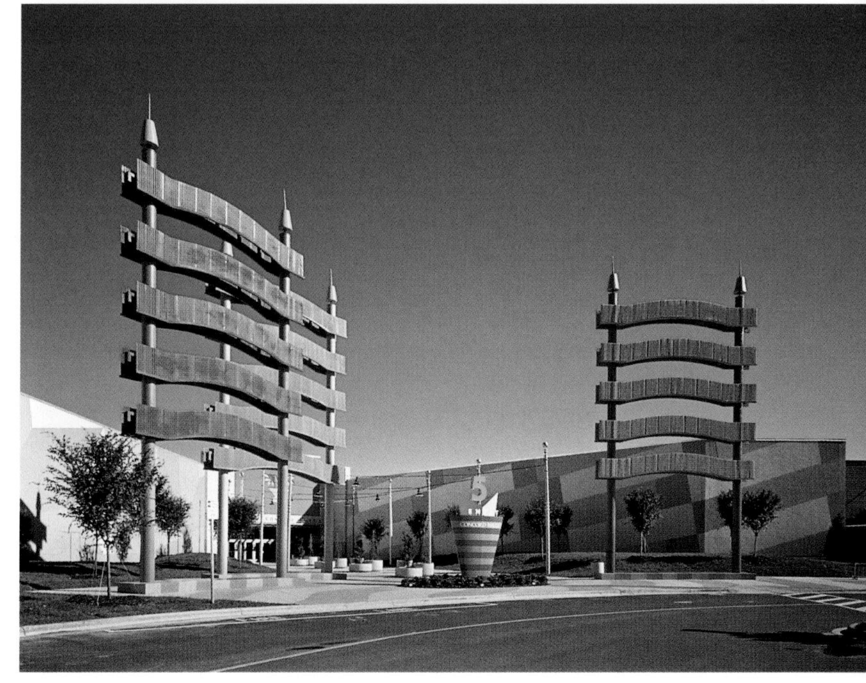

design firm

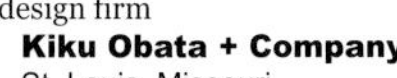

Kiku Obata + Company
St. Louis, Missouri

designers
Kiku Obata, Kevin Flynn, AIA, Dennis Hyland, AIA, Denise Fuehne, Jennifer Baldwin, Teresa Norton-Young, Gen Obata, Carole Jerome, Nikki Hite, John Scheffel, Kathleen Robert, Jeff Rifkin

client
Concord Mills/The Mills Corporation
(retail developers)

(continued)
design firm
Kiku Obata + Company
St. Louis, Missouri

design firm
Hornall Anderson Design Works, Inc.
Seattle, Washington
designers
Jack Anderson, Sonja Max, Kathy Saito, Alan Copeland
client
Impli
(media advertising technology)

design firm
Mires Design
San Diego, California
art director
Jose Serrano
designer
Deborah Hom
photographer
Carl Vandershuit
copywriter
Andrea May
client
Qualcomm
(cellular telephones & accessories)

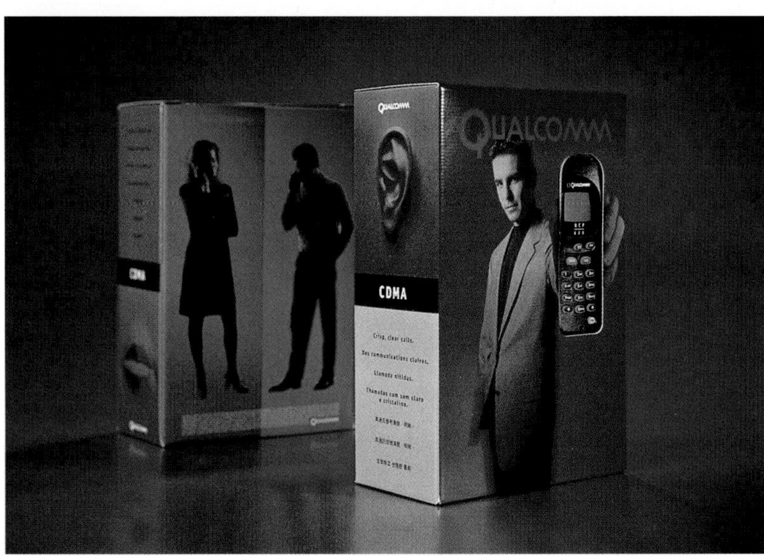

design firm
Mires Design
San Diego, California
art director
Jose Serrano
designer
Deborah Hom
photographer
Carl Vandershuit
copywriter
Andrea May
client
Qualcomm
(telecommunication)

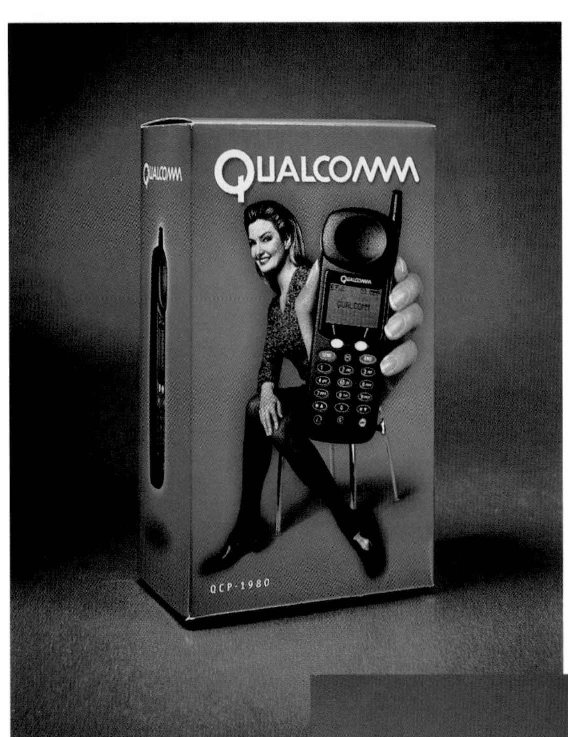

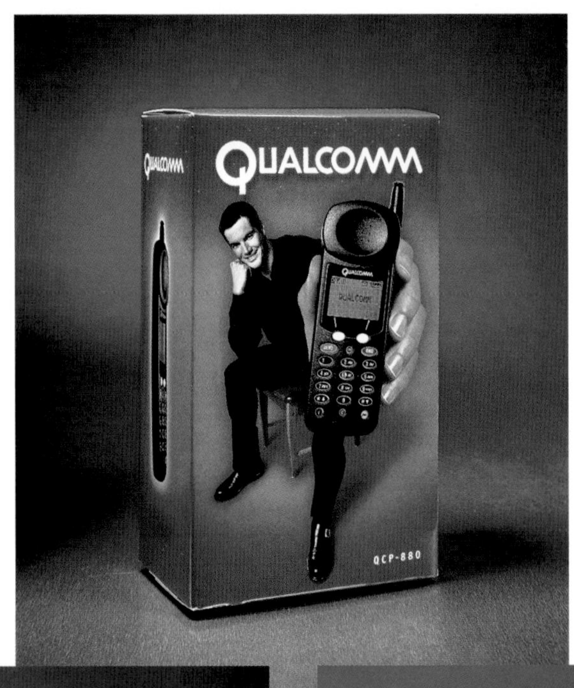

design firm
Mires Design
San Diego, California
art director
Jose Serrano
designers
Deborah Hom, David Adey
photographer
Carl Vandershuit
client
Qualcomm
(telecommunications)

NETWORK-SYMBOL

design firm
Tim Girvin Design, Inc.
Seattle, Washington
designers
Tim Girvin, Chie Masuyama, Brian Boram, Aki Morino
client
Dentsu

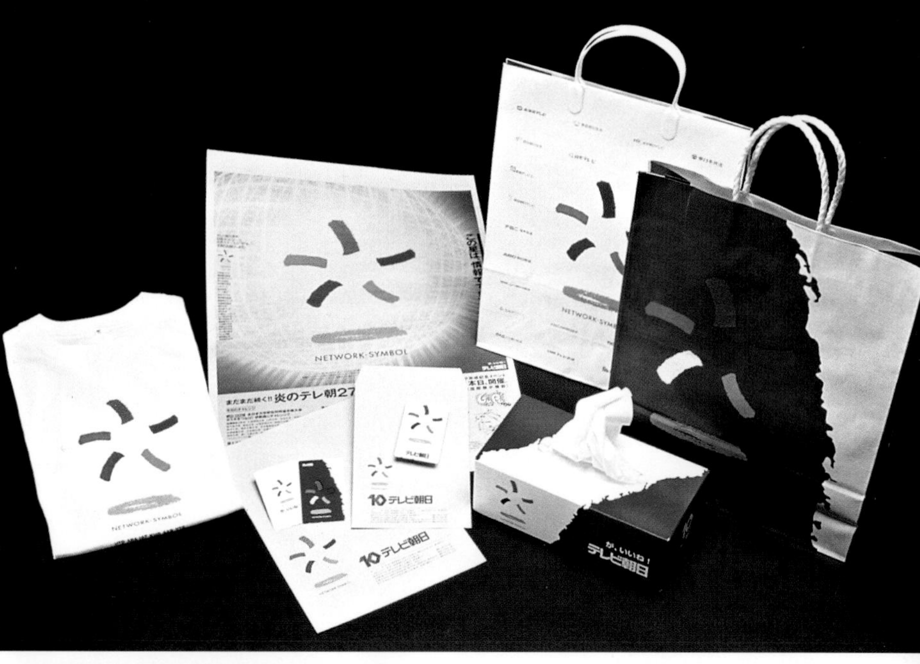

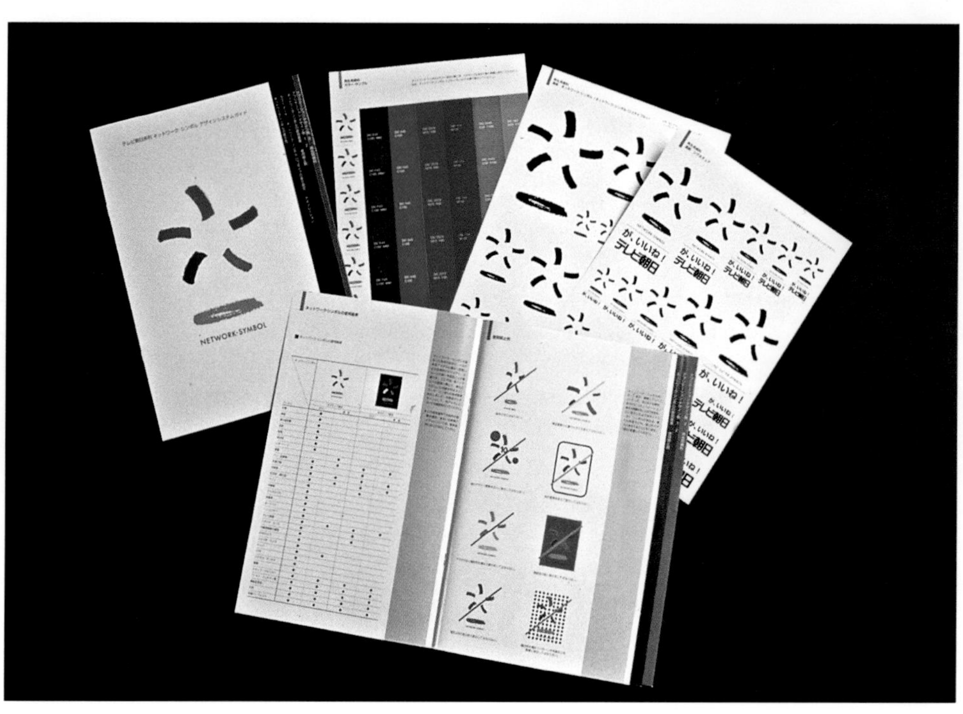

design firm
Evenson Design Group
Culver City, California
creative director
Stan Evenson
designer
Ken Loh
client
Private Exercise
(personal exercise and training facility, catering to those who need personal attention)

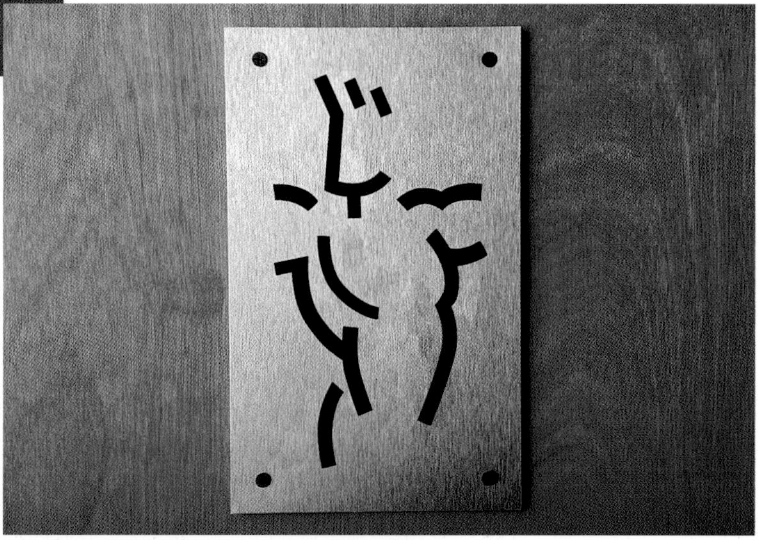

PRIVATE
EXERCISE

design firm
Boelts Bros. Associates
Tucson, Arizona
designers
J. Boelts, E. Boelts, K. Stratford,
E. Taylor, A. Arietts
client
Southwest Parks & Monuments
Association
(government)

LITTLE BIGHORN BATTLEFIELD
CHANNEL ISLANDS NATIONAL PARK
HUBBELL TRADING POST
GILA CLIFF DWELLINGS
GOLDEN SPIKE
PADRE ISLAND NATIONAL SEASHORE
SALINAS PUEBLO MISSIONS
TUMACACORI NATIONAL HISTORICAL PARK
TONTO NATIONAL MONUMENT
EL MORRO
CHACO CULTURE
EL MALPAIS NATIONAL MONUMENT
NAVAJO
BLACK CANYON OF THE GUNNISON

BLACK
CANYON
OF THE GUNNISON
NATIONAL MONUMENT

CHANNEL
ISLANDS
NATIONAL PARK

PETROGLYPH
NATIONAL MONUMENT

GILA CLIFF
DWELLINGS
NATIONAL MONUMENT

GOLDEN
SPIKE
NATIONAL HISTORIC SITE

LITTLE
BIGHORN
BATTLEFIELD
NATIONAL MONUMENT

PADRE
ISLAND
NATIONAL SEASHORE

NAVAJO
NATIONAL MONUMENT

CHACO
CULTURE
NATIONAL HISTORICAL PARK

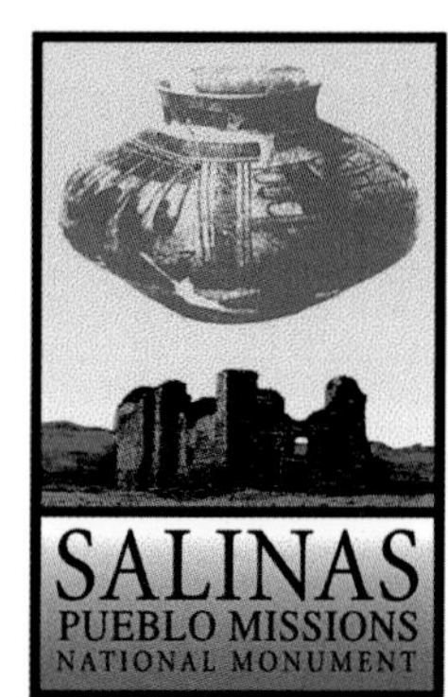
SALINAS
PUEBLO MISSIONS
NATIONAL MONUMENT

(c|t|s|n|e|t)

design firm
Mires Design
San Diego, California
art director
Scott Mires
designers
Gale Spitzley, Miguel Perez, Andrew Goddard, Jeff Samaripa, and Angela
illustrator
Miguel Perez
photographer
Carl Vanderschuit
client
CTS Net
(internet service provider)

ctsnet
Internet Services
Serious flexibility.
Serious business.
www.cts.com
OUTDOOR SYSTEMS

MTS
www.cts.com
ctsnet
Internet Services
Serious traffic.
Serious business.

ctsnet
ctsnet
ctsnet
John Villanueva
Billing Manager
ctsjov@cts.com
8913 Complex Drive
San Diego, California
92123-1413
t 858 637 3600 x1480
f 858 637 3631
www.cts.com
8913 Complex Drive San Diego, California 92123-1413 t 858.637.3600 f 858.637.3630 www.cts.com

design firm
Walsh & Associates
Seattle, Washington
designers
Miriam Lisco, Lyn Blanchard
client
Fran's Chocolates, Ltd.
(gourmet chocolates)

FRAN'S
CAFE AU LAIT
MINT
ORANGE
PEANUT BUTTER
FIXATION
NET WT. .5 OZ.
fran's
CHOCOLATES, LTD.
CAOBA NATURAL
PREMIUM MILK CHOCOLATE
fran's
CHOCOLATES, LTD.
BUCARE BLEND
ESPRESSO BITTERSWEET CHOCOLATE
fran's
CHOCOLATES, LTD.
BUCARE NATURAL
BITTERSWEET DARK CHOCOLATE
fran's
RASPBERRY SAUCE
fran's
CARAMEL SAUCE
fran's
DARK CHOCOLATE SAUCE

BEVERLY
SASSOON

design firm
Shimokochi/Reeves
Los Angeles, California
designers
Mamoru Shimokochi, Anne Reeves
client
Beverly Sassoon
(cosmetic/beauty products)

ZINERA™

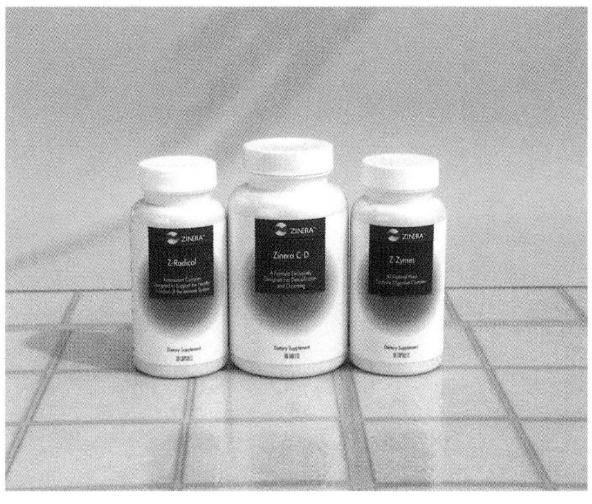

design firm
Shimokochi/Reeves
Los Angeles, California
designers
Mamoru Shimokochi,
Anne Reeves
client
Zig Ziglar Network, Inc.
(nutritional supplements)

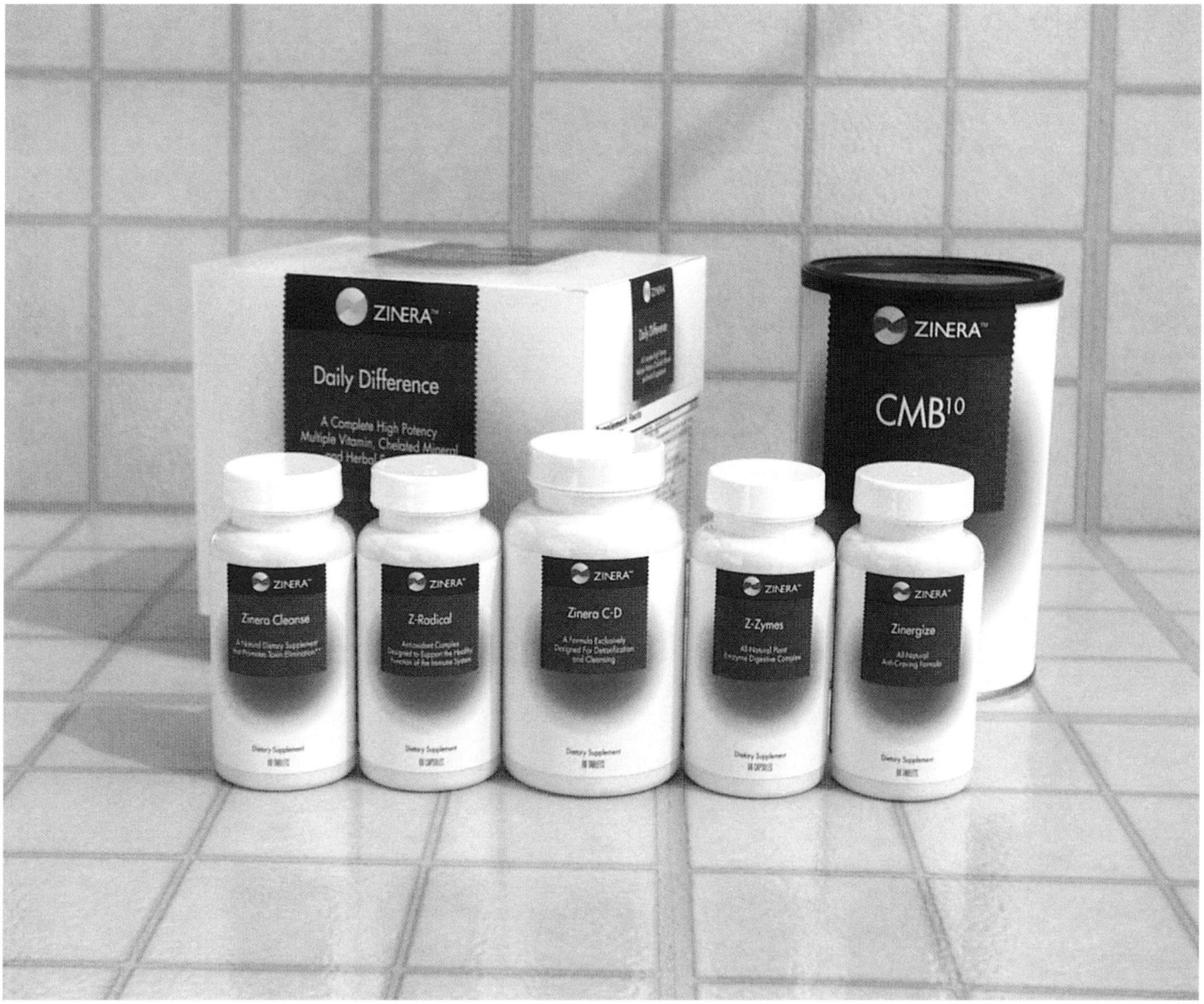

THE ELLIOTT

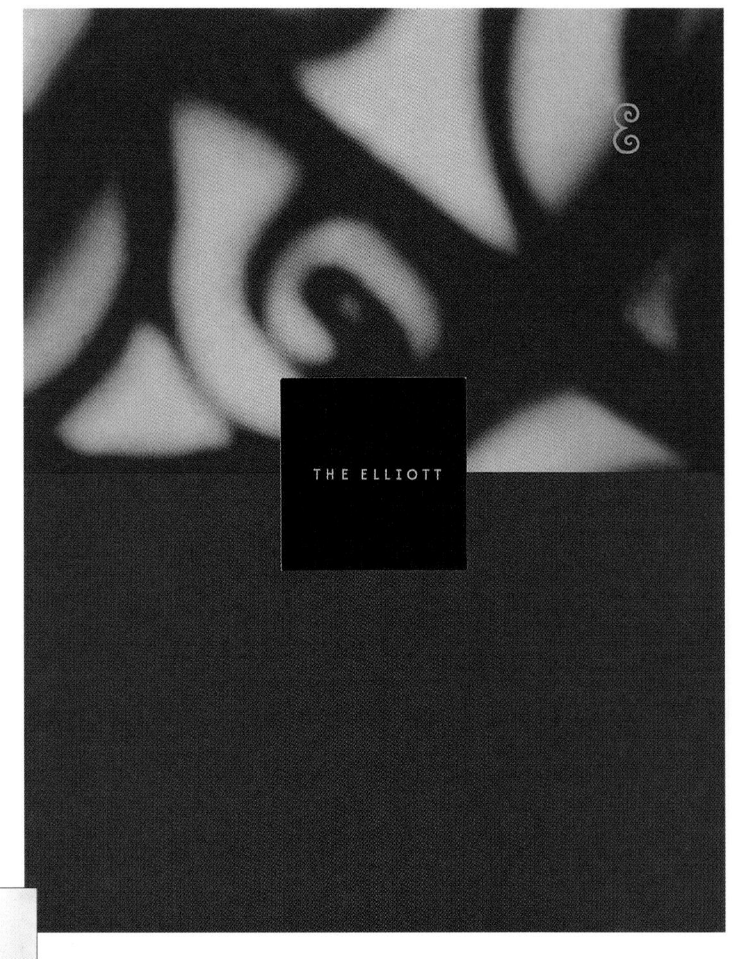

THE ELLIOTT

THE ELLIOTT

721 Pine Street
Seattle, WA 98101
t 206.262.0700
f 206.625.1221
www.elliotthotel.com

A HEDREEN HOTEL

design firm
The Traver Company
Seattle, Washington
designers
Dale Hart, Christopoher Downs,
Margo Sepanski, John Totten
client
The Elliott Hotel
(hotel industry)

T H E   E L L I O T T

THERE IS ONLY ONE ELLIOTT HOTEL. AND IT'S IN SEATTLE.

A hotel should never leave you in doubt of who you are – an honored guest – or where you are. While The Elliott's standards are international, its spirit is pure Seattle. The Elliott was created for modern travelers who want to make the most of this remarkable city. These guests expect their rooms to be superb, their stay flawless. But they also welcome surprises of a delightful kind. Above all, they want their experience here to be different. For that is one of the pleasures of travel.

A downtown hotel in a setting of extraordinary natural beauty. The Elliott surrounds you with the elements of nature: warm woods, natural stone, rich shades of blue and brown. And like the city, it's friendly, spacious, cosmopolitan and effortlessly at the center of a technological revolution.

Service? Our staff prefer the genuine smile to the raised eyebrow. Business hours? Take your pick. At The Elliott, we keep 24 of them. Mixing Seattle-style enterprising spirit with a full complement of bells and whistles, we offer round-the-clock room service and pressing, transportation, concierge service, business services and some truly awe-inspiring technology.

All together, it's an experience you'd savor anywhere on your travels. But it's only to be found at one hotel. Like Puget Sound and the snow-capped Cascades, The Elliott is one of Seattle's unique pleasures.

S T A Y.

THERE IS ONLY ONE ELLIOTT HOTEL. AND IT'S IN SEATTLE.

Open spaces. A friendly, accommodating spirit. High-tech wizardry. Reasons why meeting planners are drawn to Seattle. And why business travelers in Seattle are drawn to The Elliott, which distills the best of an extraordinary city into an extraordinary, international-class hotel.

The Elliott was created with meetings in mind. Its ballrooms, prefunction rooms and more than 25,000 square feet of meeting space are all on one floor, so you can lose yourself in your work without losing your colleagues.

Moreover, we know the way you really work: never far from your laptop. We offer high-speed network connections and power outlets at each seat in the theater, and the ability to download material from presentations. Even the guest rooms have network connections. In fact, we're Seattle's, and perhaps the country's, most tech-ready hotel. Just ask the digital concierge in your room; then use it to order tomorrow's breakfast.

At The Elliott, we're aware of the one commodity that's scarce, even in Seattle: time. We assume that you're too busy to wait in line for check-in or comb the streets for a midnight snack. That's why our only timetable is yours. We're there whenever you need us, supremely competent and ready to do the impossible at a moment's notice. After all, it's the sign of a modern, world-class hotel that you never, ever, have to lower your expectations.

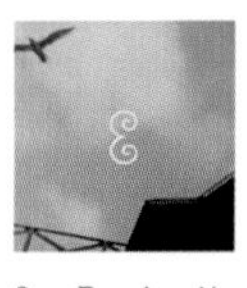

S T A Y.

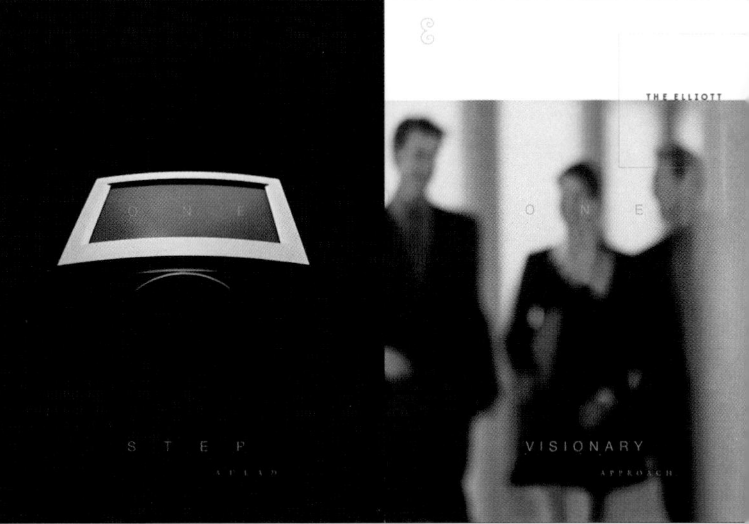

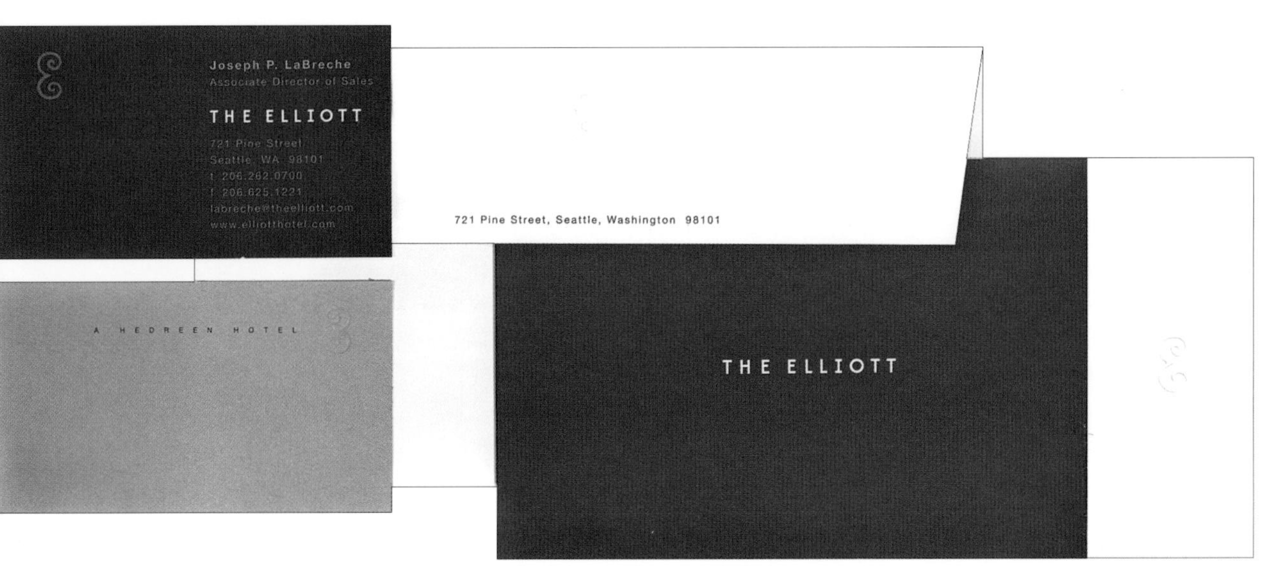

design firm
Gold & Associates
Ponte Vedra Beach, Florida
designers
Keith Gold, Jo Varra
client
Redneck Foods
(restaurant)

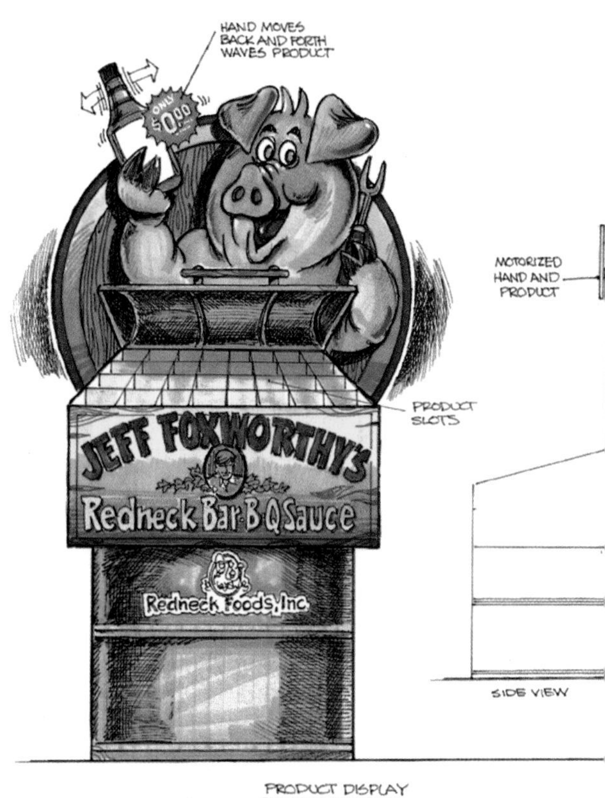

BEWARE
OF DOG

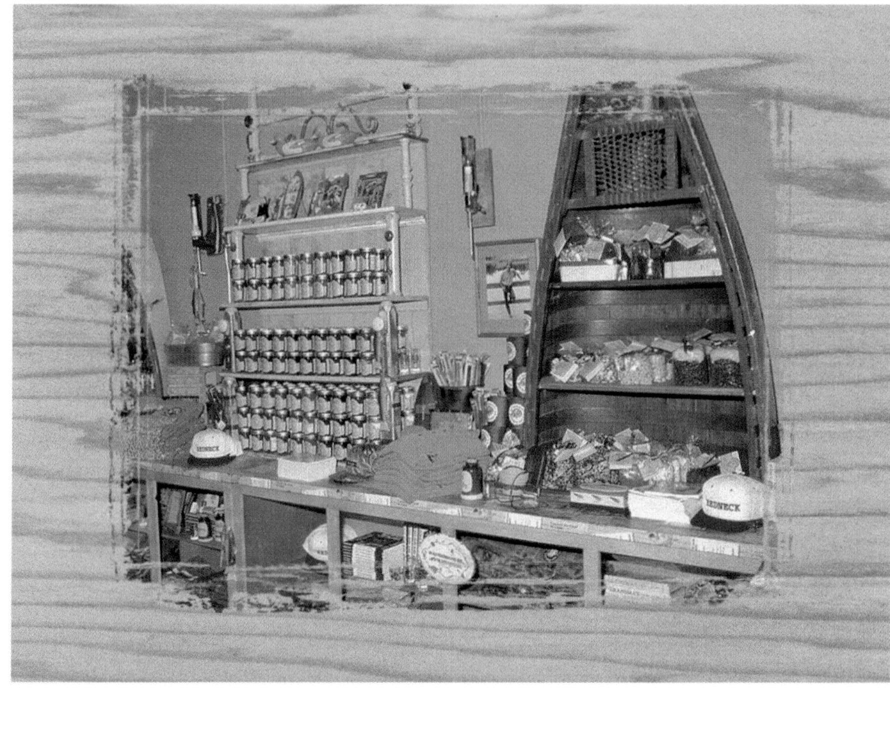
REDNECK

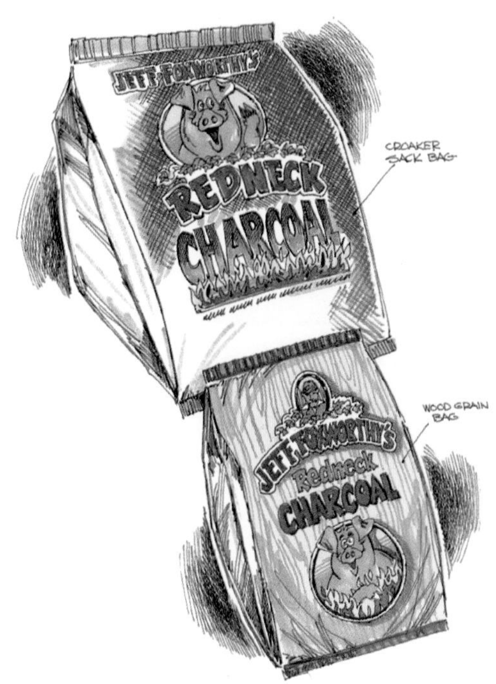
JEFF FOXWORTHY'S
REDNECK
CHARCOAL
CROAKER SACK BAG
WOOD GRAIN BAG
JEFF FOXWORTHY'S
Redneck
CHARCOAL

(continued)
design firm
Gold & Associates
Ponte Vedra Beach, Florida

WAITER & WAITRESS TAKE OUT WINDOW
CHRISTMAS LIGHTS
BAR ENCLOSED IN A TRAILER SHELL

LAWN CHAIR

U ORDER TO-GO

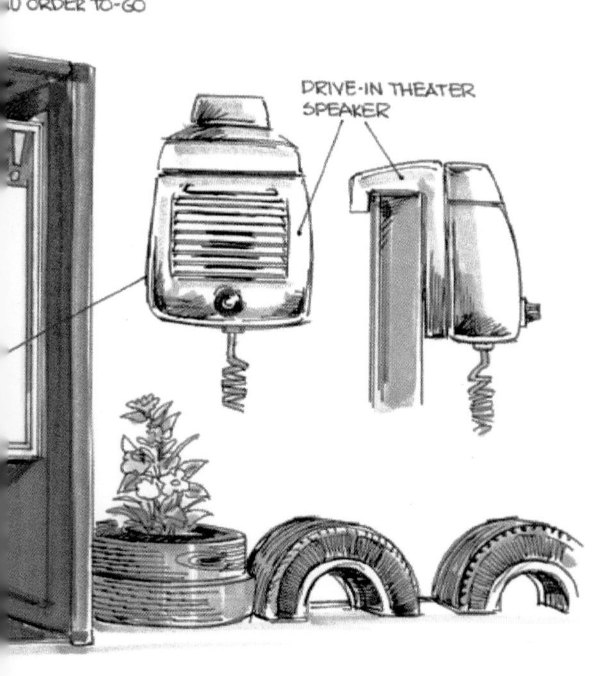
DRIVE-IN THEATER SPEAKER

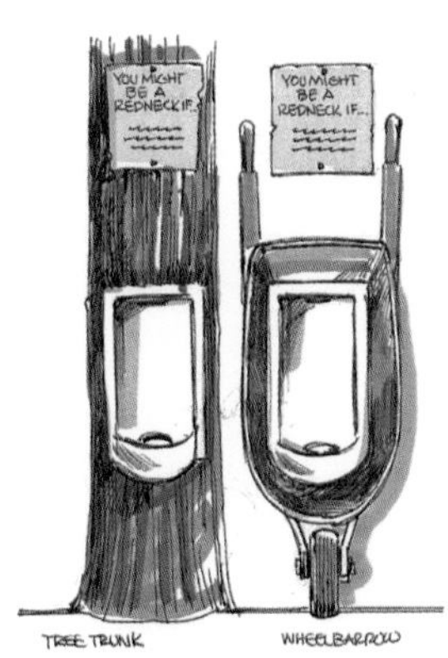
YOU MIGHT BE A REDNECK IF...
YOU MIGHT BE A REDNECK IF...
TREE TRUNK
WHEELBARROW
URINALS

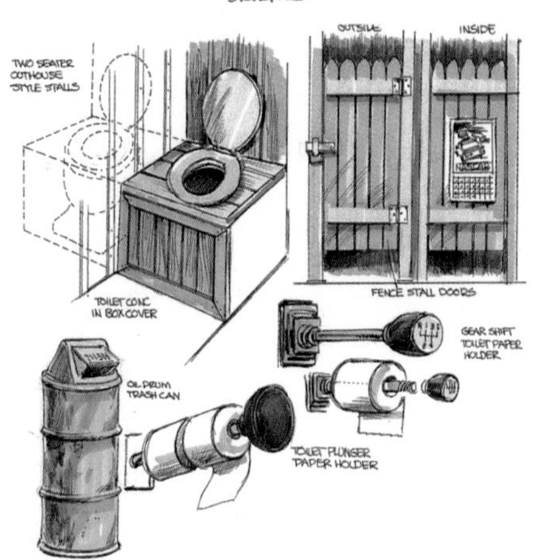
TWO SEATER OUTHOUSE STYLE STALLS
OUTSIDE
INSIDE
TOILET CONC IN BOX COVER
FENCE STALL DOORS
GEAR SHIFT TOILET PAPER HOLDER
OIL DRUM TRASH CAN
TOILET PLUNGER PAPER HOLDER

design firm
Visual Asylum
San Diego, California
designers
Joel Soleto, MaeLin Levine, Amy Jo Levine
illustrator
Linda Helton
client
Sempra Energy
(public utility)

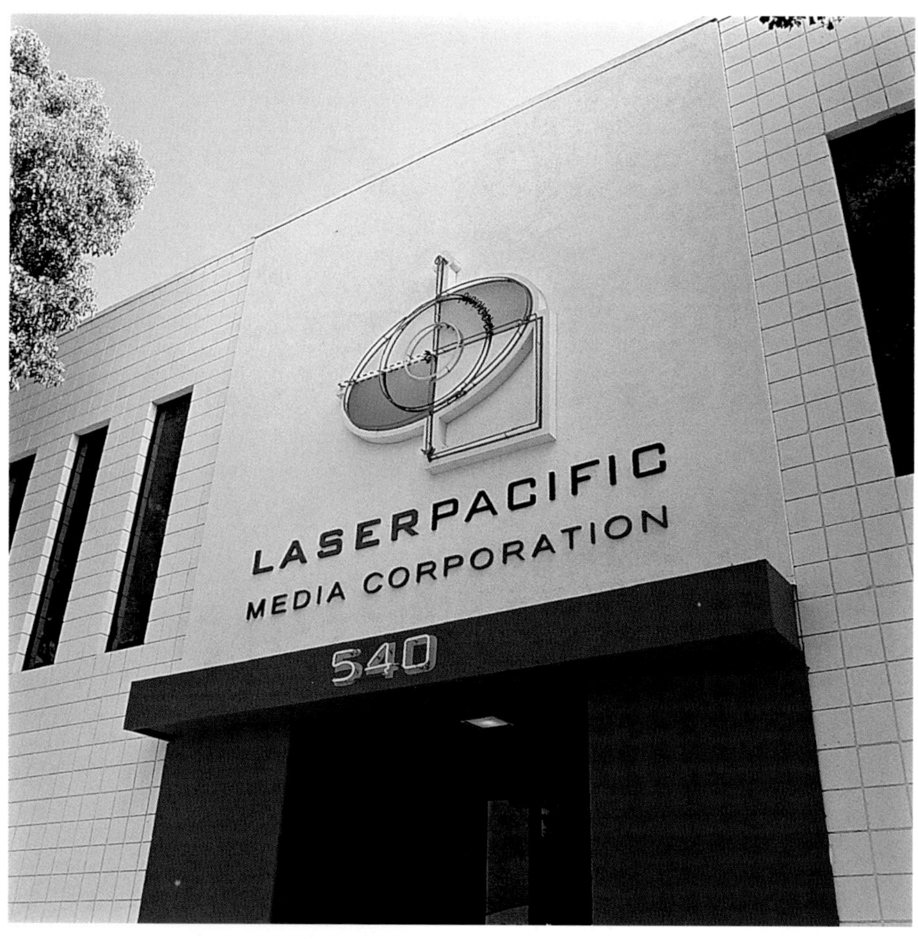

design firm
Visual Asylum
San Diego, California
designers
MaeLin Levine, Amy Jo Levine
client
Laser Pacific
(episodic television post-production house)

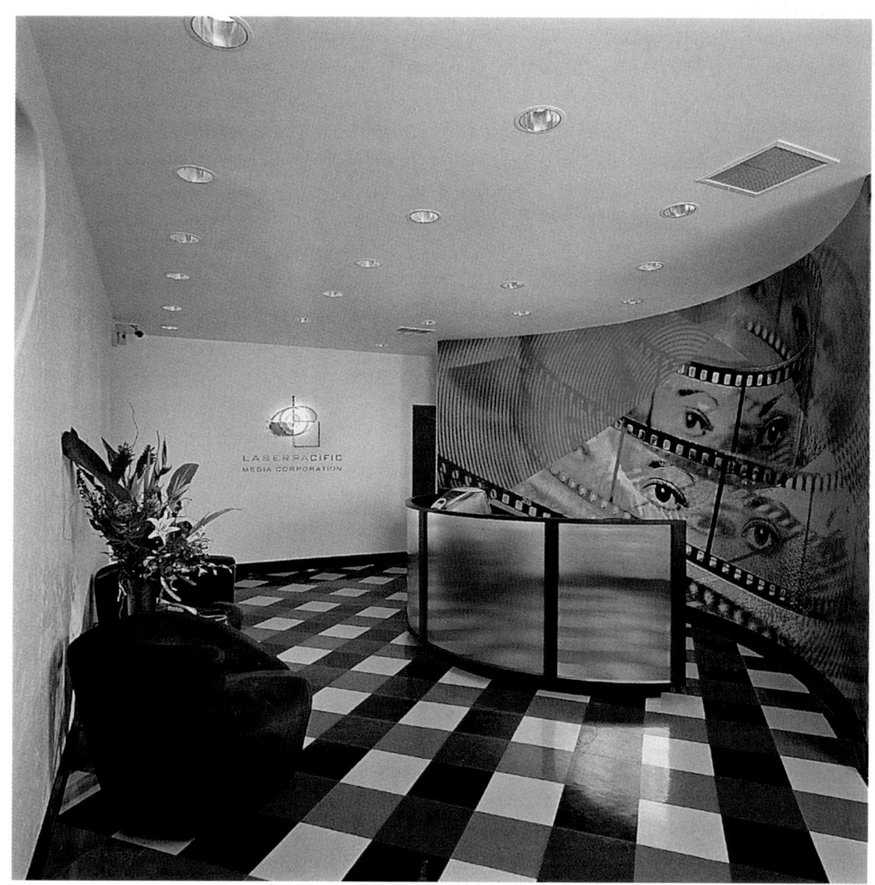

radius

design firm
Mortensen Design
Mountain View, California
art director, designer
Gordon Mortensen
client
Radius, Inc.
(hardware company)

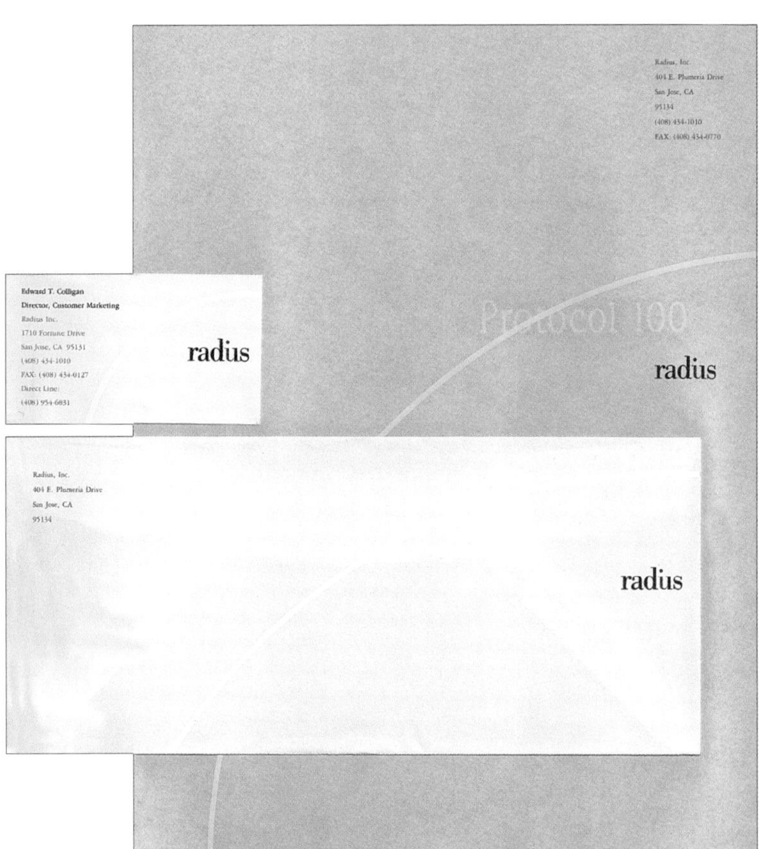

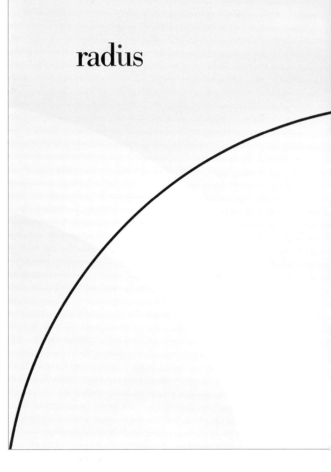

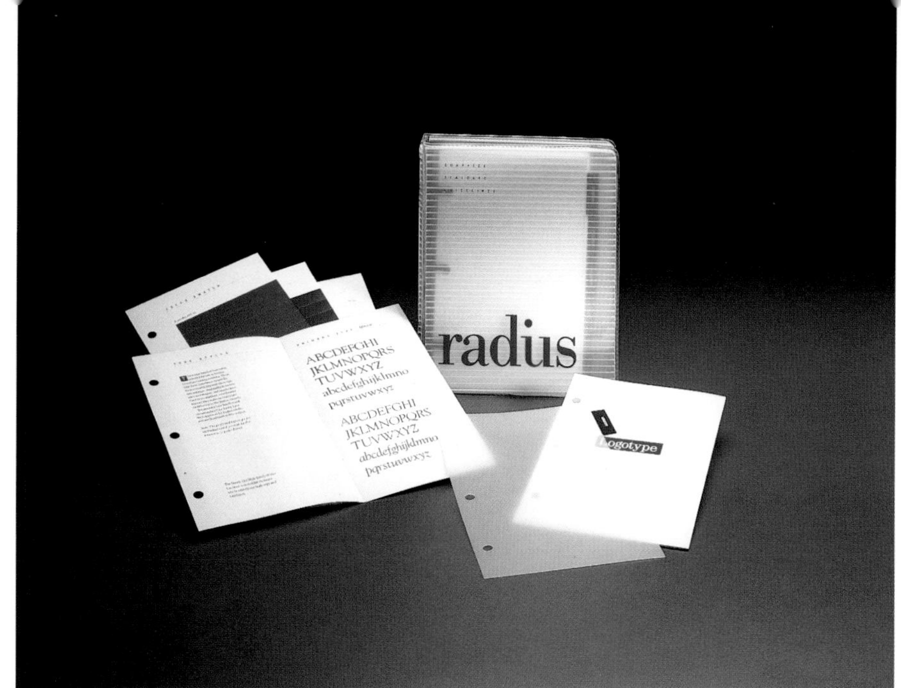

radus
ABCDEFGHI
JKLMNOPQRS
TUVWXYZ
abcdefghijklmno
pqrstuvwxyz
ABCDEFGHI
JKLMNOPQRS
TUVWXYZ
abcdefghijklmno
pqrstuvwxyz
Logotype

UNACCEPTABLE USE
radus

BUSINESS CARDS
radus

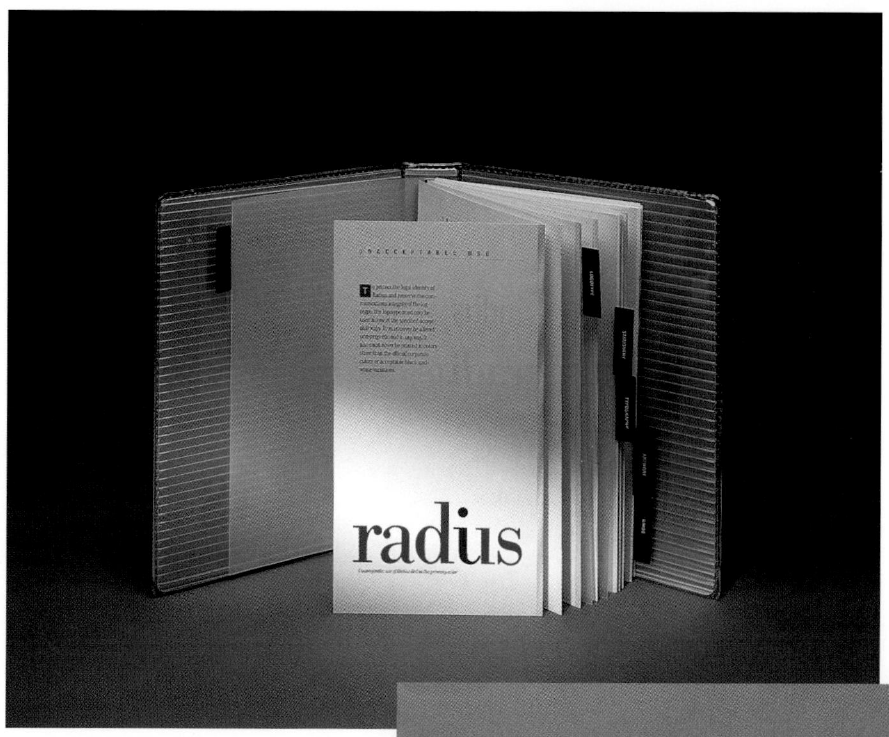

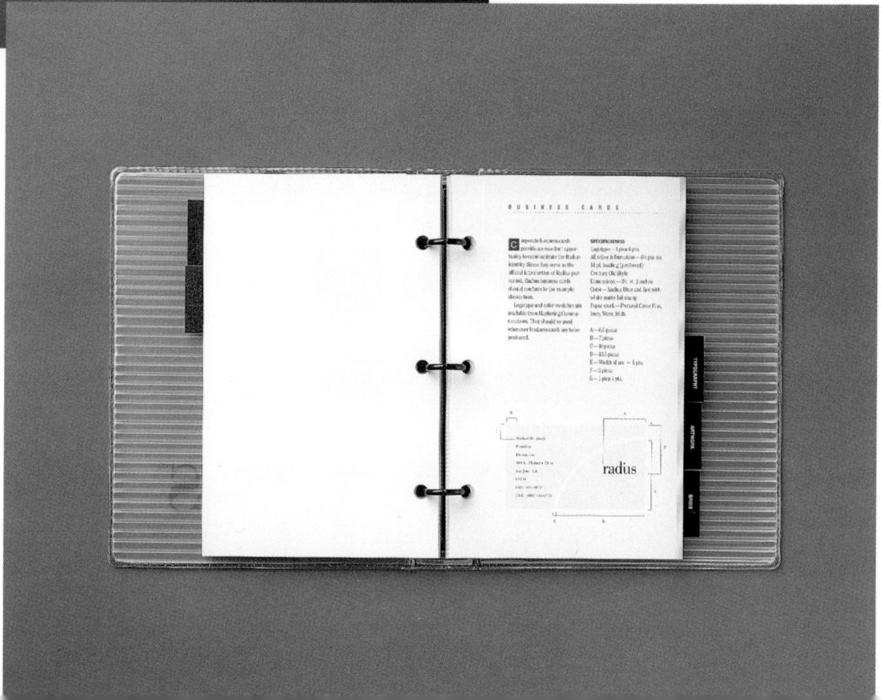

design firm
Mires Design
San Diego, California
art director
John Ball
designers
Miguel Perez, Gale Spitzley
illustrator
Miguel Perez
photographer
Mike Campos
client
Think Outside
(computer accessories)

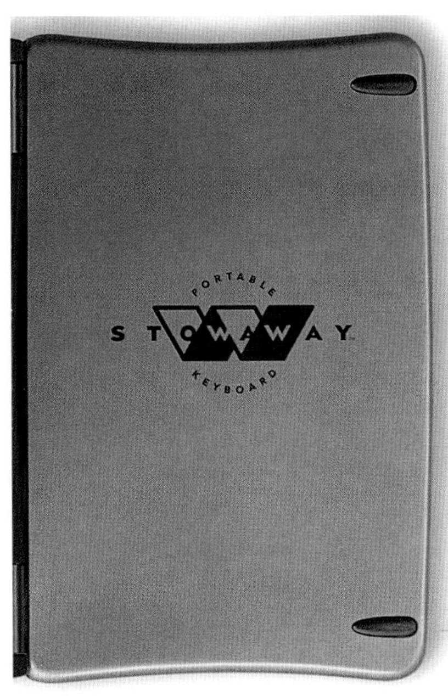

design firm
Mires Design
San Diego, California
art director
Jose Serrano
designer
David Adey
client
Exario
(vpn and telecommuter solutions)

CINNABON®

design firm
Tim Girvin Design, Inc.
Seattle, Washington
designers
Tim Girvin, Jennifer Bartlett
client
Cinnabon

design firm
Hornall Anderson Design Works, Inc.
Seattle, Washington
client
Compass Creek

>STREETSPACE.

design firm
Tom & John: A Design Collaborative
San Francisco, California
designers
Tom & John
client
Tom & John: A Design Collaborative
(graphic design)

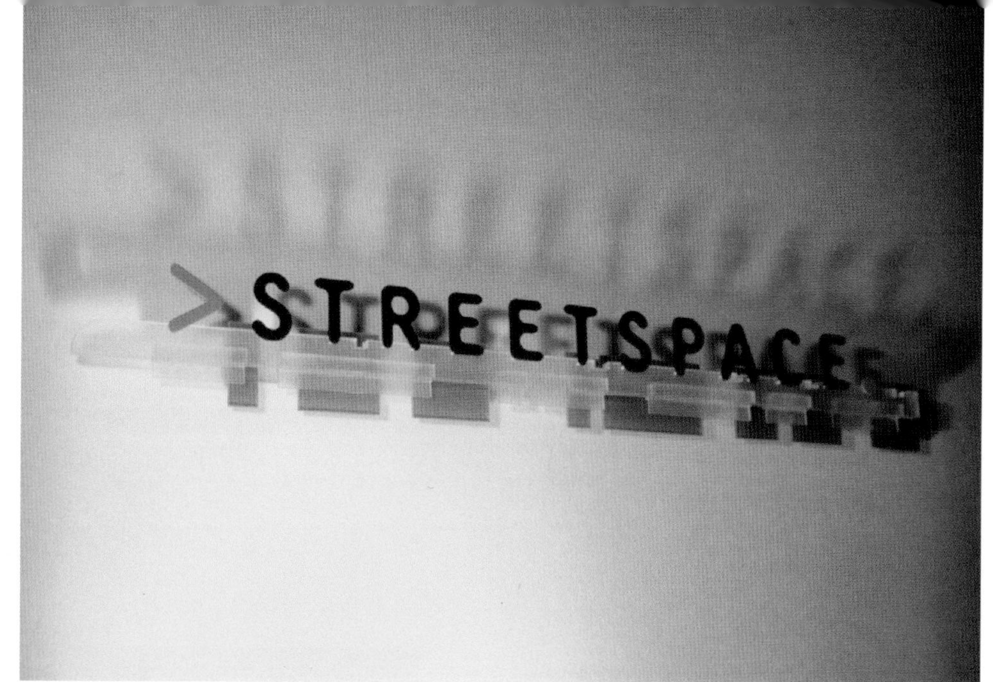
>STREETSPACE.

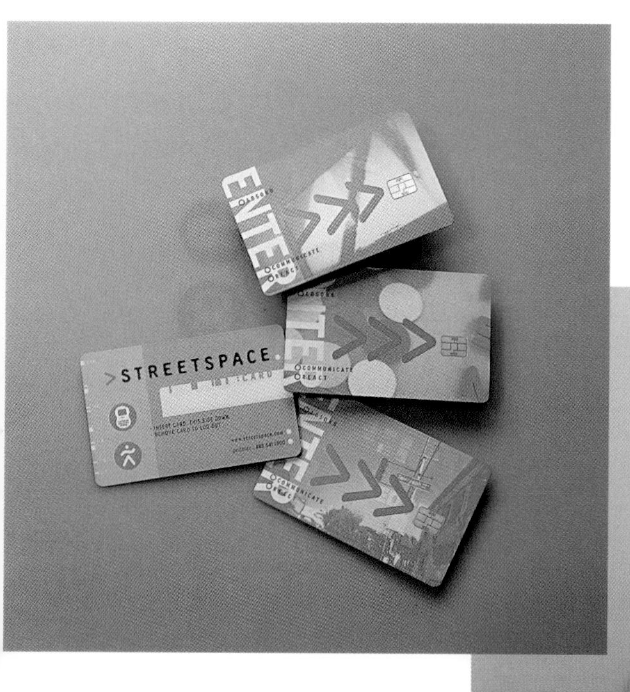
ENTER
>STREETSPACE.

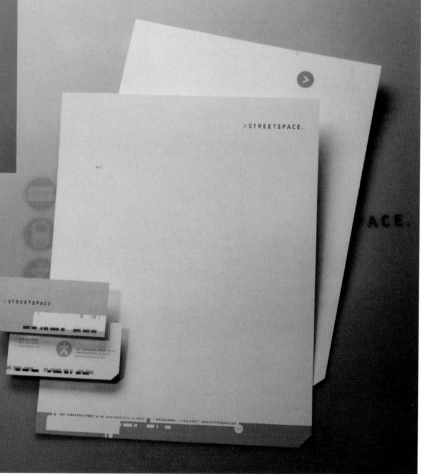
>STREETSPACE.
>STREETSPACE.

Pen & paper stationery, cards,

Pen & paper stationery, cards, invitations, accessories

design firm
Susan Meshberg Graphic Design
New York, New York
designer
Susan Meshberg
computer art
Rob Johnson
client
Pen & Paper LLC
(stationery store)

invitations, accessor

Linda Broder announces the opening of

Pen&paper

28 N. Bryn Mawr Ave
Bryn Mawr, PA 19010
tel: (610)525-6870
fax: (610)525-6831

Featuring fine stationery, invitations, greeting cards, accessories

Our awning goes up April 21st

Pen&paper stationery, cards, invitation

Adjacent to the Bryn Mawr Train Station

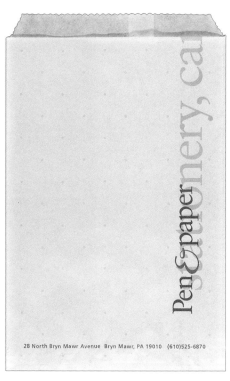

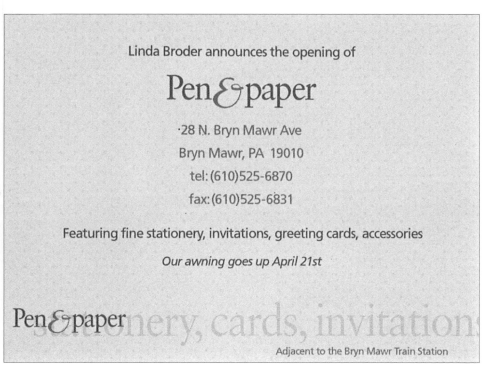

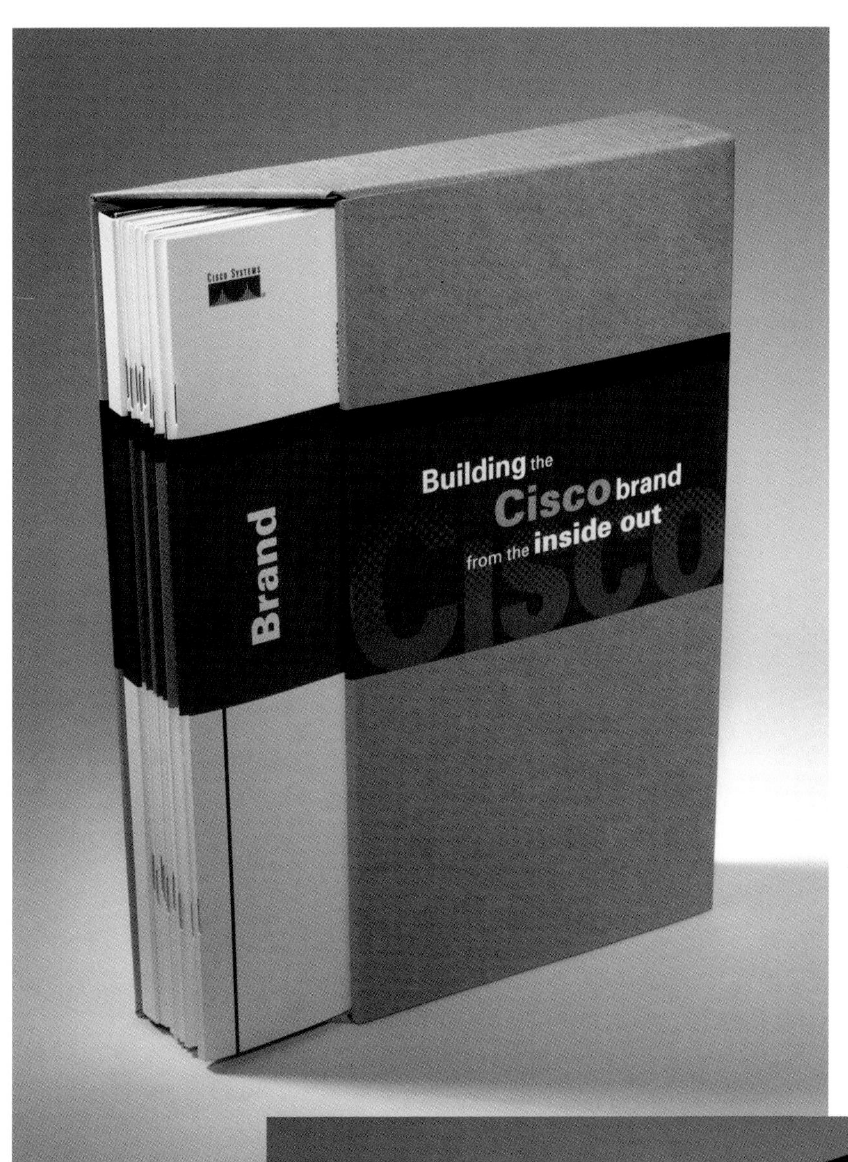

design firm
(In-House)
San Jose, California
designers
Jeff Brand, Gary McCavitt, Dennis Mancini, Donna Helliwell, Linda Mayer, Dennis Gobets, Sam Mahgod, Monique Mulbry
client
Cisco Systems
(identity system)

Building the Cisco brand from the inside out
Brand
Library
RESOURCES
The Cisco Systems Resource Library
CD
Resources
Art
Brand
Logo
Logos and Signatures
Graphic
The Graphic System
Ad
Cisco Advertising

design firm
Walsh & Associates, Inc.
Seattle, Washington
designers
Miriam Lisco, Lyn Blanchard
client
Truesoups
(food service/retail)

TRUESOUPS

TRUESOUPS

design firm
Mires Design
San Diego, California
art director
Scott Mires
designers
Miguel Perez, Gretchen Leary, Deborah Hom, Gale Spitzley
illustrators
Miguel Perez, Michael Schwab
photographer
Chris Wimpey
copywriters
Andrea May, John Robertson, Bob Taylor
client
Taylor Guitars
(premium acoustic guitars)

When I sat down to design this 25th Anniversary Limited Edition Series, I knew I couldn't just rehash one of my old designs. That may be enough for a simple collector's item, but these guitars demanded to be much more than that. And with the development of our New Technology design, I knew they could be. I discovered an incredible log of Sapele. A wood I love and a wood worthy to be used to create these guitars. And the designs are my own personal favorites. The New Dreadnought, our evolution of the old classic which offers a powerful response in all registers — and the Grand Auditorium, which yields more treble response and better definition to individual notes. Keep in mind that these guitars are not just reissues. They're not just digging up the past. They are the product of our New Technology — the culmination of 25 years of craftsmanship, ingenuity, art and technology. Play one and I think you'll agree. Guitars this good are worth the wait.

BOB TAYLOR, APRIL NINETEEN NINETY-NINE

(continued)
design firm
Mires Design
San Diego, California

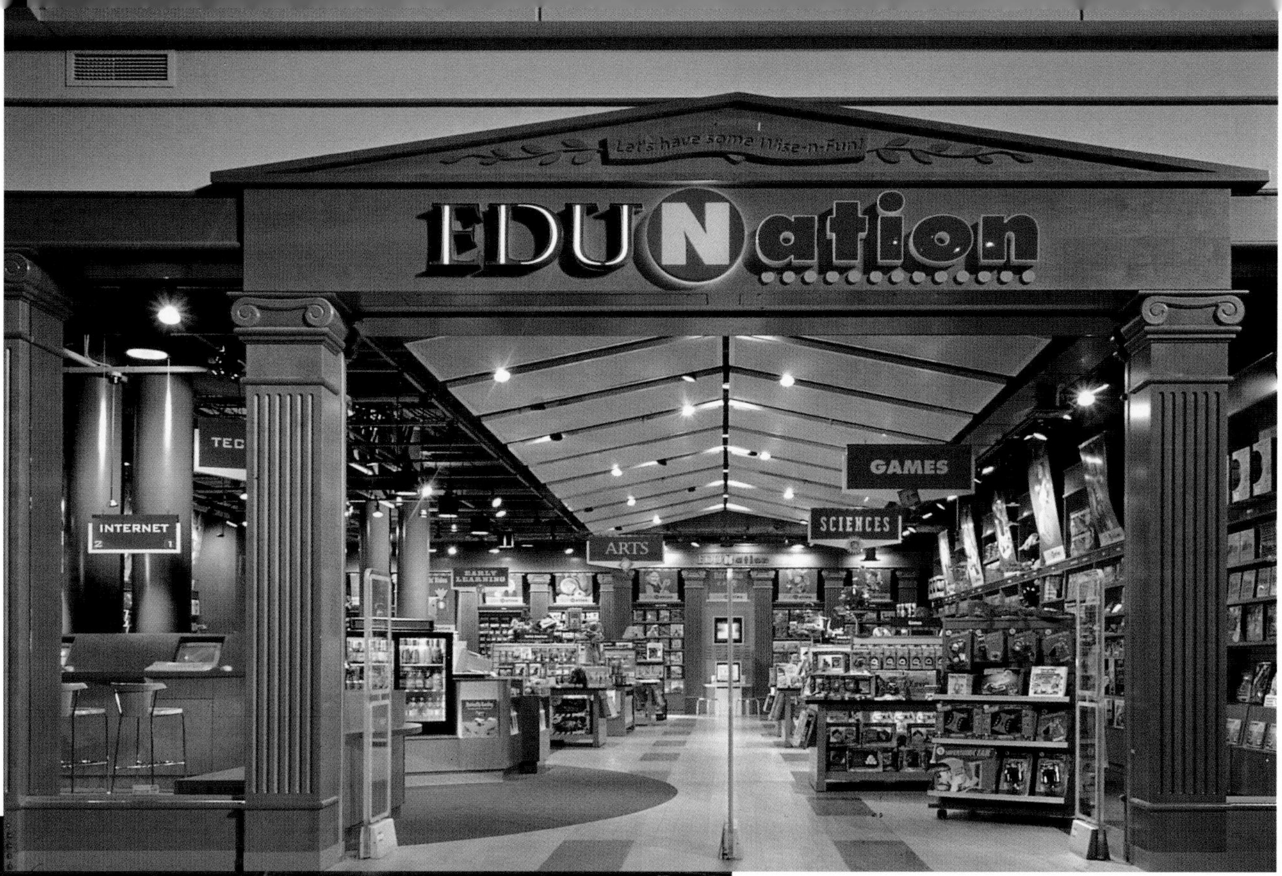

design firm
Kiku Obata + Company
St. Louis, Missouri
designers
Kiku Obata, Kevin Flynn, Idie McGinty, Tim McGinty, Rich Nelson, Chris Mueller, Beth Wallisch, Al Sacui, David Hercules, Liz Sullivan, Theresa Henrekin
client
EduNation

design firm
Sayles Graphic Design
Des Moines, Iowa
designer
John Sayles
client
1999 Iowa State Fair
(state fair)

GILLIG
PHANTOM
KNOCK YOURSELF OUT
iowastatefair.org
AUG. 12-22
IOWA STATE FAIR
77861

IOWA STATE FAIR
KNOCK YOURSELF OUT
AUG. 12-22
1999
SATURDAY, AUGUST 14
TUESDAY, AUGUST 17
THURSDAY, AUGUST 19
FRIDAY, AUGUST 20
PRCA RODEO
WEDNESDAY, AUGUST 18
iowastatefair.org

IOWA STATE FAIR
KNOCK YOURSELF OUT
1999
Des Moines Register

design firm
AERIAL
San Francisco, California
designer
Tracy Moon
client
Tribe Pictures
(entertainment)

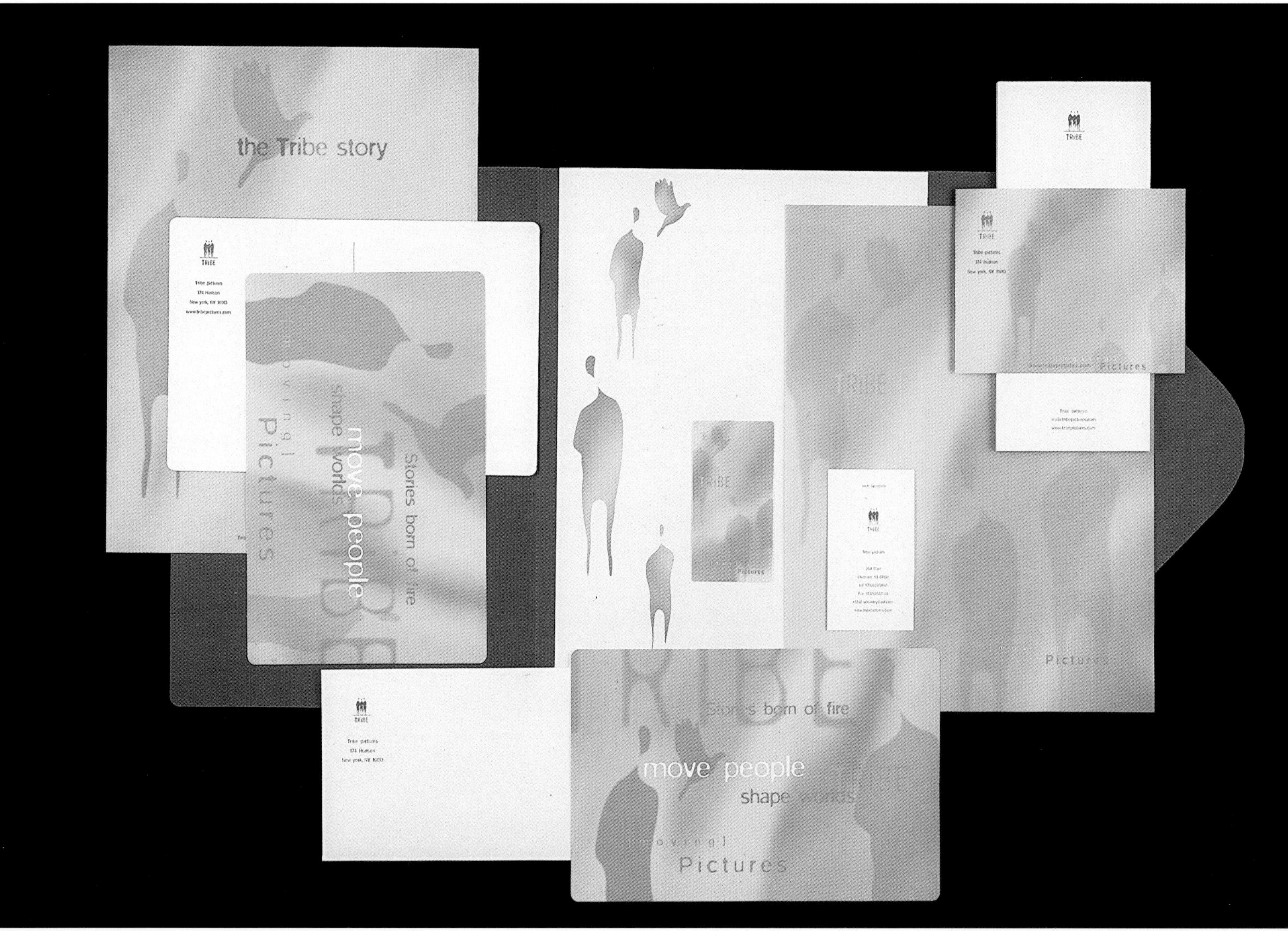
the Tribe story
Stories born of fire
move people
shape worlds
[moving]
Pictures
TRIBE

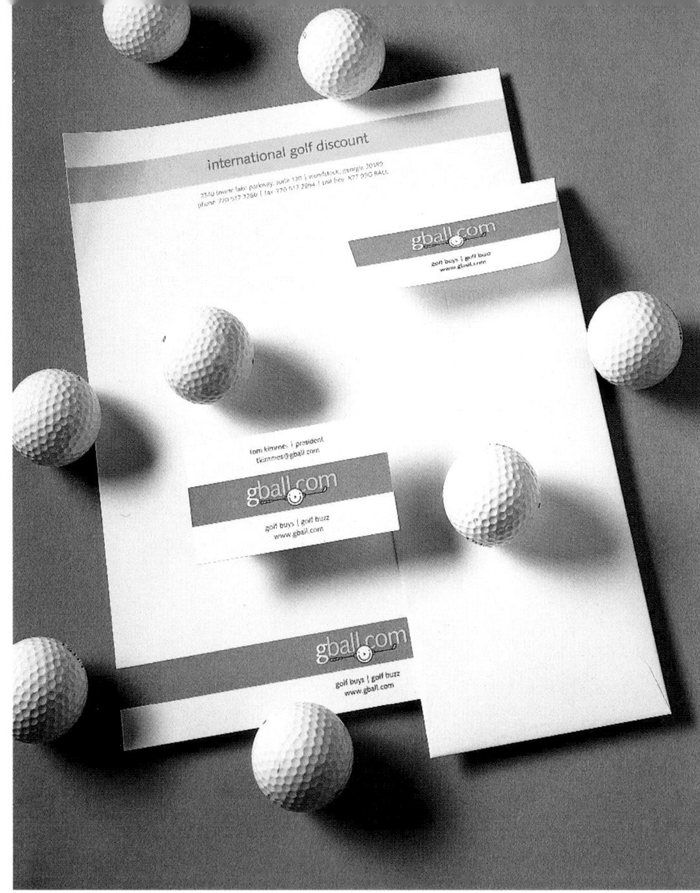

design firm
Mires Design
San Diego, California
art director
Scott Mires
designers
Miguel Perez, Gretchen Leary, Sam Grogan, Deborah Hom, Cherie Wheeler
illustrators
Tracy Sabin, Miguel Perez
copywriter
Brian Woosley
client
Gball.com
(golf web site)

Do your clients play golf?

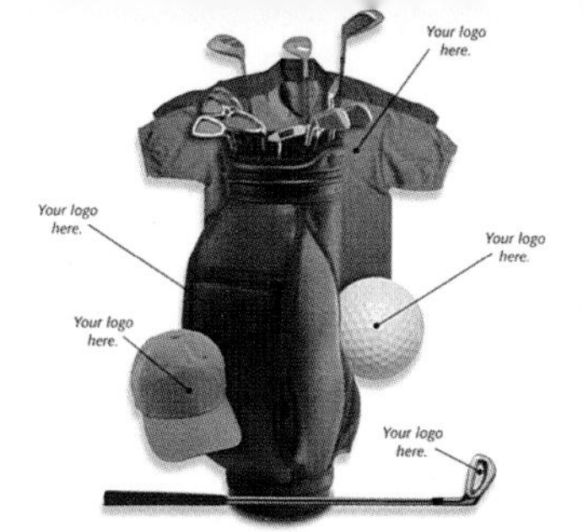

It's easy to get your customers to think about you more. Just give them some very cool golf products with your logo emblazoned on them. Call to choose from the ones you see here, or log on to see even more. 1.877.99G BALL

cool golf stuff with your logo on it™
www.gball.com/brandit

America's leading companies pay millions to put their logo on a select few players.*

*Now you can, too. (And for a whole lot less.)

Give your clients a dozen balls, and every time they tee it up they'll think of you. Especially with your logo emblazoned on each ball.

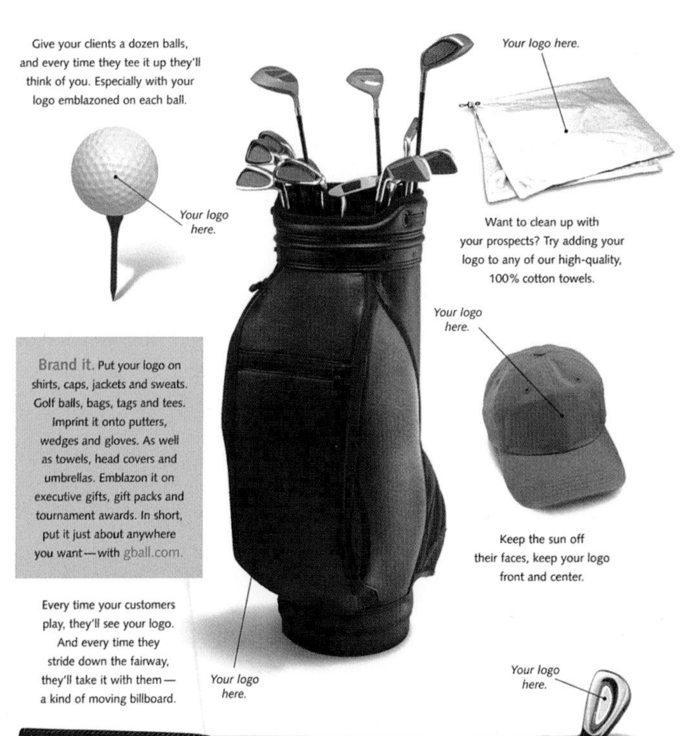

Want to clean up with your prospects? Try adding your logo to any of our high-quality, 100% cotton towels.

Brand it. Put your logo on shirts, caps, jackets and sweats. Golf balls, bags, tags and tees. Imprint it onto putters, wedges and gloves. As well as towels, head covers and umbrellas. Emblazon it on executive gifts, gift packs and tournament awards. In short, put it just about anywhere you want—with gball.com.

Keep the sun off their faces, keep your logo front and center.

Every time your customers play, they'll see your logo. And every time they stride down the fairway, they'll take it with them—a kind of moving billboard.

cool

It's younger. It's cooler. It's way more fun. That's today's golf world—and it's gball, too. Because this isn't just a company. It's a philosophy. One that captures the new outlook of the game—and of the people who play it.

More than just an online golf superstore, gball.com is a community. A place for those who love the game to voice opinions, pick up tips and get connected with today's hottest clubs and accessories. gball.com. Golf buys, golf buzz.

international golf discount

international golf discount is the bricks-and-mortar brother to gball.com. A place where golfers find the hottest new products tagged with remarkably low prices. Can't drive over? Then click over—to the community of gball.com.

2340 towne lake parkway, suite 120 | woodstock, georgia 30189
phone 770 517 2280 | fax 770 517 2854 | toll free 877 99G BALL

design firm
Art 270, Inc.
Jenkintown, Pennsylvania
designers
Sue Strohm, Dianne Mill, Carl Mill, Steve Kuttruff, John Opet
client
Curtis Institute of Music (music education)

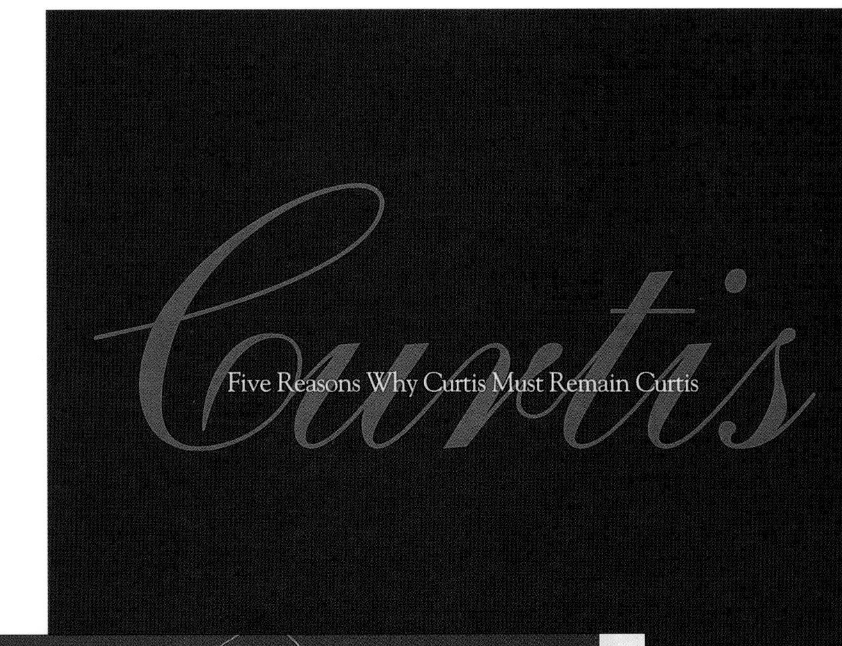

Curtis
Five Reasons Why Curtis Must Remain Curtis

TAKE NOTE

An informational update for students, faculty and staff of The Curtis Institute of Music.

CURTIS APPLICATION FORM

75
CURTIS
CELEBRATING
SEVENTY-FIVE YEARS
OF EXCELLENCE

Gary Graffman

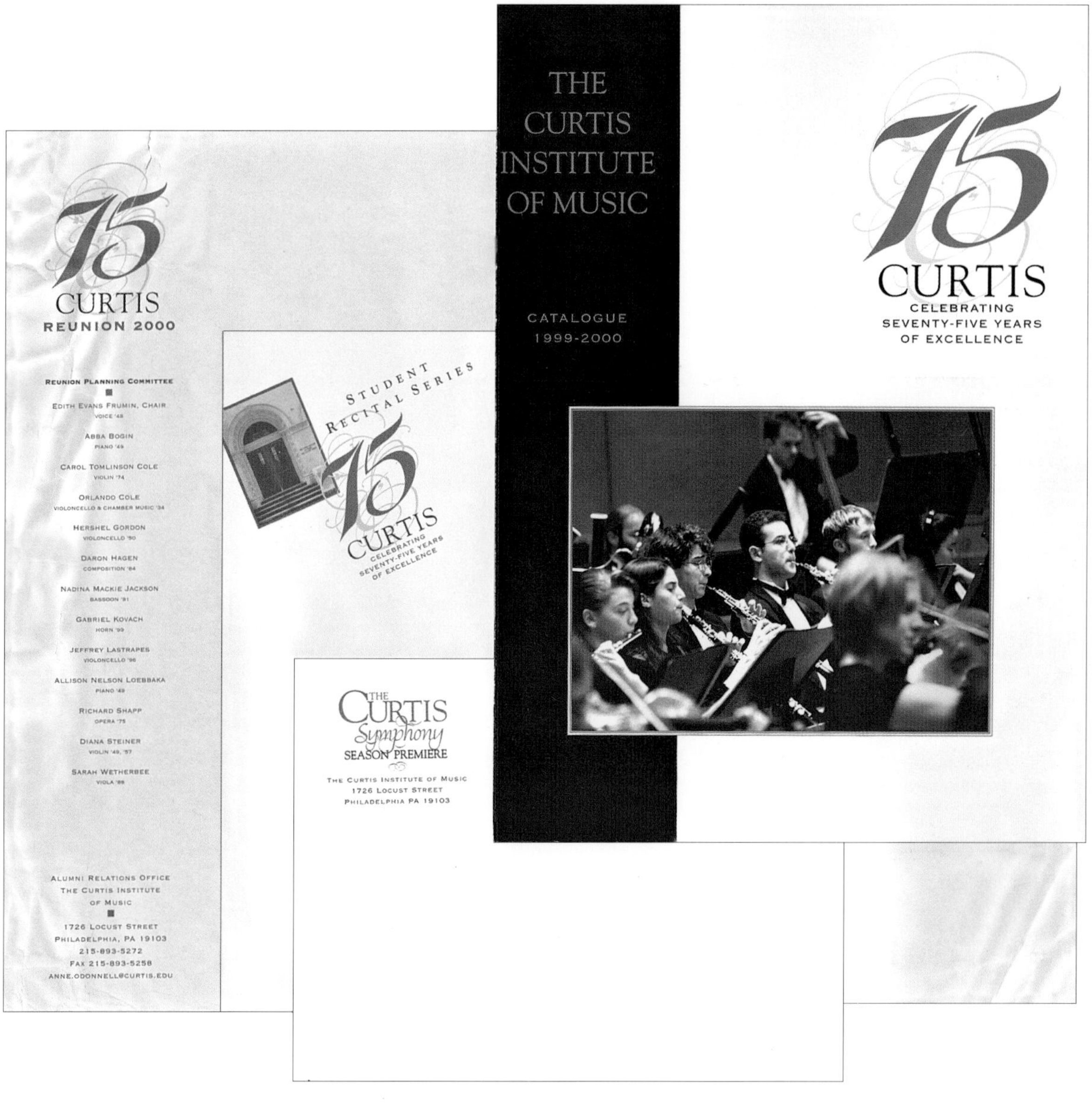

75
CURTIS
REUNION 2000

REUNION PLANNING COMMITTEE

EDITH EVANS FRUMIN, CHAIR
VOICE '48

ABBA BOGIN
PIANO '49

CAROL TOMLINSON COLE
VIOLIN '74

ORLANDO COLE
VIOLONCELLO & CHAMBER MUSIC '34

HERSHEL GORDON
VIOLONCELLO '50

DARON HAGEN
COMPOSITION '84

NADINA MACKIE JACKSON
BASSOON '91

GABRIEL KOVACH
HORN '99

JEFFREY LASTRAPES
VIOLONCELLO '96

ALLISON NELSON LOEBBAKA
PIANO '49

RICHARD SHAPP
OPERA '75

DIANA STEINER
VIOLIN '49, '57

SARAH WETHERBEE
VIOLA '88

ALUMNI RELATIONS OFFICE
THE CURTIS INSTITUTE
OF MUSIC

1726 LOCUST STREET
PHILADELPHIA, PA 19103
215-893-5272
FAX 215-893-5258
ANNE.ODONNELL@CURTIS.EDU

STUDENT RECITAL SERIES
75
CURTIS
CELEBRATING SEVENTY-FIVE YEARS OF EXCELLENCE

THE CURTIS Symphony
SEASON PREMIERE

THE CURTIS INSTITUTE OF MUSIC
1726 LOCUST STREET
PHILADELPHIA PA 19103

THE CURTIS INSTITUTE OF MUSIC

CATALOGUE
1999-2000

75
CURTIS
CELEBRATING
SEVENTY-FIVE YEARS
OF EXCELLENCE

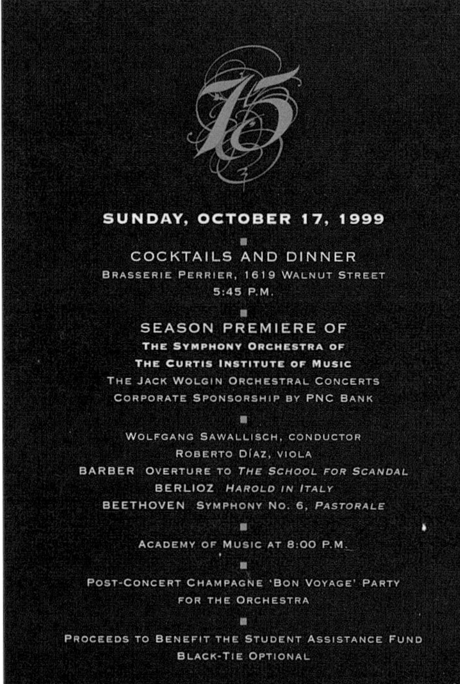
SUNDAY, OCTOBER 17, 1999
COCKTAILS AND DINNER
BRASSERIE PERRIER, 1619 WALNUT STREET
5:45 P.M.
SEASON PREMIERE OF
THE SYMPHONY ORCHESTRA OF
THE CURTIS INSTITUTE OF MUSIC
THE JACK WOLGIN ORCHESTRAL CONCERTS
CORPORATE SPONSORSHIP BY PNC BANK
WOLFGANG SAWALLISCH, CONDUCTOR
ROBERTO DÍAZ, VIOLA
BARBER OVERTURE TO THE SCHOOL FOR SCANDAL
BERLIOZ HAROLD IN ITALY
BEETHOVEN SYMPHONY NO. 6, PASTORALE
ACADEMY OF MUSIC AT 8:00 P.M.
POST-CONCERT CHAMPAGNE 'BON VOYAGE' PARTY
FOR THE ORCHESTRA
PROCEEDS TO BENEFIT THE STUDENT ASSISTANCE FUND
BLACK-TIE OPTIONAL
CELEBRATING BRILLIANT
MUSIC-MAKING
YOU ARE CORDIALLY INVITED
to a gala evening to celebrate
the 75th Anniversary of
THE PAST
The Curtis Institute of Music;
to celebrate the opening of
THE PRESENT
the 1999/2000 season of
the Curtis Symphony Orchestra;
THE FUTURE
and to wish 'bon voyage'
to the Orchestra on
its first European Tour.
THE CURTIS SYMPHONY SEASON PREMIERE
THE CURTIS Symphony SEASON PREMIERE
THE CURTIS INSTITUTE OF MUSIC
1726 LOCUST STREET
PHILADELPHIA PA 19103

(continued)
design firm
Art 270, Inc.
Jenkintown,
Pennsylvania

THE
CURTIS
INSTITUTE
OF MUSIC
W 1700
LOCUST ST

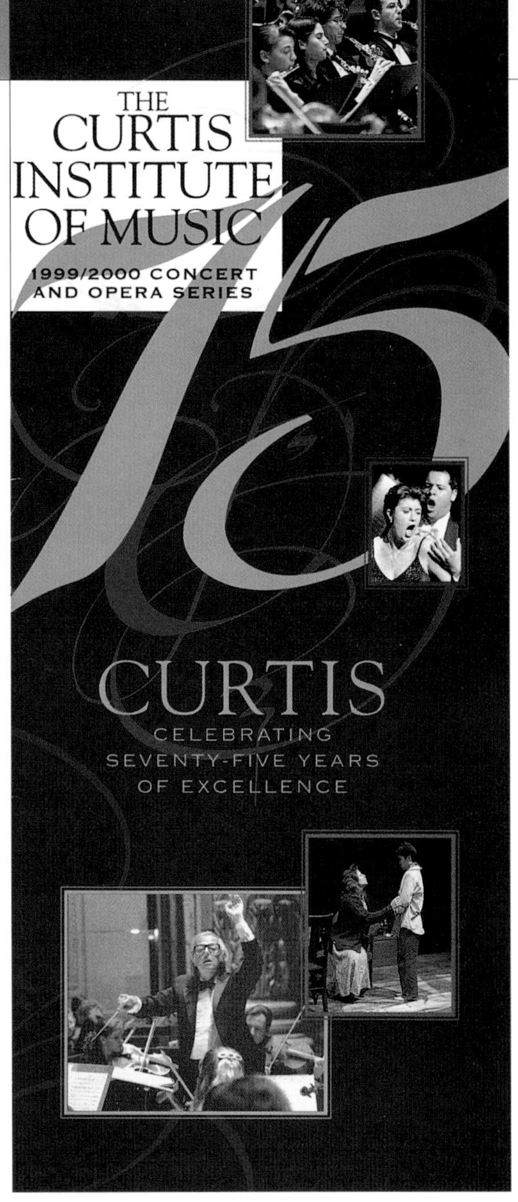
THE
CURTIS
INSTITUTE
OF MUSIC
1999/2000 CONCERT
AND OPERA SERIES
CURTIS
CELEBRATING
SEVENTY-FIVE YEARS
OF EXCELLENCE

THE CURTIS INSTITUTE OF MUSIC
SOUND FOR THE CENTURY
CAMPAIGN STEERING COMMITTEE
R. Anderson Pew
Campaign Chair
Dr. Milton L. Rock
Chair of the Board
Gary Graffman
President/Director
Shaun F. O'Malley
Chair of Major Gifts Committee
Alan R. Hirsig
Chair of the Annual Fund Committee
Richard A. Doran
Chair of the Business and Professional Associates Committee
Steven Laden
Chair of Leadership Gifts Committee
Robert Montgomery Scott
Chair of the Foundations Committee
Richard A. Shapp
Chair of the Alumni Affairs Council
Margaret A. Reese
Chair of the Board of The Friends of Curtis
Bayard R. Fiechter
Treasurer
Josiah Stevenson IV
Vice President, Development
Charles Sterne III
Director of Major Gifts and Planned Giving
Leslie Jacobson Kaye
Assistant Director of Major Gifts
Jane M. Kamp
Director of Annual Giving
THE CURTIS INSTITUTE OF MUSIC
1726 LOCUST STREET
PHILADELPHIA PA 19103
215-893-5279
FAX: 215-893-5258
1726 LOCUST STREET
PHILADELPHIA PA 19103

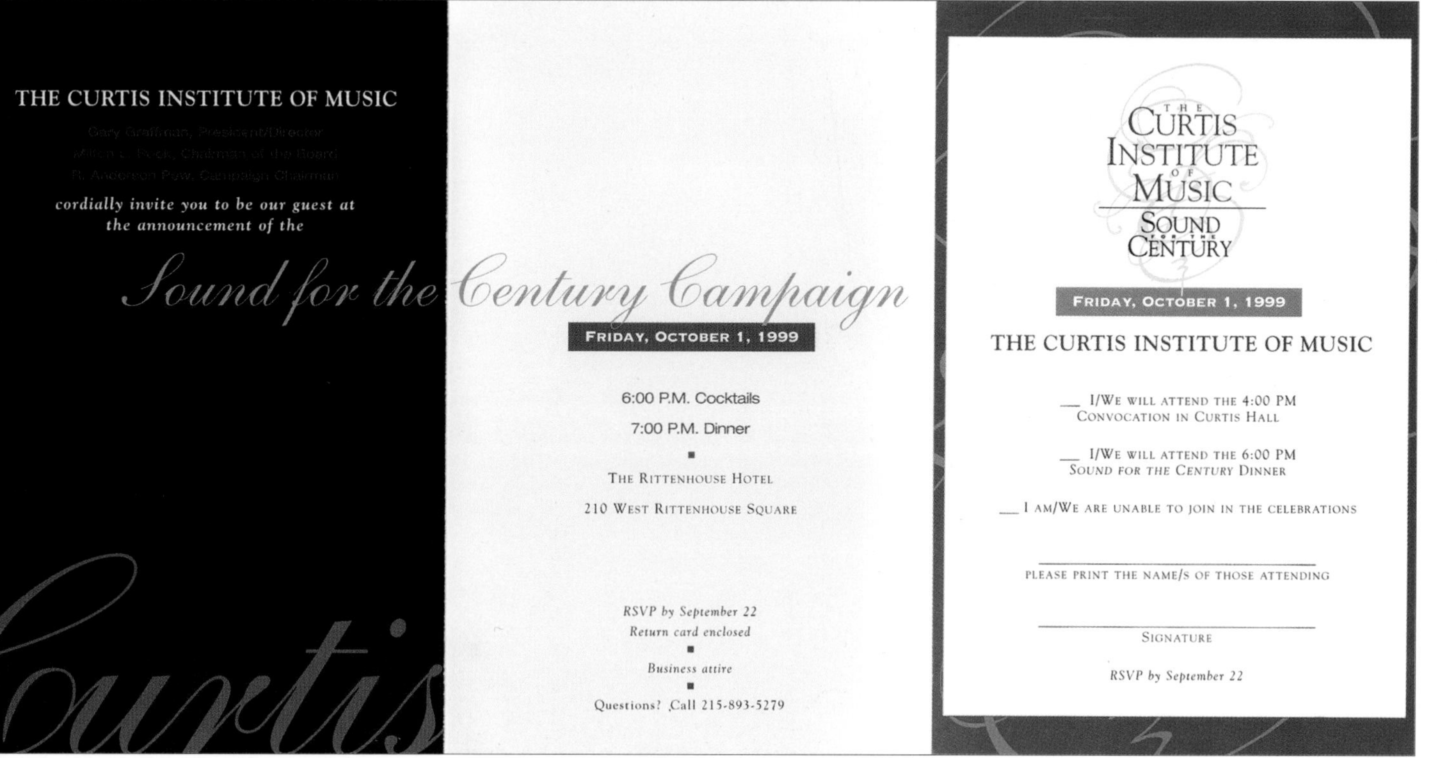
THE CURTIS INSTITUTE OF MUSIC
cordially invite you to be our guest at the announcement of the
Sound for the Century Campaign
FRIDAY, OCTOBER 1, 1999
6:00 P.M. Cocktails
7:00 P.M. Dinner
THE RITTENHOUSE HOTEL
210 WEST RITTENHOUSE SQUARE
RSVP by September 22
Return card enclosed
Business attire
Questions? Call 215-893-5279
Curtis
THE CURTIS INSTITUTE OF MUSIC
SOUND FOR THE CENTURY
FRIDAY, OCTOBER 1, 1999
THE CURTIS INSTITUTE OF MUSIC
___ I/WE WILL ATTEND THE 4:00 PM CONVOCATION IN CURTIS HALL
___ I/WE WILL ATTEND THE 6:00 PM SOUND FOR THE CENTURY DINNER
___ I AM/WE ARE UNABLE TO JOIN IN THE CELEBRATIONS
PLEASE PRINT THE NAME/S OF THOSE ATTENDING
SIGNATURE
RSVP by September 22

design firm
Mires Design
San Diego, Califorr
art director
Jose Serrano
designers
Miguel Perez, G
Joy Price, Debo
illustrator
Dan Thoner
client
Deleo Clay Tile Company
(manufacturer of clay tile)

DELEO CLAY TILE COMPANY

MANUFACTURERS OF QUALITY
Trade Mark
DELEO CLAY TILE CO.
MADE IN THE USA
EST. 1984
THROUGHBODY CLAY TILES
MISSION
When looks matter and craftsmanship counts.

DELEO
MANUFACTURERS OF QUALITY
Trade Mark
DELEO CLAY TILE CO.
MADE IN THE USA
EST. 1984
THROUGHBODY CLAY TILES
YOUR VISION IN TILE
THANK YOU

Deleo Clay Tile Co.
January 1999
Sun Mon Tue Wed Thu Fri Sat
PURE CLAY TILES MADE IN THE USA

MANUFACTURERS OF QUALITY
DELEO CLAY TILE CO.
THROUGHBODY
YOUR VISION IN TILE
MADE IN AMERICA

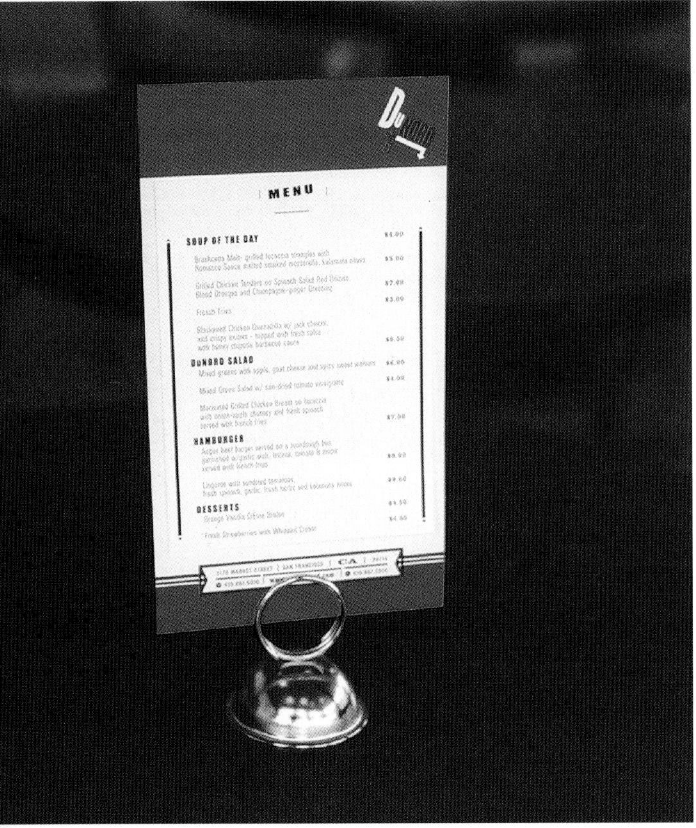

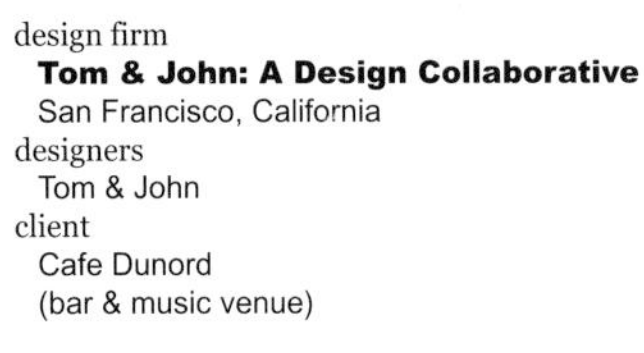
design firm
Tom & John: A Design Collaborative
San Francisco, California
designers
Tom & John
client
Cafe Dunord
(bar & music venue)

design firm
Donaldson Makoski Inc.
Avon, Connecticut
designers
Jane Heft, Debby Ryan
client
DRS Technologies

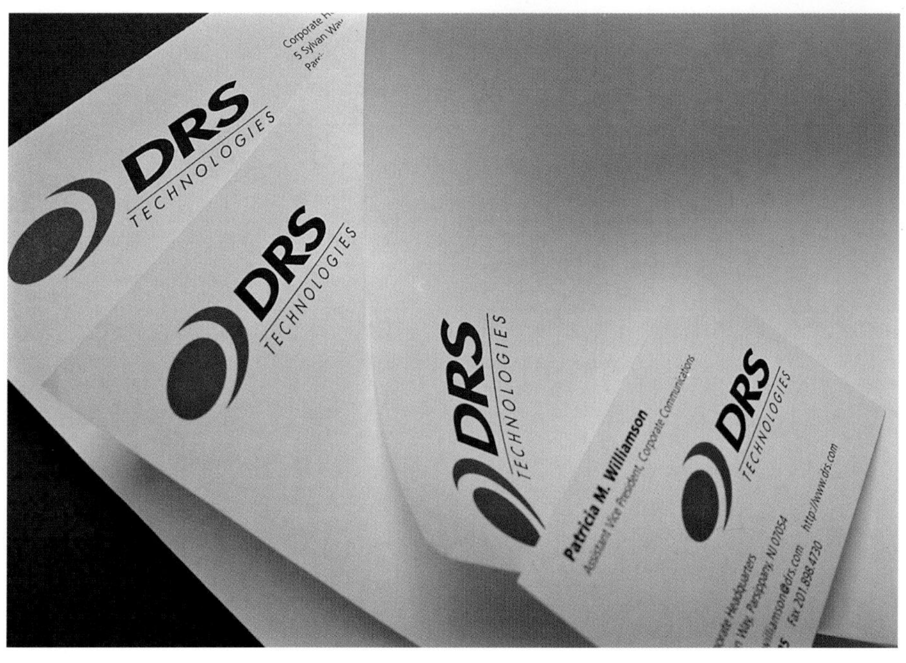

AFTER THE FALL®

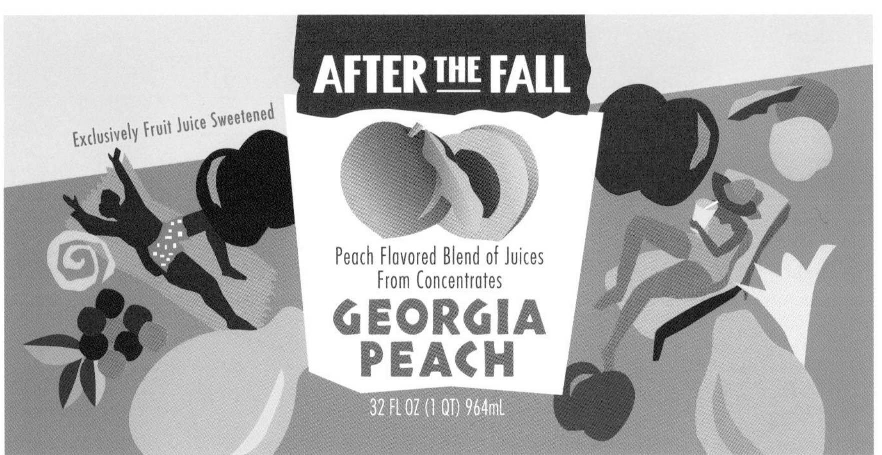

design firm
Shimokochi/Reeves
Los Angeles, California
designers
Mamoru Shimokochi, Anne Reeves
client
Smuckers Quality Beverages
(food & beverage)

P.O. BOX 369 SPEEDWAY AVENUE CHICO, CA 95927

P.O. BOX 369 SPEEDWAY AVENUE CHICO, CA 95927 TEL 530-899-5000 FAX 530-891-6397

design firm
Visual Asylum
San Diego, California
designers
MaeLin Levine, Amy Jo Levine
client
Digital Output
(service bureau)

design firm
Evenson Design Group
Culver City, California
creative director
Stan Evenson
designers
Karen Barranco, Mark Sojka, Peggy Woo
client
Reading Entertainment

SEGANET™

design firm
Mires Design
San Diego, California
art director
John Ball
designers
Miguel Perez, Pam Meierding,
Jeff Samaripa
client
Sega of America
(online video games)

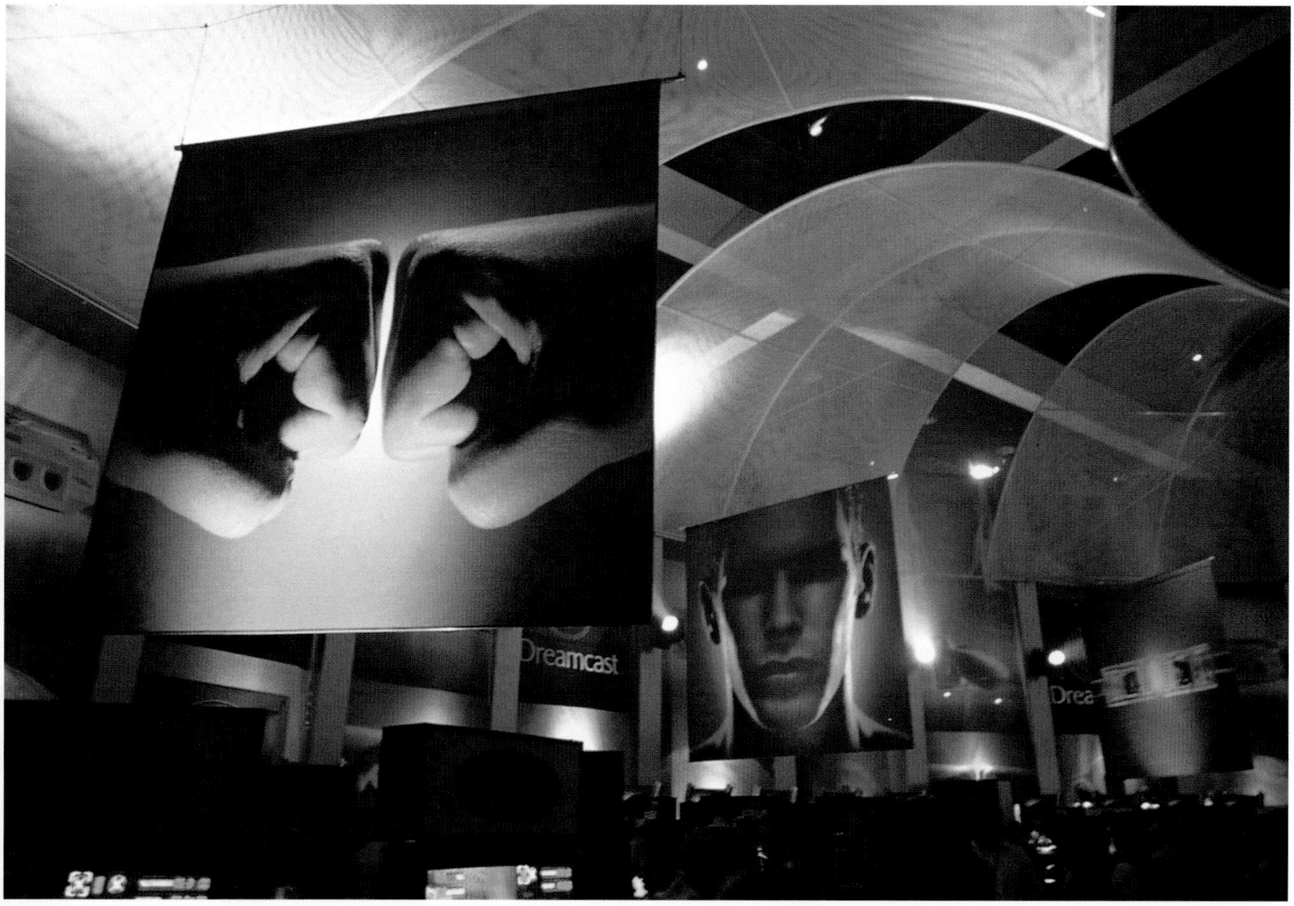
Dreamcast

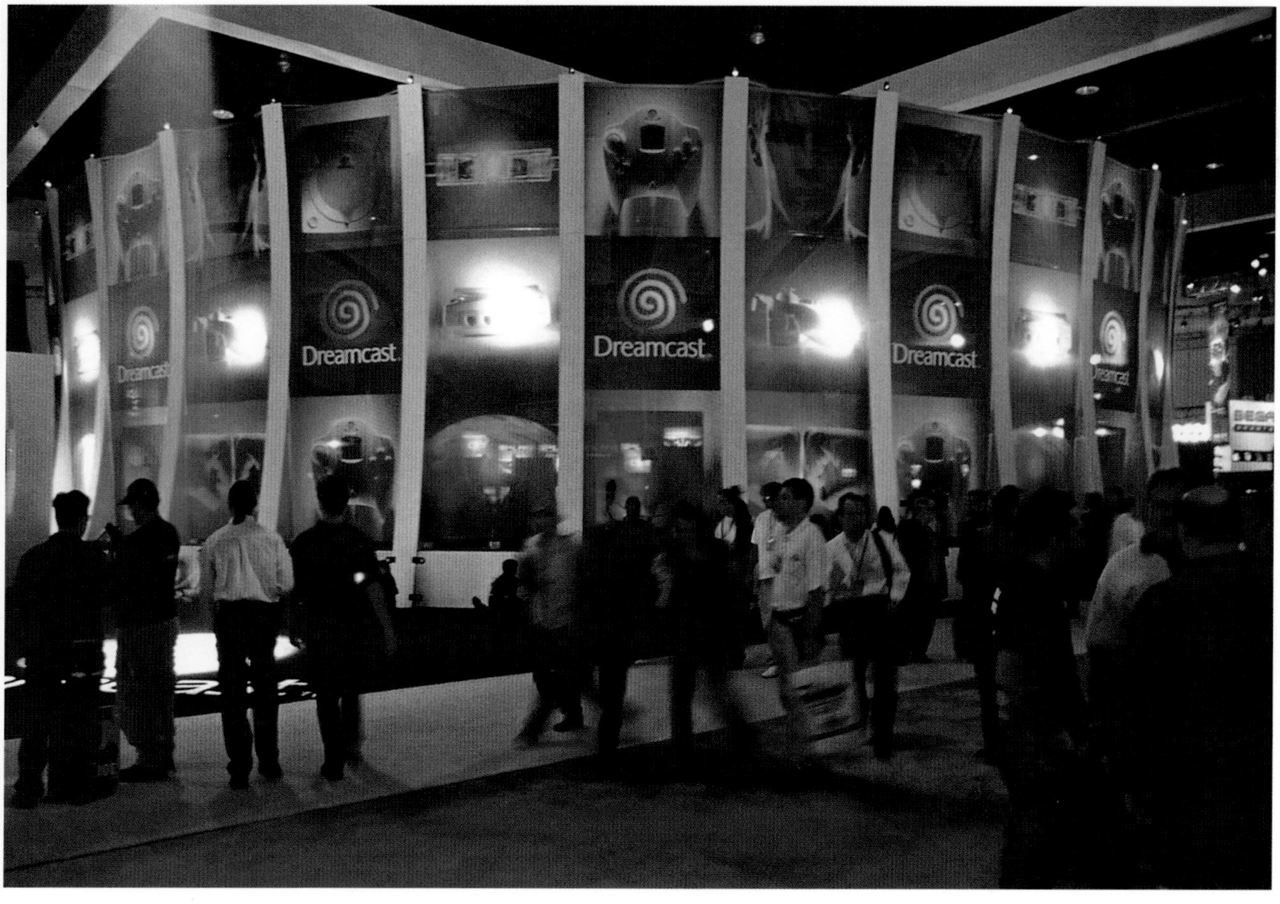
Dreamcast
Dreamcast
Dreamcast

design firm
Mark Oliver, Inc.
Santa Barbara, California
designers
Mark Oliver, Patty Devlin-Driskel
client
Breeder's Choice
(pet food manufacturer)

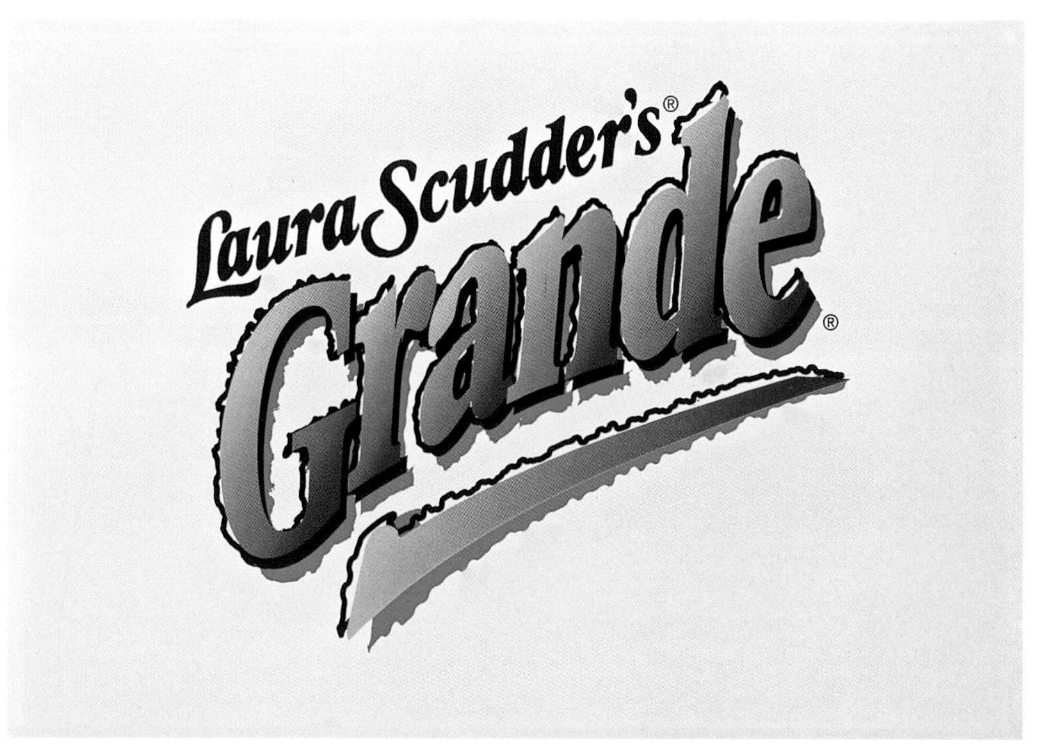

design firm
Mark Oliver, Inc.
Santa Barbara, California
designers
Mark Oliver, Brenna Pierce
client
Grande Food
(snack food manufacturer)

design firm
Susan Meshberg Graphic Design
New York, New York
designer
Susan Meshberg
computer art
Elaine MacFarlane, Jia Hwang
client
Chateau Los Boldos (Chile)
(winery)

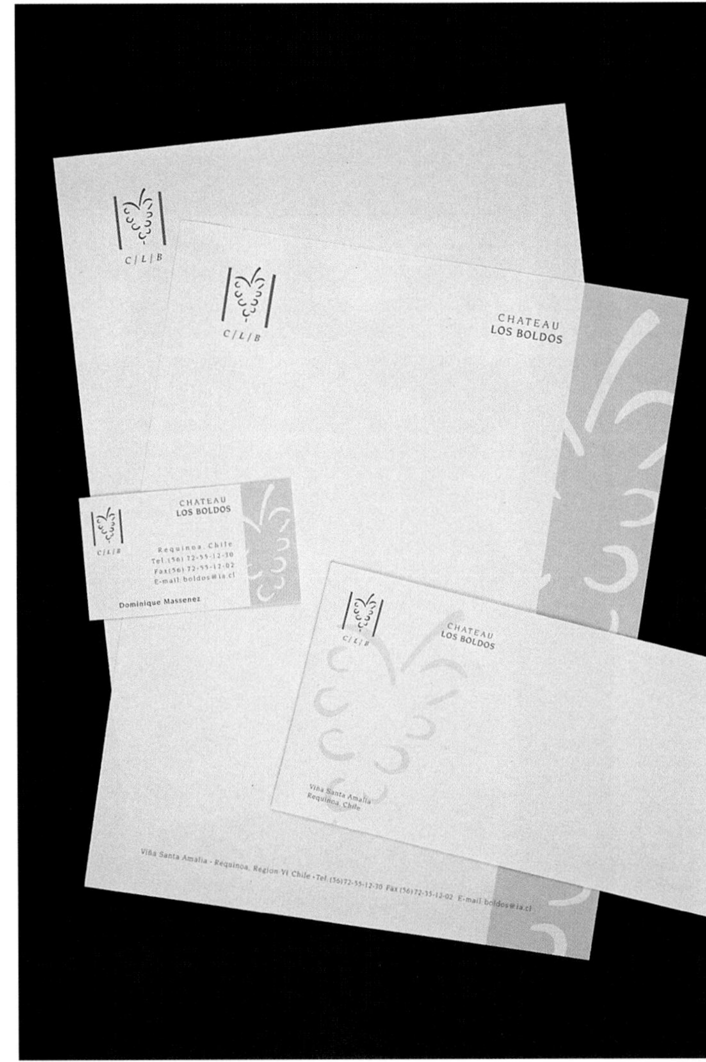

– 1 9 9 6 –
C/L/B
CHATEAU
LOS BOLDOS®
CLB RESERVE
Merlot
REQUINOA-CHILE
Mis en bouteille au Chateau
par la famille G.E. Massenez
12.5% ALC/VOL
750 ML
– 1 9 9 6 –
C/L/B
CHATEAU
LOS BOLDOS®
CLB RESERVE
Cabernet
Sauvignon
REQUINOA-CHILE
Mis en bouteille au Chateau
par la famille G.E. Massenez
12.5% ALC/VOL
750 ML

CHATEAU
LOS BOLDOS®
Merlot
CHATEAU
LOS BOLDOS®
Cabernet
Sauvignon

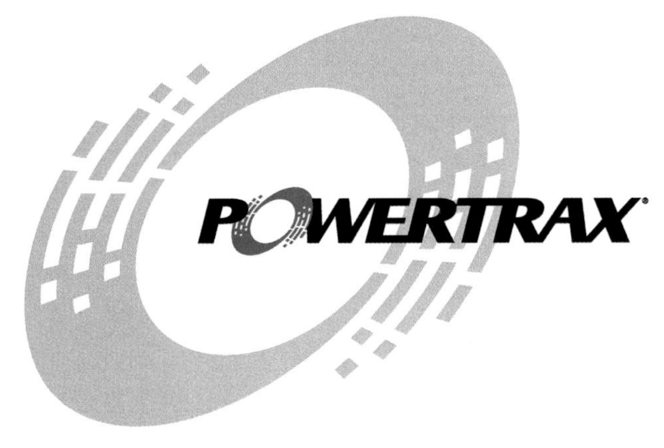

design firm
Mires Design
San Diego, California
art director
Jose Serrano
designers
Jose Serrano, Miguel Perez,
David Adey, Jeff Samaripa,
Deborah Hom, Lucas Salvatierra
illustrators
Jeff Samaripa, Miguel Perez,
David Adey, Lucas Salvatierra
photographer
Dean Siracus
client
Powertrax
(automotive traction accessories)

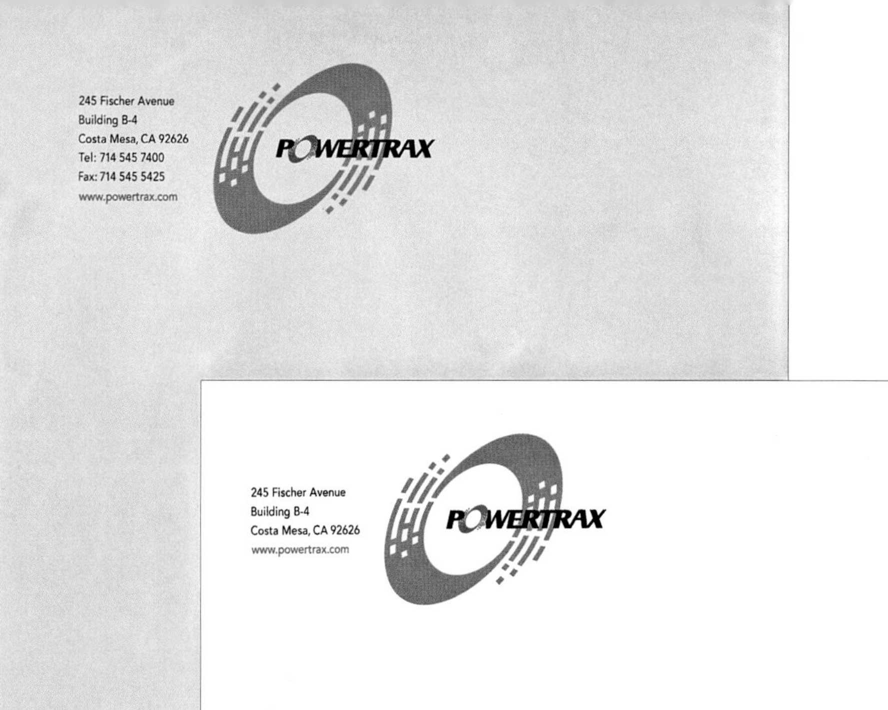
245 Fischer Avenue
Building B-4
Costa Mesa, CA 92626
Tel: 714 545 7400
Fax: 714 545 5425
www.powertrax.com
POWERTRAX
245 Fischer Avenue
Building B-4
Costa Mesa, CA 92626
www.powertrax.com
POWERTRAX

Mark V. Tyson
President and CEO
245 Fischer Avenue
Building B-4
Costa Mesa, CA 92626
www.powertrax.com
714 545 7400 x630
Fax: 714 545 5425
mtyson@powertrax.com
POWERTRAX

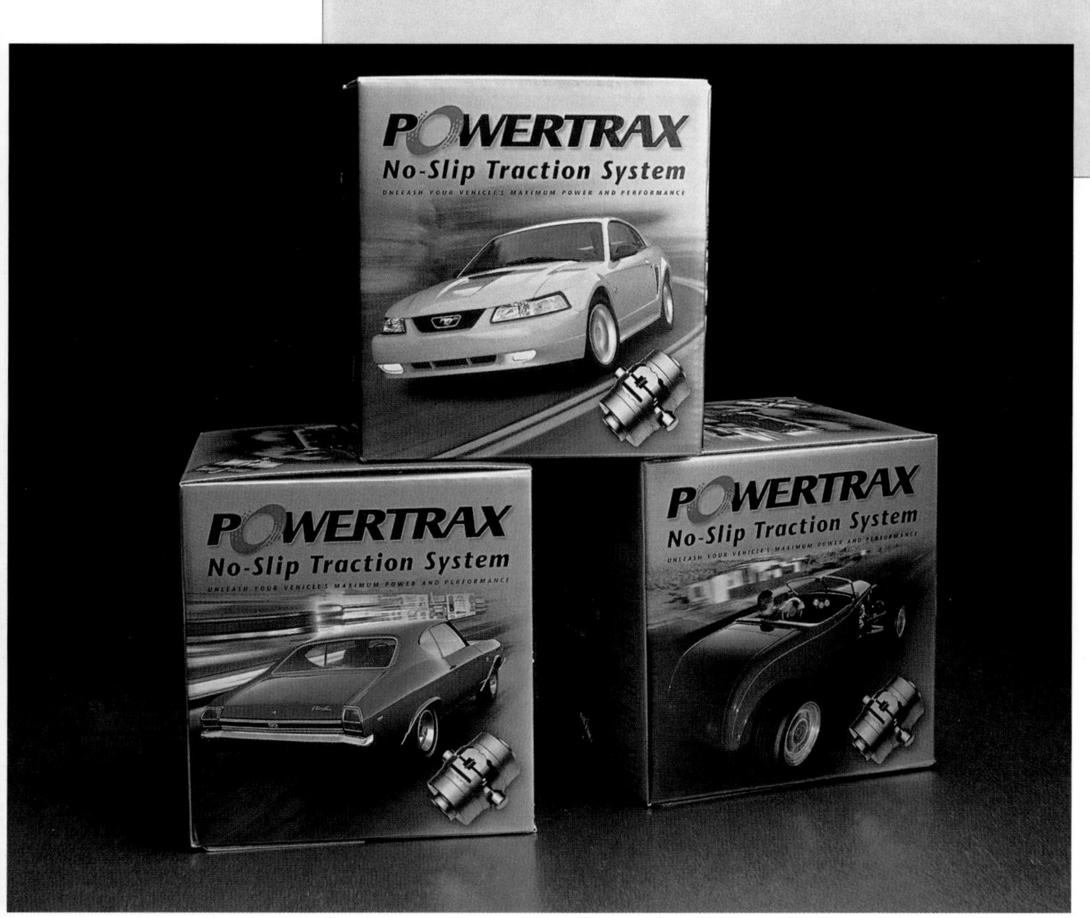
POWERTRAX
No-Slip Traction System
UNLEASH YOUR VEHICLE'S MAXIMUM POWER AND PERFORMANCE
POWERTRAX
No-Slip Traction System
POWERTRAX
No-Slip Traction System

design firm
Brand Equity International
Newton, Massachusetts
client
Zoots-"The Cleaner Cleaner"

design firm
Dotzler Creative Arts
Omaha, Nebraska
client
Lamson, Dugan, and Murray
(law firm)

LAMSON, DUGAN & MURRAY

SmartShip.com

design firm
Evenson Design Group
Culver City, California
creative director
Stan Evenson
project manager exhibit
Judy Lee
project manager logo/stationery
Karen Barranco
client
SmartShip.com
(e-commerce shipping company)

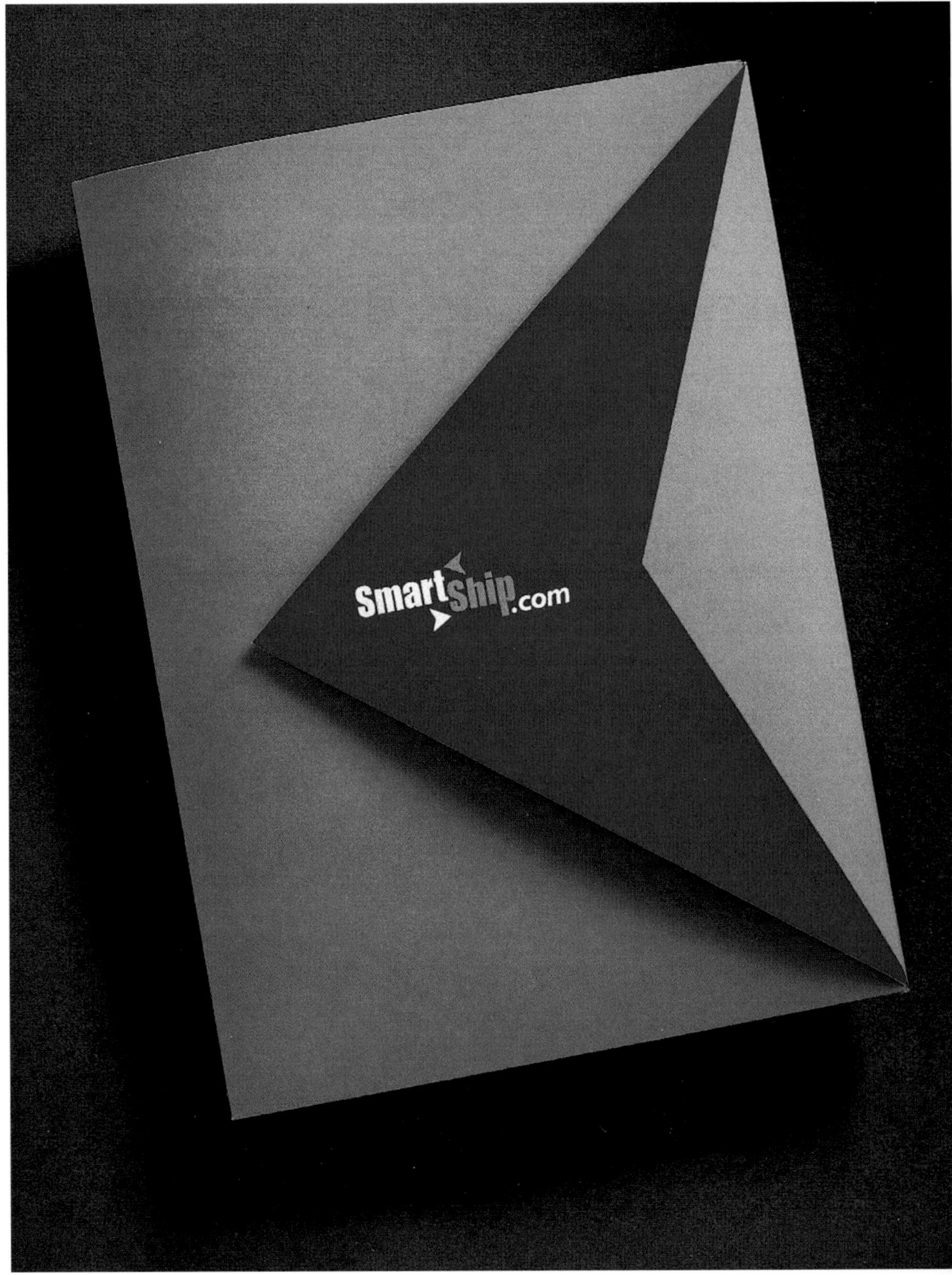

MARK HAWKINS
VP ONLINE MARKETING
SmartShip.com
6 VENTURE STE 211
IRVINE, CA 92618
TEL 949 453 9669
FAX 949 453 9399
mark@smartship.com
www.smartship.com

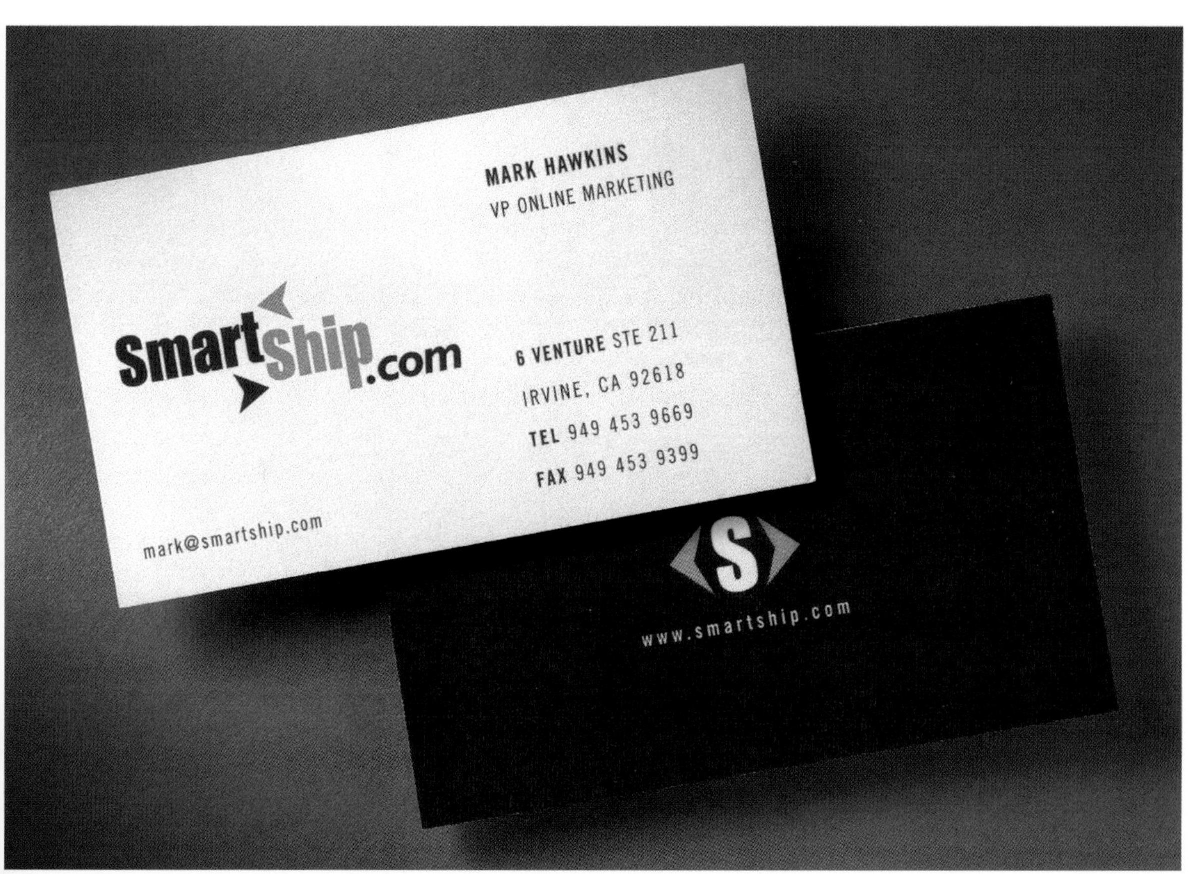

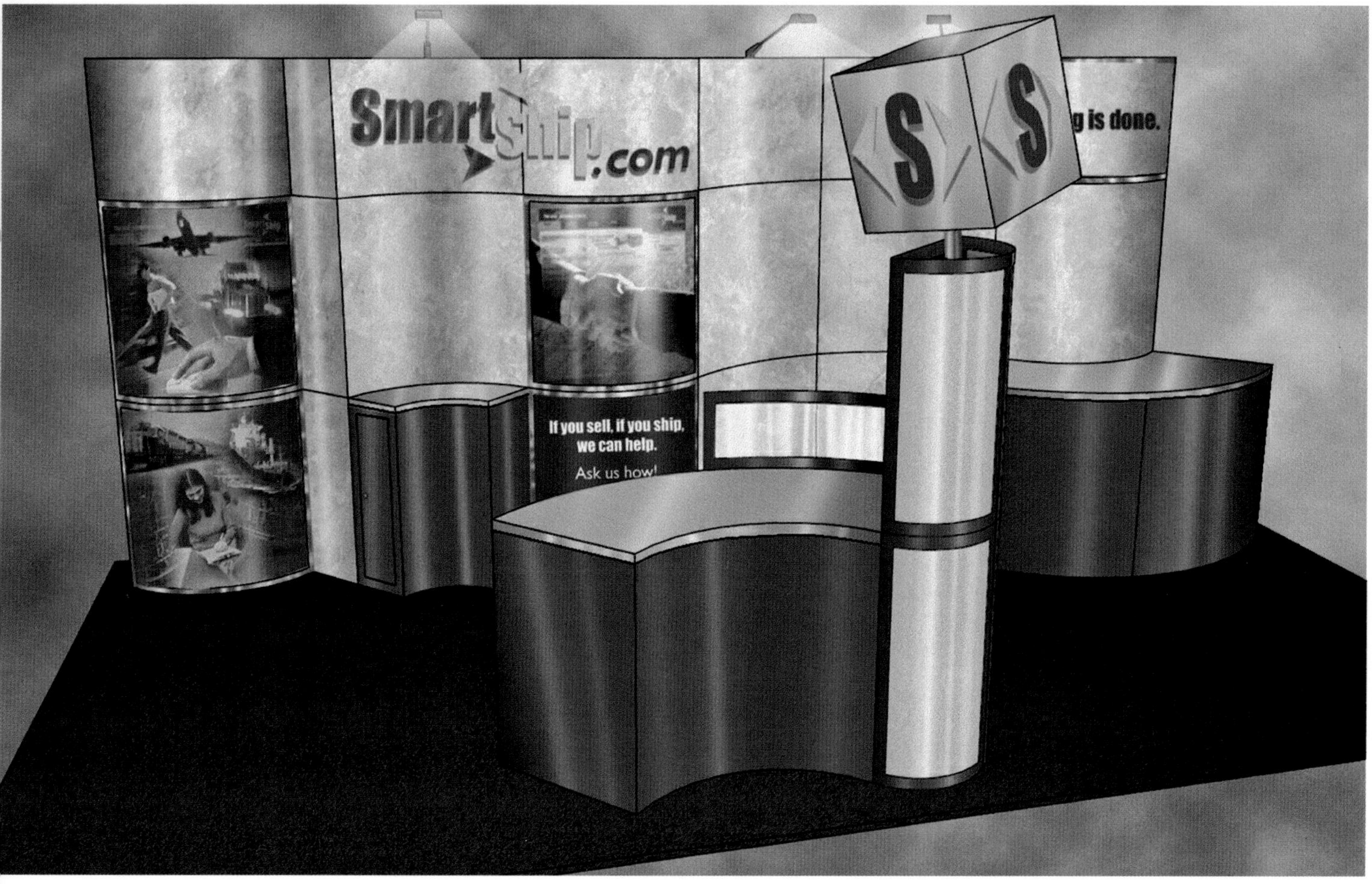

SmartShip.com
g is done.
If you sell, if you ship, we can help.
Ask us how!

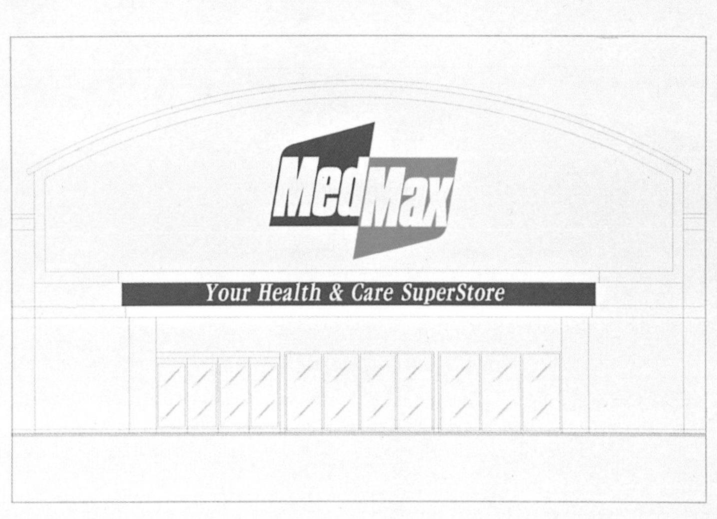

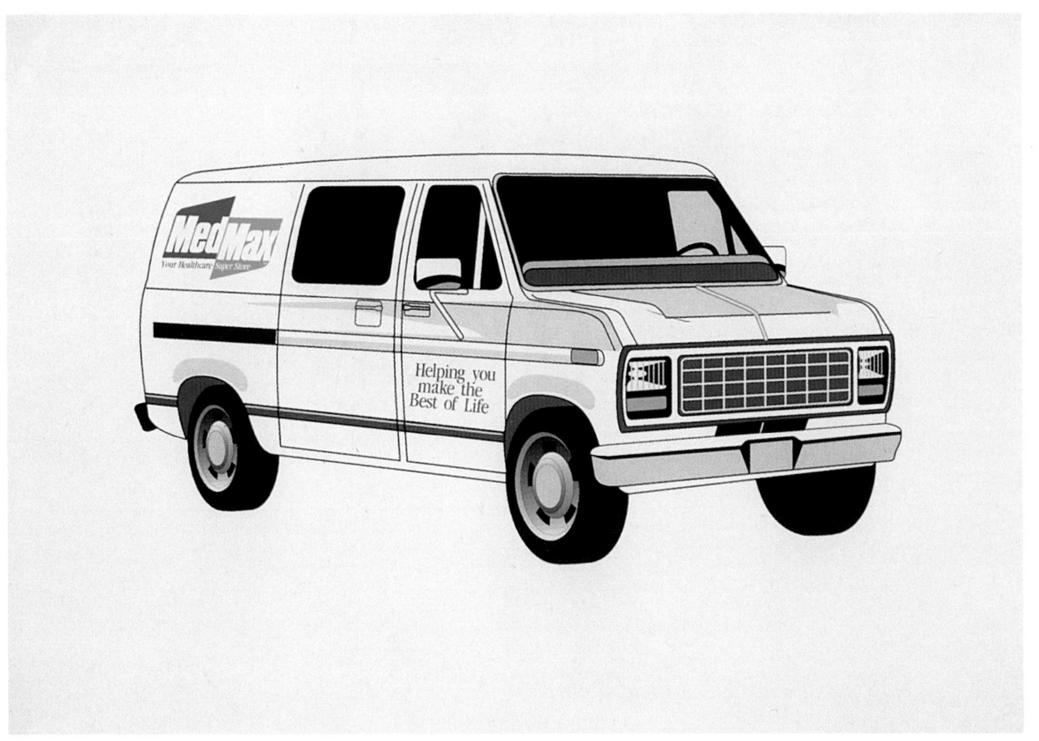

design firm
Jon Greenberg & Associates
Southfield, Michigan
vice president visual communications
Tony Camilletti
director of graphic design
Brian Eastman
client
MedMax

design firm
Baker Designed Communications
Santa Monica, California
art director
Gary Baker
designer
Michelle Wolins
client
Indymac
(real estate investment trust)

ZOKA

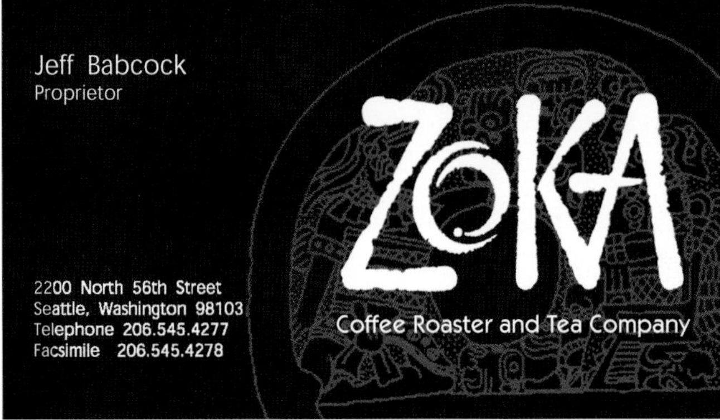

design firm
Walsh & Associates, Inc.
Seattle, Washington
designers
Miriam Lisco, Mary Ely, Lyn Blanchard
client
Zoka Coffee Roaster and Tea Company
(coffee/tea)

The ZOKA News
Summer 1997
Volume 1, Issue 1

A Newsletter About Coffee, Tea, and Happenings at Zoka Coffee Roaster & Tea Company

The Freshness Factor

Good coffee is an epic commodity, an elemental pleasure, and an exceptionally affordable luxury. Many people enjoy it, but few really understand how to get the very best out of their brewer. Zoka was established in part because it was becoming increasingly difficult to find a great cup of coffee in this City of Beans.

Many people ask us what makes our coffees so good, and the first thing we talk about is freshness. These days, most specialty coffees are sold in vacuum-packed bags that say "Fresh Roasted" on the label, but taste old, tired, or downright stale. The best things about coffee flavor are fleeting — they don't last more than a few days out of the roaster. True fresh coffee has a delicate subtle complexity that no packaging can preserve for long. Just as bread has an ephemeral dimension of flavor that must be enjoyed fresh from the oven to be fully appreciated, coffee has fantastic flavor qualities that can only be experienced within a few days of roasting. That's why we decided to roast in our shop, and encourage our customers to buy their coffee frequently in small quantities.

Of course, it also helps to have years of experience in selecting and buying fine *arabica* coffees, roasting them with care and attention in the proper type of roasting machine, and *tasting* the results. It helps to know a little about the botany of coffee and how it is cultivated and processed. It helps to visit coffee farms and mills to talk to the producers in the origin countries. It helps to understand the chemistry of roasting, how grinds are analyzed for particle size distribution and how soluble-solids concentrations and acidity are measured in brewed coffee. These things are important, but this still doesn't guarantee your satisfaction.

What really matters is what's in your cup and how you feel about it. Zoka owners Tim and Jeff have more than 30 years of coffee experience combined. They would like to put their knowledge, experience and resources to work for you, to help you achieve consistent quality and enjoyment from your coffee, and help your family and friends to fully appreciate the profound pleasures a well brewed cup of fresh *arabica* coffee can provide.

Like wine, coffee can furnish a kaleidoscope of flavor variations and nuances, some obvious, and others quite subtle. These complexities arise from the different botanical varieties, soil, climate, cultivation techniques, processing methods and a host of other variables. Unlike wine, coffee must be brewed just before serving, for the best results. Brewing is a complex and dynamic process. It requires knowledge, experience and care, as well as the proper equipment, to do well. We at Zoka would like to work with you to find the type of coffee, brewing technique and serving method that best suits your personal taste and lifestyle.

Our quest is to get back to the basic principles that first sparked the gourmet coffee revolution in the Northwest, ideas that seem to have been lost in the dramatic expansion of the industry in recent years. We want our coffees to burst forth in the cup with rich varietal character, the essences of the soil and sun, the personalities of the grower and miller, as well as the roaster, blender and brewer. And we want you to find the exquisite combination of complexities that speaks to your palate and best satisfies your culinary sensibilities. Please join us on this journey.

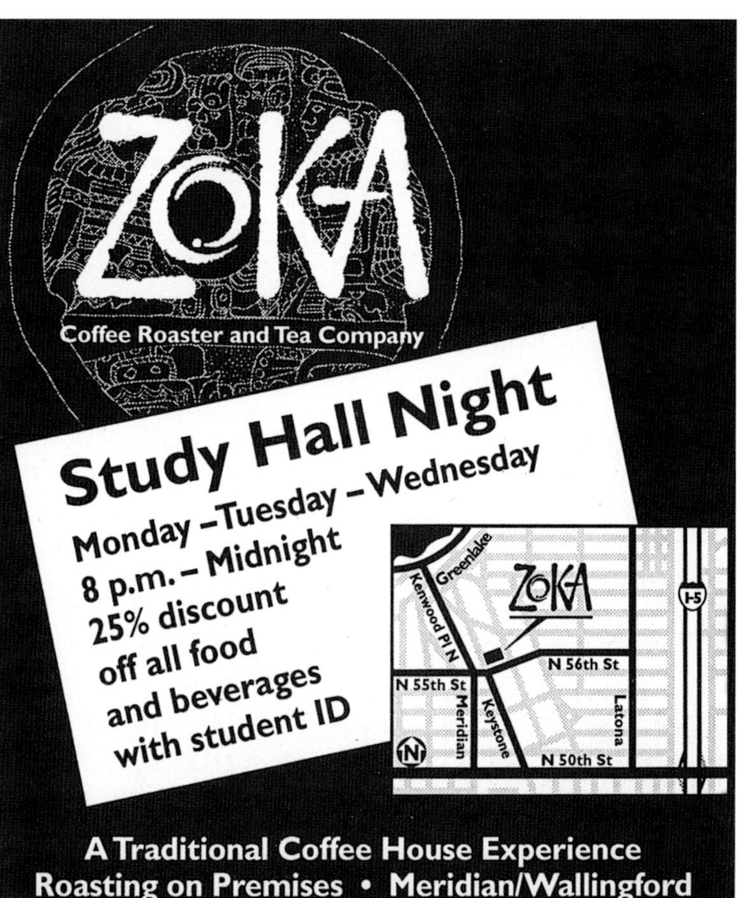
ZOKA
Coffee Roaster and Tea Company
Study Hall Night
Monday –Tuesday – Wednesday
8 p.m. – Midnight
25% discount
off all food
and beverages
with student ID
Greenlake
Kenwood Pl N
ZOKA
I-5
N 56th St
N 55th St
Meridian
Keystone
Latona
N 50th St
N
A Traditional Coffee House Experience
Roasting on Premises • Meridian/Wallingford
Hours: Open until midnight Mon.-Sat.
Open Sundays until 10
2200 North 56th Street, Seattle, WA 98103
545-4277

Coffee Roaster
ZOKA
& Tea Company

ZOKA
Coffee Roaster and Tea Company

Sonnenschein
SONNENSCHEIN NATH & ROSENTHAL

design firm
Greenfield/Belser Ltd.
Washington, D.C.
art director
Burkey Belser
designer
Jeanette Nuzum
client
Sonnenschein Nath & Rosenthal
(legal)

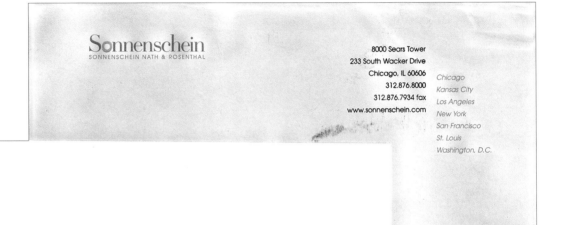

Sonnenschein
SONNENSCHEIN NATH & ROSENTHAL

8000 Sears Tower
233 South Wacker Drive
Chicago, IL 60606
312.876.8000
312.876.7934 fax
www.sonnenschein.com

Chicago
Kansas City
Los Angeles
New York
San Francisco
St. Louis
Washington, D.C.

Sonnenschein
SONNENSCHEIN NATH & ROSENTHAL

8000 Sears Tower
233 South Wacker Drive
Chicago, IL 60606

Chicago
Kansas City
Los Angeles
New York
San Francisco
St. Louis
Washington, D.C.

Sonnenschein
From the Desk of the Chairman

Financial markets are rolling, tech stocks are flying high & Y2K seems substantially behind us. Welcome to the first quarter of the year 2000.

The next mountain to climb? The evolution from bricks & mortar to e-business. We understand these new business models and both the challenges and the dangers ahead. So I've enclosed our e-business overview to help you be a part of the next big wave. If we can be of help to you, please call us at 1.800.369.0012.

Diane Quinn

Kathleen J. Brangan
Marketing Coordinator
312.876.3405
k8b@sonnenschein.com

Sonnenschein
SONNENSCHEIN NATH & ROSENTHAL

8000 Sears Tower • 233 South Wacker Dr.
Chicago, IL 60606
312.876.3151 fax
www.sonnenschein.com

Chicago
Kansas City
Los Angeles
New York
San Francisco
St. Louis
Washington, D.C.

e-business group

organization buy/sell protection jurisdiction start-ups

Netsite : http://www.sonnenschein.com/e-business/startups.htm

THE NEXT BIG THING

You want a piece of ***"the next big thing."*** Maybe it's B2B, B2C or a portal strategy. Or maybe you think you *have* the next big thing and just need the funds to produce it. Either way, you'll quickly learn that ***venture capital*** investments in e-businesses follow a unique model.

Getting in

Whether you're starting a company or investing in one, you should know the ***new business model:*** financing, goods and services are ***exchanged for equity;*** employees take warrants and stock options in lieu of salary; and talent is the most precious resource around. Do you have access to ***venture capital*** firms and other financing sources? Are ***incentive compensation*** plans in place to attract and retain top Internet talent?

Making it yours

Who owns the code and content of your site? Telecommuters, consultants and outsourcing can confuse the ownership picture. Make sure you own what you think you own.

Cashing out

Fast-paced, fast-burn e-businesses often have ***short life-spans.*** Savvy entrepreneurs have ***exit strategies*** in place on Day 1. Be ready for anything—an acquisition of your business, a bankruptcy or an IPO. Your ***corporate and financing structures*** should let you get your money out when you want it—so you'll have ***liquidity*** for your next venture.

Netsite : http://www.excite.com

excite℠

My Excite

FREE Voicemail/Email

Calendar/Address Book

Make Excite My Start Page!

Personali

New Membe

Autos

Busines

Careers

The merger of portal pioneer Excite and high-speed access provider @Home created an on-line powerhouse. Sonnenschein has assisted Excite@Home on Year 2000 matters and intellectual property litigation, as well as banner advertising, data collection, privacy and law enforcement issues throughout the United States and Europe.

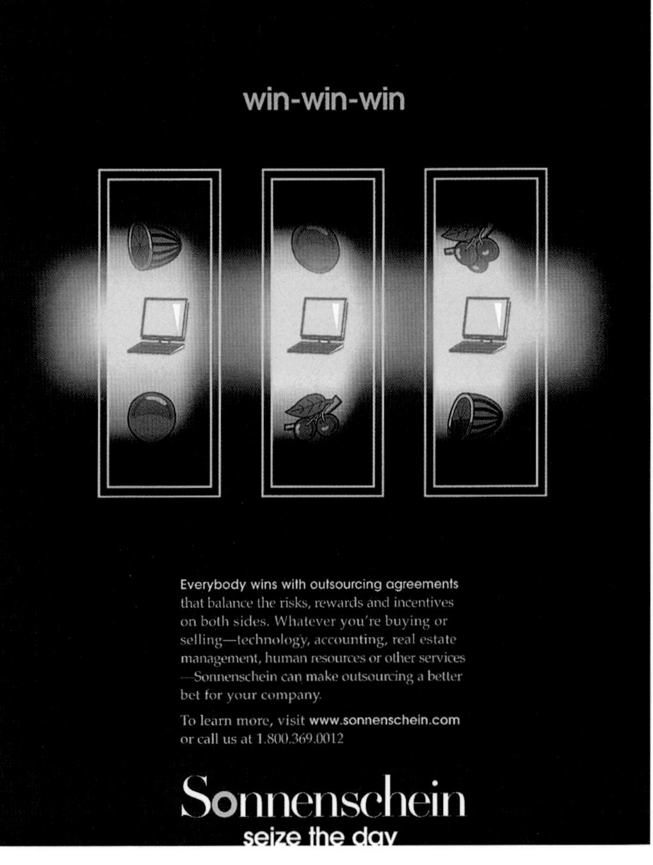

design firm
AERIAL
San Francisco, California
designers
Tracy Moon, Misty Bralver
client
Distilled Images
(dot commerce/service)

distilled images
a picture's worth

eighty-five bluxome
san francisco california 94107
t 415.618.0530 f 415.618.0531
www.distilledimages.com

distilled images
a picture's worth

leslie pritchett
ceo

eighty-five bluxome
san francisco california 94107
t 415.618.0530 f 415.618.0531
e leslie@distilledimages.com
www.distilledimages.com

distilled images
a picture's worth

leslie pritchett
ceo

eighty-five bluxome
san francisco california 94107
t 415.618.0530 f 415.618.0531
e leslie@distilledimages.com
www.distilledimages.com

distilled images
a picture's worth

peter hogg

eighty-five bluxome
san francisco california 94107
t 415.618.0530 f 415.618.0531
e peter@distilledimages.com
www.distilledimages.com

distilled images
a picture's worth

leslie pritchett
ceo

eighty-five bluxome
san francisco california 94107
t 415.618.0530 f 415.618.0531
e leslie@distilledimages.com
www.distilledimages.com

distilled images
a picture's worth

peter hogg

eighty-five bluxome
san francisco california 94107
t 415.618.0530 f 415.618.0531
e peter@distilledimages.com
www.distilledimages.com

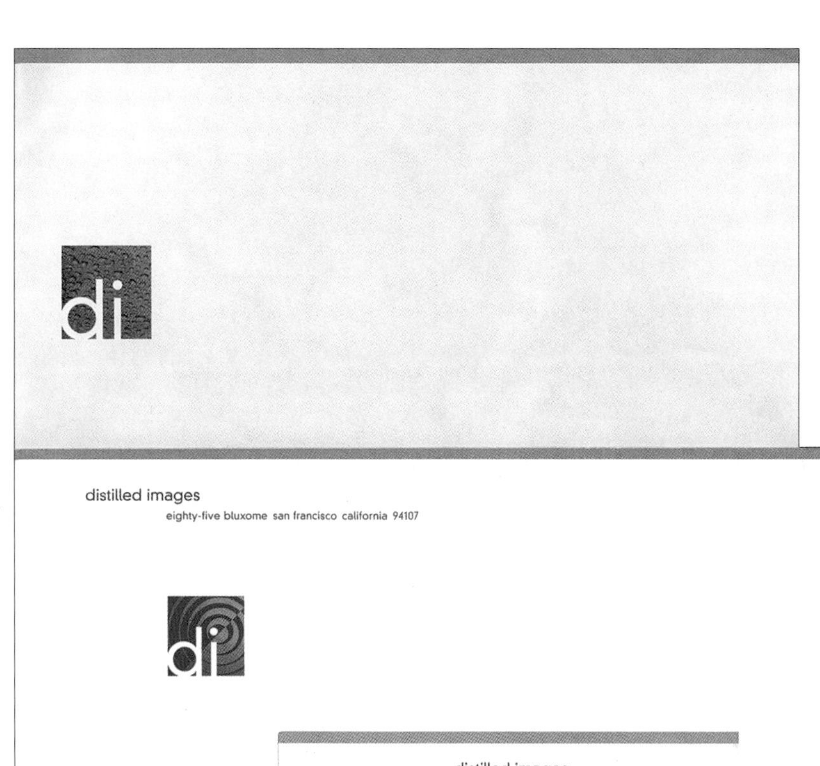
distilled images
eighty-five bluxome san francisco california 94107
distilled images
a picture's worth

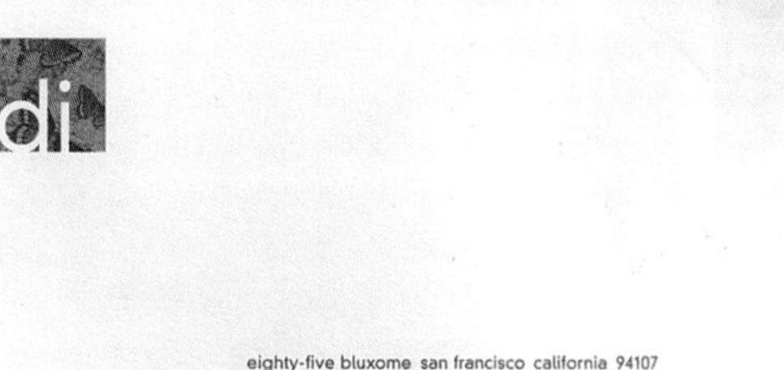
eighty-five bluxome san francisco california 94107

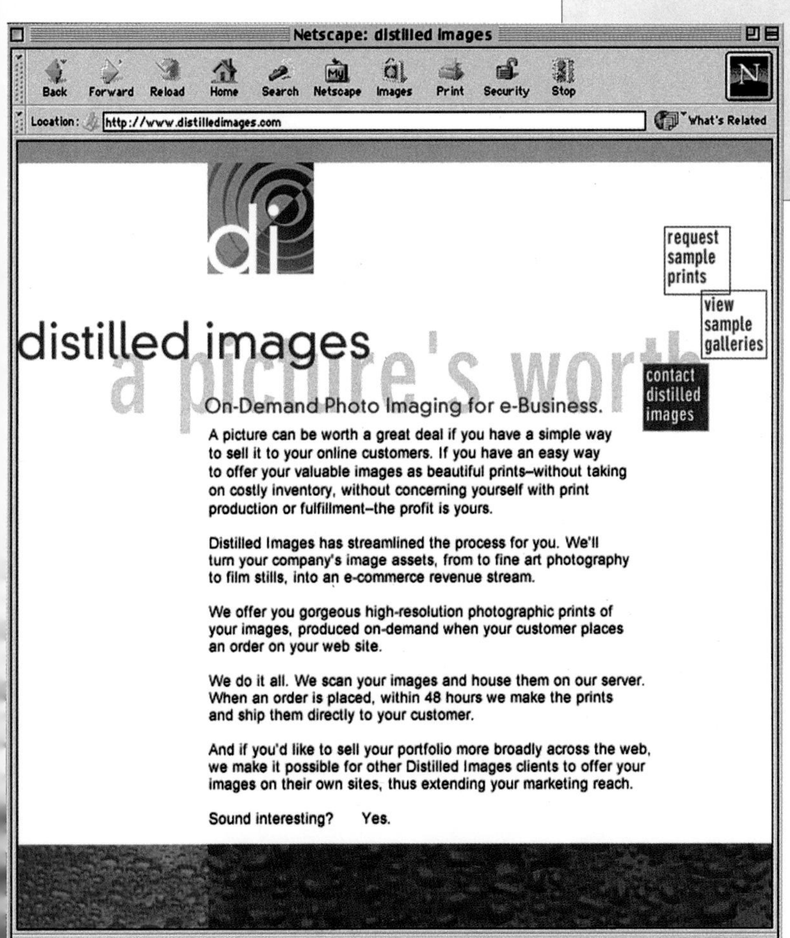
Netscape: distilled images
Back Forward Reload Home Search Netscape Images Print Security Stop
Location: http://www.distilledimages.com
What's Related
request sample prints
view sample galleries
contact distilled images
distilled images
a picture's worth
On-Demand Photo Imaging for e-Business.
A picture can be worth a great deal if you have a simple way to sell it to your online customers. If you have an easy way to offer your valuable images as beautiful prints–without taking on costly inventory, without concerning yourself with print production or fulfillment–the profit is yours.
Distilled Images has streamlined the process for you. We'll turn your company's image assets, from to fine art photography to film stills, into an e-commerce revenue stream.
We offer you gorgeous high-resolution photographic prints of your images, produced on-demand when your customer places an order on your web site.
We do it all. We scan your images and house them on our server. When an order is placed, within 48 hours we make the prints and ship them directly to your customer.
And if you'd like to sell your portfolio more broadly across the web, we make it possible for other Distilled Images clients to offer your images on their own sites, thus extending your marketing reach.
Sound interesting? Yes.

design firm
Sayles Graphic Design
Des Moines, Iowa
designer
John Sayles
client
Phil Goode Grocery Store
(specialty convenience store)

SQUEEZED
Goode
Juice

Goode
GRINDE™
COFFEE

HOT
Goode
FOOD

O
Goode
N
COLDER

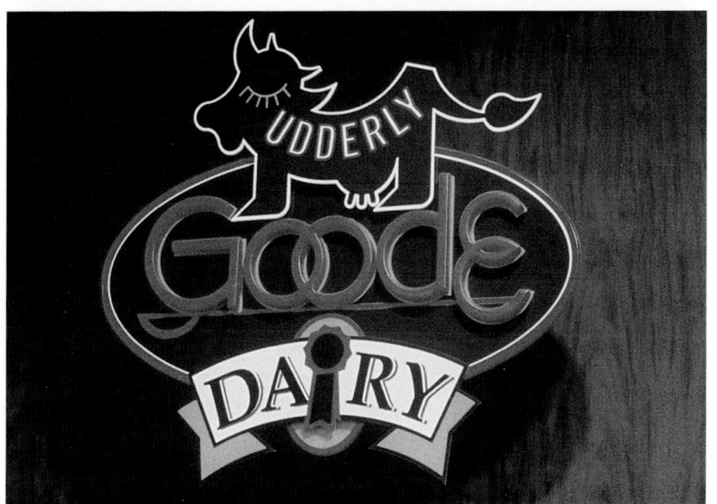
UDDERLY
Goode
DAIRY

COLD
Goode
SODA

design firm
Addis Group
Berkeley, California
designers
Rick Atwood, James Eli, Ariel Villasol,
Joanne Hom, David Leong
client
Gordon Biersch Restaurants & Brewery

Gordon Biersch

Gordon Biersch
Gordon Biersch

MÄRZEN
PILSNER
HEFEWEIZEN
Gordon Biersch®
BREWING COMPANY
Gordon Biersch

INDEX

Design Firms

A

Addis Group 380
AERIAL 61, 342, 376
Art 270, Inc. 346

B

Baker Designed Communications 109, 215, 371
BBK Studio 118
Belyea 206, 207, 212
Boelts Bros. Associates 232, 306
Brand Equity International 17, 226, 366
Bright/Point Zero 263

C

Cisco Systems (In-House) 332
CommArts 208, 211, 260, 284
CROXSON Design 36

D

David Carter Design Assoc. 58, 59, 149
David Lemley Design 242, 252
Desgrippes Gobé & Associates 246
Design Guys 55, 178
Deskey Associates 282
DeSola Group, Inc. 39
Dever Designs 251
Donaldson Makoski Inc. 353
Dotzler Creative Arts 85, 105, 367
Doyle Partners 197, 237

E

EAT Advertising & Design 8, 129, 184, 220, 253
Evenson Design Group 78, 240, 304, 357, 368
Extraprise Group, Inc. 12, 18

F

Flanders + Associates 233

G

Gardner Design 50, 51, 64, 65, 70, 71, 80, 81, 86, 87, 94, 99, 106, 114, 122, 123, 134, 169, 181, 192
Gold & Associates 151, 316
Graphic Solutions 158
Greenfield/Belser Ltd. 14, 20, 26, 32, 40, 43, 199, 374

H

Hans Flink Design Inc. 52, 120, 137, 144, 159, 170, 180, 186, 189
Hanson Associates, Inc. 277
Herbst Lazar Bell INC 259
Herip Associates 227
Hornall Anderson Design Works, Inc. 22, 46, 74, 96, 100, 168, 172, 218, 238, 239, 248, 249, 256, 257, 268, 281, 288, 299, 327
Hunt Weber Clark Assoc., Inc. 76, 77, 83

I

Interbrand 38, 293, 295
IXL 267

J

Jensen Design Associates 171
JGA, Inc. 90, 154, 216, 290
John Milligan Design 202
Jon Greenberg & Associates 370

K

Karlsberger 45
Kiku Obata + Company 204, 213, 230, 297, 339

L

Larsen Design + Interactive 119
Larsen Design Office, Inc. 236
LAT Diseño Grafico 292
Laura Coe Design Assoc 92, 112, 124, 164
Lipson Alport Glass & Assoc. 194, 195, 224, 225
Lister Butler Consulting Inc. 283
Love Packaging Group 56, 57, 110, 121, 148

M

Maffini & Bearce 203
Malcolm Grear Designers 130, 136, 138, 156, 182, 214
Mark Oliver, Inc. 234, 360, 361
McElveney & Palozzi Design Group Inc. 62, 63, 72, 73, 82
Michael Niblett Design 200
Michael Orr + Associates, Inc. 30
Michael Patrick Partners 88, 98, 102
Mires Design 6, 162, 196, 245, 264, 294, 300, 301, 308, 324, 325, 336, 338, 344, 350, 358, 364
Mortensen Design 24, 322
Mossimo In-House Graphics 258

P

Paprika Communications 152
Pink Coyote Design, Inc. 187
Pittard Sullivan 271

R

RKS Design, Inc. 243

S

Sasaki Associates 289
Sayles Graphic Design 28, 44, 66, 116, 160, 166, 190, 201, 228, 254, 279, 340, 378
Shimokochi/Reeves 312, 313, 354
Sibley Peteet 193
Smart Design Inc. 265
Stein & Company 270
Studio Morris LA/NY 262
Studio Izbickas 141, 179
Susan Meshberg Graphic Design 330, 362
Sussman/Prejza & Co., Inc. 176, 188

T

Tharp Did It 4, 274, 280, 286
The Focus Group 48
The Leonhardt Group 175
The Traver Company 42, 140, 314
Tilka Design 222
Tim Girvin Design, Inc. 223, 231, 303, 326
The Wyant Simboli Group, Inc. 145
Tom & John: A Design Collaborative 328, 352
Tom Fowler, Inc. 174

V

Visual Asylum 320, 321, 356

W

WalkerGroup/CNI 244
Wallace Church ass., inc. 147, 269, 272
Walsh & Associates, Inc. 10, 34, 142, 310, 334, 372
Woodson & Newroth 276

Clients

Symbols

1997 Iowa State Fair 44
1998 Iowa State Fair 228
1999 Iowa State Fair 340

A

Abacus 59
ACIS 32
Active Motif 112
Alphabet Soup 279
Alpine World Championships, The 284
Ambrosia Wine 12
Ameren Corporation 230
American Association of Museums 251
American Cancer Society 190
Anacomp 6
Arena Stage 162
Art Institute of Boston, The (Edible Art) 1997 233
Aspen Traders 134
Atlanta Committee for the Olympic Games 130
Auto Craft 70
Avalanche Popcorn 192
Avenue A 100

B

Bank Boston 38
Baptist Health Care 226
BBK Studio 118
beau monde 148
Beckman Coulter, Inc. 263
Bell Atlantic 39
Bellagio Hotel & Casino 193
Best Cellars 257
Beverly Sassoon 312
Blue Chair Design 43
Boelts Bros Associates: 10th Anniversary ID 232
Bogart Golf 74
Boullioun Aviation Services 46
Breeder's Choice 360
British Airways 295
Brown Shoe Company 204
Buena Vista College 166
Buster Brown + Co. 213

C

Cafe Dunord 352
Chateau Los Boldos 362
Chugach Heritage Center 142
Cinnabon 326
Cisco Systems 332
City of Santa Monica 176
Clarify 102
Cleveland Indians, The 227
Coca-Cola Company, The 224
Colgate-Palmolive Co. 52
Compass Creek 327
Concord Mills/The Mills Corporation 297
Cowley County Community College 123
CPI Business Groups 82
Creative Center, The 85
Cruise West 207
CTS Net 308
Cubby's Coffee House 78
Curtis Institute of Music 346
Custom Building Products 238
CW Gourmet/Mondeo 256
Cymerc Exchange 18

D

Dade Behring 225
David Lemley Design 252
Deleo Clay Tile Company 264, 350
Dentsu 303
Des Moines "Firstar Nitefall On The River" 254
Développements Germain-des-Prés 152
Digital Navigation Corporate ID 270
Digital Output 356
Distilled Images 376
Doskocil 94
DRS Technologies 353

E

EduNation 339
Elliott Hotel, The 314
Eric Long 259
ESM Consulting Engineers 42
Exario 325
Excel 50, 51, 169

F

Finlandia Vodka Americas, Inc. 277
Fisher Companies Inc. 175
Foster Pepper Shefelman 249
Fran's Chocolates, Ltd. 310
FreemanWhite, Inc. 182

G

Gardner Design 87
Gball.com 344
GE Capital Services, Center for Learning and Organ 145
GeoForm 121
Gettuit.com 281
Gianna Rose 160
Gillette Co., The 147
Glazed Expressions 201
Go Boulder 208, 211
Gold & Associates 151
Gordon Biersch Restaurants & Brewery 380
Goulston & Storrs 199
Grande Food 361
Greenfield/Belser Ltd. 40
Guess? Inc. 246

H

Handspring, Inc. 24
handyvan 280
Hardware.com 168
Harnetts 179
Hawthorne Lane 77
Henry Ford Museum and Greenfield Village 154
Hot Sox 262

I

IBC Creative Services of Unilever HPC 174
Impli 299
Indymac 371

K

Kabloom 17
Kansas City Art Institute-Artspace 129
Kansas Joint Replacement Institute 106
Kansas Speech-Language-Hearing-Association 65
Karlsberger 45
Kimpton Hotel + Restaurant Group 76, 83
Kmart 197
Knowledge Exhange 188

L

Lamson, Dugan, and Murray 367
Landgrant 158
Lascco 234
Laser Pacific 321
Laura Coe Design Assoc 164
Leatherman Tool Group 218
LeBoulanger 4
LeRoy Village Green 63
Les Piafs 206
Liechtenstein Global Trust 283
Loomis, Fargo, & Co. 48
Love Packaging Design 110
Luminate 98

M

Mansion at MGM Grand, The 58
Mashreq Bank 244
Maveron 248
Maxfli 272
Mayer Bros. 62

Mead Johnson Nutritionals 180
MedMax 370
MegaFab 71
Michael's Grill 220
Mossimo, Inc. 258
Motorola, Inc. 194
Mulvanny Architects 34
Museum of Art, Rhode Island School of Design 138

N

NetworkOil, Inc. 36
New Bedford Whaling Museum 136
New England Patriots 240
NextRx Corporation 172
Nike, Inc. 196
Novell, Inc. 239
Novellus Systems, Inc. 119, 236

O

Ommegang Brewery 237
One Reel 242
Organized Living 184

P

P.S. the Letter 200
PANoRAMA Baking Company 274
Paramount Inc. "Buddy Bar" 56
Paul Chauncey Photography 122
PB&J Restaurants/Great Chefs of the Midwest 8
PB&J Restaurants/Yahooz 253
Peabody & Arnold LLP 14
Pen & Paper LLC 330
Pfizer Inc. 120, 189
Pharmacia + UpJohn 293
Phil Goode Grocery Store 378
Pittard Sullivan 271
Pivotal 64
Polaroid 265
Polly-O Italian Cheese Co. 269
Powertrax 364
Prairie State Bank 81
Printmaster 80
Pritzker Realty Group LLC 195
Private Exercise 304

Q

Qualcomm 300, 301

R

Reading Entertainment 357
Redley 140
Redneck Foods 316
Restaurant.com 267
RKS Design, Inc. 243
Robeks Juice 171
Rue 21 90

S

S1 Corporation 88
SafeGuard Health Enterprises, Inc. 215
Sakson & Taylor 10
Sasaki Associates 289
Sayles Graphic Design 28
Schaffer's Bridal Shop 116
Scripmaster 114
Sega of America 358
Sempra Energy 320
Setter Leach & Lindstrom 222
Shurgard 231
SmartShip.com 368
Smuckers Quality Beverages 354
Somnograph 181
Sonnenschein Nath & Rosenthal 374
Southern Comfort 294
Southwest Parks & Monuments Association 306
Space Needle 96
Speed Art Museum, The 214
St. Peter's University Hospital 187
Step Up To Life 105
Steven Kent Winery, The 286
Stockpot Soups 223
Stuffbak.com 260
SupplyPro 92
Syracuse University Athletic Department 202

T

Tabacalera de Espana 156
Talbots 141
Tallgrass Beef 86
Target Stores 55, 178
Taylor Guitars 336
Taylor Made Golf Co. 124
Tenet Health Care 109
Teplik Laser Surgery Centers 276
The Alpine World Championships 284
The Art Institute of Boston (Edible Art) 1997 233
The Cleveland Indians 227
The Coca-Cola Company 224
The Creative Center 85
The Elliott Hotel 314
The Gillette Co. 147
The Mansion at MGM Grand 58
The Speed Art Museum 214
The Steven Kent Winery 286
Therapon 57
Think Outside 324
Timbuktuu Coffee Bar 66
Tom & John: A Design Collaborative 328
Tonkon Torp LLP 26
Tribe Pictures 342
Truesoups 334
Turabo Medical Group 292
Tiger Lily 268

U

U.S. Airways 282
Unilever HPC USA 137, 144, 170, 186
United Health Services 30
University Village 288
Upstate Farms Inc. 72

V

Veenendaal Cave 212
Verde Communications 245
Violet.com 61
Virtuoso 149
Viziworx 99

W

Wallace's Bookstores 216
Wells Fargo "Innoventry" 22
Whitehall-Robins 159
Womble Carlyle Sandridge & Rice 20

X

X-IT Products LLC 203
Xelus 73

Z

Zehnders of Frankenmuth 290
Zig Ziglar Network, Inc. 313
Zoka Coffee Roaster and Tea Company 372
Zoots—"The Cleaner Cleaner" 366